Walking the Good Road

The Gospels and Acts
...with Ephesians

D1490244

FIRST NATIONS VERSION

This book is the second publication of a larger project called The First Nations Version Project, a translation of the New Testament by First Nations People for First Nations People. More information is available at www.firstnationsversion.com.

Great Thunder Publishing, USA

For information on special pricing for bulk orders:

Website: www.firstnationsversion.com/fnv-bulk-orders

Cover Art: Antonia Maria Hudson
Cover Design: Terry M. Wildman

Table of Contents

First Nations Version Project:
New Testament

Welcome to the second publication of the First Nations Version Project: New Testament, *Walking the Good Road: The Gospels and Acts with Ephesians - First Nations Version*. We are thrilled that this publication completes half of the New Testament.

Our first publication of *Luke and Ephesians: First Nations Version* was well received and over 3000 copies have been sold or given away. We thank the Foursquare Missions Press for printing 1000 for distribution on many reservations in the US. This is a small beginning, but interest is growing.

Please remember that this translation is a work in progress. We are inviting constructive feedback on the work we have done so far. This feedback will be evaluated and reflected in the final print. We are also inviting any First Nations Bible scholars and Greek scholars to help us improve this translation.

The following organizations have been actively using the First Nations Version: Arise Ministries, Cru Nations, Foursquare Missions Press, InterVarsity Native Ministries, and Lutheran Indian Ministries.

Desired Results

This project was birthed out of a desire to provide an English Bible that connects, in a culturally sensitive way, the traditional heart languages of the over six million English-speaking First Nations people of North America.

Why English? It is estimated that about 90% of First Nations people do not speak their tribal language, and even fewer can read it. This is the result of several generations of governmental assimilation policies that attempted to eradicate our over-250 languages spoken in North America.

This translation is not intended to be tribally specific, but to present the Scriptures in a general way, attempting to represent some of the simple yet profoundly beautiful ways our languages can be expressed in English.

We are aiming for a style that is easy to read, with an attempt to present, in writing, the cadence and feel of an oral storyteller. A contextual approach will be adhered to, using English word choices and idiomatic phrases that are culturally relevant, with an effort to refrain from a stereotypical or culturally degrading simplicity.

Why the Name First Nations Version?

The term 'First Nations,' while mostly used in Canada for the original inhabitants of the land, is increasingly being accepted and used by many Native Americans in the U.S. and by indigenous peoples worldwide. Following this trend, the name First Nations Version was chosen for this translation.

Partnering Organizations

OneBook, a Canadian organization dedicated to helping indigenous peoples all over the world translate the Bible for themselves, is providing financial support, along with the tools and training needed for a high quality translation. They have partnered with Rain Ministries, located in the U.S., to facilitate this translation. Wycliffe Associates of Orlando, Florida, also served this project by providing technical support and funding in its initial stages.

Church Engagement and Ownership

The First Nations Version of the New Testament is being produced in response to the consistently positive feedback given to the initial translation efforts. As samples were shared in churches and other venues, those who heard these samples began asking for more. Pastors, evangelists, missionaries, Native elders, and others began to ask if a complete Bible would be translated using this contextual approach.

It was Rain Ministries, a ministry that has been sharing the Good Story of Jesus with First Nations people for more than a decade, that had initiated this project. When OneBook became aware of the interest in this translation from those in Native churches, they partnered with Rain Ministries to help create the First Nations Version New Testament.

A small circle of interested Native American and First Nations pastors, church leaders and church members gathered together to begin the work of translation. They decided on the method of translation, created the first key-terms that would be used, and participated in the translation, checking, reviewing and editing of the Gospel of Luke.

A larger circle of pastors, church leaders and members, along with some bible scholars, participated in reviewing the draft version of Luke. Their input has been valuable in improving this edition.

We welcome and encourage any pastors, church leaders, Bible scholars and others to participate and provide feedback as we work toward the completion of the rest of the New Testament.

The First Nations Version New Testament belongs to all the churches, and it is especially for those involved in contextual ministry with Native North Americans.

Our Translation Council

A translation council has been selected from a cross-section of Native North Americans—elders, pastors, young adults and men and women from differing tribes and diverse geographic locations. This council also represents a diversity of church and denominational traditions to minimize bias.

Our initial group, forming our translation council, consists of twelve First Nations individuals representing tribes from these diverse geographical regions. This council determined the style and method of translation to be used and continues to be involved in ongoing translation, review and cultural consultation. From this group a smaller council was chosen to determine the key terms to be used.

The members of our initial translation council are listed below, with the exception of one, along with their North American tribal heritages:

Barry D. Belindo — Kiowa/Navajo/Pawnee/Choctaw
Garland Brunoe — Wascoe/Ojibwe
Gordon Campbell — Kalispel/Spokane/Nez Perce
Shándíín Church — Diné/Pokagon Band Potawatomi
Alvin Deer — Kiowa/Creek
John GrosVenor — Cherokee
Antonia Hudson — Kiowa/Navajo/Pawnee/Choctaw
Bryan Jon — Ojibwe
Dale and Charlotte Tsosie — Diné (Navajo)
Terry M. Wildman — Ojibwe/Yaqui

The following ministries have also given of their time to participate in this project:

Mending Wings
Rain Ministries
Lutheran Indian Ministries

Other First Nations Involved

Besides the members of our council, many other First Nations people have had input into this translation as reviewers, cultural consultants, and community feedback participants.

All in all, the tribal heritages represented include, but are not limited to: Apache, Assiniboine, Blackfeet, Cherokee, Creek, Desert Cahuilla, Cayuga, Hopi, Kalispel, Klickitat, Lakota, Mohawk, Métis, Miami, Navajo, Nez Perce, Odawa, Ojibwe, Pawnee, Piaute, Plains Cree, Potawatomi, Northern Cree, Tlingit, Tohono O'odham, Western Cree, Yankton Sioux, Spokane, Wascoe and Yaqui.

Many others will also be included in the reviewing process when the opportunities are available.

Here are the names of some of the others who have helped in the review process: Dylan and Trish Hamilton (Diné), Courtland Hopkins (Lakota/Diné), Kimberlee Medicine Horn Jackson (Yankton Sioux), Josh Manriquez (Paiute/Assiniboine), Warren Petoskey (Odawa/Lakota), Rashawn Ramone (Diné), Dion Unangwanwuntaqa Sahneya (Hopi), Sonya Skan (Métis/Tlingit), Raymond Torres (Desert Cahuilla).

Consultant Support People

Alongside our translation council are a number of support people who are consultants on this project. Dave Ohlson, our primary consultant, brings to us his over 45 years of Biblical translation experience with indigenous cultures.

State-of-the-art translation software and expertise is also provided by David Duncan. He offers to us training and technical support on all the software and sets up our text for printing.

These partners are committed to having the First Nations people do the actual work of translation and review, while they provide experience, expertise, help and feedback.

We also give our thanks to Elsa Henderson who has volunteered many weeks and hours of her time providing expertise in punctuation and grammar for the entire project. Her heart for our First Nations People is full of Creator's love. She has also covered this translation with prayer from the beginning.

Community Checking and Feedback

Our hope is that this translation will be used widely by the Native churches in North America. To facilitate this, about 1300 draft versions of Luke were printed and distributed to Native churches, leaders, and many others both in Canada and the US, asking for review and feedback. Our translation council was instrumental in ensuring widespread community testing in Native communities. The feedback has been overwhelmingly positive and many great suggestions have been incorporated into this current printing.

For more information and how you can support this project, please visit the following webpages:

www.firstnationsversion.com

www.onebook.ca/projects/fnv/

Reader Aids

Use of Italics

In an attempt to present the scriptures as a living and moving narrative, at times we have added reasonably implied statements within, above and below the text. For this we used our imagination as we tried to picture what may have been the reaction in the voices and faces of the participants. These added statements are not intended to change the meaning of the text, but rather to bring clarity. For further clarity these additions are in italics to distinguish them from the text of Scripture.

History, Culture and Geography

At times we also inserted comments about the history, culture and geography within the story to add depth and understanding. This is for those without a historical understanding of the Jewish culture that is found in the New and Old Testaments. All these additions are also in italics to distinguish them from the text of Scripture.

Names of Persons and Places

We decided to follow our Native naming traditions and use the meaning of names for persons and places in this Great Story. In our community feedback, this practice was affirmed and appreciated. Most reviewers liked the standard English versions of the names in parentheses, while a few did not. We experimented with many options and finally decided to reduce the size of the font for the standard English names. Leaving the names in the text this way, instead of in footnotes, keeps the eye on the text, and helps the reader's eye to more easily skip over it, if so desired.

Prologue

The Great Spirit is known among our First Nations people in North America by many names: the Great Mystery, Creator, Maker of Life, Giver of Breath, and by many other names from our tribal languages. Names like these have been chosen in the retelling of this story to honor the simplicity and beauty of our Native understanding of the One Above Us All.

In the beginning the Great Spirit made all things seen and unseen. He made the world above and the earth below. He created all the spirits to be his messengers and helpers. He also made the sun, moon and stars, and all plants and animals. The winged-ones who fly in the sky, the four-legged ones who walk on the ground, every creeping thing that crawls—all were shaped and molded by his hands.

Creator made the first two-leggeds, a man and woman and placed them in the Garden of Beauty and Harmony (Eden) to be caretakers of the earth. But the evil snake, a spirit sometimes called Accuser (Satan), also entered the Garden of Beauty and Harmony (Eden). He opposed the Great Spirit and twisted the words of Creator. He planted a seed of doubt into their minds, so they ate the fruit of the only tree the Great Spirit had told them not to eat from. By listening to this evil spirit and disobeying the Maker of Life, the first two-leggeds brought death with all its bloodshed, violence and destruction to all the generations of mankind that would follow.

The life of beauty and harmony was lost, and the circle of life was broken. A powerful curse came upon the ground that affected all living things. Spiritual and physical death came to all; and the hearts of human beings became broken, twisted together with good and evil. They could no longer live in harmony upon the land and began to follow evil ways, hurting and killing one another.

Creator revealed the effects that would come from the curse brought by the ancient snake. Then he made a promise to all mankind: that he would one day send another human being, born of a woman, who would crush the head of the ancient snake and restore human beings and all of creation back to the life of beauty and harmony again.

Creator found a man whom he would choose to make a Peace Treaty with, named Father Of Many Nations (Abraham). He had twelve sons who became the twelve tribes of Wrestles With Creator (Israel).

When Father Of Many Nations (Abraham) and his wife were too old to have children, the Great Spirit gave them a son. They named him He Made Us Laugh (Isaac), because they laughed when Creator told them they would have a child. He Made Us Laugh (Isaac) had a son whom he named Heel Grabber (Jacob), because he grabbed his twin brother's heel when he was being born. The Great Spirit later gave him a new name, Wrestles With Creator (Israel), because he wrestled with a spirit-messenger from Creator.

Wrestles With Creator (Israel) had twelve sons who became twelve tribes. After four hundred winters of mistreatment and slavery to a foreign nation, the Great Spirit set them free through Drawn From The Water (Moses), who became the Lawgiver.

The Great Spirit made a Peace Treaty with the tribes and gave them their own Land of Promise, ceremonies to purify them, and feasts to teach them to celebrate his goodness. He also gave them their Tribal Law that was carved into tablets of stone, and a Sacred Tent Lodge where they would perform their ceremonies.

Creator wanted to be their only Chief, but the tribes wanted a human chief so they could be like the nations around them. This grieved Creator, but he gave them what they wanted. Most of these chiefs became arrogant and misrepresented the Great Spirit, but there were a few good ones. One of these chiefs was Much Loved One (David). He had a good heart toward Creator and the people, even though he, at times, also strayed from the path.

Creator had chosen the tribes to be a light to other nations; but they failed to keep his Peace Treaty, broke his laws, and misrepresented him to others. He sent many prophets to turn the hearts of the tribes back to the right ways, but they did not listen and their hearts became like stone.

Finally, the protection of Great Spirit was removed from them and he allowed them to be conquered by other nations. They were conquered by the people of Village of Confusion (Babylon). The tribes were taken captive and removed from their homeland. Their Sacred Lodge was destroyed and their Village of Peace (Jerusalem) was left in ruins.

After 70 years, a small remnant returned to their homeland and rebuilt the Sacred Lodge. But the elders wept because it was pitiful in comparison to the original Sacred Lodge built by the great chief Stands In Peace (Solomon).

Through the generations that followed, many powerful nations ruled over the tribes. The most recent were the People of Iron (Romans). Their government took control of the tribes and dominated them for nearly two generations.

The People of Iron (Romans) forced their treaties on the tribes, but did allow some freedoms. They could practice their own spiritual ways, build gathering houses called synagogues and maintain a Sacred Lodge to perform their ceremonies and make their prayers.

This government also allowed them to have their own tribal chiefs. But over many years these chiefs became corrupt and were controlled more by the ways of the People of Iron (Romans) than by their ancient Sacred Ways.

The people were oppressed and feared this powerful government with its many soldiers and weapons of war. They kept praying that the Great Spirit would fulfill the age-old prophecies and send the Chosen One, whom they hoped would be a great warrior chief to destroy the People of Iron (Romans) and set them free.

The right time had finally come for Creator to fulfill his ancient prophecies and promises and send his Chosen One.

But he would not come in the way the tribes expected.

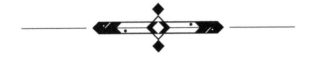

Behold! The time will come when I will
make a New Peace Treaty with the northern
tribes of Wrestles With Creator and the
southern tribes of Give Him Honor.
This Peace Treaty will be different from the
one I made with their ancestors when I took
them by the hand and walked them out
of Black Land. They did not honor
that Peace Treaty, so I had to turn
away from them. But here is the
New Peace Treaty I will make with them.
I will plant my laws in their minds and carve
them into their hearts. I will be their Great
Spirit and they will be my people,
My Sacred Family.

From the Great Spirit
To the tribes of Wrestles With Creator

Jeremiah Chapter Thirty-One
Verses Thirty-One to Thirty-Three

Gift From Creator
Tells the Good Story

Gospel of Matthew

FIRST NATIONS VERSION

FIRST NATIONS VERSION

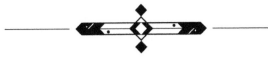

Gift From Creator Tells the Good Story

(Gospel of Matthew)

His Tribal Ancestry

1 Here is the record of the ancestry of Creator Sets Free (Jesus)—the Chosen One—a descendant of Much Loved One (David) and of Father Of Many Nations (Abraham).

From Father Of Many Nations (Abraham) to Much Loved One (David), his ancestors were:

2 Father Of Many Nations (Abraham), He Made Us Laugh (Isaac), Heel Grabber (Jacob), Give Him Honor (Judah) and his brothers, 3 He Breaks Through (Perez) and his brother First Light (Zerah) whose mother was Fruit Of Palm Tree (Tamar),

Circle of Teepees (Hezron), He Is Lifted Up (Ram), 4 Noble Relative (Amminadab), Talks With Snakes (Nahshon), He Makes Peace (Salmon), 5 Moves With Strength (Boaz) whose mother was Boastful Woman (Rahab),

He Works Hard (Obed) whose mother was Beautiful Friend (Ruth), Original Man (Jesse), 6 who was the father of the great chief Much Loved One (David).

From Much Loved One (David) to the removal to Village of Confusion (Babylon), the ancestors of Creator Sets Free (Jesus) were:

Much Loved One (David), Stands In Peace (Solomon) whose mother Daughter Of Seven (Bathsheba) was the wife of Fire From Creator (Uriah), 7 Big People Maker (Rehoboam), He Is My Father (Abijah),

Gathers The People (Asa), 8 He Makes Wrongs Right Again (Jehoshaphat), Creator Is Above (Jehoram), My Great Power (Uzziah), 9 Creator Has No Equal (Jotham), Held By Creator (Ahaz),

He Will Be Strong (Hezekiah), 10 He Made Them Forget (Manasseh), Burden Bearer (Amon), Good Medicine (Josiah), 11 Chosen By Creator (Jeconiah) and his brothers at the time of the removal to Village of Confusion (Babylon).

¹²From the removal to Village of Confusion (Babylon) to the birth of Creator Sets Free (Jesus), his ancestors were:

Chosen By Creator (Jeconiah), Ask Creator (Shealtiel), Born In Village of Confusion (Zerubbabel), ¹³Father Boasts In Him (Abihud), He Builds Up (Eliakim),

He Helps Him (Azor), ¹⁴Stands With A Good Heart (Zadok), Makes Him Strong (Akim), Power Of Creator (Eliud), ¹⁵Creator Helps Him (Eleazar),

Gifted By Creator (Matthan), Heel Grabber (Jacob), ¹⁶He Gives Sons (Joseph) who was the husband of Bitter Tears (Mary) who gave birth to Creator Sets Free (Jesus) who is the Chosen One.

¹⁷And so there were fourteen generations from Father Of Many Nations (Abraham) to Much Loved One (David), fourteen more generations from Much Loved One (David) until the removal to Village of Confusion (Babylon), and then fourteen more from the removal to Creator Sets Free (Jesus), the Chosen One.

Birth of the Chosen One

¹⁸Here is the story of how the Chosen One was born:

His mother, Bitter Tears (Mary), had been promised in marriage to He Gives Sons (Joseph). But before they came together in marriage, while still a virgin, she found out that she was carrying a baby in her womb from the Holy Spirit.

¹⁹Because He Gives Sons (Joseph) was a man of honor, and did not want to bring her trouble and open shame, he thought about secretly releasing her from the marriage promise.

²⁰As he wondered about these things, a messenger from the Great Spirit appeared to him in a dream and said, "He Gives Sons (Joseph), descendant of Much Loved One (David), do not be afraid to take Bitter Tears (Mary) to be your wife, because the Holy Spirit has given her this child. ²¹She will give birth to a son. You will name him Creator Sets Free (Jesus), because he will set his people free from their bad hearts and broken ways."

²²This gave full meaning to the words of Creator spoken long ago by the prophet, ²³"A young virgin will be with child and give birth to a son. They will call his name Immanuel, ᵃ which *in our tribal language* means Creator Is With Us."

²⁴When He Gives Sons (Joseph) woke up, he followed the guidance given him in the dream and took Bitter Tears (Mary) to be his wife. ²⁵But he did not have sexual relations with her until after the child was born, and he named the child Creator Sets Free (Jesus).

Seekers Of Wisdom

2 It was during the days of the *bad hearted* Chief Looks Brave (Herod)ᵇ that the Chosen One was born in the village of House of Bread (Bethlehem) in the Land of

---

a 1:23 Isaiah 7:14   b 2:1 Also known as Looks Brave (Herod) the Great

Promise (Judea). After his birth Seekers Of Wisdom (Magi) traveling *on a long journey* from the East came to Village of Peace (Jerusalem).

2 They began to ask around, "Where is the one who has been born to be chief of the tribes of Wrestles With Creator (Israel)? We saw his star where the sun rises and have come to honor and bow down before him."

3 When Chief Looks Brave heard this, he and all who lived in Village of Peace (Jerusalem) were troubled. 4 He called a council of all the head holy men and scroll keepers and asked them where the Chosen One was to be born.

5 "In House of Bread (Bethlehem), the village of the great chief Much Loved One (David)," they answered. "This is what the ancient prophet said: 6 'But you, O House of Bread (Bethlehem), in the Land of Promise (Judea), even though you are small, you have a good reputation with the chiefs who watch over the land; and so from you will come a Great Chief who will guide my chosen people—the tribes of Wrestles With Creator (Israel).'*c*"

7 Then Looks Brave (Herod) called a secret council with the Seekers Of Wisdom (Magi) to find out when the star first appeared. 8 He then sent them to House of Bread (Bethlehem) and told them, "Look everywhere for the child. Find him and tell me where he is, so that I may also come and honor him."

9 After listening to Looks Brave (Herod), the Seekers Of Wisdom (Magi) went their way. 10 When they saw the star rising in the East, they jumped with joy, and with glad hearts they followed until the star stopped and rested over the place where the child was. 11 They went into the house and saw the child and his mother, Bitter Tears (Mary). As soon as they saw the child, they bowed down to the ground to honor him. Then they opened their bundles and gifted him with gold, sweet smelling incense, and bitter ointment of myrrh.

Escape to Black Land

12 The Seekers Of Wisdom (Magi) were warned in a dream not to go back to Looks Brave (Herod), so they returned to their homeland by a different road.

13 After the Seekers Of Wisdom (Magi) had gone, a spirit-messenger from Creator warned He Gives Sons (Joseph) in a dream. "Rise up!" he said *urgently.* "Take the child and his mother and go quickly to Black Land (Egypt) and remain there until I tell you to leave. Looks Brave (Herod) is searching for the child to kill him!"

14 That night He Gives Sons (Joseph) took the child and his mother and fled for their lives to Black Land (Egypt). 15 They remained there until the death of Looks Brave (Herod). This gave full meaning to Creator's ancient prophecy: "I will call for my son from Black Land (Egypt)."*d*

16 When Looks Brave (Herod) realized he had been outsmarted by the Seekers Of Wisdom (Magi),

---

c 2:6 Micah 5:2   d 2:15 Hosea 11:1

he was full of rage. Using the knowledge he had gained from them, he gave orders for all male children in House of Bread (Bethlehem) under two winters of age to be put to death. [17] This gave full meaning to another ancient prophecy spoken by Lifted By Creator (Jeremiah): [18] "A sound of weeping and wailing is heard in Highland (Ramah). Sheep Woman (Rachel) is shedding tears for her children. No one can bring her peace, because her children have been taken from the land of the living."[e]

Dream Guidance

[19] After Looks Brave (Herod) died, a spirit-messenger from Creator appeared again to He Gives Sons (Joseph) in a dream while he was still in Black Land (Egypt). [20] The spirit-messenger said to him, "Get up and take the child and his mother back to the land of the tribes of Wrestles With Creator (Israel), for the ones who were trying to take the child's life are dead."

[21] He Gives Sons (Joseph) got up, took the child and his mother and began to go where he was told. [22] On the way, when he heard that Rules The People (Archelaus), the son of Chief Looks Brave (Herod) had become the new chief, he became afraid.

After being warned in another dream, he took a different path to their home through Circle of Nations (Galilee), [23] to an *out-of-the-way village most people looked down on, called* Seed Planter Village (Nazareth). This gave full meaning to the words of the prophets, "He will be called a Seed Planter (Nazarene)."

3 *Many long winters had now come and gone. Creator Sets Free (Jesus) was now thirty winters old—a mature man. The People of Iron (Romans) had many new rulers and governors, and the tribes of Wrestles With Creator (Israel) had a new chief holy man for the Sacred Lodge.*

He Shows Goodwill

In those days a man named He Shows Goodwill (John) appeared in the desert places of the Land of Promise (Judea). He began to speak out a message *that was loud and clear,* [2] "It is time to return to the right ways of thinking. Creator's Good Road from above is close—*it is time to begin walking on it.*"

[3] The prophet Creator Will Help Us (Isaiah) told about him long ago when he said, "A voice is howling in the desert, 'Clear the pathways! Make the path straight for the coming of the Great Chief!'[f]"

[4] He Shows Goodwill (John) came wearing a buffalo robe, with a deer hide[g] sash around his waist. The food he ate was grasshoppers and wild honey.

[5] The people were coming from Village of Peace (Jerusalem), from all over the Land of Promise (Judea) and the territory surrounding the river Flowing Down (Jordan). [6] They came admitting to their bad hearts and broken ways and participated in the purification ceremony.

---

e 2:18 Jeremiah 31:15   f 3:3 Isaiah 40:3   g 3:4 Lit., garments of camel's hair and a leather belt

Spiritual Leaders Warned

7 When he saw the Separated Ones (Pharisees) and Upright Ones (Sadducees) in the crowd watching, he cried out to them, "You nest of poisonous snakes! Who warned you to run and hide from the coming storm? 8 You are like trees without fruit. Prove to others, by the way you live, that you have returned to the Good Road. 9 Do you think you can say, 'Father Of Many Nations (Abraham) is our ancestor?' Don't you know the Great Spirit can make these stones into his children? 10 The tomahawk is already at the root of the trees, and the ones that have no good fruit will be cut down and tossed into the fire.

Purification Ceremony With Fire

11 "I perform the purification ceremony with water, for the ones who have returned to the right way of thinking. But there is one you do not know, who is right here with you, and even though he comes after me, he is much greater. I am not even worthy to bend down and untie his moccasins. He is the one who will perform the purification ceremony with the fire of the Holy Spirit! 12 His harvest basket is in his hands, to separate the grain from the husks. He will store the good grain in his barn, but the husks he will burn up with a fire no one can put out."

This is My Much Loved Son

13 He Shows Goodwill (John) then looked up and saw Creator Sets Free (Jesus) wading out into the water of the river Flowing Down (Jordan). He had come from Circle of Nations (Galilee), *a journey of many days,* for the purification ceremony, 14 but He Shows Goodwill (John) tried to stop him.

"Why are you coming to me?" he asked *humbly.* "I am the one who should come to you."

15 "This is the way it should be, for now," Creator Sets Free (Jesus) answered. "It is the right thing to do, *to bring honor to the ways of Great Spirit.*"

He Shows Goodwill (John) agreed to perform the ceremony. 16 As soon as Creator Sets Free (Jesus) came up from the water, he saw the sky open. The Spirit of Creator came down like a dove and rested on him. 17 A voice from the sky spoke *like distant thunder,* "This is my much loved Son who makes my heart glad!"

Tested by the Evil Trickster

4 Creator Sets Free (Jesus) followed the guidance of the Spirit, who took him into the desert wilderness to be tested by Accuser (Satan), the evil trickster snake.

In the story of creation, the first man and woman lived in a Garden of Beauty and Harmony. A sly and crafty snake came to them and twisted the words of the Great Spirit to deceive them. They listened to the snake, lost the life of beauty and harmony and fell under the curse of death. This snake, who opposes Creator's Good Road, is the ruler of all evil spirits.

2 For forty days and nights Creator Sets Free (Jesus) ate nothing; *his body*

became weak and his hunger grew strong.

[3] When the evil snake *saw that Creator Sets Free (Jesus) was weak and hungry, he* came to him *and whispered in his ear.*

"Are you the Son of the Great Spirit?" he hissed. "Prove it by turning these stones into bread."

[4] "The Sacred Teachings are clear," Creator Sets Free (Jesus) said. "Human beings cannot live only on bread, but on all the words that come from the mouth of the Great Spirit."[h]

[5] The evil trickster then took him to the Great Spirit's Sacred Lodge in Village of Peace (Jerusalem). He set him at the very top, *high above the village.*

[6] "Prove you are the Son of the Great Spirit and jump down from here!" the evil snake taunted him. "Do not the Sacred Teachings also say, 'His spirit-messengers will watch over you to keep you from harm. They will even keep your foot from hitting a stone.'[i]?"

[7] "Yes," Creator Sets Free (Jesus) said back to him, "but they also say, 'Do not test the Great Spirit.'[j]"

[8] Once more the evil trickster took him to a high mountain and showed him all the great nations of the world with their power and beauty.

[9] "All of these I will give you," the snake said *smoothly,* "if you will highly honor me and walk in my ways!"

[10] "Get away from me, Accuser (Satan)!" he responded. "For it is written in the Sacred Teachings, 'The Great Spirit is the only one to honor and serve.'[k]"

[11] The evil trickster could think of nothing more to test him with, so he slithered away to wait for another time.

Then spirit-messengers came to give comfort and strength to Creator Sets Free (Jesus).

He Shows Goodwill Jailed

[12] After that, Creator Sets Free (Jesus) heard that He Shows Goodwill (John) was put in jail, so he left that place to return to Circle of Nations (Galilee). [13] He left his home in Seed Planter Village (Nazareth) and went to live in Village of Comfort (Capernaum) by the sea. This was in the territory of the tribes of Honored Dwelling (Zebulun) and He Will Wrestle (Naphtali).

[14] The ancient prophecy of Creator Will Help Us (Isaiah) had finally found its full meaning. [15] "In the territory of the tribes of Honored Dwelling (Zebulun) and He Will Wrestle (Naphtali), toward the great waters to Circle of Nations (Galilee) where many Nations dwell— [16] the ones who sit in darkness, where death casts a great shadow, have seen the light of a new sunrise."[l]

The Good Road is Close

[17] From that time forward Creator Sets Free (Jesus) began to speak out, "Creator's Good Road from above

---

h 4:4 Deuteronomy 8:3   i 4:6 Psalm 91:11,12   j 4:7 Deuteronomy 6:16   k 4:10 Deuteronomy 6:13
l 4:16 Isaiah 9:1-2

is close, it is time to change your thinking and begin your great journey."

His First Followers

18 Creator Sets Free (Jesus) was walking by the shoreline of Lake of Circle of Nations (Sea of Galilee) when he saw two fishermen throwing out their nets. They were One Who Hears (Simon), also named Stands On The Rock (Peter), and his brother Stands With Courage (Andrew).

19 He said to them, "Come, walk the road with me, and I will show you how to fish in a new way—for two-leggeds."

20 They dropped their nets right then and became his followers.

21 As Creator Sets Free (Jesus) was leaving, he saw two other brothers, He Takes Over (James) and He Shows Goodwill (John), the sons of Gift Of Creator (Zebedee). They were sitting with their father in a canoe getting their nets ready for fishing. 22 Creator Sets Free (Jesus) called out to them, and they dropped their nets, left their father, and also became his followers.

Demonstrating the Good Road

23 Creator Sets Free (Jesus) traveled throughout Circle of Nations (Galilee). He was teaching in their gathering houses, and telling everyone the beautiful story of Creator's Good Road. He was healing the people of every kind of sickness and disease. 24 His reputation as a healer spread as far as Bright Sun (Syria). Then they brought to him the ones tormented with evil spirits, along with people who suffered from seizures, and he healed them. He even healed the crippled and paralyzed among them.

25 Large crowds from all directions began to seek after him—too many to number! They came from Circle of Nations (Galilee) and Ten Villages (Decapolis), and from Village of Peace (Jerusalem), and the Land of Promise (Judea), and from beyond the river Flowing Down (Jordan).

5 When Creator Sets Free (Jesus) saw this great crowd, he went back up into the mountainside and sat down to teach the people. His followers came to him there, 2 so he *took a deep breath,* opened his mouth and began to share his wisdom with them *and teach them how to see Creator's Good Road.*

Blessings of the Good Road

3 "Creator's blessing rests on the poor, the ones with broken spirits, the Good Road from above is theirs to walk.

4 "Creator's blessing rests on the ones who walk a trail of tears, for he will wipe the tears from their eyes and comfort them.

5 "Creator's blessing rests on the ones who walk softly and in a humble manner; the earth, land and sky will welcome them and always be their home.

6 "Creator's blessing rests on the ones who hunger and thirst for wrongs to be made right again; they will eat and drink until they are full.

7 "Creator's blessing rests on the ones who are merciful and kind to others; their kindness will find its way back to them—full circle.

8 "Creator's blessing rests on the pure of heart, for they are the ones who will see the Great Spirit.

9 "Creator's blessing rests on the ones who make peace; it will be said of them, 'They are the children of the Great Spirit!'

10 "Creator's blessing rests on the ones who are hunted down and mistreated for doing what is right, for they are walking the Good Road from above.

11 "Others will lie about you, speak against you, and look down on you with scorn and contempt, all because you walk the road with me. This is a sign that Creator's blessing is resting on you. 12 So let your hearts be glad and jump for joy, for you will be honored in the world above. You are like the prophets of old, who were treated in the same way by your ancestors.

Salt and Light

13 *As you walk the Good Road with me,* you are the salt of the earth, *bringing cleansing and healing*[m] *to all.* Salt is a good thing, but if it loses its saltiness, how will it get its flavor back? That kind of salt has no worth and is thrown out.

14 *As you walk the road with me,* you are a light shining in this dark world. A village built on a hill cannot be hidden. 15 No one hides a torch under a basket. Instead it is lifted up high on a pole, so all who are in the house can see it. 16 In the same way, let your light shine by doing what is good and right. When others see, they will give honor to your Father—the One Above Us All.

Fulfilling the Sacred Teachings

17 *"When you hear my words,* you may think I have come to undo the Law given by Drawn From The Water (Moses) and the words of the prophets. But I have come to honor them and show everyone their true meaning. 18 I speak from my heart, as long as there is a sky above and an earth below, not even the smallest thing they have said will fade away, until everything they have said has found its full meaning and purpose.

19 "Anyone who turns away from these instructions and tells others to do the same will be looked down on, as a small one, on Creator's Good Road from the world above. But the ones who do them and teach others to do the same, they will be looked up to as great ones.

20 "I will say this to you, unless you have a better reputation than the scroll keepers and the Separated Ones (Pharisees), you will not find the path that leads to the Land of Creator's Good Road from above."

Creator Sets Free (Jesus) then began to help the people see how the full meaning and purpose of the Law and the Prophets applied to them.

---

m 5:13 2 Kings 2:19-22

Respect Toward All

21 "You have heard that our ancestors were told long ago, 'Do not take another person's life,'n and 'whoever does will have to answer to the council.'o 22 But I tell you, every one who is angry toward a fellow human being will have to give an answer to the tribal council. If they speak with disrespect to someone, saying, 'You hollow head!' they will also face the tribal council. If they curse someone by saying 'You damn fool!' they may end up in the Valley of Smoldering Fire. 23 So if you are offering a gift *at Creator's Ceremonial Lodge,* and there remember that a Tribal Member has something against you, 24 leave your gift and go make things right. Then you can come back and finish the ceremony."

Resolving Conflict With Dignity

25 "If someone has a complaint against you and takes you before the village council, work out an agreement before you get there. *You know how to decide things for yourselves.* The council might decide against you and turn you over to the ones who have the power to put you in prison. 26 The truth is, there is no way out of there until honor has been restored."p

Honoring Our Women

Most women in the time of Creator Sets Free (Jesus) were dominated by the men and were often treated like property and looked down on with disrespect.

27 *So he said to the men,* "You have heard the saying, 'You must not have sexual relations with another man's wife.'q 28 But I tell you this, any man who looks at a woman and wants his way with her has already done so in his heart.

"This is not how the Great Spirit wants us to see our sisters. 29 If your right eye sees in this wayr—gouge it out and throw it away! 30 If your right hand does harm to hers—cut it off and throw it away! It is better to lose a part of your body, than for your whole body to be thrown into the Valley of Smoldering Fire.

31 "Drawn From The Water (Moses) said, 'If you put away your wife you must give her divorce papers.'t 32 Let me tell you why. Anyone who puts away his wife, *without giving her divorce papers,* makes her unfaithful when she remarries, unless she was unfaithful already. Then anyone who marries her is having sexual relations with another man's wife."

In those days men would 'put away' their wives without divorcing them, leaving them destitute and unable to properly remarry.

No Solemn Promises

33 "You have heard the ancestors were told, 'When you make a solemn promise, you must keep it to honor the Great Spirit.'u 34 But I

---

n 5:21 Exodus 20:13   o 5:21 Deuteronomy 16:18   p 5:26 Lit., until the debt is paid in full
q 5:27 Exodus 20:14   r 5:29 Lit., offends you   s 5:30 Lit., offends you   t 5:31 Deuteronomy 24:1
u 5:33 Leviticus 19:12

say this to you, do not make any solemn promises. Do not say, 'I promise by the world above,' for it is Creator's seat of honor, 35 or 'I promise by the earth below,' which is the resting place for his feet. Or 'I promise by Village Of Peace (Jerusalem),' for it belongs to the Great Spirit Chief. 36 Do not even say, 'I promise by my own head.' Can you make even one hair on your head become white or black? 37 Your simple 'yes' or 'no' is enough. To say more is to speak with a forked tongue like the evil trickster snake.

Eye for an Eye?

38 "You have also been told, 'Take an eye for an eye and a tooth for a tooth.'ᵛ 39 But I tell you, do not fight back. *Violence will not be defeated by more of the same.* If someone strikes the right side of your face, turn to him the other side also. 40 If someone takes you to council for your shirt, give him your vest also. 41 If anyone, *even a soldier of the People of Iron (Romans),* forces you to carry his bundle one mile, *show the strength of your heart and* carry it two. 42 Give to the one who asks for help, and do not turn away from the one who wants to borrow from you.

Love Your Enemies

43 "You have been told to love only your own people and to despise others as your enemy.ʷ 44-45 But I tell you, treat your enemies with love and respect and send up good prayers for the ones who make trouble for you and bring you pain. This will show that you are full grown children of your Father from above, who sends his blessing of rain on the ones who do right and the ones who do wrong.

46 "If you love and show respect only to the ones who do the same, how does that bring honor to you? Even tribal tax collectors do these things. 47 If you welcome only friends, how are you different from others? Even 'Outsiders' from other nations do these things.

48 "By loving and blessing all people, you will be walking in the footsteps of your Father from the world above, who is perfect in all his ways.

The Way to Do Good

6 "Beware of doing good just so people can see you, for then you will receive no honor from your Father from above, *who is the Creator.* 2 When you give gifts to the poor and do good things for others, do not brag about it on the village pathways or in the gathering houses, like those who put on a false face, pretending to be something they are not. The truth is, they honor only themselves and they will get nothing more.

3-4 "But when you help others who are in need, do it in secret. Do not even tell your left hand what your right hand is doing. Then your Father who sees all things will honor you.

---

v **5:38** Exodus 21:24, Leviticus 24:20   w **5:43** Leviticus 19:18

The Way to Pray

5 "When you send your words to the Great Spirit, do not be like the ones who love to stand up and pray with a loud voice in the gathering houses and along the village pathways, hoping to be seen by others. The truth is, they have their honor already. They will get no more. 6 Instead, find a quiet hiding place where no one can see or hear you and send your prayers to your Father in secret. He will see what you have done and honor you.

7-8 "When you pray, do not be like the people from the Outside Nations, who use empty words over and over again, thinking their many words will help them be heard. Your Father, the Creator, already knows what you need even before you ask.

9 "Instead, when you send your voice to the Great Spirit, here is how you should pray:

"O Great Father, the one who lives above us all, we honor your name as sacred and holy.

10 "Bring your Good Road to us, where the beauty of your ways in the world above is reflected in the earth below.

11 "Provide for us day by day—the elk, the buffalo, and the salmon; the corn, the squash, and the wild rice; all the things we need each day.

12 "Release us from the things we have done wrong, in the same way we release others for the things done wrong to us.

13 "Guide us away from the things that tempt us to stray from your Good Road, and set us free from the evil one and his worthless ways.

14 "Remember, our Father from the world above will release you from your wrongdoings in the same manner you release others from theirs. 15 But if you fail to release others, then this keeps your Father, the Creator, from releasing you.

The Way to Fast

16 "When you go without food to seek spiritual things, do not be like the ones who put on a false face. They hang their heads down and darken their faces to look as if they are going without food. They only want people to notice them and think they are spiritual. I speak from my heart, they already have their *false* honor—they will get no more. 17 But when you go without eating, put on your headdress and wash your face, 18 so others won't notice. But know that your Father from above, who sees in secret, will honor you.

The Way to See Possessions

19 "Take care not to store up possessions on earth that can be spoiled by worms, eaten by moths, or stolen by thieves. 20 Instead, *give away your possessions to the ones in need,* then you will be storing up great possessions in the world above, where nothing can be lost or stolen. 21 For where you store your valued possessions is where your heart will be."

Good Eye or Bad Eye

Among the tribes of Wrestles With Creator (Israel) a greedy person was said to have a bad eye and unable to see the Good Road. A generous person was said to have a good eye, full of light and able to clearly see the Good Road.

[22] *So he said to them,* "Light shines into the body through the eye. If your eye is clear, your whole being is full of light. [23] But, if your eye is bad, then your whole being is full of darkness. If the only light you have is darkness, then the darkness is very great!

[24] "No one can be loyal to two rival chiefs. You will have to choose between them. You will either hate one chief and love the other, or honor one and resent the other. You cannot be loyal to the Great Provider and to possessions at the same time.

Worry is the Wrong Path

[25] "This is why I am telling you not to be troubled about getting enough to eat or drink, or what to wear. Is eating, drinking and clothing yourself all there is? Does your life not have more meaning than this?

[26] "Look to the winged-ones who soar on the wind. Do they plant seeds and gather the harvest into a storehouse? No! But the Great Spirit gives them plenty to eat. Do you not know he cares even more for you? [27] Can worry add even one more step to the length of your life's journey?

[28] "Why do you trouble yourself with what to wear? Have you seen how the wildflowers grow in the plains and meadows? Do you think they work hard and long to clothe themselves? [29] No! I tell you not even the great chieftain Stands In Peace (Solomon), wearing his finest regalia, was dressed as well as even one of these.

[30] "If Creator covers the wild grass in the plains with such beauty, which is here today and gathered for tomorrow's fire, will he not take even better care of you? Why is your faith so small? [31] There is no need to say, 'What will we eat? What will we drink? What will we wear?' [32] This is what the Nations *who have lost their way* have given their hearts to, but your Father from above knows you need these things.

[33] "If you will make Creator's Good Road your first aim, representing his right ways, he will make sure you have all you need for each day. [34] So do not worry about tomorrow's troubles. It is enough to trust Creator to give you the strength you need to face today.

Seeing Others Clearly

7 "If you do not want to be judged, then do not judge others; [2] for the way you judge others will come back to you—full circle. [3] *Think of it this way,* how can you see the speck of wood in someone else's[x] eye when you can't see a log in your own eye? [4] How can you say, 'Here, let me help you,' when you can't see that you need even more help? [5] Stop pretending to be something you are not! If you will be honest about yourself, you will then see clearly enough to help others.[y]

---

x 7:3 Lit., your brother's   **y 7:5** Lit., your brother

Wisdom for Sacred Things

6 "Take care not to give what is sacred to the ones who will turn on you and treat you with disrespect. For who would toss an eagle feather into the dirt to be trampled on?

Keep Dancing Your Prayers

7 "Let your prayers rise like smoke to the Great Spirit, for he will see and answer you. Every step is a prayer, and as you dance upon the earth for the things you seek, the way will open before you. In the same way, as you search for the true ancient pathways, you will find them. 8 Answers will come to the ones who ask, good things will be found by the ones who search for them, and the way will open before the ones who keep dancing their prayers."

Creator Sets Free (Jesus) took a loaf of bread and a fish from a basket. He lifted the bread up high for all to see.

9 "What father, if his son wanted bread, would give him a stone to eat?"

Then he lifted the fish up high.

10 "If he asked for a fish would he give him a snake?

11 "If fathers with bad hearts know how to give good gifts to their children, then how much more will the Creator, who is your loving Father from above, give good gifts to the ones who ask?

The Meaning of My Teachings

12 "Here is the meaning of what I have been saying: whatever good thing you want others to do for you is what you should do for them. This is the whole purpose of the instructions given by Drawn From The Water (Moses) and the words spoken by the prophets.

Small Gate and Narrow Way

13-14 *"To walk Creator's Good Road you must* enter this small gate and walk a narrow path that leads to the good life; only a few find and walk this road. But the gate is large and the path is wide that leads to a bad end—many walk this road.

15 "Some *who walk this wide road* represent themselves as sheep, but inside they are hungry wolves. Watch out for these false prophets. 16 You will know them by their fruit. Do grapes come from a thorn bush or pears from thistles? 17-18 Will a sick tree give good fruit or a healthy tree bad fruit? No! Healthy trees give good fruit and sick trees give bad fruit. 19 It is the trees with bad fruit that are cut down and used to make a fire. 20 When you see the fruit of their ways, you will know them.

21 "Not everyone who calls me their Great Chief is walking the Good Road from the world above. The ones who do what my Father from the world above wants are the ones walking this road.

22 "On that day, *the time when Creator reveals all hearts,* many will say to me, 'O Great Chief, did we not speak for you, force out evil spirits, and do great things all in your name—representing you?'

23 But this is what I will have to say to them, 'Who are you? Go away from me, you who do what you know is wrong, for you never truly knew me.'z

Wise and Foolish

24 "The ones who listen to me and walk in my ways are like a wise man who built a grand lodge on solid ground. 25 The rain poured down, the streams flowed, and the strong winds came. They all beat against the lodge, but it stood strong against the storm. Nothing could shake it, for it was built on solid ground.

26 "The ones who hear my words but do not walk in these ways are like another man, a foolish one, who built his lodge on top of the sand. 27 When the storm came against it, the lodge crashed to the ground, and all that was in it was lost."

28-29 Creator Sets Free (Jesus) was finished for the day with his teachings and wise stories. All the people were amazed and had great respect for him, for he was not like the other spiritual leaders—the scroll keepers. He spoke with true wisdom and dignity, showing he had the right to represent the Great Spirit.

Power to Cleanse and Heal

8 A great crowd of people followed Creator Sets Free (Jesus) as he walked down from the mountainside. 2 A man with a skin disease all over his body came up to Creator Sets Free (Jesus). He humbled himself, bowed down and pleaded with him, "Honored One! If you want to, you can heal and cleanse me."

3 "I want to!" Creator Sets Free (Jesus) said as he reached out and touched the man.

Tribal Law says that anyone who touches anything unclean would also be unclean and in need of cleansing. a But Creator Sets Free (Jesus), instead of becoming unclean himself, cleansed the man with his touch.

"Be clean!" he added, and right away the disease left the man and he was healed.

4 Creator Sets Free (Jesus) instructed the man, "Tell no one! Take the traditional ceremonial gift and show yourself to a holy man. Then have him perform the cleansing ceremony given by the lawgiver Drawn From The Water (Moses). This will show others that you have been healed and made ceremonially clean again."

Faith From A Head Soldier

5 As Creator Sets Free (Jesus) walked into Village of Comfort (Capernaum), a head soldier from the People of Iron (Romans) came up to him. 6 "Honored One," the head soldier begged, "my household servant that I care deeply about is lying in bed, unable to move and in great pain."

7 "I will come to your house and heal him," Creator Sets Free (Jesus) told the man.

8 But the head soldier, *knowing the tribal traditions,* said to him,

---

z 7:23 Lit., I never knew you.   a 8:3 Leviticus 22:6

"Honored One, I am not worth the trouble that coming to my house would bring to you. If you will only speak the word, I know my servant will be healed, ⁹ for I am also a man under orders with many soldiers under me. I say to this one, 'Go,' and he goes, and to another, 'Come,' and he comes. My servants do what I say."

¹⁰ Creator Sets Free (Jesus) was amazed at this answer. He turned to the ones who were following him and said to them, "I speak from my heart, I have never seen such great faith, not even among the tribes of Wrestles With Creator (Israel)."

He let his words sink deep into the hearts of the people listening.

¹¹ Then he said, "Listen closely, for I tell you that this man is only one of many who will come from the four directionsᵇ to sit in a great lodge and feast with our ancestors. They will sit down with Father Of Many Nations (Abraham), He Made Us Laugh (Isaac), and Heel Grabber (Jacob) in the Land of Creator's Good Road from above. ¹² But the ones who were first born to walk the Good Road will be forced out into the night. Outside in the darkness, they will howl with tears and grind their teeth together in anger and frustration."

¹³ Creator Sets Free (Jesus) then turned to face the head soldier.

"Go home" he said to him, "Your faith in me has healed your servant."

And right then the head soldier's servant was healed!

In the Home of Stands on the Rock

¹⁴ Creator Sets Free (Jesus) *and his close followers* came to the home of Stands On The Rock (Peter). The mother-in-law of Stands On The Rock (Peter) was sick in bed with a fever. ¹⁵ When Creator Sets Free (Jesus) saw her, he reached out and touched her hand. Right then the fever left her. She *felt so good she* got up and made a meal for them.

¹⁶ Later that day, when the sun was going down, many who were tormented by evil spirits were brought to him. He spoke to the spirits, forced them out with a word, and healed the ones who were sick. ¹⁷ All this was done to bring full meaning to the ancient prophecy spoken by Creator Will Help Us (Isaiah), "He took upon himself our sickness and carried the weight of our diseases."ᶜ

Cost of Following

¹⁸ Creator Sets Free (Jesus) saw the great number of people around him and gave his followers instructions *to prepare a canoe* to cross over to the other side of the lake.

¹⁹ On the way to the lake a scroll keeper walked up to him, "Wisdomkeeper," he said, "I will follow you wherever you want to go."

²⁰ He answered the man, "The foxes live in their holes, the winged-ones who fly above us live in their nests, but the True Human Being has no place to lay his head."

---

b 8:11 Lit., East and West   c 8:17 Isaiah 53:4

²¹ Another follower said to Creator Sets Free (Jesus), "Honored One, let me first go home to my father *until it is time* to bury him."

²² "Let the ones who are *spiritually* dead bury their dead," he said to the man. "You come and walk the road with me."

Power Over Storms

²³ *They came to the lake and* Creator Sets Free (Jesus) and his close followers climbed into a canoe and began to paddle across the lake.

A dark and menacing storm began to move in quickly and the sound of distant thunder rolled over the waters. They paddled harder trying to get to the other shore before the storm hit.

²⁴ Suddenly the violent storm overtook them and threatened to sink the large canoe, but Creator Sets Free (Jesus) had fallen into a deep sleep. ²⁵ *In desperation* they woke him up.

"Wisdomkeeper!" they cried out. "We are fighting for our lives! Save us!"

²⁶ "Why are you full of fear?" he asked them, "Is your faith so small?"

He stood up and spoke sharply to the wind and the raging water. At his words a great peace fell upon the surface of the waters.

²⁷ His followers were greatly amazed. They shook their heads and said to each other, "What kind of man is this? Even the wind and the waves do what he says."

Power Over Evil Spirits

²⁸ When they finished crossing the lake, they came to the territory of the people of the village of Honors End (Gadara). As soon as Creator Sets Free (Jesus) stepped from the canoe, two men coming from the burial caves, who were tormented by evil spirits, came up to him. These men were so violent that no one dared to pass through that area.

²⁹ "Son of the Great Spirit!" they shrieked. "What do you want from us? Are you here to torment us before Creator's chosen time?"

³⁰ In the distance a large herd of pigs was feeding *on a hillside.* ³¹ The evil spirits spoke through the men. "If you must force us out," they begged, "then send us into that herd of pigs."

³² "Be gone!" he said, giving them permission.

The evil spirits left and entered into the herd of pigs. Then the whole herd stampeded down the steep hill headlong into Lake of Circle of Nations (Sea of Galilee) and drowned in the deep water.

³³ The ones who were watching over the pigs rushed away, *shaken and afraid.* They went to the village and told everyone all that happened.

³⁴ When they heard this, the whole village went out to find Creator Sets Free (Jesus); and when they found him, they begged him to leave their land.

Who Can Forgive Broken Ways?

9 So Creator Sets Free (Jesus) *and his close followers* climbed back into the canoe and crossed over to the other side of the lake and went to the village where he was staying.

² Some people there came carrying a crippled man lying on a sleeping mat and brought him to Creator Sets Free (Jesus). When he saw their faith in him, he said to the crippled man, "Be brave, my son, you are released from your broken ways."

³ When they heard this, some of the scroll keepers began to grumble among themselves. "This man is speaking against the Great Spirit and his ways!"

⁴ In his spirit, Creator Sets Free (Jesus) knew what they were thinking.

"Why are your hearts so full of dark thoughts?" he said to them. ⁵ "Is it easier to tell a crippled man, 'Get up and walk,' or to say to him, 'You are released from your broken ways'?"

The crowd grew quiet as all eyes turned to Creator Sets Free (Jesus), waiting to see what he would do.

⁶ "This is how you will know that the True Human Being has the right to forgive bad hearts and broken ways on this earth." He turned to the crippled man and said, "Get up, roll up your sleeping bundle and walk home."

⁷ So the man stood up and began to walk home. ⁸ Then great respect and awe filled the hearts of all who were there. They gave honor to the Great Spirit for giving such authority to human beings.

A Tribal Tax Collector Follows Him

⁹ Creator Sets Free (Jesus) left there, and as he walked on, he saw a tribal tax collector named Gift From Creator (Matthew/Levi) sitting at his tax booth.

Tribal tax collectors were often tribal members who were given the right to collect taxes for the People of Iron (Romans). They could force their own people, under the threat of violence, to pay them. To make a living, they would take more than the People of Iron (Romans) required. But many of them became greedy and took even more than they were permitted. They were hated and looked down on by the people.

Creator Sets Free (Jesus), *to the surprise of all, walked up to the tribal tax collector and* said to him, "Gift From Creator (Matthew/Levi), come and walk the road with me."

So he got up from his tax booth, left it all behind, and began to walk the road with Creator Sets Free (Jesus). ¹⁰ In the house of Gift From Creator (Matthew/Levi), Creator Sets Free (Jesus) and his followers were sitting down at the table eating with the guests. Among the guests were many tax collectors and outcasts.

The Separated Ones (Pharisees) called certain people outcasts. They used their strict interpretation of Tribal Law as a way to point them out. These outcasts were not permitted to enter the gathering houses. They were looked down on and despised by the Separated Ones (Pharisees). Outcasts included tribal tax collectors, prostitutes, people who ate and drank too much, the ones with diseases that made them ceremonially unclean, and anyone who was not a member of the tribes of Wrestles With Creator (Israel).

[11] When the Separated Ones (Pharisees) saw Creator Sets Free (Jesus) eating with outcasts, they complained to his followers saying, "Why does your wisdomkeeper eat with tribal tax collectors and outcasts?"

[12] Creator Sets Free (Jesus) overheard them and said, "People who are well do not need medicine; it is for the ones who are sick. [13] Go and learn this wise saying, 'What I want is kindness and mercy, not animal sacrifices.'[d] I have not come for the ones with good hearts. I have come to the help the outcasts find the path back home again."

New Wineskins for New Wine

[14] Some of the followers of He Shows Goodwill (John) came to Creator Sets Free (Jesus) and asked him, "Why do your followers feast instead of going without food and praying often, like we and the Separated Ones (Pharisees) do?"

[15] "Do you expect wedding guests to be sad and go without eating when the groom is hosting a feast?" he asked. "The time will come when he is gone; then they will be sad and go without eating.

[16] "No one uses a new piece of cloth to patch an old garment; it would shrink and make the tear worse. [17] No one puts new wine into an old wineskin, for the new wine would burst the old skins. Then the wine would be lost and the skins ruined. New wineskins are what is needed; then both wine and skins are preserved."

He said this to show that the old ways of the spiritual leaders did not reflect the beauty of the new way he was bringing.

Come and Heal My Daughter!

[18] As Creator Sets Free (Jesus) was speaking, a tribal leader came and humbled himself before him.

"My little girl has just crossed over to death! But I know that if you will come and lay your hands on her, she will live again."

[19] So Creator Sets Free (Jesus) and his followers went with him. [20] There was a woman following with the crowd who had been bleeding in an unusual way for more than twelve winters.

This would have made her ceremonially unclean and untouchable according to Tribal Law.

She came up close behind Creator Sets Free (Jesus), reached out her hand and touched the fringe of his

---

d 9:13 Hosea 6:6

outer garment; 21 for she had said to herself, "If I can only touch his clothes, I know I will be healed."

22 Creator Sets Free (Jesus) turned around and looked at her *with kindness in his eyes* and said, "Take courage daughter, your faith has made you well."

Right then the blood stopped flowing, and she was healed!

Power over Death

23 When they arrived at the tribal leader's home, Creator Sets Free (Jesus) saw the noisy crowd of mourners and flute players.

24 "Go from here!" he said. "This little girl is not dead; she only sleeps."

But they scorned and laughed at him, *for they knew she was dead.*

25 After they had gone, Creator Sets Free (Jesus) went inside the house, took the little girl by the hand and she stood up. 26 And the story of this began to spread far and wide.

Two Blind Men

27 As Creator Sets Free (Jesus) left from there, two blind men followed after him. They were calling out to him, "Be kind to us, descendant of Much Loved One (David)."

28 The blind men, *with the help of others,* followed him into a house; so Creator Sets Free (Jesus) asked them, "Do you believe I can make your eyes see?"

"Yes, Wisdomkeeper," was their answer.

29 He reached out, touched their eyes and said to them, "Your trust in me will make it so."

They staggered back and rubbed their eyes.

30 He had healed them! They could see! Creator Sets Free (Jesus) gave them a stern warning and said, "Tell no one about this."

31 But *in their excitement, they didn't listen, and* they told the news far and wide about what Creator Sets Free (Jesus) had done for them.

Powerful Medicine

32 As they went from there, someone brought a man to Creator Sets Free (Jesus) who could not speak because of an evil spirit. 33 When the spirit was forced out of him, the man began to speak. All the people were amazed and said, "In all the history of the tribes of Wrestles With Creator (Israel) no one has ever seen this kind of powerful medicine."

34 But the *spiritual leaders from the* Separated Ones (Pharisees) said, "It is the ruler of evil spirits that gives him the power to force out spirits."

Chief of the Harvest

35 Creator Sets Free (Jesus) continued to walk about and visit the villages. He taught in their gathering houses, helped people to understand about Creator's Good Road, and healed people from every kind of sickness and disease.

36 When he saw the great number of people needing help, he was moved in his spirit with great compassion for them. He knew they were pushed

down with no one to help and scattered about like sheep without a shepherd to watch over them.

37 So he said to the ones who walked the road with him, "There is a great harvest in front of us, but only a few to gather it in. 38 Pray to the Great Spirit Chief of the harvest, so he will send out more helpers into the fields."

Twelve Message Bearers

10 *Since there were originally twelve tribes of Wrestles With Creator (Israel), this may be why he chooses twelve message bearers.*

Creator Sets Free (Jesus) then gathered his twelve message bearers together *to prepare them for this great harvest.* He gave them authority over evil and unclean spirits, to force them out of people and to heal all kinds of sickness and disease.

2 Here are the names of the twelve that he chose to be his special message bearers:

First there was One Who Hears (Simon), who was also called Stands On The Rock (Peter), and his brother Stands With Courage (Andrew). Then he chose He Takes Over (James) and his brother He Shows Goodwill (John), who are the sons of Gift Of Creator (Zebedee).

3 He also chose Friend Of Horses (Philip) and Son Of Ground Digger (Bartholomew) and Looks Like His Brother (Thomas/Didymus) along with Gift From Creator (Matthew/ Levi), the tribal tax collector.

Then he chose He Takes Over (James), the son of First To Change (Alphaeus), along with Strong Of Heart (Thaddaeus/ Jude) and 4 One Who Listens (Simon) the Man On Fire (Zealot). And last of all, Speaks Well Of (Judas), *also known as* Village Man (Iscariot), who later betrayed him.

Instructing His Message Bearers

5 Before Creator Sets Free (Jesus) sent out his twelve message bearers *to represent him,* he gave them these instructions:

"It is not the time to go to the Outside Nations or to the villages of the people of High Place (Samaria). 6 Instead, go to *your own people*— the lost sheep of the tribes of Wrestles With Creator (Israel).

7 "This is what I want you to say to them: 'Creator's Good Road from above is close, reach out and take hold of it!' 8 Heal all who are sick, cleanse the ones with skin diseases, raise the dead, and force evil spirits out of people. Give away the things I have given to you and ask no price for your service.e

9 "Take no trading goods with you or coins for your money pouches. 10 Take no traveling bundle, moccasins, or extra clothes to wear, not even a walking stick, because the ones who work hard in the harvest fields deserve to be fed and cared for.

---

e 10:8 Lit., Freely you have received, freely give.

¹¹"Whenever you enter a camp or village, find an honorable person who will give you lodging. ¹²When you come to their dwelling, greet the family with respect. ¹³If they are people of honor, your greeting of peace will rest on them. ¹⁴But if no one in that village welcomes you or listens to your message, then go from there and shake the dust from your moccasins. ¹⁵The truth is, on the day when the fate of that village is decided, it will be worse for them than it was for Village of Bad Spirits (Sodom) and Village of Deep Fear (Gomorrah).

Sheep Among Wolves

¹⁶"Look and listen! I am sending you out like sheep into a pack of wolves, so be as crafty as snakes but as harmless and gentle as doves. ¹⁷Look out for men with bad hearts, for they will bring you before their councils, and whip you with leather straps in their gathering houses. ¹⁸You will also be dragged before government rulers and leaders—all because you are representing me—and in this way through you both the tribes of Wrestles With Creator (Israel) and the People of Iron (Romans)ᶠ will hear my message.

¹⁹"When this happens, do not be afraid or worry about what you will say, or how you will say it. ²⁰When that time comes, you will be given the words to say; for it is not you who will speak, but the Spirit of your Father will speak through you.

Betrayal and Hatred

²¹"Brother will betray brother and parents will betray their children, even putting them to death. Children will turn against their parents and have them killed. ²²The time will come when all will hate you because you represent me and carry my name; but remember, it is the ones who never give up and make it to the end of the road that will be rescued and made whole.

²³"If they hunt you down in one village, leave there and go to the next one. I speak from my heart, the True Human Being will come before you finish going through all the villages in the land of the tribes of Wrestles With Creator (Israel).

²⁴"Followers are not greater than the one they follow, so then you who are my followers will be treated in the same bad ways they treat me; ²⁵so consider it an honor that you will be treated the same as your Wisdomkeeper. If they have called the Chief of the council house Worthless Ruler (Beelzebul),ᵍ how much worse will they speak of the members of his council?

²⁶"Do not fear their threats. For their evil ways will be found out, even what they say and do in secret will be made clear for all to see.

²⁷"The things I have told you in secret at night, make them known when the sun rises! What I have whispered in your ears, stand on the rooftops and shout out loud for all to hear!

---

f 10:18 Lit., Gentiles   g 10:25 Another name for Accuser (Satan)

Do Not Fear Your Opponents

28 "Have no fear of your opponents, for they can only kill the body, but not your inner being. Instead, fear the one who can bring an end to your entire being*h* in the Valley of Smoldering Fire.

29 "Two small winged-ones could be traded for two poorly beaded earrings, but not one can fall to the ground unless your Father, the Creator, knows it. 30-31 Are you not worth more to him than many small winged-ones? He knows the number of hairs on your head, so do not fear the ones who stand against you.

32 "All who represent me before others I will represent before my Father from above. 33 But the ones who disown me will be disowned before my Father above.

Families Will Fight Like Enemies

34 "Do you look for me to bring peace to this *troubled* land? 35 The message I bring will pierce like the blade of a long knife. It will turn a son against his father, a daughter against her mother, and a daughter-in-law against her mother-in-law. 36 In their own homes they will fight like enemies—all because of me.

37 "The ones who choose their father or mother, son or daughter, over me dishonor me. 38 The ones who fail to pick up their cross and walk the road with me do not know my worth. 39 The ones who care only for their own life will fail to find life, but the ones who will lay down their life for me will find true life.

40 "The ones who welcome you welcome me, and the ones who welcome me welcome the one who sent me. 41 If you welcome a prophet for who he is, you will receive the honor he brings. If you welcome a good-hearted person, you will receive the good that he brings. 42 I speak from my heart, even a drink of water given to a small one who follows me will bring great honor to the one who has given it."

11 After instructing his twelve followers, Creator Sets Free (Jesus) left there to teach and announce his message in the surrounding villages.

Are You the One?

2 From prison He Shows Goodwill (John) heard about the things the Chosen One was doing. So he sent two of his followers to ask Creator Sets Free (Jesus), 3 "Are you the one we are waiting for, or should we look for someone else?"

4 Creator Sets Free (Jesus) told them, "Go back to He Shows Goodwill (John) and tell him about the things you have seen with your own eyes and heard with your own ears. 5 The blind can see again, the lame can walk, the ones with skin disease have been cleansed! Ears that cannot hear have been opened, the dead have come back to life

---

h **10:28** Lit., both body and soul

again, and the poor are being told the Good Story! [6] Creator's blessing and goodwill rests on the one who does not stumble and leave the path because of me."

Honoring He Shows Goodwill

[7] When the messengers left, Creator Sets Free (Jesus) spoke to the people about He Shows Goodwill (John):

"What were you looking for in the desert wilderness? A frail reed blowing in the wind? [8] Did you see a man in soft clothes? No!—for the ones who wear soft clothes live soft lives. [9] Were you looking for a true prophet? Yes! He is a true prophet but also much more! [10] He is the one spoken of in the Sacred Teachings, 'Look! I am sending my messenger ahead of you. He will clear the path before you.'[i]

[11] "I speak from my heart, He Shows Goodwill (John) who performed the purification ceremony is a true human being. No one born of a woman has ever been greater, but now the smallest one who walks Creator's Good Road from above is greater than he.

[12] "From the time of He Shows Goodwill (John) until now, Creator's Good Road from above has been under attack, and the violent ones are trying to force their way upon it. [13] The Law and the Prophets spoke until he came. [14] If you can accept it, he is Great Spirit Is Creator (Elijah), the one the prophets said would come.[j] [15] If you have ears to hear, you will understand.

[16] "This generation, what can I compare them to? They are like children at a trading post, teasing each other, saying, [17] 'You didn't dance when we played the drum! You didn't cry when we played a sad flute song.'

[18] "He Shows Goodwill (John) did not feast or drink wine, but they say, 'He has an evil spirit.' [19] The True Human Being comes feasting and drinking and they say, 'He eats too much and is a drunk, a friend of tribal tax collectors and outcasts!' But wisdom is like a mother who knows what her children are doing and can see right through them."

Village Warnings

[20] Then Creator Sets Free (Jesus) began to warn about what would happen to the villages that saw his greatest signs and wonders, but did not receive his message.

[21] "Sorrow and trouble will come to you, Village of Secrets (Chorazin), and the same for you, House of Fishing (Bethsaida). If the ancient villages of Rock Land (Tyre) and Hunting Grounds (Sidon) had seen the powerful signs you have seen, they would have humbled themselves long ago and with great sorrow turned their hearts back to Creator's ways. [22] So then, it will be worse for you in the day when you face your end.

[23] "As for you, Village of Comfort (Capernaum), do you think you will be lifted up to the world above? No! You will be brought down low, to the Dark Underworld of Death. If Village of Bad Spirits (Sodom) had seen the

---

i **11:10** Malachi 3:1   j **11:14** Malachi 4:5

powerful signs you have seen, that village would have remained to this day. ²⁴But the day of their end will be better than yours."

Father and Son

Creator Sets Free turned his eyes to the sky and sent his voice to the Great Spirit.

²⁵"I honor you, O Great Father, Maker of earth and sky," he prayed, "for you have hidden these things from the ones who are wise in their own eyes, but have shown them to the humble of heart. ²⁶Yes, my Father, it has made your heart glad to see this day come."

Then he turned to the ones who walked the road with him.

²⁷"My Father has put everything into my hands," *he said with a solemn voice.* "Only the Father knows the Son and only the Son knows the Father. No one can know the Father *in his fullness* unless the Son makes him known."

Then he lifted his eyes to the horizon as if he was speaking to all the world.

²⁸"Come close to my side, you whose hearts are on the ground, you who are pushed down and worn out, and I will refresh you. ²⁹Follow my teachings and learn from me, for I am gentle and humble of heart, and you will find rest from your troubled thoughts. ³⁰Walk side by side with me and I will share in your heavy load and make it light."

Chief of the Day of Resting

12 During that time on a Day of Resting, Creator Sets Free (Jesus) and his followers were walking through a field of grain. The men were hungry, so they plucked some grain, rubbed the husks off in their hands and began to eat.

²When the Separated Ones (Pharisees) saw what they were doing, they said to him, "Why do your followers do what is not permitted on the Day of Resting?"

³He answered them, "Have you not heard about the time long ago when the great chief Much Loved One (David) was hungry? ⁴How he and his followers went into the Sacred Lodge and ate the ceremonial bread? Tribal Law says that only the holy men are permitted to eat this bread.

⁵"Have you not read in Tribal Law that the holy men who perform the ceremonies in the Sacred Lodge are permitted to ignore the sacredness of the Day of Resting—without blame?

⁶"Listen to me! The one standing before you is greater than the Sacred Lodge! ⁷If you understood this saying, 'I want kindness and compassion, not ceremonial sacrifices,'ᵏ you would not have blamed the innocent ones. ⁸For the True Human Being is Chief over the Day of Resting!"

Healing on the Day of Resting

⁹Creator Sets Free (Jesus) left there and went to their gathering

---

k 12:7 Hosea 6:6

house; [10] there he saw a man with a shriveled and useless hand.

The Separated Ones (Pharisees) had been keeping a close eye on him. Then they saw him looking at the man with the useless hand.

Trying to find a reason to accuse him, they asked, "Is it permitted to heal on the Day of Resting?"

Creator Sets Free (Jesus) knew what they were scheming.

[11] "Is there anyone here who would not help his sheep out of a ditch it fell into, even on the Day of Resting?" he challenged them. [12] "A human being has more value than a sheep! That is why it is permitted to do good on the Day of Resting!"

[13] Then he turned to the man and said, "Stretch out your hand."

He stretched it out, and it was the same as his good hand!

[14] The Separated Ones (Pharisees) stormed out of there and began to scheme together about how to have Creator Sets Free (Jesus) killed. [15] But he knew what they were doing, so he left that place. A large number of people went with him and he healed all who were sick, [16] but he warned them not to tell others who or where he was.

An Ancient Prophecy Fulfilled

[17] Another ancient prophecy of Creator Will Help Us (Isaiah) had now found its full meaning:

[18] "Here is the one I have chosen, who does all I ask and makes my heart glad. I have made my stand with him and love him as a father loves a son. My Sacred Spirit will rest on him and give him a message that will right the wrongs done to all people. [19] He will not make loud arguments on the village pathways, but will speak with humble dignity. [20] He will not break a bruised reed. He will not snuff out a smoldering fire. He will never give up until all wrongs have been made right again! [21] All Nations will hear of his reputation and put their trust and hope in him."[l]

The Separated Ones Accuse Him

[22] They brought a man to Creator Sets Free (Jesus) who, tormented by an evil spirit, could not see or speak. He healed the man, who could then see and speak again. [23] The large crowd was amazed and said, "Could this be the promised descendant of chief Much Loved One (David)?"

[24] When the Separated Ones (Pharisees) heard what the people were saying, they said, "No! His power over evil spirits comes from the Worthless Ruler (Beelzebul), the one who rules over all evil spirits."

[25] Creator Sets Free (Jesus) knew what they were thinking and said to them, "A nation warring against itself comes to a bad end. Villages or clans warring against each other will not survive. [26] If Accuser (Satan) is warring against himself, how will he continue to rule?

---

l 12:21 Isaiah 42:1-4

27 "If it is by his power that I force out evil spirits, by what power do your children do these things? So then they are the ones who will decide against you. 28 But if I force out evil spirits by Creator's Spirit, then the Great Spirit's Good Road has come close to you.

Defeating the Strongman

29 "Who can enter the strongman's house and take away his goods, unless he first defeats him? He will then tie him up and take what is in his house.

30 "The one who is not fighting with me fights against me. The one who does not help me gather scatters and makes things worse.

In this spiritual war there is no unclaimed territory.

31 "That is why I say to you, the wrongdoings and evil speaking that mankind has done will be forgiven them. 32 Anyone who speaks against the True Human Being will be forgiven. But speaking evil of the Holy Spirit will not be forgiven, in this present world, nor in the one that is coming.

Good and Bad Fruit

33 "You must grow a good tree to get good fruit. If you grow a bad tree, you get bad fruit; for a tree is known by its fruit."

Then with fire in his eyes Creator Sets Free (Jesus) turned to the Separated Ones (Pharisees) and spoke with a voice like thunder.

34 "You nest of poisonous snakes! How can you who are evil speak any good things? What is in your hearts will come out of your mouths. 35 Good people speak from the good medicine stored in their hearts. Evil people speak from the bad medicine stored in their hearts. 36 But I tell you, when the day comes for the final decision, human beings will have to give an answer for every worthless word spoken. 37 The words that come out from your hearts will decide for or against you when you stand before the Great Spirit."

An Unusual Sign

38 Then some of the scroll keepers and Separated Ones (Pharisees) spoke back to him.

"Wisdomkeeper," they demanded, "show us a powerful sign *to prove who you are.*"

But Creator Sets Free (Jesus) turned their words back on them, for they had just seen him do a powerful sign.

39 "Only a worthless and unfaithful generation would keep demanding signs," he answered. "The only sign that you will be given is the sign of the prophet Wings Of Dove (Jonah). 40 Just as he was in the belly of a great fish for three days and nights, the True Human Being will be in the womb of the earth for three days and nights.

41 "When the time comes for the final decision to be made about the people living today, the people of Village of Changed Minds (Nineveh) will stand in agreement against them. What they did will show your guilt, because they changed their hearts and minds when they heard

the message of Wings Of Dove (Jonah). Look! One who is greater than he stands before you now.

42 "The female chief of the South[m] will also be there to stand against the people of today. Her reputation will show your guilt, for she journeyed from a land far away to listen to the wisdom of the great chief Stands In Peace (Solomon). Look! One greater than Stands In Peace is standing right in front of you.

43 "When an evil spirit goes out of a person, it wanders through dry and desolate lands, looking for a place to rest. When it finds none, 44 it says, 'I will go back to the house I left.' It returns to find the house empty, swept clean and put in order. 45 The spirit then finds seven other spirits, more evil than itself, who all go in and live there, making the person worse than before. This is how it will be for the generation of people living today."

All My Relatives

46 While Creator Sets Free (Jesus) was speaking to the people, his mother and brothers were outside wanting to talk with him. 47 Someone noticed and told him, "Your relatives are here, waiting outside to see you."

48 "Who are my relatives?" he asked the person who told him.

49 Then he *looked around the circle of people,* lifted his hands toward his followers and said, "Here they are! 50 The ones who walk in the ways of the Great Spirit are my relatives— my mother, brothers and sisters."

The Stories Begin

13 Later the same day Creator Sets Free (Jesus) left that place and found a quiet spot to sit by Lake of Chief Garden (Gennesaret). 2 Once again, people began to gather around him. The number of people was so great that he sat down in a canoe *and pushed out a little ways from the shore.* The people gathered at the shoreline on the water's edge and sat down to listen to him.

The Great Storyteller began to tell his stories, teaching people about Creator's Good Road.

Story of the Seed-Planter

3 Here is one of the many stories he told them: *"Listen!"* he said. "A seed-planter went to plant some seeds and began to scatter them about on the ground.

4 "Some seeds fell on the village pathway, and the winged-ones pecked at the seeds and ate them all.

5 "Some of the seeds fell on the rocks where there was only a little dirt. The plants sprouted up quickly, 6 but when the sun came out, they dried up because they had no roots.

7 "Other seeds fell into the weeds, and thistles sprouted around the seeds and choked the life out of them.

8 "But some seeds fell on good ground, grew strong, and gave a harvest. Some gave one hundred times what was planted, some sixty, and others thirty. 9 The ones who have ears, let them hear and understand!"

---

m 12:42 Queen of Sheba

Why Teach With Stories?

[10] The ones who walked the road with him came to him and asked, *"Wisdomkeeper,* tell us why you use stories to teach the people?"

[11] He answered them, "To you the honor has been given to understand about the mysterious ways of Creator's Good Road from above. This honor is not given to those who are not ready for it. [12] The ones who understand will gain wisdom and be ready for more—much more. But the ones who do not understand or walk in the ways of wisdom will lose even the little they have.

[13] "This is the reason I tell the stories, 'for they have eyes that do not see, ears that do not hear,'[n] and hearts that do not understand.

[14] "These are the ones who give full meaning to the words of the prophet Creator Will Help Us (Isaiah) when he said, 'They will hear but not understand the meaning; they will see without knowing what it is they see. [15] Their hearts of stone have made their ears dull and their eyes dim. If only they would see with their eyes and hear with their ears, they could open their hearts to the Maker Of Life and he would heal them.'[o]

[16] "But Creator's blessing rests on you, for you have eyes to see and ears to hear. [17] I speak from my heart, there were many prophets and good-hearted people who longed to see what you see and hear what you hear, but never did."

The Meaning of the Story

[18] "So then," he said to his followers, "listen with your hearts and I will tell you the meaning of the story of the seed-planter.

[19] "The seed in this story is the message from the Great Spirit about his Good Road.

"The seed planted on the village pathway represents the ones who hear but do not understand the message. The evil trickster sneaks up and snatches it from their hearts.

[20] "The rocky ground represents the ones who hear and receive the message with a glad heart, [21] but because they have no roots, their faith is shallow and does not last. As soon as the message brings them trouble or opposition, they stumble and fall away.

[22] "The seed planted among the weeds and thistles represents the ones who have heard the message, but they are too busy worrying about their earthly existence. The desire for more and more possessions leads them down a false path, and they never grow into mature human beings.

[23] "The good ground represents the ones that, when they hear the message, understand it, and let it grow in their hearts to produce a harvest; some one hundred times as much, some sixty, and some thirty."

Weeds in the Garden

[24] Creator Sets Free (Jesus) told the people another story. He said,

---

n 13:13 Jeremiah 5:21   o 13:15 Isaiah 6:9-10

"Creator's Good Road from above is like a man who scattered good seed in his garden. 25 But during the night, while his family slept, an enemy sneaked in and scattered bad seeds in with the good ones. 26 When the plants began to grow, the weeds also grew with them.

27 "When the family's garden workers saw the weeds, they said to the man, 'Honored One, didn't you plant good seeds in your garden? Where did these weeds come from?'

28 "The man answered, 'An enemy has done this.'

"'Should we go and dig out the weeds?' the workers asked.

29 "'No,' the man said, 'they are too hard to tell apart now. You might dig out the good plants with the bad. 30 Wait and let them grow together until it is time for the harvest. At that time I will tell the workers: First go and gather the weeds into bundles for burning, then gather the grain into my storehouse.'"

More Stories

31 Creator Sets Free (Jesus) then told them more stories about the Good Road: "The Good Road from Above is also like a man who plants a single grain of mustard seed, 32 one of the smallest of seeds. But when planted in a garden, it grows larger than all the other plants and takes over the garden.p It becomes a great tree with many branches, large enough for the winged-ones who soar in the sky to find lodging in its shade.

33 "Again, think of the Good Road from Above to be like the yeast a grandmother uses when she makes bread dough. She mixes a little yeast into a large amountq of flour. Then the yeast spreads throughout the dough, causing it to rise."

34 Creator Sets Free (Jesus) would use only stories *like these* when he spoke to the crowds; he taught nothing to the crowds without using a story. 35 This brought full meaning to the ancient prophecy, "I will tell many stories, stories of the ancient ways, things hidden since the beginning of the world."r

Meaning of the Good and Bad Seeds

36 When he was finished, Creator Sets Free (Jesus) left the crowds and went into the house where they were staying. The ones who walked the road with him went in with him and asked, "Tell us the meaning of the story about the good and bad seeds in the garden."

37 "The True Human Being is the one who plants the good seeds," he answered. 38 "The garden is *all the nations of* the world. The good seeds are the children of the Good Road. The weeds are the children of the worthless ways of the world, 39 and the enemy who plants the bad seeds is the evil one. The harvest is the end of this world cycle, and the helpers are spirit-messengers.

40 "The weeds will be burned when this world cycle is complete. 41 The True Human Being will send

---

p 13:32 The mustard plant was used as an herbal medicine.　　q 13:33 Lit., 3 measures, about 13 liters　　r 13:35 Psalm 78:2

his messengers to remove the stumbling stones from the Good Road, along with all who hold onto their bad-hearted ways. 42 They will be gathered into bundles and used to feed the fire of a great oven. There they will weep many tears and grind their teeth together in anger and frustration. 43 Then the ones who are in good standing will shine like the sun in the Land of the Father's Good Road. The ones with ears should hear and understand."

More Good Road Stories

44 "The Good Road from Above is like a hidden treasure a man finds buried in a field. He buries it back into the ground and is then happy to go and trade everything he has for that field.

45 "The Good Road from above is also like a trader in goods who is looking for the finest of beads.s 46 When he finds one of great beauty and worth, he trades all his goods so he can have it.

47 "Here is another way to see the Good Road from Above: A large fishing net is let down into the great waters. Many different kinds of fish are caught in it. 48 When it is filled up, the fishermen pull it to shore. Then they sit down and separate the good fish into baskets and throw away the bad fish.

49 "It will be the same when this world cycle ends. The spirit-messengers from Creator will be sent to separate the ones who are in good standing from the ones who

have bad hearts. 50 The bad-hearted ones will then be thrown into a pit of fire where they will weep with many tears and grind their teeth together in anger and frustration."

51 Then Creator Sets Free (Jesus) asked his followers, "Now do you understand the things I am saying to you?"

"Wisdomkeeper," they said, "we do understand."

52 He smiled and said to them, "Every scroll keeper who has learned to walk in the ways of Creator's Good Road is like the head of a family, an elder who opens the medicine pouch of his heart, sharing wisdom that is both new and old, bringing new understanding to the old ways."

His Own Village Rejects Him

53 When Creator Sets Free (Jesus) was through telling his stories, he traveled to his boyhood home of Seed Planter Village (Nazareth). 54 There he entered the local gathering house and began to teach the people, and they were amazed at his words.

"Where did this man get his wisdom from?" they asked. "Who gave him this powerful medicine? 55 Is this not the son of the wood carver? Is his mother not Bitter Tears (Mary)? And his brothers He Takes Over (James) and He Gives More (Joseph) and He Hears (Simon) and Speaks Well Of (Judas) 56 and all his sisters—are they not here living among us?"

57 And so the people stumbled from the path because of him.

s 13:45 Lit., pearls

Creator Sets Free (Jesus) *with a sad heart* said to them, "A prophet is given honor everywhere except in his own village, among his own clan, and in his own house."

58 So he did not do many works of power there because they failed to put their trust in him.

Looks Brave and Creator Sets Free

14 Looks Brave (Herod), who ruled the territory of Circle of Nations (Galilee), began to hear reports about Creator Sets Free (Jesus).

2 He said to his servants, "This man must be He Shows Goodwill (John) who performed the purification ceremony; he has returned from the world of the dead. That is why he can do these powerful things."

The Death of He Shows Goodwill

3-4 Looks Brave (Herod) had arrested He Shows Goodwill (John) and put him in chains because he had been speaking against him for breaking Tribal Law by living with Daring Woman (Herodias), the wife of Friend of Horses (Philip), who is the brother of Looks Brave's (Herod).

5 Looks Brave (Herod) would have put He Shows Goodwill (John) to death right then, but he was afraid of what the people would do, for they honored him as a prophet.

6 When the birthday of Looks Brave (Herod) came, the daughter of Daring Woman (Herodias) danced before all the guests. Looks Brave (Herod) was so pleased 7 he made a solemn promise to give her whatever she wanted. 8 Her mother jumped at the chance and told her daughter what to ask for.

The daughter said to Looks Brave (Herod), "Give me, here and now, the head of He Shows Goodwill (John) in a basket!"

9 The heart of Looks Brave (Herod) fell to the ground. But he had made a solemn promise before all of his guests; 10 so he sent a soldier to the prison, had him cut off the head of He Shows Goodwill (John), 11 put it in a basket and bring it to the girl, who then gave it to her mother.

12 The followers of He Shows Goodwill (John) took his body and gave him a proper burial. Then they went and told Creator Sets Free (Jesus).

Creator Sets Free Retreats

13 When Creator Sets Free (Jesus) heard how He Shows Goodwill (John) had been put to death, he found a canoe and went off to a deserted place to be alone for a while. But the crowds of people, when they heard about it, went after Creator Sets Free (Jesus) from their villages; 14 and when he came to shore, they were waiting for him. He felt deeply for them, so he healed the ones who were sick.

He Feeds Five Thousand

15 When the evening came, his followers said to him, "This is a deserted place and the day is almost over. Let's send the people away to

the villages in the countryside so they can find food to eat."

Creator Sets Free (Jesus) looked around at the great crowd of people, for there were over five thousand who had gathered there.

16 "There is no need to send them away," he said to his followers. "You feed them."

His followers could not believe their ears!

17 *With one voice* they said to him, "All we have is five loaves of bread and two fish!"

18 "Bring them to me," he told them.

19 Then he had all the people sit down on the grass. He took the five loaves of bread and two fish *and held them to the sky.* He looked up, gave thanks to the Great Spirit, and began to break the bread into smaller pieces, which he gave to his followers to give to the people. 20 Everyone ate until they were full! When they were done, they gathered the leftovers—twelve baskets full! 21 Not counting the women and children, there were about five thousand men who had eaten.

Water Walker

22 Right away Creator Sets Free (Jesus) had his followers get into the canoe and go ahead of him to the other side of the great lake, while he sent the people back to their homes.

23 After that he went up into the mountainside to be alone while he sent his voice to the Great Spirit. He stayed there and prayed as the sun set and the stars came out.

24 His followers were still in the canoe far from land. The wind blew strong against them, and the waves pounded the canoe and began to toss it about.

25 Late into the night, just before the morning light, Creator Sets Free (Jesus) came near them, walking on the water! 26 When his followers saw him, they cried out in terror, "It is a ghost-spirit!"

27 But he heard their cries and called out to them, "Do not fear, take heart. It is I."

28 "Wisdomkeeper, is it you?" Stands On The Rock (Peter) shouted back to him. "If so, tell me now to come to you on the water."

29 "Come!" he said to him *without any hesitation.*

With reckless abandon Stands On The Rock (Peter) climbed over the side of the canoe and began to walk on the water toward him.

The wind howled and the waves splashed against him as he made his way toward Creator Sets Free (Jesus).

30 But when he felt how strong the wind was, fear took hold of him. He began to sink, and cried out, "Wisdomkeeper, save me!"

31 Creator Sets Free (Jesus) quickly reached out and took hold of him. "Man of small faith," he said, "what made you hold back and doubt me?"

32 The wind stopped blowing as they climbed into the canoe. 33 They all bowed low to honor him, saying, "Truly, you are the Son of the Great Spirit."

All Who Touch Him Are Healed

34 They came to shore at Lake of Chief Garden (Gennesaret). 35 When the people there recognized him, they sent messengers to all the surrounding villages, and the people brought to him all who were sick. 36 They begged him to let them touch the fringe on his outer garment—and all who touched it were healed.

Conflict Over Traditions

15 *The teachings of Creator Sets Free (Jesus) were becoming a great concern to the spiritual leaders in Village of Peace (Jerusalem). So messengers were sent to spy on him and try to find ways to accuse him and make him look bad in the eyes of the people.*

Some of the Separated Ones and scroll keepers came to Creator Sets Free (Jesus) from Village of Peace (Jerusalem).

2 "Why do your followers not keep the traditions given by the elders and wash their hands before they eat?" they accused him.

3 Creator Sets Free (Jesus) asked them, "How is it that you use your traditions to ignore the instructions given by the Great Spirit? 4 For he said, 'Give honor to your father and your mother'*t* and 'The one s who speak evil against them must die.'*u* 5 But your tradition says, 'If you give to the Great Spirit the gifts that were meant for your father and mother, 6 you no longer have to honor them.' This is only one of the many ways you use your traditions to do away with the instructions given by the Great Spirit."

He paused and let them think about what he had said. Then with fire in his eyes he raised his voice and spoke sharply to them.

7 "Your false faces do not fool me!" he said *loud enough for all to hear.* "The prophet Creator Will Help Us (Isaiah) was talking about you when he said, 8 'These people honor me with their lips but their *hard, cold* hearts are far away from me. 9 Their prayers are empty words and their ceremonies are for show. The things they tell others to do are only rules made up by weak human beings.'"*v*

10 Creator Sets Free (Jesus) then gathered the people around him and said, "Listen with your hearts and understand what I tell you. 11 There is nothing you can take into your mouth that will make you impure. It is what comes out of your mouth that makes you impure."

12 Then his followers came to him and said, "Don't you know what you said insulted the Separated Ones (Pharisees)?"

13 "Every plant that has not been planted by my Father from above will be pulled out by the roots," he answered. 14 Then he warned them, "The Separated Ones (Pharisees) are blind guides; the ones who follow them are also blind, and they will both fall into a ditch. You will do well to stay away from them."

---

t 15:4 Exodus 20:12; Deuteronomy 5:16   u 15:4 Exodus 21:17; Leviticus 20:9   v 15:9 Isaiah 29:13

¹⁵ Then Stands On The Rock (Peter) said to him, "Tell us the meaning of the wise-saying *about what is pure and impure.*"

¹⁶ "Do you still not understand," he answered, ¹⁷ "that when food enters the mouth it goes into the stomach, *not the heart,* and then out of the body? ¹⁸ It is what comes out from the mouth, from deep inside, that makes people impure. ¹⁹ It is from the heart that come things like the taking of lives, unfaithful marriages, uncontrolled sexual desires, stealing, lying and speaking against the Great Spirit. ²⁰ It is things like these that make you impure, not failing to wash your hands when you eat."

A Lowland Woman

²¹ From there Creator Sets free (Jesus) journeyed into the territory of Rock Land (Tyre) and Hunting Grounds (Sidon) *along the coast of the Great Middle Sea (Mediterranean) north of Circle of Nations (Galilee).*

²² A Lowland Woman (Canaanite) from that territory came to Creator Sets Free (Jesus).

"Honored One! Descendant of Much Loved One (David)," she cried out to him. "Have pity on me, for my daughter is tormented by an evil spirit."

²³ Creator Sets Free (Jesus) gave no answer to the woman.

His followers came to him and begged him, "Send her away, for she is bothering us with her loud crying."

²⁴ He then said *to the woman,* "I was sent only to the lost sheep of the tribes of Wrestles With Creator (Israel)."

²⁵ She came close and gave honor to him by bowing down at his feet. "Honored One," she begged him, "help me."

²⁶ "The children's food should not be given to the dogs," he said to her.

²⁷ "That is true, Honored One," she answered, "but even the dogs can feed on the crumbs from the table of their Honored One."

²⁸ "*Dear* woman," he answered back, "your answer shows how great your faith is! What you have asked for will be yours"—and her daughter was healed from that time forward.

The Great Healer

²⁹ Creator Sets Free (Jesus) journeyed from there past Lake of Circle of Nations (Sea of Galilee) to a mountainside where he sat down to rest.

³⁰ Once again great crowds of people came, bringing to him the lame, the blind, the ones who could not walk or speak, and many more. They laid them down at the feet of Creator Sets Free (Jesus) and he healed them all. ³¹ When they saw the healings, the crowds were filled with wonder and amazement and gave honor and thanks to the Great Spirit of the tribes of Wrestles With Creator (Israel).

He Feeds Four Thousand

Creator Sets Free (Jesus) spent the next three days healing the sick and injured. People came from the Ten Villages (Decapolis) and surrounding area where many people from Outside Nations lived. The number of people had grown to over four thousand.

32 Creator Sets Free (Jesus) called his followers to his side and said to them, "I have pity in my heart for all these people, for they have been with us for three days with no food. *Some of them have come from a great distance, and* if I send them away hungry, they might lose their strength and faint."

33 "This is a lonely and desolate place," they answered him. "Where could we find enough food to feed all these people?"

34 "How much food do we have?" he asked.

"We have seven loaves of bread and a few small fish," they answered.

35 Creator Sets Free (Jesus) instructed all the people to sit down on the ground. 36 He then took the seven loaves and the fish, gave thanks and broke them into pieces. He gave them to his followers and they gave them out to the people.

37 Everyone ate as much as they wanted, and when they were done eating, his followers gathered up the leftovers—seven baskets full! 38 They had fed four thousand men, besides women and children.

39 After sending the crowds away to their homes, he climbed into the canoe *with his twelve followers* and went to the territory of Creator's High Lodge (Magdala).*w*

Signs of the Times

16 The Separated Ones (Pharisees) and Upright Ones (Sadducees) came again to Creator Sets Free (Jesus) to put him to the test *and find something to accuse him with.*

"Show us a powerful sign from the world above," they demanded, *"to prove to us who you are."*

Creator Sets Free (Jesus) was growing weary of their ongoing attacks, but as always he was able to answer them with great wisdom.

2 *He looked to the west.* "When the sun is setting you say, 'The sky is red. It will be a good day tomorrow.'" *He then turned to the east.* 3 "At the sunrise you say, 'The sky is dark and red. There will be a storm today.'"

Then he turned to look into the faces of the spiritual leaders.

"You understand what the earth and sky are saying, but you are blind to the message of the season you live in. 4 It is the bad-hearted and unfaithful people of today who look for signs, but the only sign they will be given is the sign of the prophet Wings Of Dove (Jonah)."*x*

After saying this, he left them and went on his way.

Confusion About Bread

He and his followers took their canoe to cross again to the other side of the lake.

5 When they came to shore, his followers realized that they had forgotten to bring bread with them.

---

w **15:39** Or in some manuscripts, Magadan   x **16:4** Jonah 1:17-2:10

⁶Creator Sets Free (Jesus) said to them, "Be on the lookout for the yeast of the Separated Ones (Pharisees) and the Upright Ones (Sadducees)."

⁷His followers tried to understand why he said this. They said to each other, "Is it because we forgot to bring more bread?"

⁸When Creator Sets Free (Jesus) heard them, he said, "Why are you talking like this? Why are you worried that you forgot to bring bread? Is your faith so small? ⁹Do you have no understanding? Have you forgotten so soon how many baskets of broken pieces were left over when I fed the five thousand with five loaves? ¹⁰How about the seven basketfuls left over when I fed the four thousand?"

¹¹"How do you not understand that I was not talking about bread? Beware of the yeast of the Separated Ones (Pharisees) and the Upright Ones (Sadducees)!"

¹²They finally understood he was talking about the teachings of the Separated Ones (Pharisees) and the Upright Ones (Sadducees), not about yeast in bread.

You Are the Chosen One!

They journeyed on and came into the territory of Ruler of Horsemen (Caesarea Philippi).

This territory was ruled by Chief Looks Brave (Herod) under the authority of the Ruler of the People of Iron (Caesar). There was a cave and a deep bottomless pit there that was called by the local people "The Gate of the Dark Underworld of Death" This was a place of bad medicine and lying spirits.

¹³When they came into this place, Creator Sets Free (Jesus) asked the ones who were walking the road with him, "Who do the people think the True Human Being is? What are they saying?"

His followers looked around at each other and then back to Creator Sets Free (Jesus).

¹⁴"Some say He Shows Goodwill (John) *who performed the purification ceremony,"* they answered. "Others say Great Spirit Is Creator (Elijah), or even Lifted By Creator (Jeremiah), or one of the other prophets."

He then lowered his voice and spoke in a more serious tone.

¹⁵"So tell me," he asked them. "How do you see me? Who do you say that I am?"

Silent faces stared back at him. They began to look at each other and some looked down to the ground. The moment of truth had come, but no one dared to speak. Then suddenly a voice pierced through the silence.

¹⁶"You are the Chosen One," One Who Hears also called Stands On The Rock (Simon/Peter) answered, "the Son of the living Creator!"

¹⁷Creator Sets Free (Jesus) *smiled at him and* said, "One Who Hears (Simon), Son Of Wings Of Dove (Bar-Jonah), Creator's blessing rests on you, for flesh and blood did not help you see, but my Father from above opened your eyes. ¹⁸*For this reason* I have given you the name

Stands On The Rock (Peter),[y] and upon this great rock[z] I will make my Sacred Family strong; and the powers[a] of the Dark Underworld of Death (Hades) will not stand against them.

The Secrets of the Good Road

19 "I am giving you the secrets[b] to *the mysteries of* Creator's Good Road from above. The things you do not allow on earth will be what Creator does not allow. The things that you allow on earth will be what Creator allows."

20 He then instructed his followers not to tell anyone that he was the Chosen One.

Accuser Tests Him Again

21 Creator Sets Free (Jesus) then began to tell his followers that he must go to the Village of Peace (Jerusalem) where the elders, the head holy men and the keepers of the scrolls will make him suffer many things and then kill him, and that on the third day he will return from the dead.

22 But Stands On The Rock (Peter) pulled him away from the others and spoke sharply to him, "Wisdomkeeper, do not even think this way! This must never happen to you!"

23 "Get out of my way, Accuser (Satan), you evil trickster!" he said to Stands On The Rock (Peter). "You have become a stone to trip over and make me stumble on my path.

Your thoughts are against the Great Spirit, for his ways are not the ways of human beings."

Creator Sets Free (Jesus) knew that his follower's thinking was being affected by Accuser (Satan).

Walking the Road of the Cross

24 "To walk the road with me," Creator Sets Free (Jesus) said to his followers, "you must turn away from your own path, and always be ready to carry your cross with me to the place of ultimate sacrifice. 25 The ones who hold on to their lives will not find life, but the ones who are willing to let go of their lives, for me and my message, will find *the true* life. 26 How will it help you to get everything you want, but lose this life? Is there anything in this world worth trading for your life?

27 "When the True Human Being comes, along with his spirit-messengers, after being honored by his Father, he will then give to everyone the honor they deserve for what they have done.

28 "I speak from my heart, there are some of you standing here today who, before you die, will see the True Human Being coming and bringing with him *the power of* his Good Road."

He Talks to the Ancestors

17 Six days later, Creator Sets Free (Jesus) took *only* Stands On The Rock (Peter), He Takes Over

---

y **16:18** Greek, petros, meaning a small rock or stone   z **16:18** Greek, petra, meaning a huge rock
a **16:18** Lit., gates   b **16:19** Lit., keys

(James) and his brother He Shows Goodwill (John) up on a great high mountain. ² Right there before them his appearance began to change. His clothes turned bright white and his face began to shine like the sun.

³ Then before their eyes *two ancestors appeared— the lawgiver* Drawn From The Water (Moses) and *the ancient prophet* Great Spirit Is Creator (Elijah). They were talking with Creator Sets Free (Jesus).

They all stared in wide-eyed wonder not knowing what to say. Then Stands On The Rock (Peter) found his voice.

⁴ "Wisdomkeeper," he said out loud, "this is a good place to stay. If you want, I will put up three tipis— one for you, one for Drawn From The Water (Moses), and one for Great Spirit Is Creator (Elijah)."

⁵ While he was still speaking, a bright cloud covered them. A voice spoke from the cloud, saying, "This is my much loved Son, the one who makes my heart glad. Listen to him!"

⁶ They all fell on their faces in fear, ⁷ but Creator Sets Free (Jesus) laid his hands on them and said, "Do not fear! Stand to your feet."

⁸ When they looked around, *the cloud was gone, the men were gone,* and all they could see was Creator Sets Free (Jesus) standing alone in front of them.

⁹ As they walked down the mountainside, he instructed them to tell no one what they had seen until after the True Human Being had come back to life from the dead.

During the long walk down the mountain, the three followers had a lot to think about. Perhaps they were wondering about the ancient prophecies and how they related to what they had just seen.

¹⁰ They asked him, "Why do the scroll keepers say that Great Spirit Is Creator (Elijah) must be first to come?"

¹¹ "It is true," he answered, "Great Spirit Is Creator (Elijah) is the first to come to return all things to their original purpose, ¹² but I am telling you that he has already come— but no one recognized him. They did whatever they wanted with him, just as the Sacred Teachings foretold. It is also foretold that they will treat the True Human Being in the same way; they will look down on him and turn their faces away from him."

¹³ Then his followers understood he was talking about He Shows Goodwill (John) who performed the purification ceremony.

A Generation With No Faith

They continued down the mountain to rejoin the other followers. When they arrived, there was a crowd of people there waiting for them.

¹⁴ From the crowd of people a man came to Creator Sets Free (Jesus) and humbled himself before him.

¹⁵ "Wisdomkeeper!" the man said *with desperation in his voice.* "Take pity on my son. An evil spirit has taken hold of him and makes him suffer greatly; he often falls into

the fire or the water. 16 I brought him to your followers, but they failed to heal him."

17 "The people of this generation are bent and twisted with no faith! How much longer will I have to put up with you?" Creator Sets Free (Jesus) cried out. Then he said, "Bring the boy to me."

18 He spoke sharply to the evil spirit and it left the boy, and right then he was healed.

19 Later when Creator Sets Free (Jesus) was alone with his followers, they asked him, "Why couldn't we force the evil spirit out of him?"

20 "It is because of your weak faith," he answered and then said to them, "I speak from my heart, if you had faith like a mustard seed, you could tell this mountain to move from here to there and it would do what you say. Nothing would be too hard for you. 21 But it takes praying and going without food, to make you ready to force out a spirit of this kind."c

The Road Ahead

22 While they were in Circle of Nations (Galilee), Creator Sets Free (Jesus) gathered his followers together.

"The True Human Being will soon be taken and handed over to men 23 who will kill him," he told them, "but on the third day he will come back to life from the dead."

This filled his followers with sorrow and dread.

Dues for the Sacred Lodge

From there he and his followers walked to Village of Comfort (Capernaum) where Stands On The Rock (Peter) and his brother Stands With Courage (Andrew) lived.

24 When they came into Village of Comfort (Capernaum), some of the men who collected the money for the Ceremonial Lodge *that was in Village of Peace (Jerusalem)* came to Stands On The Rock (Peter).

"Does your Wisdomkeeper pay his dues for the Lodge?" they asked.

25 "Yes, he does," he answered them.

When he returned to his house, before he could say a word about what happened, Creator Sets Free (Jesus) said to him *using his family name,* "Tell me, One Who Hears (Simon), do the rulers of the land collect taxes or dues from their own family members or from others? How do you see it?"

26 "From others," Stands On The Rock (Peter) answered.

"So then," he said back to him, "the family members do not have to pay; 27 but, to keep from insulting them, *we will pay.* Go to the lake and open the mouth of the first fish you catch, and you will find a silver coin. Use that to pay the dues for both of us."

Who is Truly Great?

18 The ones who walked the road with Creator Sets Free (Jesus) came to him. "Who is

---

c 17:21 Verse 21 is not found in most ancient manuscripts.

the greatest one on Creator's Good Road from above?" they asked.

2 He had a small child come to him and stood the child in front of them.

3 "I speak from my heart," he said to them, "unless you become like a little child, you will not find the pathway onto the Good Road. 4 The ones who humble themselves, like this little child, will become great ones in the Land of Creator's Good Road."

He then lifted up the child into his arms.

5 "The ones who represent me and welcome a little child—like this one—welcome me."

Stumbling Stones

Then he spoke in a more serious manner.

6 "But for the ones who put a stumbling stone in the path of one of these little ones who trust in me, it would be better for them to have a great stone tied to their necks and be drowned in the deep waters! 7 This world of sorrow and pain will make many stumble, but how terrible it will be for the ones who go along with it!

8 "So, if what your hand or foot does makes you stumble from the path, cut it off and throw it away! It is better to walk this life without a hand or foot than to be thrown into the fire that never stops burning.

9 "If what your eye sees makes you stumble on the path, then gouge it out and throw it away! It is better for you to walk this life with only one eye than to be thrown into the Valley of Smoldering Fire.

10 "So do not look down on even one of these little ones, for their spirit-messengers in the world above always look upon the face of my Father, the one who is above us all. 11 For the True Human Being has come to rescue the lost ones."[d]

The Worth of the Little Ones

12 "How do you see it?" he asked them. "If a man has one hundred sheep and one of them wanders away, will he not leave the ninety-nine on the mountainside to go and find the lost one? 13 If he finds that lost one—I speak from my heart—he will find more joy for that one than for the ninety-nine that were not lost. 14 In the same way your Father from the world above does not want to lose even one of these little ones.

Handling Conflict

15 "If a Tribal family member[e] wrongs you, go to him alone and tell him. If he listens, then you have won him back. 16 If he cannot see the wrong, then go to him with one or two others who have seen the wrong, so he can hear them. 17 If he still will not listen, take him before the Sacred Family Council. If he will not hear the council, then he will be the same to you as an outsider or a tribal tax collector.

18 "I speak from my heart, what has been decided in the world above is what you will decide on earth.

---

d 18:11 Verse 11 does not appear in most ancient manuscripts.   e 18:15 Lit., brother

19-20 From my heart I will say it again this way: When two or three have gathered together on earth to represent me, I will be there *in spirit to guide you.* Then, *under my guidance,* whatever two or more of you agree upon and ask for will be done by my Father from above."

A Question About Forgiveness

21 Stands On The Rock (Peter) came close to Creator Sets Free (Jesus). "Wisdomkeeper," he asked, "how many times must I forgive a brother or sister who does wrong to me? Is seven times enough?

22 "Not just seven times," Creator Sets Free (Jesus) answered, "but seventy times seven."

Story About Forgiveness

To help them see more clearly into the ways of forgiveness, he told them this story:

23 "So then, Creator's Good Road is like a ruler who wanted to collect the money owed to him by his hired servants. 24 The first one brought to him owed ten thousand horses.*f* 25 The man could not repay him, so the ruler ordered that the man, his family and all he owned be sold to pay for the debt.

26 "The servant fell to his knees before him and said, 'Ruler, give me time and I will repay all that I owe!'

27 "The ruler felt sorry for the servant, set him free and released him from his debt.

28 "But that same servant went to one of his fellow servants who owed him only a small horse blanket.*g* He took hold of the man's throat and said, 'Pay me all that you owe!'

29 "The man humbled himself, bowed down and pleaded, 'Please, give me more time and I will repay you!'

30 "But the man would not even listen. He threw him into prison until he could pay all that he owed. 31 When his fellow servants saw this, it made their hearts fall to the ground. They went to the ruler and told him the sad story.

32 "The ruler had the man brought to him and said, 'You worthless servant! *How could your heart be so cold?* I forgave you all your debt because you begged me to. 33 Why would you not do the same for your fellow servant?'

34 "The ruler was angry with him and put him in prison to be punished until his debt was paid in full."

Creator Sets Free (Jesus) looked deep into the eyes of the ones who walked the road with him.

35 "My Father from above is warning you that the same thing will happen to you, unless, from your heart, you each forgive your fellow human beings."

19 After Creator Sets Free (Jesus) had finished speaking in the territory of Circle of Nations (Galilee), he left there and went to the territory of the Land of Promise (Judea) beyond the river Flowing

---

f **18:24** About sixteen years of wages   g **18:28** About a day's wages

Down (Jordan). [2] Once again large crowds came to him there, and he healed them.

Marriage and Divorce

Like hungry wolves the Separated Ones (Pharisees) began to come in packs and test him with questions about Tribal Law, hoping to trap him. They knew that among the spiritual leaders there was much disagreement about how to interpret the instructions about marriage and divorce.

[3] Some of the Separated Ones (Pharisees) came to him. "Does our Tribal Law permit a man to put away his wife for any and every reason?" they asked.

[4] "Have you not read in the Sacred Teachings," Creator Sets Free (Jesus) asked them, "that, in the beginning of creation, from one human being the Great Spirit made two—one male and one female. [5] This is why a man will leave his father and mother and be joined to his wife. Together they become one flesh, [6] no longer two, but one body joined together.[h] No human being should tear apart what Creator has put together."

Like sly coyotes they smiled at each other. They were sure that he could not answer their next question.

[7] "Why then," they asked him, "does Drawn From the Water (Moses), in the Law, instruct that a man give his wife divorce papers before sending her away?"

[8] "It is because of your cold hearts of stone that Drawn From the Water (Moses) permitted this," he answered, "but this was not the Great Spirit's original plan for men and women.

[9] "But here is how I will answer you," he told them. "Any man who sends his wife away *without divorce papers* and marries another is guilty of being unfaithful to her, unless she was the one who was not faithful."

[10] The ones who walked the road with *him shook their heads and* said, "If this is so, between husband and wife, then it must be better not to marry."

[11] "Not many can hold to this teaching," he answered them, "but only those to whom it has been gifted. *There are many reasons for not getting married.* [12] Some are born with no desire or ability for marriage. Some have lost their ability from what has been done to them. Others choose not to marry so they can put all their strength into walking the Good Road from above. The ones who have this gift are able to walk in this wisdom."

Little Children and the Good Road

[13] The people were bringing their little children to Creator Sets Free (Jesus) so he would lay his hands on them and pray, but his followers spoke harsh words to the ones bringing them.

---

h 19:6 Genesis 1:27

¹⁴ "Let the little children come to me!" Creator Sets Free (Jesus) said to his followers. "Do not turn them away. Creator's Good Road from above belongs to the ones who are like these children."

¹⁵ He then took the children into his arms, laid his hands on them, *blessed them* and then went on his way.

Possessions or the Good Road

¹⁶ As he was walking on down the road, a man came to him. "Wisdomkeeper," he asked, "what good must I do to find the life of the world to come that never fades away?"

¹⁷ "Why do you ask me about what is good?" he asked the man. "There is only one who is good—*the Great Spirit.* If you want this life, then follow the instructions *given in our Tribal Law.*

¹⁸ "Which instructions?" the young headman asked.

"You already know them," Creator Sets Free (Jesus) answered. "Do not take away the life of another, do not be unfaithful in marriage, and do not take what is not yours. Be honest in all you say and do, and never cheat a fellow human being. ¹⁹ Give honor and respect to your father and mother, and love your fellow human beings as much as you love yourself."

²⁰ "*Wisdomkeeper,*" the man answered, "from my youth I have followed all of these instructions. What have I left undone?"

²¹ "Only one thing remains," he answered. "Take all of your possessions and give them to the ones who have none, then you will have great possessions in the world above."

Creator Sets Free (Jesus) then gave the man the same invitation that he gave to his message bearers.

"Come," he said to the man, "and walk the road with me."

²² But when the young man heard this, his heart fell to the ground. He hung his head and walked away, for he had many possessions.

Help to Walk the Good Road

²³ "I speak from my heart," Creator Sets Free (Jesus) then said to his followers, "Finding the way onto the Good Road from above is a hard thing for the ones who have many possessions. ²⁴ It would be easier for a moose[i] to squeeze through the eye of a *beading* needle."

²⁵ His followers could not believe what they were hearing. "How then can anyone find and walk the Good Road?" they asked.

²⁶ Creator Sets Free (Jesus) set his eyes firmly on them and said, "With two-leggeds this is impossible, but all things are possible with the help of the Great Spirit—for nothing is impossible for him."

²⁷ Then Stands On The Rock (Peter) spoke up, "We have left all our possessions, and our relatives, to walk the road with you! What will become of us?"

---

i 19:24 Lit., camel

28 "I speak to you from my heart," he answered, "in the new world that is coming, the True Human Being will sit in his place of honor, and you who have walked the road with me will sit in twelve places of honor, deciding what is good and right for the twelve tribes of Wrestles With Creator (Israel).

29 "All who have given up their homes and families because they represent me will receive back much more[j] than they have lost, and the life of the world to come that never fades away will be theirs.

For they now belong to Creator's Sacred Family that will care for them.

30 "But *remember*, many who are first *in this present world* will be last in the world to come, and many who are last *in this present world* will be first in the one to come."

20 *To help them to better understand what he was saying, Creator Sets Free (Jesus) told them another story about Creator's Good Road.*

Workers in a Vineyard

"Creator's Good Road from above is like this tribal member who managed a large vineyard. He went out early in the morning to find people to harvest the grapes." 2 After they agreed with him on the amount for a full day's pay, he sent them to work.

3 "A few hours later he went to the trading post and saw people there doing nothing.

4 "He told them, 'If you will join the workers in my field, I will pay you well.'

5 "So they went to work. Then, about midday, and again at mid-afternoon, he went out and found others and did the same. 6 "Finally, when the day was nearly done, he found a few more people doing nothing.

"'Why aren't you working?' he asked them.

7 "'No one has hired us,' they answered. He agreed to pay them fairly, and sent them to work.

8 "At the end of the day, the headman said to his manager, 'Bring the workers in from the field and pay them, beginning from last to first.'

9 "He paid the workers hired at the end of the day a full day's wage. 10 When the workers who were hired at the start of the day were paid, they expected to receive more, but were paid the same amount.

11 "'We have worked all day in the scorching heat,' they complained to the manager. 12 'Why should we be paid the same as the ones who worked only one hour?'

13 "'I am not being unfair with you, my friend,' he said to one of them, 'Did we not agree on the amount of a full day's wages? 14 Take your pay and go *in peace*. If I want to pay

---

j **19:29** Lit., one hundred times as much

these men the same, what is that to you? 15 Am I not permitted to be generous with what is mine? Or are you jealous because I have done a good thing?'"

Creator Sets Free (Jesus) let his followers think about the story for a moment.

16 "That is why I told you before," he reminded them, "the last will be first and the first will be last."

A Solemn Reminder

17 As they journeyed on toward the Village of Peace (Jerusalem), he stopped on the way and gathered his followers around him.

18 "We are on our way up to the Village of Peace (Jerusalem)," he reminded them. "There the True Human Being will be handed over to the head priests and scroll keepers, who will put him to death. 19 They will condemn him to death and hand him over to the People of Iron (Romans).*k* They will treat him shamefully, whip him with cords of braided cowhide, and kill him by nailing him to a cross.

"But remember, he added, "on the third day he will defeat death and live again."

The Good Road is About Serving Others

20 The mother of He Takes Over (James) and He Shows Goodwill (John), *who are the sons of Gift of Creator (Zebedee),* came close to Creator Sets Free (Jesus) and humbled herself before him to make a request.

21 "What do you want from me?" he asked.

"Promise me," she said, "that my two sons will have an honored place when your Good Road comes—one on your right hand, the other on your left."

22 "You do not know what you are asking," he said to her.

He turned to her sons and asked them, "Can you drink the cup of suffering that I will drink, or endure my purification ceremony?"

"We are able!" they answered.

23 "Yes, you will drink from my cup of suffering," he said to them, "but the place of honor on my right and left hand is not mine to give. My Father will give this honor to the ones he has chosen."

24 When the other ten message bearers heard this, they began to look down on the two brothers.

25 So Creator Sets Free (Jesus) called them together and said, "Other nations, *like the People of Iron (Romans),* have rulers. They like to show their power over people and push them around. 26 But this will not be the way of the ones who walk with me. The ones among you who would be great must humble themselves and serve all the others. 27 And the ones who want to be first must become the household slave of all. 28 In the same way, the True Human Being did not come to be served by others, but to offer his life in the place of many lives, to set them free."

---

k 20:19 Lit., Gentiles

Two Blind Men See Again

The road to Village of Peace (Jerusalem) took them through Moon Village (Jericho).

²⁹ As they walked out from Moon Village (Jericho), a large crowd of people trailed after them. ³⁰ Not far from the village there were two blind men sitting on the side of the road.

When the blind men heard that Creator Sets Free (Jesus) was passing by, they cried out to him, "Honored One! Descendant of Much Loved One (David), have pity on us!"

³¹ The people in the crowd scolded them and said, "Be quiet!"

That only made them cry out louder, "Honored One! Descendant of Much Loved One (David), have pity on us!"

³² Creator Sets Free (Jesus) stopped walking and called out to them, "What do you want from me?"

³³ "Honored One," they said, "open our eyes, that we may see."

³⁴ He felt pity for them, so he touched their eyes, and right then their eyes were opened and they could see! So they went with him down the road.

21 *Creator Sets Free (Jesus) and the ones who walked the road with him were coming to the end of their journey. As they neared Village of Peace (Jerusalem), he began to make preparations for what would be his final week with his followers. It was now time to complete the work the Great Spirit had sent him to do.*

Grand Entry

They came to House of Unripe Figs (Bethphage) at the foot of Olive Mountain, near Village of Peace (Jerusalem). There he sent two of his followers ahead of him.

² "Go into the village ahead of us," he instructed them. "As soon as you enter, you will find a donkey tied there with her colt. Untie them and bring them to me. ³ If anyone asks you what you are doing, say to them, 'Our Wisdomkeeper has need of them,' and the owner will release them to you."

⁴ This took place to show the full meaning of the ancient prophecy, ⁵ "Speak these words to the daughter of Strong Mountain (Zion): 'Behold, your Chief is coming to you, in a humble way, riding upon a donkey—a colt still with its mother.'"[l]

⁶ His followers did as they were told. When they arrived at the village, they found everything just as he had said. ⁷ They brought the donkey colt to Creator Sets Free (Jesus), laid their outer garments on the colt, and he sat down on them.

⁸ From the large crowd many began to cut branches from nearby trees and spread their outer garments on the road in front of him. ⁹ The crowd circled around him, front and back, and began to shout:

"Hosanna!—*Set Us Free!*—to the descendant of Much Loved One (David)!"

---

l 21:5 Zechariah 9:9-10

"Blessed is the one who comes representing the Great Spirit!"

"Hosanna to the highest one!"

This humble Chief did not fit the image of a conquering ruler. Instead of a warhorse he rode upon a donkey colt. No mighty warriors rode next to him; no dignitaries came out to meet him. It was mostly the common people who welcomed him that day.

10 When he rode through the gate entering the Village of Peace (Jerusalem), the whole village was in an uproar!

"Who is this?" they asked.

11 "He is Creator Sets Free (Jesus), the prophet from Seed Planter Village (Nazareth) in Circle of Nations (Galilee)," the crowd answered.

Sacred Lodge Keeper

12 Creator Sets Free (Jesus) rode into the village and to the Sacred Lodge. He entered the Lodge and began to force out the ones who were selling and buying *ceremonial animals*. He then tipped over the tables of the money-handlers and the seats of the ones who were selling the *ceremonial* doves.

13 "It is written *from the words of the prophets,"* he cried out, "'My Lodge will be called a house of prayer for all nations, but you have turned it into a hideout for thieves!'*m*"

The ancient prophecies had now found their full meaning, for this was the area of the Lodge called Gathering Place for the Nations. It was here that other nations could come to learn about the Great Spirit and his ways. The holy men were keeping the Outside Nations who wanted to learn of Creator's ways from entering into this Holy Place. They were stealing the ways of the Great Spirit from the Nations.

14 After that, people who could not see or walk came to him at the Lodge, and he healed them. 15 The children came to him there, shouting for joy, "Hosanna to the descendant of Much Loved One (David)!"

The children then made a circle around him and laughed, danced and sang songs.

But when the head holy men and the scroll keepers saw the wonderful things he did and heard the children shouting *and singing,* they burned with anger 16 and said to him, "Do you hear what these children are saying?"

"I hear them," he answered, "but have you not heard what the ancient Sacred Teachings say? 'From the mouths of little children and nursing babies you have created praise.'*n*"

17 Then Creator Sets Free (Jesus) left Village of Peace (Jerusalem) and returned to House of Figs (Bethany) *where he was lodging.*

A Fig Tree With No Fruit

18 The next morning, as he was returning to Village of Peace (Jerusalem), he became hungry. 19 He saw a fig tree on the side of the

---

m 21:13 Isaiah 56:7; Jeremiah 7:11   n 21:16 Psalm 8:2

road and went to it; but when he came to the tree, he found only leaves.

He spoke to the tree, "You will never again grow fruit!" and the fig tree began to wither away right then and there.

[20] When the ones who walked the road with him saw the tree withering, they were amazed.

"How did it dry up and wither so quickly?" they asked.

[21] "I speak from my heart, if you put all your trust in the Great Spirit and do not doubt *that the Knower Of Hearts hears you,*" he answered them, "not only will you do what was done with this fig tree, but even if you speak to this mountain and say, 'Be lifted up and go into the great waters,' it will happen. [22] So when you send your prayers to the Great Spirit, believe that he hears you, and whatever you ask for will be yours."

Questioned by the Spiritual Leaders

[23] When he arrived at the Lodge, the head priests *were waiting for him.* They, and the ruling elders of the people, came to him.

"By what right do you do these things?" they challenged. "Who gave you this right?"

[24] "First you must answer one question from me," he challenged back, "then I will tell you what gives me the right. [25] The purification ceremony performed by He Shows Goodwill (John), was it from the world above, or did it come from human beings?"

They put their heads together and talked it over. "If we say it is from the world above, he will say to us, 'Why then did you not believe him?' [26] But if we say it is from human beings, we fear what this crowd would do, for they are sure He Shows Goodwill (John) was a prophet."

[27] So they answered him, "We do not know."

"So then," Creator Sets Free (Jesus) said to them, "neither will I tell you what gives me the right to do these things."

Story of Two Sons

Then, since they would not answer him, he told them the answer to his own question about He Shows Goodwill (John)—with a story.

[28] "How do you see it?" he asked them. "A man with two sons came to one of his sons and said, 'Son, will you work in my vineyard today?' [29] At first the son told him 'No,' but later changed his mind and went to work.

[30] "Then the man went to his other son and asked him the same. He told his father, 'Yes, I will,' but never went.

[31] *Creator Sets Free (Jesus) looked right at the spiritual leaders and asked,* "Which of the two sons did what his father wanted?"

They said to him, "The first one."

"I speak truth from my heart," he said to them, "tribal tax collectors and those who sell sexual favors will find their way onto Creator's

Good Road ahead of you! ³² He Shows Goodwill (John) came to show the good way, but you refused to hear him. You saw how the tribal tax collectors and those who sell sexual favors put their trust in him, but not even this changed your mind to believe him."

Story of the Vineyard

³³ "Hear me," he said to them, "and I will tell you another story.

"There was a tribal member who planted a vineyard. He put a hedge around it, dug a pit to crush the grapes, and built a treehouse from which to watch over all the vines. He then rented the vineyard out to other tribal members *for a share of the grapes*. Then he traveled far away to another land.

³⁴ "When harvest time came, the tribal member who owned the vineyard sent trusted messengers to gather his share of the grapes; ³⁵ but the renters took hold of the messengers. They fiercely beat one, killed another and even threw stones to kill another.

³⁶ "Then the vineyard owner sent even more messengers than at first, but they did the same to them.

³⁷ "Finally he sent his son to them, thinking, 'They will respect my son.'

³⁸ "But when they saw that he had sent his son, they said to each other, 'This vineyard will one day belong to this son. If we kill him, we can take the vineyard for ourselves.'

³⁹ "So they dragged him out of the vineyard and murdered him."

Creator Sets Free (Jesus) turned to face the spiritual leaders.

⁴⁰ "When he returns, what will the owner of this vineyard do?" he asked them.

⁴¹ They answered him, "He will bring those bad-hearted ones to a bad end and then rent out the vineyard to others who will be honorable and give him the share of the harvest he deserves."

Stumbling Over the Chief Pole

⁴² "Are you blind to the Sacred Teachings?" he said to them. "Have you not read this: 'The tree the lodge builders threw away has become the Chief Pole. This is what the Great Spirit has done, and it will fill us with wonder'ᵒ?

⁴³ "So I say to you that Creator's Good Road will be torn from you and given to a people who will bring its fruit to a full harvest; for the ones who stumble over this Chief Pole will be broken into pieces; ⁴⁴ and when it falls on them, they will be crushed *and scattered like dust in the wind.*"

⁴⁵ When the head holy men and the Separated Ones (Pharisees) heard his stories, they realized they were about them. ⁴⁶ They wanted to arrest Creator Sets Free (Jesus), but feared the people, since they considered him a prophet.

---

o 21:42 Psalm 118:22-23

A Rejected Invitation

22 Creator Sets Free (Jesus) continued to speak to them using stories like this one:

2 "Creator's Good Road from above is like a chief who prepared a wedding feast for his son. 3 When the feast was ready, he sent out trusted messengers to gather the ones who had been invited, but no one came.

4 "So he sent out others with this message: 'I am serving my best beef fresh from the herd. So come, the wedding feast for my son has been prepared!'

5 "But some ignored the messengers and returned to their work, 6 while others mistreated them and even killed them.

7 "When the chief found out what they had done, he was filled with rage and sent his warriors to kill those murderers and burn their village to the ground.

8 "Then the chief told his messengers, 'The wedding feast is ready, but the ones invited have proved they have no honor. 9 Waste no time, go out into the village pathways and invite all you find to come to the feast.'

10 "So they went and did as they were told and gathered as many as they could find, whether honorable or bad-hearted. So the lodge was filled with many wedding guests *for his son.*

11 "When the chief came in to see the guests, he saw someone who was not wearing the proper regalia *that was provided for the guests at the wedding feast.* 12 He said to the guest, 'How did you get in here without the proper regalia? "There was nothing the man could say.

By not wearing the outfit provided, the man was dishonoring the chief and his son.

13 "The chief called his warriors and said to them, 'Bind him with leather straps from head to foot and throw him outside into the darkness, to weep and grind his teeth in anger.'

14 "So you can see," Creator Sets Free (Jesus) said, "many are invited, but few accept his invitation."[p]

The Separated Ones Attack

15 The Separated Ones (Pharisees) began to scheme against Creator Sets Free (Jesus). 16 They sent their followers along with some of the Friends of Looks Brave (Herodians) to spy on him.

"Wisdomkeeper," they said to him, "we know you always speak the truth about the Great Spirit and represent him well. You show respect to human beings and treat them all the same. 17 Tell us what is right, should our tribal members pay taxes to the Ruler of the People of Iron (Caesar)? Yes or no?"

18 He could see right through them; he knew what they were up to!

"Why are you putting me to the test? I can see behind your false faces!" he answered. 19 "Show me

---

p **22:14** Lit., Few are chosen.

one of their silver coins used to pay the tax *and let me take a close look at it.*"

They found a silver coin and handed it to him.

He took a good long look, holding it up to the sky to see it clearly. Then he turned the face of the coin toward them.

20 "Whose image and words are carved into this coin?" he asked.

21 "The Ruler of the People of Iron (Caesar)," they answered.

He *handed the coin back to them and* said, "Then give to this ruler the things that are his, and give to the Great Spirit the things that belong to the Great Spirit."

22 When they heard his answer, they were amazed at his wisdom and *hung their heads in silence as they* walked away.

The Upright Ones Attack

23 Later that same day some of the Upright Ones (Sadducees), who say that the dead do not rise again, came to Creator Sets Free (Jesus) to question him also.

24 "Wisdomkeeper," they said, "in our Tribal Law, Drawn From the Water (Moses) gave us these instructions: 'If a Tribal Member should die before having children, then his brother should marry his widow and give her children to carry on his brother's name.'

25 "In a family of seven brothers," they continued, "the oldest took a wife, but died without children.

26 The next brother married her, but he also died with no children. A third brother married her, and like his other brothers, he died with no children. The same happened to all seven of them, 27 and, last of all, the woman also crossed over to death. 28 So, when they all come back to life in the new world, whose wife would she be, since all seven brothers married her?"

29 "You are asking the wrong question," Creator Sets Free (Jesus) answered back. "You do not understand the Sacred Teachings or the power of the Great Spirit. 30 When the dead rise to life, there will be no marriage, for they will be like the spirit-messengers from the world above."

31 Then he added, "You say you do not believe the dead will rise again. But have you not read what was told by the Maker of Life: 32 'I am the Great Spirit of Father Of Many Nations (Abraham), of He Made Us Laugh (Isaac), and of Heel Grabber (Jacob)'[q]?

"He is not the Great Spirit of the dead, but of the living."

33 All the people who heard him were amazed by his teaching.

The Greatest of the Instructions

34 When the Separated Ones (Pharisees) heard how he silenced the Upright Ones (Sadducees), they put their heads together and came up with a plan. 35 One of them, who was an expert in Tribal Law, would put him to the test.

---

q 22:32 Exodus 3:6

³⁶ The expert came to him. "Wisdomkeeper," he asked, "which instruction in our Tribal Law stands first?"

³⁷ Creator Sets Free (Jesus) answered him, "'You must love the Great Spirit from deep within, with the strength of your arms, the thoughts of your mind, and the courage of your heart.'ʳ ³⁸ This is the first and greatest instruction.

³⁹ "The second is like the first," he added. "'You must love your fellow human beings in the same way you love yourselves.'ˢ ⁴⁰ The Law and the words of the prophets all find their full meaning in these two instructions."

He Silences His Adversaries

⁴¹ While the Separated Ones (Pharisees) were still gathered near him, he asked them this question, ⁴² "How do you see the Chosen One? Who is he descended from?"

"He is the son who is descended from Much Loved One (David)," they answered.

⁴³ "How can the scroll keepers call him the descendant of Much Loved One (David)," he asked, "when Much Loved One (David) himself, speaking by the power of the Spirit, called the Chosen One his Honored Chief? ⁴⁴ For in the book of Sacred Songs he said, 'The Honored Chief said to my Honored Chief, "Sit down beside me at my right hand, my place of greatest honor, until I bring your enemies under my loving power."ᵗ'?"

He paused to let them think about his words.

⁴⁵ Then he said, "If Much Loved One (David) calls the Chosen One, 'My Honored Chief,' how can the Chosen One be his descendant?"

⁴⁶ None of the spiritual leaders could answer him. From that time on, no one dared to challenge him with another question.

His great wisdom had silenced the ones who were against him.

Bad Spiritual Leaders

23 *Creator Sets Free (Jesus) cared deeply about the people, so he began to warn the people and his followers about the bad spiritual leaders.*

¹⁻² "The Separated Ones (Pharisees) and the scroll keepers *are leading you down the wrong path!*" he said to the people and his followers. "When they speak, they represent the lawgiver Drawn From the Water (Moses), ³ so listen when they speak the truth and do what they say, but do not walk in their ways. They fail to do the things they demand of others ⁴ and tie heavy *spiritual* loads on their backs, too much for them to carry, but will not lift even one finger to help them.

⁵ "They want to look important to others, so to look spiritual they wear large and fancy medicine pouches and long fringes on their outfits. ⁶ They love to dress up in fine regalia, sit in the seats of honor at the gathering houses, ⁷ and have people call them 'wisdomkeeper' at the trading posts."

---

r 22:37 Deuteronomy 6:5   s 22:39 Leviticus 19:18   t 22:44 Psalm 110:1

Then he turned to instruct the ones who walked the road with him.

The Great Will Serve

8-10 "Titles like 'wisdomkeeper,' 'chief,' and 'spiritual guide' are not for you. There is only one true Wisdomkeeper, Chief and Spiritual Guide—the Chosen One—and you all belong to his family; so call no one on earth by the title 'father,' for only the Great Spirit is truly the Father of us all. 11 The great ones among you will be servant of all. 12 The ones who put themselves above others will be brought down low; the ones who humble themselves will be lifted up."

Then he turned again and began to boldly confront the bad spiritual leaders.

Sorrow and Trouble

13 "Sorrow and trouble is waiting for you scroll keepers and Separated Ones (Pharisees), for you have hidden from the people the way onto the Good Road from above. You have failed to walk the Good Road yourselves, and, even worse, you have barred the way for others who were trying to find the way.

14 "Sorrow and trouble will come your way, you scroll keepers and Separated Ones (Pharisees), for with many words you make long empty prayers and you trick widows into giving you their homes and possessions. You will come to a bad end when your fate is decided. *u*

15 "Sorrow and trouble await you blind guides with false faces, for you journey far and wide, across the great waters, to find one person who will change to your ways. When you have won him over, he becomes twice as bad as you are, a true son of the Valley of Smoldering Fire.

16 "And to the blind guides who say, 'A promise made outside the Lodge can be broken, but one made inside must be kept,' 17 you are so foolish and blind! It is not the Lodge that makes the promise good, but it is the Great Spirit over the Lodge who sees and hears all promises.

18 "Or you say, 'A promise made before a ceremony can be broken, but one made during a ceremony must be kept.' 19 Are you so blind? Can you not see that the Great Spirit sees and hears all promises and expects you to keep them?

20-22 "It matters not if a promise is made inside or outside the Lodge, or before or during a sacred ceremony. All promises on the earth below or in the world above are made before the eyes of the Great Spirit, who sees and hears everything.

23 "Sorrow and trouble wait for you scroll keepers and Separated Ones (Pharisees), with false faces you are careful to do what Tribal Law says by giving a tenth of each little herb in your garden, but you ignore the more important instructions like justice, kindness and honesty. 24 You are spiritually blind guides,

---

u 23:14 Most manuscripts leave out verse 14.

for you strain out a small flea *from your water pouch,* but swallow a whole moose.ᵛ

25 "Sorrow and trouble will be your end, you scroll keepers and Separated Ones (Pharisees), for you wash the outside of your cups and bowls, but on the inside your hearts are full of greed and selfish ways. 26 You blind Separated Ones (Pharisees)! First clean the inside of your cup, then the outside of the cup will become clean also.

27 "Sorrow and trouble will be waiting at the end of the trail for you Separated Ones (Pharisees) and scroll keepers who hide behind false faces. You are like burial caves that have been painted white to look good on the outside, but on the inside you are full of dead men's bones and rotting things. 28 You may look good to others, but you are full of falsehood and worthless ways.

29 "Sorrow and trouble will be waiting at the end of the trail for you Separated Ones (Pharisees) and scroll keepers who hide behind false faces. You put great decorated stones on the burial grounds of the prophets and the ones who walked upright—the ones your ancestors killed.

An Ominous Warning

30 "You say, 'If we had lived in the days of our ancestors, we would not have participated with them when they shed the blood of the prophets.'

31 But you are speaking against yourselves, for you are admitting that you are the descendants of the ones who killed them, 32 and you will finish what your ancestors started! 33 You nest of poisonous snakes! How will you escape the bad end of the Valley of Smoldering Fire?"

34 "That is why I am sending to you prophets, wisdomkeepers and scroll keepers. You will whip some of them in your gathering houses; others you will nail to a cross. You will threaten them and pursue them from village to village *until you shed their blood.* 35 Then you will be guilty of shedding the innocent blood of all who have lived on the earth from His Breath Goes Up (Abel), who was killed by his brother,ʷ to Creator Will Remember (Zechariah), the son of He Will Be Blessed (Barachiah), who was put to death in the courtyard of the Sacred Lodge.ˣ

36 "I speak the truth from my heart, all these things will happen to this generation.

O Village of Peace!

A dark cloud cast a shadow over Creator Sets Free (Jesus), and a look of pain and sorrow came upon his face.

37 "Jerusalem, O Village of Peace!" *he cried out loud for all to hear,* "You who kill the prophets and stone to death the ones sent to you! How I have longed to gather your children

---

v 23:24 Lit., camel   w 23:35 Abel was the second son of Red Clay (Adam), the first human to be killed by another. See Genesis 4:1-16 for the story.   x 23:35 Lit., between the altar and the sanctuary

together, like an eagle gathers her young under her wings, but you would not have it. 38 Look! Your house has fallen and will be left in ruins! 39 I speak from my heart, you will not see me again until you say, 'Blessed is the one who comes representing the Great Spirit!'"

The Sacred Lodge Will Fall

24 As Creator Sets Free (Jesus) made his way out of the Sacred Lodge, his followers began to point out to him all the buildings that surrounded the Sacred Lodge.

As he stopped and looked around at the Lodge and all its buildings, a look of great sadness came over his face.

2 "Take a good long look, for I speak truth from my heart—all of these will fall to the ground. Not one log or stone will be left standing against another."

Signs of the End

3 *Later that day* Creator Sets Free (Jesus) sat down *to rest* on the side of Olive Mountain.

From there he could look across the valley past the walls of Village of Peace (Jerusalem) and see the Sacred Lodge.

Some of his followers came to him privately. "Wisdomkeeper," they asked *with worried faces,* "when will these things happen? What will be the sign of your coming that will bring an end to this age we live in?"

4 "Beware of those who would lead you down a false path,"

Creator Sets Free (Jesus) warned them, 5 "for many will come falsely representing who I am, and say, 'I am the Chosen One,' and many will follow them to a bad end.

6 "When you hear of wars and stories of war breaking out, do not fear, for all of this must happen; but the end will not come all at once. 7 There will be tribal wars, and nations will make war against other nations. Food will be scarce and the earth will shake in many places— 8 but this is only the beginning of the time of sorrow, like a woman feeling the pains of birth.

9 "Because you represent me, you will be looked down on by all the nations; they will hunt you down and kill you, all because you follow me. 10 When this happens, many will stumble on the path and even hate and betray each other.

11 "Then many false prophets will rise up and lead many down false paths. 12 Because evildoers will grow strong, the love in many hearts will grow cold— 13 but the ones who stand firm *in their faith* to the end will be rescued and made whole.

14 "The Good News about Creator's Good Road will be told in truth for all the nations of this world to hear. Then the end will come.

A Time of Sorrow and Trouble

15 "When you see the 'horrible thing that destroys,' that the prophet Creator Will Decide (Daniel) told about,*y* making its stand against

---

y 24:15 Daniel 9:27; 11:31; 12:11; Luke 21:20; Mark 13:14

the place that is holy—the reader will understand the meaning—[16] you will then know it is time for those who live in the Land of Promise (Judea) to escape to the mountains. [17] If you are on your rooftop, go—without taking time to get anything from your house. [18] Workers in the fields should not even go back to get their outer garments. [19] It will be a terrible time for women who are pregnant or nursing their babies. [20] Pray that it will not happen in winter or on a Day of Resting.

[21] "It will be a time of trouble and sorrow like no other. A worse time has not been seen since the world was created—and there will never be a time like this again. [22] If that terrible time was allowed to reach the end of the trail, no one would survive, but for the sake of Creator's chosen ones those days will be cut short.

[23] "In those days if anyone says to you, 'Look, the Chosen One is over here,' or 'Look, he is over there,' pay no attention to him, [24] for false Chosen Ones will rise up and fake prophets will appear. They will provide great signs and omens to mislead the people. Even Creator's chosen ones will be tempted to believe them.

[25] "Remember that I have warned you ahead of time! [26] So if they say, 'The Chosen One is in the desert wilderness,' do not go with them there. Or if they say, 'The Chosen One is hidden in a secret place,' do not believe them. [27] For when *the sign of*[z] the True Human Being appears, it will be like lightning when it flashes across the sky from the east to the west.

[28] *"In the same way that gathering vultures*[a] *are a sign of dead bodies, so these things are a sign of the end.*

[29] "Then, right after that time of trouble and sorrow, 'the sun will no longer shine, the moon will go dark, the stars will fall from the sky, and the powers in the world above will tremble.'[b]

[30] "This is when the sign of the True Human Being will appear in the sky. Then all the tribes of the land will weep in anguish when they see the True Human Being riding on the clouds and coming with great honor and power. [31] Then he will send out his spirit-messengers who will blow the eagle bone whistle[c] to gather his chosen ones from the four winds. From one end of the sky the other."

Wisdom From a Fig Tree

[32] "Listen to this fig tree and hear what it is saying to you: When its branches get soft and leaves appear, you know that summer will soon be here. [33] In the same way when you see all these things happening, you will know that the time is almost here. [34] I speak from my heart! All of this will happen to this generation, during the lifetime of the people who live today. [35] The earth and sky, as we know them, will fade away, but my words will never fade!

---

z 24:27 See verse 30.   a 24:28 The word for 'vulture' can also be translated 'eagle.'
b 24:29 Isaiah 13:10; 34:4   c 24:31 Lit., loud trumpet, or in Hebrew 'shofar' meaning 'ram's horn'

Always Be Ready

36 "But no one knows the day or hour that these things will take place. Not the spirit-messengers from the world above, not even Creator's own Son, but only the Great Spirit—our Father from above—knows.

37-38 "When the True Human Being comes, it will be like it was in the days before the great flood in the time of One Who Rests (Noah). In those days the people were eating and drinking and getting married until the day that One Who Rests (Noah) entered the great wooden canoe. 39 No one knew what was happening until the flood waters came, washed them away and drowned them all. It will be the same when the True Human Being appears.

40 "During that time two men will be working in the field; one will be taken away and the other left. 41 Two women will be husking corn; one will be taken away and the other left. 42 So be on the lookout, because you never know when your Honored Chief will arrive.

43 "But know this: If the elder of a family had known at what part of the night the thief was coming, he would have stayed awake and stopped the thief from breaking in. 44 Just like this elder, you must be ready, for the True Human Being will not come at the time you expect him to.

Who Will Be Wise?

45 "Who will be the wise one, worthy of trust? Will it be the uncle who was told to feed and care for the family while the elder is away?

46 A great blessing will come to that uncle when the elder returns and finds him doing so. 47 I speak from my heart, he will invite that uncle to live with the family and share everything.

48 "But what if the uncle says to himself, 'It will be a long time before he returns,' 49 then begins to abuse the family and invites the local drunks to eat and drink with him?"

Creator Sets Free (Jesus) paused to let his followers think about the answer and then continued.

50 "The elder will return at a time the uncle does not expect. 51 He will then put him out of the family to share the fate of the ones who wear false faces. There the uncle will weep with them as they grind their teeth together in anger and frustration."

Wise and Foolish Young Women

25 "When that time comes, the ones who are walking Creator's Good Road from above will be like ten young unmarried women who took their ceremonial torches and went out to welcome the groom. 2 Five of them were foolish and five were wise. 3-4 The wise women took an extra clay pot of oil along for their torches, but the foolish ones did not bother to bring any.

5 "The groom did not come when expected, and they all fell asleep as they waited. 6 Then suddenly, in the dark of the night, someone cried out, 'Look! The groom is coming, let us go welcome him!'

7 "All the women woke up to prepare their torches, *but the oil in the torches had run out.*

8 "The foolish ones said to the wise, 'Give us some of your oil so our torches won't go out.'

9 "The wise ones answered back, 'There is not enough for all of us. *Hurry,* go to the village and trade for some more.'

10 "They hurried away to get more oil; but while they were gone, the groom came and all the guests went into the lodge for the wedding feast, and the gate was closed.

11 "A while later the other women came to the gate and said to the gatekeeper, 'Honored one, O honored one, open the door and let us come in.'

12 "But he said to them, 'I truly do not even know who you are—*why should I let you in?*'"

Creator Sets Free (Jesus) finished the story with these words of wisdom.

13 "Here is what I am saying to you, *be prepared like the wise women in this story and* always be ready, for you do not know the time of day or night that the True Human Being will appear."

Story of the Trusted Tribal Members

14 "Here is another way to see how the Creator's Good Road from above will come: It is like a tribal headman preparing for a long journey. He gathered three trusted tribal members together to give them charge of his goods during his journey.

15 "He gave five herds of horses[d] to one, two herds to another, and one herd to the third man, giving each one according to his ability to make a good trade. After that he left on his journey.

16 "The man with five herds of horses went to work right away, traded well and earned five more herds. 17 In the same way the one with two herds used them to gain two more. 18 But the one who had only one, kept the herd well hidden and safe from thieves.

19 "Many moons passed before the headman returned from his journey. He gathered the trusted tribal members together to see how well they had traded.

20 "The one given five herds came forward and said, 'Look, I have gained five more!'

21 "'You have served me well, my good and trusted friend,' the headman said, 'You have done well with a small amount, now I will give you much more. Come and live with my family and enjoy all I have.'

22 "Then the man to whom he gave two herds came forward and said, 'You gave me two herds, but I have four to give back to you.' 23 The headman honored him and did the same for him as the one with ten.

24 "Then the man to whom he had given one herd came to him and

---

d 25:15 Lit., five talents. A talent was worth at least 15 years of wages.

said, "Headman, I knew you have a reputation of being a harsh man, taking what you did not plant and gathering what is not yours. 25 I was afraid, so I hid the herd away to keep them safe for you—here they are!"

26 "The headman said to him, 'You *have broken the trust I gave you, and* have proven you are lazy and no good. *I have no use for you any longer.* If you knew I was a harsh man, 27 why didn't you ask the trading post to trade for them so there would be something to show for them when I returned?'

28 "So he told them to take the herd from him and give it to the one who had ten 29 and said, 'The ones who do well with what they are given will be given more, but the ones who do nothing with it will lose even what they have been given.' 30 Then he had the man thrown out of his house into the darkness outside, the place where they weep and grind their teeth together in anger and frustration."

Fate of the Nations

31 "When the True Human Being comes in all of his power and glory, along with all of his spirit-messengers, he will sit down in his place of honor. 32 All nations will be gathered and come before him. He will choose between them like a shepherd separates the sheep from the goats. 33 He will put the sheep on his right side and the goats to his left.

34 "Then the Chief will say to the sheep on his right, 'The blessing of my Father rests upon you. Come into the Land of Creator's Good Road that has been prepared for you from the beginning of the world. 35 For I was thirsty and you gave me drink, I was hungry and you fed me, I was a stranger and you gave me lodging. 36 When I needed clothes, you gave me something to wear; when I was sick, you took care of me; and when I was in prison, you visited me.'

37-39 "'When did we do all these things for you?' the ones in good standing asked.

40 "'I speak from my heart,' he answered them, 'whatever you did for the least important of my fellow human beings[e] who needed help, you did for me.'

41 "Then the Chief will say to the goats on his left, 'Go away from me, you who have bad hearts,[f] into the fire that burns everything up, made for the evil trickster snake and his messengers. 42 For when I was hungry, you gave me nothing to eat; when I was thirsty you gave me no drink; 43 and when I was a stranger, you turned me away. When I needed clothes, you gave me nothing to wear, and when I was sick and in prison, you failed to visit me.'

44 "'Honored One,' they questioned, 'when was it that we saw you like this and did nothing?'

45 "'I speak from my heart,' he answered back, 'when you did not help the ones who needed it most, you failed to help me.'

---

e 25:40 Lit., my brothers   f 25:41 Lit., accursed ones

[46] "Then the goats will go away to the punishment of the world to come that has no end, and the sheep will enter the life of the world to come that will never fade away."

The Council Decides His Fate

26 After he had finished speaking about these things, Creator Sets Free (Jesus) said to the ones who walked the road with him, [2] "As you know, the Passover festival will begin after two days. It is during this time that the True Human Being will be taken captive and then killed on the cross."

[3] At that time the head holy men and the elders of the people gathered in the lodge of Hollow In The Rock (Caiaphas), the chief holy man. [4] They schemed together to take Creator Sets Free (Jesus) captive on the sly and then kill him.

[5] "We should not do this during the festival," they said, "or there could be an uprising among the people."

Prepared for Burial

[6] Creator Sets Free (Jesus) went to House of Figs (Bethany) to the home of He Hears (Simon), a man who had suffered from a skin disease. [7] While there, a woman with a pottery jar full of costly, sweet-smelling ointment came to Creator Sets Free (Jesus) and poured it over his head as he sat on the floor near the table.

[8] His followers, when they saw this, became angry and said to each other, "Why waste this costly ointment? [9] It could have been traded for food and goods to give to the ones who have none."

[10] Creator Sets Free (Jesus) heard them and said, "Why are you troubling this woman? She has done a good thing for me. [11] You can help the poor any time, for they will always be with you, but I will not. [12] By pouring this sweet-smelling ointment on my body, she has performed a preparation ceremony for my burial. [13] I speak from my heart, when the Good Story is told all over the world, her story will also be told to remember what she has done."

[14] It was then that Speaks Well Of (Judas) son of Village Man (Iscariot), one of the twelve, left and went to the head holy men. [15] "How much is he worth to you," he asked them. "What price will you pay if I turn him over to you?"

They agreed on thirty pieces of silver and paid him. [16] So from then on he looked for a good time to betray Creator Sets Free (Jesus).

Preparing for the Ceremonial Meal

[17] It was now the first day of the Festival of Bread Without Yeast. His followers came to Creator Sets Free (Jesus) and asked, "Where do you want us to go to prepare for the eating of the ceremonial Passover meal?"

[18] "Go into the village," he instructed them, "and there you will meet a certain man and say to him: Our Wisdomkeeper says, 'My

time has now come. I will eat the Passover meal with my followers here in your home.'"

19 They did as he said and made everything ready for the ceremonial meal.

The Ceremonial Meal Begins

20 As the sun was setting, Creator Sets Free (Jesus) sat down around the table with his twelve followers. 21 During the meal he spoke out, "I speak from my heart, one of you will turn against me."

22 They were all worried and troubled by this and began to ask him one by one, "Wisdomkeeper, am I the one?"

23 "It is the one who dipped his hand into the dish with me that will turn against me," he said with a look of sorrow. 24 "The True Human Being must walk the path chosen for him, as the Sacred Teachings have said; but it will not go well for the one who betrays him. It would be better if that one had never been born."

25 Speaks Well Of (Judas), the betrayer, looked at Creator Sets Free (Jesus) and asked, "Wisdomkeeper, you do not think I am the one, do you?"

"You have said it with your own words," he answered back.

A New Peace Treaty

26 Then, during the meal, Creator Sets Free (Jesus) took some of the bread, *lifted it up* and gave thanks.

He broke it into pieces, gave some to each of his followers and said, "This is my body, take it and eat it."

27 Then he took a cup of wine, *lifted it up* and gave thanks. He gave it to his followers and said, "Drink from this cup, all of you, 28 for this is my life-blood of the *New* Peace Treaty, poured out to release many people from their broken ways.

29 "I tell you now, I will not drink from the fruit of this vine again until I drink it with you in a fresh and new way when we walk together on my Father's Good Road."

30 Then, after they sang a ceremonial song together, they walked to Olive Mountain.

The Sheep Will Scatter

As they walked to Olive Mountain, Creator Sets Free (Jesus) began to warn his followers about what they would face in the night ahead.

31 "This very night all of you will stumble on the path and turn away because of what will happen to me. The Sacred Teachings have made it clear, 'Attack the shepherd and the sheep will scatter.'g 32 But after I have risen from the dead, I will go ahead of you to Circle of Nations (Galilee)."

33 Stands On The Rock (Peter) answered him, "Even if all others stumble and turn away, I will not!

34 "I speak from my heart," Creator Sets Free (Jesus) said back to him, "before the rooster crows, you will deny three times that you know me."

---

g 26:31 Zechariah 13:7

[35] *"Not so, my Wisdomkeeper!,"* Stands On The Rock (Peter) replied. "Even if I must die with you, I will never turn away!"

Then all of his followers said the same thing.

Praying in the Garden

[36] Creator Sets Free (Jesus) and his followers came to the place called Where the Olives Are Crushed (Gethsemane), *a garden with many olive trees.*

"Sit here," he told his followers, "while I go over there and pray."

[37] He then took with him Stands On The Rock (Peter) and *He Takes Over (James) and He Shows Goodwill (John),* the two sons of Gift Of Creator (Zebedee), to a place not far from the others.

As Creator Sets Free (Jesus) began to send his voice to the Great Spirit, he became deeply troubled and full of sorrow.

[38] "My heart is full of sorrow to the point of death," he said to his three followers that were with him. "Stay here and watch over me."

[39] He went a little ways from them, dropped his face to the ground and prayed. "O Great Father," he cried out, "is there a way to take this cup of bitter suffering away from me? But I want only your way, not mine."

[40] He then got up and found his followers sleeping.

"Could you not stay awake with me for even one hour?" he said to Stands On The Rock (Peter). [41] "Stay awake and pray so that you will be able to face the rough trail ahead of you. Your human body is weak, but your spirit is strong."

[42] Once again he went from them and prayed, "My Father, if this is the only way, then, as you desire, I will drink *deeply* of this bitter cup."

The night was silent and cold as Creator Sets Free trembled and prayed. The powers of darkness were pressing in hard. After a while he returned to the three followers who were supposed to be praying.

[43] He found them and saw that their eyes were heavy with sleep, [44] so he went away from them a third time and prayed the same words.

[45] He then returned to his followers and said to them, "Why are you still sleeping? The time is upon us! The True Human Being has been betrayed into the hands of the ones with bad hearts. [46] Rise up! We must go! Look! The one who has turned against me is here!"

Betrayed at the Hands of His Follower

[47] Right then, while Creator Sets Free (Jesus) was speaking, a crowd of people stormed into the garden. Speaks Well Of (Judas), one of the twelve, was leading the way. Along with the betrayer came the large crowd, sent from the head holy men and elders of the tribal council, carrying clubs and long knives.

The air was filled with the smell of burning torches as the crowd pushed their way forward.

48 The betrayer had given them a sign, "Take hold of the one I greet with a kiss, and arrest him."

49 Speaks Well Of (Judas) walked right up to Creator Sets Free (Jesus).

"Greetings, Wisdomkeeper," he said, and then kissed him.

50 "My friend," Creator Sets Free (Jesus) said *to his face,* "Do what you came to do."

The crowd moved in and took hold of Creator Sets Free (Jesus) to arrest him. 51 But then one of his followers drew his long knife from its sheath and cut off the ear of the servant of the chief holy man.

52 "Put away your long knife," he said to his follower, "for all who take up weapons will also die by them! 53 Do you not know that if I called out to my Father, he would send to me many thousands*h* of spirit-messengers. 54 But if I did, how would the ancient prophecies that foretold this find their full meaning?"

55 Creator Sets Free (Jesus) then turned to the ones who had come to take him and said, "Why do you come at me with clubs and long knives as if I were a thief? Did I not sit with you every day in the Sacred Lodge? Why did you not take me then? 56 But now the words of the prophets have come true and found their full meaning."

After *hearing him say* this, all his followers turned and ran away.

His Trial by the High Holy Man

57 The ones who had arrested him dragged him away and brought him to Hollow In The Rock (Caiaphas), the chief holy man. The scroll keepers and elders *of the Grand Council* had gathered there *to question him.*

58 Stands On The Rock (Peter) followed from a safe distance until they came to the courtyard of the chief holy man. He then went inside through the gate, sat down next to the lodge guards, and waited to see what would happen.

59 The head priests and the Grand Council kept trying to find someone who would speak against Creator Sets Free (Jesus) falsely so they could put him to death, 60 but found none *who could agree,* even though many came forward and spoke lies against him.

Finally two men came forward 61 and said, "We heard him say, 'I can tear down Creator's Sacred Lodge and build it again in three days.'"

62 The chief holy man stood up before all. He said to Creator Sets Free (Jesus), "Have you no answer to these accusations?"

63 Creator Sets Free (Jesus) remained silent before all—*and said nothing to defend himself.*

Hollow In The Rock (Caiaphas) was frustrated! His face became red with anger and his voice thundered.

---

h 26:53 Lit., twelve legions, about sixty thousand

"On your honor before the living Creator—speak the truth!" he demanded. "Tell us if you are the Chosen One, the Son of the Great Spirit!"

The room became silent. Time seemed to stand still. The air was filled with tension as they waited for his answer. When he spoke, every ear and eye in the room was fixed on him, for he must now answer.

64 "What you have said is right!" he answered them. "But listen to this: From now on you will see the True Human Being sitting at the right hand of the Great Power when he comes riding the clouds of the world above!"[i]

65 *They could not believe their ears!* The chief holy man tore his outer garments and cried out, "He is guilty! His words have insulted the Great Spirit!"

He turned to the council of elders and said, "You have heard it with your own ears! Why do we even need witnesses? 66 What does the council have to say?"

With one voice the council answered, "Death is what he deserves!"

67 Then they spit in his face, struck him with their fists, and others slapped him *with the back of their hands.* 68 "Prophesy to us, Chosen One," they taunted him. "Tell us who struck you!"

69 Stands On The Rock (Peter) was still outside sitting in the courtyard.

A servant girl looked at him and said, "I saw you when you were with Creator Sets Free (Jesus) in Circle of Nations (Galilee)."

70 "What!" he denied before them all. "I don't know what you are talking about."

71 Then he went toward the gate, and another servant-woman saw him and said out loud to all, "This man was with Creator Sets Free (Jesus) from Seed Planter Village (Nazareth)."

72 "I swear to you," he denied with a sacred oath, "I do not know this man!"

73 A short time later some of the men came up to him. "You must be one of his followers," they said. "The way you speak gives you away."

74 Stands On The Rock (Peter) cursed and swore out loud, "What are you all saying? I do not know this man you are talking about."

Right then a rooster began to crow, 75 and then he remembered what Creator Sets Free (Jesus) had told him, "Before the rooster crows, you will deny three times that you know me."

Stands On The Rock (Peter) ran out of the gate and wept bitter tears *as he stumbled down the road.*

27 As the sun began to rise, the head priests and council elders laid out their plans to kill Creator Sets Free (Jesus). 2 Then they tied cowhide strips around him again and dragged him away

---

i 26:64 Daniel 7:13-14

to turn him over to the governor from the People of Iron (Romans)— Spear Of The Great Waters (Pilate).

The Betrayer Takes His Own Life

3 When Speaks Well Of (Judas), the one who betrayed Creator Sets Free (Jesus), saw they had decided to have him killed, he was overcome with sorrow. He changed his mind and took the thirty pieces of silver back to the head holy men and the elders.

4 "I have done wrong!" he told them. "I have betrayed the blood of an innocent man."

"What do we care?" they said back to him. "You did this to yourself."

5 He threw the thirty pieces of silver on the floor of the Sacred Lodge and ran away in sorrow. He then left them and hanged himself.

As the light of the sunrise grew brighter on the horizon, his lifeless body could be seen hanging from the branch of a tree. He could not live with what he had done.

6 They picked the silver pieces up from the floor and said, "It is not permitted to put them in the storehouse of the Sacred Lodge, for it is blood money."

The head holy men didn't know what to do with the pieces of silver.

7 So they counseled together and used the silver to purchase a clay field, that had been used for making pottery, to use as a burial ground for outsiders. 8 From that time on it has been called the Field of Blood.

9 This gave full meaning to the words of the prophet Lifted By Creator (Jeremiah), "He was sold out for thirty pieces of silver by the tribes of Wrestles With Creator (Israel). This is how much they thought his life was worth. 10 With the silver they bought a field of clay, as instructed by the Great Spirit."*j*

On Trial by the People of Iron

11 Creator Sets Free (Jesus) now stood before the governor of the People of Iron (Romans) for questioning.

"Are you the chief of the tribes of Wrestles With Creator (Israel)?" the governor asked him.

"It is as you say," he answered.

12 Then the head holy men began to accuse him, but he gave them no answer.

13 *"Why are you silent?"* Spear Of The Great Waters (Pilate) asked him, "Do you not hear their accusations?"

14 But Creator Sets Free (Jesus) answered not one word, which amazed the governor.

Who Shall Be Released?

15 It was a tradition during the Passover festival to release to the crowd one criminal, whomever they wanted. 16 At that time they were holding a prisoner with a

---

j **27:10** Jeremiah 32:6-9

deadly reputation whose name was Son Of His Father (Barabbas).

17 "Which one shall I release?" the governor raised his voice to the crowd. "Son Of His Father (Barabbas) or Creator Sets Free (Jesus), who is called the Chosen One?"

18 Spear Of The Great Waters (Pilate) said this because he knew the head holy men and elders had handed over Creator Sets Free (Jesus) because they were jealous of his reputation with the people.

When the governor of the People of Iron (Romans) would make his final decision about the guilt and fate of a person, he would sit upon a great rock carved into a seat. This seat was called the Stone of Deciding.

19 While he was sitting there, a messenger came from his wife with these words: "Do no harm to this innocent man, for today I had a dream about him that troubles me greatly."

20 But the head holy men and the elders talked the crowd into asking for Son Of His Father (Barabbas) to be released and to have Creator Sets Free (Jesus) put to death.

21 Once more the governor asked the crowd, "Whom do you want me to release?"

"Son Of His Father (Barabbas)!" the crowd roared back.

22 "Then what would you have me do with Creator Sets Free (Jesus), who is called the Chosen One?" he asked them.

With one voice they shouted, "Nail him to the cross!"

23 "But what wrong has he done to deserve this?" he asked them again.

But their voices grew louder and louder, "Nail him to the cross!"

24 Spear Of The Great Waters (Pilate) could see that their minds would not be changed. He was worried that the crowd might turn violent, *so he decided to give them what they wanted.* He washed his hands in a vessel of water in front of all the people and said, "This man's blood is not on my hands. It is on yours!"

25 "Let his blood be on us and on our descendants!" they answered him back.

Condemned to a Violent Death

26 So the governor released Son Of His Father (Barabbas) to them. He then turned over Creator Sets Free (Jesus) to the soldiers to be whipped with cowhide strips and then nailed to the cross.

The People of Iron (Romans) used a whip with many strips of leather, each braided together with bone and metal. The victim would be tied to a large rock, exposing his bare back, and then lashed. The pieces of bone and metal would rip and tear the skin from the body, leaving the victim almost lifeless.

Beaten and Mocked by the Soldiers

²⁷ The governor's soldiers dragged Creator Sets Free (Jesus) into the great hall of his headquarters, *k* and all the soldiers there gathered around him. ²⁸ They stripped off his clothes, wrapped a fancy purple and red Chief Blanket around him, ²⁹ and twisted together a headdress from a thorn bush and pressed it onto his head. Then they put a Chief's Staff in his right hand and began to bow down before him.

"Honor to the chief of the tribes of Wrestles With Creator (Israel)!" they mocked him, *making a big show of it, insulting him with cruel words and twisted faces.*

³⁰ They spit on him, took his Chief's Staff and clubbed him with it. Then they took turns beating him on his head, over and over again. ³¹ When they were done, they stripped him of the Chief Blanket, put his own garment back on him, and took him away to nail him to the cross.

The People of Iron (Romans) used a wooden pole, with a crossbeam attached, to punish criminals and anyone who dared to rise up against their empire. The cross was used as an instrument of terror and torture to keep the people in fear of the People of Iron (Romans). It was one of the most painful and cruel ways to die ever created by human beings. Their feet were fastened with iron nails to the tree-pole and their hands to a crossbeam attached to the pole—where they remained until dead.

His Trail of Tears

The soldiers then put a heavy crossbeam on the back of Creator Sets Free (Jesus). But he stumbled under the weight, because he was weak from the beating he had endured, too weak to bear the burden.

³² On the way they came across He Hears (Simon), from Strong Wall (Cyrene) *in northern Africa.* The soldiers forced him to carry the cross for Creator Sets Free (Jesus).

Nailed to the Cross

³³ They came to Place of the Skull (Golgotha) ³⁴ and gave him wine mixed with bitter herbs to drink; but after tasting it, he would not drink it. ³⁵ *They stripped him of his garments* and, after they nailed his hands and feet to the cross, they gambled for his clothes. ³⁶ The soldiers then sat down and kept watch over him.

³⁷ Above his head on the crossbeam, *carved into a piece of wood,* was the accusation against him:

THIS IS CREATOR SETS FREE
CHIEF OF THE TRIBES OF
WRESTLES WITH CREATOR

³⁸ Then they also nailed two outlaws to their crosses, one on his right side, the other on his left.

---

k 27:27 The Praetorium

Mocked by His Own People

[39] As people walked by and saw him, they spoke arrogantly to him, wagged their heads [40] and said, "You who thought you could tear down the Sacred Lodge and rebuild it in three days—can you even save yourself? If you are the Son of the Great Spirit, then come down off that cross!"

[41] The head holy men, the scroll keepers and the elders all joined in.

[42] "He set others free," they said, "but he can't even free himself. So he is the chief of the tribes of Wrestles With Creator (Israel), is he? Let him come down from the cross now, and then we will believe in him! [43] He said, 'I am the Son of the Great Spirit,' so let the one he has put his trust in come and rescue him now—if he wants him."

[44] Even the thieves who were dying next to him joined in with the others and threw insults at him.

A Time of Darkness

[45] At the sixth hour of the day clouds moved in and covered the land with darkness until the ninth hour.[l]

[46] That is when Creator Sets Free (Jesus), speaking in his native language, cried out loud, "Eli, Eli, lama sabachthani"—which means, "O Great Spirit, my Creator, why have you left me alone?"[m]

[47] Some of the people standing there heard him and said, "He is calling on the prophet, Great Spirit Is Creator (Elijah), to help him."

[48] One of them ran and soaked a cloth with the bitter wine, put it on a staff and put it to his mouth. [49] But the others said, "Wait, let's see if Great Spirit Is Creator (Elijah) will come and save him."

He Breaths His Last

[50] But right then Creator Sets Free (Jesus), *with his dying breath,* lifted his voice *one last time* and with a loud cry gave up his spirit.

[51] Suddenly the earth began to quake. Large rocks cracked and shattered. Then in the Sacred Lodge the great heavy blanket that hung over the entry to the most holy place was torn from top to bottom.

For the first time the inner chamber, where only the chief holy man could go, was open to all.

[52-53] The burial caves opened *as the stones that covered them broke into pieces.* After Creator Sets Free (Jesus) returned to life from the dead, many of the bodies of the holy ancestors were raised to life from their sleep of death. They came out from their burial caves and appeared to many in the Sacred Village of Peace (Jerusalem).

[54] When the head soldier of the People of Iron (Romans) and his soldiers who were guarding Creator Sets Free (Jesus) felt the earth shake and saw what was happening all around them, they trembled with fear and said, "This man must truly be the Son of the Great Spirit!"

---

l **27:45** From noon till 3:00 p.m.   m **27:46** Psalm 22:1

Women Who Served Him

55 Many of the honored women who had walked the road with him from the time he was in Circle of Nations (Galilee) were there, watching from a distance. These were some of the women who had served him during his journeys. 56 Strong Tears (Mary) of the village of Creator's High Lodge (Magdala) and Brooding Tears (Mary), the mother of He Takes Over (James) and He Gives More (Joseph), were among them, and also the mother of the two sons of Gift Of Creator (Zebedee).

Buried in a New Burial Cave

57 A while before sunset He Gives More (Joseph) from the tribal village of High Mountain (Arimathea), who was also one who followed Creator Sets Free (Jesus), 58 went to Spear Of The Great Waters (Pilate). He asked for the body of Creator Sets Free (Jesus) *so he could prepare it properly for burial.* The governor then gave him permission to take the body.

59 He took the body and ceremonially wrapped it in a traditional way using a clean soft blanket. 60 He then laid the body of Creator Sets Free (Jesus) in his own burial cave freshly cut from the rock hillside. He rolled a large stone in front of the cave and left.

Soldiers Guard Him

61 Strong Tears (Mary) of the village of Creator's High Lodge (Magdala) and Brooding Tears (Mary) were also there sitting across *the garden* from the tomb.

62 The next day, which was after the Day of Preparing, the head holy men and the Separated Ones (Pharisees) came to Spear Of The Great Waters (Pilate).

63 "Honored One," they said to him, "When he was still alive, that human trickster Creator Sets Free (Jesus) said, 'On the third day I will come back from the dead.' 64 We must put an end to his lies or his followers could take his body away and tell the people he has come back from the dead, making things worse for all of us. So we are asking that you order your soldiers to guard the burial cave."

65 He said to them, "Take with you a good number of my soldiers and set them to guard the burial cave securely."

66 So they went and placed a seal over the great stone and set the guards to watch.

A New Sunrise for a New World

28 Then on *Sunday,* the first day of the week following the Day of Resting, as the sun began to rise, Strong Tears (Mary) of the village of Creator's High Lodge (Magdala) and Brooding Tears (Mary) went to the see the burial cave.

2 Suddenly the earth began to shake, and a spirit-messenger from the world above came down from the sky, walked to the burial cave, rolled the stone away—and sat down on it! 3 He was shining as bright as a flash of lightning, and his regalia was pure white like *freshly fallen* snow.

[4] The soldiers staggered back, trembling with fear, and fell to the ground like dead men.

[5-6] "Do not fear!" the spirit-messenger said to the women, "The one you are looking for is not here. Creator Sets Free (Jesus), who was killed on the cross, has come back to life again—just as he said. Look! Here is where they laid him. [7] Now hurry and go tell his followers that he has risen from the dead. Tell them he is going ahead of them to Circle of Nations (Galilee) and they will see him there. Now remember what I have told you!"

He Appears to the Women

[8] The women ran from the burial cave to bring the good news to his followers. Their hearts were trembling with fear and great joy. [9] Suddenly, Creator Sets Free (Jesus) was standing in front of them.

"It's a good morning!" he *smiled and* said to them.

They came close, held tightly to his feet, and gave great honor to him.

[10] "Do not fear!" he told them. "Go and tell my brothers to go to Circle of Nations (Galilee), and there they will see me."

The Soldiers are Paid to Keep Quiet

[11] After the women had left the burial cave, some of the soldiers who were guarding the place went to Village of Peace (Jerusalem) and reported everything to the head holy men. [12] So they gathered a council together to make a plan.

They decided to pay the soldiers well to make up a story: [13] "Tell the people that his followers came and stole his body while you were sleeping. [14] Don't worry about the governor hearing about this. We will pay him whatever it takes to keep you from trouble."

Normally the People of Iron (Romans) would have put to death any soldiers who would have let someone steal a body they had been ordered to guard.

[15] So the soldiers took the money and did as they were told, and even to this day their story has been told far and wide among all the tribes.

Final Instructions

It was now time for Creator Sets Free (Jesus) to return to the world above. It had now been forty days since he had come back to life again. So he gathered his followers, one last time, to give them their final instructions.

[16] So there remained eleven of his followers who journeyed to Circle of Nations (Galilee). There, at the mountain where Creator Sets Free (Jesus) had told them to go, they met with him. [17] When they saw him, they gave to him the honor he deserved—but there were some who still doubted.

[18] "The right to all the powers of the world above and the earth below has been given to me," he told them. [19] "So now I am sending you into all nations to teach them how to walk the road with me. You will represent me as you perform

the purification ceremony with them, initiating them into *the life of beauty and harmony represented in* the name of the Father, Son and Holy Spirit. 20 You will then teach them all the ways that I have instructed you to walk in."

Creator Sets Free (Jesus) then looked into their faces with love and great affection. He lifted his hands toward them and spoke these final blessing words over them.

"Never forget," he said *as he began rise up into the world above.* "I will always be with you, *your invisible guide,* walking beside you, until the new world has fully come."

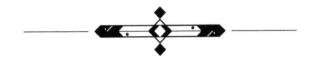

*As I lay awake during the night, I was
given many sacred visions. In one vision
I looked and saw what appeared to be a True
Human Being. He was riding on the clouds of
the world above and was brought into the
council house of the Ancient Of Days. He
stood before the Ancient Of Days and was
gifted with great authority over all the earth,
with honor that outshines the sun, and with
power that reaches beyond all the directions.
All clans, tribes, nations and languages will
honor and serve this Chosen One above all
others. His Chiefly Rule will last beyond the
end of all days. For it will be a Good Road
that can never fade away
or come to a bad end.*

*A Sacred Vision from the Great Spirit
To the tribes of Wrestles With Creator*

*Daniel Seven
Verses Thirteen and Fourteen*

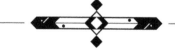

War Club

Tells the Good Story

Gospel of Mark

FIRST NATIONS VERSION

FIRST NATIONS VERSION

War Club
Tells the Good Story
(Gospel of Mark)

The Good Story Begins

1 This is the Good Story about the Chosen One, Creator Sets Free (Jesus), who is the Son of the Great Spirit. This story began long ago and was foretold in the Sacred Teachings by the ancient prophet Creator Will Help Us (Isaiah).

² "Behold!" Creator Will Help Us (Isaiah) said, *as he spoke the words of the Great Spirit.* "I am sending my messenger ahead of you to prepare the way. ³ He will be a voice howling in the desert wilderness, 'Clear away the stones and make a straight path for the coming of the Honored One!'" *ᵃ*

Purification Ceremony

⁴ And so the messenger appeared in the desert wilderness. He came to tell everyone to turn from their wrong ways of thinking and return to the ways of the Great Spirit. The messenger's name was He Shows Goodwill (John). He came to perform the purification ceremony to show people that they had been released from their broken ways.

⁵ From the surrounding territory of the Land of Promise (Judea) and from Village of Peace (Jerusalem), all the people came to him to participate in his purification ceremony performed in the river Flowing Down (Jordan). As they came, they were admitting to their bad hearts and broken ways.

Preparing the Way

⁶ He Shows Goodwill (John) came wearing buffalo skin*ᵇ* garments, with a cowhide sash around his waist. The food he ate was grasshoppers and wild honey.

⁷ "I am preparing the way for the one who is greater and more powerful than I," he announced to all. "I am not even worthy to bend down and untie his moccasins. ⁸ I perform the purification ceremony with water, but he will perform the purification ceremony with the Holy Spirit!"

---

a 1:3 Isaiah 40:3   **b 1:6** Lit., camel's hair

78

Creator Sets Free Comes Forward

⁹ It was in those days that Creator Sets Free (Jesus) came from his home in Seed Planter Village (Nazareth) in the territory of Circle of Nations (Galilee), to have He Shows Goodwill (John) perform for him the purification ceremony.

Creator Sets Free (Jesus) was a full grown man of about thirty winters. The time had come for him to show himself to all the people and begin his great work. He waded out into the river to have He Shows Goodwill (John) perform the ceremony.

¹⁰ As soon as Creator Sets Free (Jesus) came up from the water, he saw the sky open. The Spirit of Creator came down like a dove and rested on him. ¹¹ Then a voice from the sky spoke *like distant thunder,* "This is my Much Loved Son who makes my heart glad!"

His Vision Quest

¹² Right then and there the Spirit drove Creator Sets Free (Jesus) into the desert wilderness. ¹³ For forty days and nights he remained there, surrounded by wild animals and being tested by Accuser (Satan)—the ancient trickster snake. Spirit-messengers also came there to give him strength and comfort.

The Message of the Good Road

¹⁴ Then later, after He Shows Goodwill (John) was arrested, Creator Sets Free (Jesus) traveled to the territory of Circle of Nations (Galilee) to tell the Good Story.

¹⁵ "The time has now come!" he said to the people. "Creator's Good Road is right in front of you—it is time to return to the right ways of thinking and doing! Put your trust in this Good Story I am bringing to you."

His First Followers

¹⁶ As he walked along the shore of the Lake of Circle of Nations (Sea of Galilee), he saw two men, One Who Hears (Simon) and Stands With Courage (Andrew), throwing their nets into the lake; for they were fishermen.

¹⁷ "Come! Walk the road with me," he called out to them, "and I will teach you a new way of fishing—for two-leggeds instead of fish!"

¹⁸ Right then and there they dropped their nets and began to walk the road with him.

¹⁹ He walked a little further down the shore and saw two more men, the brothers He Takes Over (James) and He Shows Goodwill (John), the two sons of Gift Of Creator (Zebedee). They were sitting in their canoe and mending their nets. ²⁰ Right away he called out for them to walk the road with him; so they dropped their nets, left their father behind with the hired help, and also became followers of Creator Sets Free (Jesus).

New Teaching for New Medicine

Once a week the people would come together at the local village gathering house to learn the ways of the Great Spirit.

21 Creator Sets Free (Jesus) took his new followers and went to Village of Comfort (Capernaum). When the next Day of Resting came, he went to the gathering house and began to teach the people. 22 They were amazed at his manner of speaking, for, unlike the scroll keepers, he spoke *clearly and boldly* as one with authority.

23 Suddenly, a man controlled by an unclean spirit cried out loud, 24 "Creator Sets Free (Jesus) from the Seed Planter Village (Nazareth), what are you doing here? Have you come to put an end to us? I know who you are! You are the Holy One from the Great Spirit!"

25 Creator Sets Free (Jesus) spoke sharply to the spirit. "Be silent!" he said. "Come out of him!"

26 The unclean spirit shook the man, threw him to the ground and, howling with a loud voice, came out of him.

27 The people were dumbfounded and began to ask each other, "What is this teaching? What new medicine is this? He even tells the unclean spirits what to do—and they do it!"

28 His reputation spread like wildfire into the territory of Circle of Nations (Galilee) and to all the surrounding territories.

Power Over Sickness

29 As soon as they left the gathering house, they went to the home of One Who Hears (Simon) and his brother Stands With Courage (Andrew). He Takes Over (James) and He Shows Goodwill (John) were with them.

30 The wife of One Who Hears (Simon) was there. Her mother was sick in bed with a bad fever, so they asked Creator Sets Free (Jesus) to help her. 31 He went and stood by her, took her by the hand, and lifted her up. The fever left her *and she was healed*. Then *with a glad heart* she went to prepare a meal for them.

32 Later that day, when the sun was going down, many sick people were brought to him, along with those who were tormented by evil spirits. 33 The whole village had gathered outside the door.

34 He healed many with different illnesses and set others free from evil spirits; but he didn't permit the spirits to speak, for they knew who he was.

35 Early the next morning, before the sunrise, he left and found a quiet, out-of-the-way place to be alone and pray. 36 One Who Hears (Simon) and the others 37 found him and said, "Everyone is looking for you!"

38 "It's time to go to the other villages and tell them the Good Story," Creator Sets Free (Jesus) said to them, "for that is what I came to do."

39 So he traveled about all the territory of Circle of Nations (Galilee). He taught in their gathering houses and forced out many evil spirits.

He Heals A Man With Skin Disease

40 *While in one of the villages*, a man with a skin disease all over his body

came to Creator Sets Free (Jesus). He humbled himself, bowed down and pleaded with him, "Honored One! If you want to, you can heal and cleanse me."

Under Tribal Law anyone with a skin disease was considered ceremonially unclean and could not participate in ceremonies or attend meetings at the gathering houses. If someone touched or was touched by an unclean person, they would be considered unclean until the sun set that day. So to help people avoid this, the diseased person was required to shout, "Unclean! Unclean!"

⁴¹ Creator Sets Free (Jesus), stirred with compassion, reached out and touched the man. "I want to!" he said. "Be cleansed!"

⁴² And right away the disease left him and he was made clean.

⁴³ Creator Sets Free (Jesus) sent him away at once with a warning. ⁴⁴ "Tell no one!" he instructed. "Go and show yourself to a holy man, so he can see with his own eyes, and have him perform the cleansing ceremony given to us by the lawgiver Drawn From The Water (Moses)."

But the man chose not to follow his instructions.

⁴⁵ Instead, he spread the news about his healing far and wide. Soon Creator Sets Free (Jesus) was unable to show his face in the local villages, so he stayed away from them. But the people continued to come to him from all the directions.

Healing at Village of Comfort

2 After many days Creator Sets Free (Jesus) went back to Village of Comfort (Capernaum), but word got out that he had returned home. ² So many people had gathered in the house that there was no more room; even the entrance was blocked. Creator Sets Free (Jesus) began to teach the people there ³ when four men came carrying a paralyzed man on a sleeping mat, ⁴ but they couldn't get past the crowd. In their desperation, they climbed up to the rooftop and broke through the roof right above Creator Sets Free (Jesus). They lowered the paralyzed man down, sleeping bundle and all.

⁵ When he saw their faith in him, he said to the paralyzed man, "Young man, you are released from your broken ways, *and the things in your heart that are not true to Creator's Good Road.*"

Who Can Forgive Broken Ways?

⁶ There were some scroll keepers there who began to wonder in their hearts, ⁷ "Who is this man to speak against the Great Spirit with such disrespect? Who but the Maker Of Life can release a man from his wrongdoings?"

Under Tribal Law the only way to be forgiven for broken ways or wrongdoings was to go to the Sacred Lodge and have a ceremony performed by a holy man. By releasing this man from his broken ways Creator Sets Free (Jesus) was claiming to have the right to do this himself, which, to the spiritual leaders, was wrong.

8 In his spirit, Creator Sets Free (Jesus) knew right away what they were thinking and said to them, "Why are your hearts full of these thoughts? 9 Is it easier to tell a paralyzed man, 'Get up and walk,' or to say to him, 'You are released from your wrongdoings'?"

The room became quiet as he waited for an answer from them.

10 "This is how you will know that the True Human Being has the right to forgive bad hearts and wrongdoings on this earth."

11 He turned to the paralyzed man and said, "Get up, roll up your sleeping bundle and walk home."

12 Right away the man stood up, and, in front of them all, he rolled up his sleeping bundle and walked out.

Great amazement filled the hearts of all who were in the house as they gave praise to Creator.

"Who has ever seen this kind of mysterious and powerful medicine?" they asked.

Eating With Outcasts

13 After this, Creator Sets Free (Jesus) went once again to walk by the lake shore. A large crowd followed him there, so he was teaching them. 14 As he walked the shore, he saw a tribal tax collector named He Brings Together (Levi), the son of First To Change (Alphaeus) sitting at his tax booth.

"Come," Creator Sets Free (Jesus) said to him, "and walk the road with me."

So He Brings Together (Levi) got up from his tax booth, left that life behind him, and became a follower of Creator Sets Free (Jesus).

Tribal tax collectors were often tribal members who were given the right to collect taxes for the People of Iron (Romans). They could force their own people, under the threat of violence, to pay them. To make a living, they would take more than the People of Iron (Romans) required. But many of them became greedy and took even more than they were permitted. They were hated and looked down on by the people.

15 Creator Sets Free (Jesus) went to a feast at the home of He Brings Together (Levi) and sat down to eat with the guests. There were many other tribal tax collectors and other outcasts also sitting with Creator Sets Free (Jesus) and his close followers—for he had many followers who were also outcasts.

16 When the Separated Ones (Pharisees) and the scroll keepers saw Creator Sets Free (Jesus) eating with outcasts, they complained to his close followers saying, "Why does your wisdomkeeper keep company with tribal tax collectors and other outcasts?"

17 Creator Sets Free (Jesus) overheard them and said, "People who are well do not need medicine. I have not come to the ones who are already walking the good road, but to help the dark-hearted and broken ones find the way back home."

New Ways For Old

It was a common practice among the tribal people to go without food to help their prayers and for other spiritual reasons. Sometimes it was done out of sadness and sorrow for a friend or a family member's troubles.

18 Some of the followers of He Shows Goodwill (John) and the Separated Ones (Pharisees) were ceremonially going without food, so they came to Creator Sets Free (Jesus).

"Why do your followers feast," they questioned him, "instead of going without food and praying often like we do?"

19 "Do you expect wedding guests to be sad and go without eating when the groom is hosting a feast?" he answered. "No! As long as the groom is there with them, they will feast! 20 But the time will come when he is taken from them; then they will be sad and go without eating."

They still didn't understand, so he gave them a wise saying.

21 "No one uses a new piece of cloth to patch an old garment; it would shrink and make the tear worse. 22 No one puts new wine into old wineskins, for the new wine would burst the skins. New and fresh wineskins are what is needed."

Chief Over the Day of Resting

23 On a Day of Resting, Creator Sets Free (Jesus) and his followers were walking through a field of grain. The men were hungry, so as they walked, they plucked some grain to eat.

24 When the Separated Ones (Pharisees) saw what they were doing, they said to him, "Why do your followers do what is not permitted on the Day of Resting?"

25 He answered them, "Have you not heard about the time long ago when *the great chief* Much Loved One (David) was hungry? 26 How he and his followers went into Creator's Ceremonial Lodge, when Father Of Plenty (Abiathar) was the chief holy man, and ate the ceremonial bread? Only the holy men are permitted to eat this bread.

27 "Human beings were not made for the Day of Resting. Instead, the Day of Resting was made for human beings. 28 So then, the True Human Being is Chief over the Day of Resting!"

Doing Good on the Day of Resting

3 Creator Sets Free (Jesus) then went to their gathering house to teach. A man was there with a shriveled and useless hand. 2 The Separated Ones (Pharisees) kept a close eye on Creator Sets Free (Jesus) to see if he would heal the man on the Day of Resting, so they could accuse him.

3 Creator Sets Free (Jesus) said to the man with the useless hand, "Stand up and come forward."

4 Then he turned to the Separated Ones (Pharisees) and asked, "On the Day of Resting is it permitted to

help or to harm, to rescue life or destroy it?"

They just glared at him and said nothing, *sneering in their hearts.*

⁵ There was fire in his eyes as he looked around the room. His anger turned to sorrow when he saw their hearts of stone. He turned to the man and said, "Stretch out your hand."

He stretched it out, and it was the same as his good hand!

⁶ The Separated Ones (Pharisees) stormed out right away and went straight to the Friends of Looks Brave (Herodians) to conspire with them about how to do away with Creator Sets Free (Jesus).

Creator's Chosen Servant

⁷ Creator Sets Free (Jesus) and the ones who walked the road with him left that place and went to the lake. ⁸ Word about him drew large crowds from Circle of Nations (Galilee), Land of Promise (Judea) and Village of Peace (Jerusalem). They also came from Red Land (Idumea), from the territory beyond the river Flowing Down (Jordan), and from Rock Land (Tyre) and Hunting Grounds (Sidon).

⁹ He asked his followers to keep a canoe close by, in case the crowd pressed in too close and crushed him. ¹⁰ His reputation as a healer had made the sick desperate to reach out and touch him.

¹¹ When the ones with evil spirits saw him, they would fall down at his feet and wail, "You are the Son of the Great Spirit!"

¹² But he warned them over and over again not to tell anyone who he was.

He did not want evil spirits spreading news about him.

Twelve Message Bearers

¹³ Creator Sets Free (Jesus) went up the mountain and gathered to himself some of his followers. ¹⁴⁻¹⁵ He chose twelve of them—to learn his ways by being with him, so he could send them out to tell the Good Story and to have the power to force out evil spirits—and he called them message bearers.

¹⁶ Here are the names of the twelve he chose:

Stands On The Rock (Peter), the name he gave to One Who Hears (Simon), ¹⁷ He Takes Over (James) the son of Gift Of Creator (Zebedee) and his brother He Shows Goodwill (John), whom he also called Sons of Thunder,

¹⁸ Stands With Courage (Andrew), Friend Of Horses (Philip), Son Of Ground Digger (Bartholomew), Gift From Creator (Matthew), Looks Like His Brother (Thomas),

He Takes Over (James) the son of First To Change (Alphaeus), Strong Of Heart (Thaddaeus), One Who Listens (Simon) the Man On Fire (Zealot), ¹⁹ and Speaks Well Of (Judas), the one who would betray him.

He Has Lost His Mind

²⁰ Creator Sets Free (Jesus) then returned to his house in Village of Comfort (Capernaum). Just like before, a large crowd gathered

there—so many that he and his followers were not even able to eat. ²¹ When his relatives heard about this, they tried to take him away from there, because the people were saying, "He has lost his mind!"

Accused by the Spiritual Leaders

²² The scroll keepers from Village of Peace (Jerusalem) were there also.

"He stands with Worthless Ruler (Beelzebul)," they accused him, "for his power to force out evil spirits comes from the one who rules over them."

²³ So Creator Sets Free (Jesus) gathered them around himself and spoke to them with wise sayings like these:

"How can Accuser (Satan), that evil trickster, force out evil spirits? Can he defeat himself? ²⁴ If a nation wars against itself, that nation cannot stand. ²⁵ A family that fights against itself will fall. ²⁶ In the same way, if Accuser (Satan) rises up against himself, then how will he continue to rule?

²⁷ "No one can enter the house of a strongman and take away his goods, unless he first defeats him; then he can take away his goods.

²⁸ "I speak from my heart, mankind will be released from all their wrongdoing and evil speaking, ²⁹ but whoever speaks evil of the Holy Spirit will not be released. This wrongdoing will follow them into the world to come and to the end of all days."

³⁰ He said this because they were saying to Creator Sets Free (Jesus), "He has an evil spirit."

All My Relatives

³¹ Then his mother and brothers came to him outside the house and sent word to him to come out to them. ³² The crowd that was sitting *in a circle* around him said, "Look, your relatives are outside looking for you."

³³ "Who are my relatives?" he asked them ³⁴ as he looked around at the circle of people. "Here they are! ³⁵ The ones who walk in the ways of the Great Spirit are all my relatives—my mother, brothers and sisters."

Seed Planter Story

4 Creator Sets Free (Jesus) returned to the lakeshore and once again a very large crowd gathered around him. They pressed in so close that he got into a canoe and pushed out a little way from shore, while the people stayed at the shoreline. ² He then began to tell them stories to teach them about the Great Spirit's ways.

³ "Listen!" he said. "A seed planter went to plant some seeds and began to scatter them about on the ground.

⁴ "Some seeds fell on the village pathway, *but people walked on them*, and the winged-ones pecked at the seeds and ate them all.

⁵ "Some of the seeds fell on the rocks where there was only a little dirt. The plants sprouted up quickly, ⁶ but when the sun came out, they

dried up because the roots were not deep enough.

7 "Other seeds fell into the weeds, and thistles sprouted around the seeds and choked the life out of them. None of these plants grew for a harvest.

8 "But some seeds fell on good ground, grew strong, and gave a harvest of thirty, sixty, and even one hundred times as much.

9 Then he said, "Let the one who has ears hear the meaning of this story."

The Reason For Stories

10 Later, when the twelve message bearers and other followers were alone with him, they asked why he taught with stories.

11 He answered them, "To my close followers the honor has been given to understand about the mysterious ways of Creator's Good Road. This honor is not given to those who are not my close followers. The stories are to help them, 12 because, 'When they look, they cannot see clearly what is in front of them; and when they hear, they do not understand the meaning. If they did, then they would return to Creator and be released from their broken ways.'c"

Meaning of the Seed Planter Story

13 "If you do not understand this story, then how will you understand any of my stories?" he answered.

14 "The seed planter's seed in this story is the message about Creator's Good Road.

15 "The village pathway represents the ones who hear but do not understand the message. Accuser (Satan), the trickster snake, sneaks up and snatches it away from them.

16 "The rocky ground represents the ones who hear and receive the message with a glad heart, 17 but because they have no roots, their faith is shallow and does not last. As soon as the message brings them trouble or opposition, they stumble and lose their way.

18 "The weeds and thistles represent the ones who have heard the message, 19 but they are too busy worrying about their earthly existence. This makes them stray away from the Good Road, wanting more and more possessions, thinking this will make them happy. The message is choked and their faith stops growing.

20 "The good ground represents the ones with good and pure hearts. When they hear and understand the message, they hold on tightly to it until it grows into a harvest— thirty, sixty and even one hundred times as great!

Light Shines in the Darkness

21 "No one hides a torch behind a blanket or under a sleeping bundle. No! A torch belongs up high on a pole, where it can give light to everyone. 22 Nothing that has been hidden can stay a secret, and what

---

c 4:12 Jeremiah 5:21; Isaiah 6:9-10

has been covered up in darkness will be exposed by the light. 23 The ones who have ears—hear this!"

24 Then he added, "You must listen with an open heart. 25 The ones who do so will gain wisdom and be ready for more—much more. But the ones who close their hearts *to my teaching,* even what little they have will be taken away.

More Stories About the Good Road

26 "Here is another way to see Creator's Good Road," he said. "It is like a man who plants seed into the earth. 27 Day or night, awake or asleep, the seed grows without the man knowing how or doing anything. 28 The earth makes the seed grow without any help—first the stem, then the head, and finally the grain appears. 29 Once it is ripe, the time has come, and right away it is harvested.

30 "What is Creator's Good Road like?" he asked. "What can I compare it to? What story will help us see its meaning?

Mustard Seed Wisdom

31-32 "It is like a single grain of mustard seed,*d* one of the smallest of seeds. But when planted in a garden, it grows larger than all the other plants and takes over the garden. It becomes a great tree with many branches, large enough for the winged-ones who soar in the sky to find lodging in its shade."

33 So Creator Sets Free (Jesus) taught the people with many stories like these. He would tell them as much as they were able to hear. 34 He would only use stories to teach the crowds, but then in private he would tell the full meaning to the ones who walked the road with him.

Power Over Storms

35 On that same day as the sun began to set, Creator Sets Free (Jesus) said to followers, "Let's cross over to the other side of the lake."

36 So they left the crowd and climbed into the canoe with him and pushed off from shore along with some other canoes. 37 A storm was moving in, and a fierce wind drove the waves into the canoe and threatened to swamp it.

They paddled harder trying desperately to keep the canoe from sinking, but the wind and waves were too much for them. They were filled with fear and about to sink and needed help from their Wisdomkeeper.

38 But Creator Sets Free (Jesus), *weary from a long hard day,* was in the back of the canoe—sleeping on a soft blanket! They shook him awake and cried out loud, "Wisdomkeeper! Don't you care that we are fighting for our lives?"

39 He stood up and spoke sharply to the wind and said to the raging waters, "Calm down and be still!"

---

d 4:31-32 The mustard plant was used as an herbal medicine.

Right then and there the wind died down and a great peace fell upon the surface of the water.

40 He then *turned to his followers* and said to them, "Why have you given yourselves over to fear? Where is your faith?"

41 They all began to tremble with fear. They shook their heads with wonder and whispered to each other, "Who is this man? Even the wind and the waves do what he says!"

Territory of Many Spirits

5 When they finished crossing the lake, they came to the territory of Many Spirits (Gerasenes)*e f*. 2 As soon as Creator Sets Free (Jesus) stepped from the canoe, a man who was tormented by an unclean spirit came up to him. 3 This man had been living at the local burial grounds, and no one could bind him, not even with iron chains.

4 The people of the village had tried to capture the man and tie him down, but he would tear their ropes and break their chains. No one was strong enough to overpower him. 5 Day and night he wandered about the burial grounds and into the mountains. He would never stop wailing and cutting himself with sharp stones. 6 When the man saw Creator Sets Free (Jesus) from a distance, he ran up to him and fell down before him.

7 "Creator Sets Free (Jesus), Son of the One Above Us All, what are you going to do with us?" the unclean spirits cried out through the man.

"Promise me by the Great Spirit that you will not torment us."

8 The unclean spirits said this because Creator Sets Free (Jesus) had said to the man, "Come out of him, you unclean spirit!"

9 Then Creator Sets Free (Jesus) asked, "What is the name of the spirit you represent?"

"Our name is Many Soldiers,"*g* the evil spirits answered, "for our numbers are great."

The spirits feared Creator Sets Free (Jesus) and knew he could force them out of the man.

A Heard of Pigs

10 They kept begging him not to send them out of the territory. 11 There was a large herd of about two thousand pigs feeding nearby on the side of a mountain.

12 "Send us to those pigs over there," they begged, "so we can enter into them."

13 So he gave them permission. The unclean spirits then came out of the man and entered into the herd of about two thousand pigs. Then the whole herd stampeded down the mountainside headlong into the lake and drowned *in the deep water, making a frightful scene.*

14 The local ones who were watching over the pigs rushed away, shaken and afraid. They went to the nearby village and told everyone all that happened. As word spread, people came from the villages and the countryside to see for themselves.

---

e 5:1 The actual meaning of the name Gerasenes is unknown.   f 5:1 Some manuscripts have Gadarenes and some Gergesenes.   g 5:9 Lit., Legion, a segment of the occupying army of the People of Iron (Romans) of about 5000 soldiers

Set Free and Made Whole

¹⁵ There they found the man who had been tormented by the unclean spirits, sitting quietly at the feet of Creator Sets Free (Jesus). He was clothed and in his right mind. The people trembled with fear ¹⁶ as they listened to the story of how the man was set free and to the story about the pigs. ¹⁷ So they begged Creator Sets Free (Jesus) to go away from their land.

¹⁸ As Creator Sets Free (Jesus) was climbing into his canoe to leave, the man who had been set free from the evil spirits begged him to take him along.

¹⁹ But Creator Sets Free (Jesus) would not permit it and said to the man, "Return home to your family and friends. Tell them all the good and kind things the Great Spirit has done for you."

²⁰ The man went his way and told the story far and wide in all the territory of the Ten Villages (Decapolis) of what Creator Sets Free (Jesus) had done for him—and all who heard were amazed.

A Desperate Request

²¹ Creator Sets Free (Jesus) *and his followers* canoed back to the other side of the lake. As soon as he arrived, a great crowd began to gather around him at the lakeshore.

²² A man named He Gives Light (Jairus), a headman of the local gathering house, *pushed his way through the crowd and* fell down on his knees in front of Creator Sets Free (Jesus).

²³ "My little girl is almost dead!" he begged him urgently. "She is my only daughter. Please come and lay your hands on her that she may be healed and live!"

²⁴ So Creator Sets Free (Jesus) went with him. The crowd also trailed along, pressing in around him from all sides.

Who Touched Me?

²⁵ There was a woman in the crowd who had been bleeding for more than twelve winters. ²⁶ She had spent all she had, putting up with medicine men who were not able to heal her, and she was getting worse.

Under Tribal Law this woman would be considered unclean and even the things she touched would be unclean also, isolating her from friends and family. She would not be able to marry or participate in the gathering house for prayer.

²⁷ When she heard about Creator Sets Free (Jesus), she pressed through the crowd and came up close behind him. She reached out her hand and touched his outer garment, ²⁸ for she had said to herself, "If I can only touch his clothes, I know I will be healed."

²⁹ She touched him, and right away the blood stopped flowing and she felt in her body that she was healed.

³⁰ Creator Sets Free (Jesus) stopped suddenly, turned and looked around the crowd and said, "Who touched my clothes?" For he was aware that power had gone out from him.

Fear gripped the heart of this woman, for she had not announced herself as unclean, and even worse she had touched a spiritual leader. The crowd might turn against her or even have her stoned to death. So she remained silent and said nothing.

31 His followers *looked around, shrugged their shoulders and* said to him, "You can see that the crowds are pushing and shoving you. How can you say, 'Who touched me?'"

32 Creator Sets Free (Jesus) continued to look around to see who had touched him. 33 The woman knew she could hide no longer, so she came forward trembling with fear, fell to the ground in front of him and told the whole truth.

34 "Daughter," he said to her *with great loving kindness in his eyes*, "your faith *in me* has made you well. Now go in peace, for you have been healed of your disease."

Power Over Death

35 While Creator Sets Free (Jesus) was still speaking, some messengers came from the home of the headman of the gathering house.

"Your little girl has crossed over to death," they said *with sad faces.* "Why trouble the Wisdomkeeper any longer?"

The man's heart fell to the ground and grief began to creep over him.

36 But Creator Sets Free (Jesus) paid no attention to what was said.

"Do not fear!" he said to the headman, "Trust in me alone, *and all will be well.*"

37 He would not permit any to go with him except Stands On The Rock (Peter), He Takes Over (James) along with his brother He Shows Goodwill (John)—*his most trusted message bearers.*

38 As they came near the house of the headman, they saw and heard an uproar! People were weeping and wailing loudly.

39 When he entered into the house, Creator Sets Free (Jesus) said to them, "Why are you making such a noise? Do not weep; the child is not dead. She only sleeps."

40 But they only scorned and laughed at him, *for they knew she was dead.*

Wake Up!

So he put them all out of the house except his most trusted message bearers and the father and mother. He went with them into where the girl lay, 41 took hold of her hand and said in his native language, "Talitha cumi," meaning, "Little girl, wake up!"

42 She stood up right away and began to walk; she was twelve winters old. Her father and mother stood there, amazed beyond words, *weeping for joy, for their little girl was alive!*

43 Creator Sets Free (Jesus) had them give her some food to eat and then firmly told them not to tell anyone what had happened.

His Own Village Rejects Him

6 Creator Sets Free (Jesus) and his followers left there and went to Seed Planter Village (Nazareth),

where he grew up as a boy. ² On the following Day of Resting at the local gathering house, he began to teach the people. When they heard him, they were amazed and wondered at his words.

"Where did he learn about these things?" they asked *with contempt in their voices.* "Who gave him this wisdom and ability to perform such powerful medicine? ³ Is he not the wood carver, son of Bitter Tears (Mary) and brother to He Takes Over (James), He Gets More (Joses), Speaks Well Of (Judas) and He Hears (Simon)? Look, his sisters are also here with us!"

And so, they were offended and turned their faces away from him.

⁴ "A prophet is given much honor," he said to them, "except in his own village, among his own clan and relatives, and even in his own family."

⁵ Because of this he could do no great miracles among them, except to touch and heal a few sick people. ⁶ He was troubled by their lack of trust in him. So he left his boyhood village and went about teaching in other villages.

He Sends His Message Bearers

⁷ He then gathered his twelve message bearers together, gave them power over unclean evil spirits, and began to send them out two by two. ⁸ He told them to take nothing with them except a walking stick—no traveling bundle, food or money pouches. ⁹ They were to wear only one outer garment and have one pair of moccasins for their feet.

¹⁰ "When you come to a village, stay in one home until you leave. ¹¹ If no one in that village welcomes you or will listen to your message, then go from there and shake the dust from your moccasins as a sign against them."

¹² So the twelve went out traveling two by two, and everywhere they went, they told people to return to Creator's right way of thinking. ¹³ They forced out evil spirits and poured herbal oils on many who were sick and healed them.

Looks Brave Wonders About Him

¹⁴ The reputation of Creator Sets Free (Jesus) reached the ears of Chief Looks Brave (Herod). Some told him, "He Shows Goodwill (John) has come back from the world of the dead. That is why he can work so much power!"

¹⁵ At the same time others said, "He must be Great Spirit Is Creator (Elijah)," and still others said, "He is a prophet! Just like one of the ancient prophets."

¹⁶ But Looks Brave, after hearing all this, said, "He Shows Goodwill (John), the one whose head I cut off, has come back from the dead *to haunt me.*"

¹⁷⁻¹⁸ He said this because he was the one who had He Shows Goodwill (John) arrested and put in prison. He Shows Goodwill (John) had spoken out against Looks Brave (Herod) for marrying the wife of his brother Friend of Horses (Philip).

"It is not permitted in the Sacred Teachings for you to be with your brother's wife!" he told Looks Brave (Herod).

19 So Daring Woman (Herodias) held this against He Shows Goodwill (John) and wanted to kill him. 20 But Looks Brave (Herod) knew he was a man that walked in an upright and holy manner, so he was afraid and protected him. From time to time Looks Brave (Herod) liked to sit and listen to He Shows Goodwill (John), even though his words troubled him.

A Day of Sorrow

21 Daring Woman (Herodias) was waiting for a chance to have him killed. This chance came on the birthday of Looks Brave (Herod). He had a great feast prepared to celebrate his birthday and invited government officials, head soldiers and important dignitaries from Circle of Nations (Galilee).

22-23 The daughter of Daring Woman (Herodias) came in and danced before them. pleasing Looks Brave (Herod) and all the guests.

"Ask anything from me and I will give it to you," he said to her, making a solemn promise, "up to half of all that I rule over."

24 So she went out to her mother and said, "What shall I ask for?"

"Ask for the head of He Shows Goodwill (John), the one who performs the purification ceremony," she replied *with a sly grin on her face.*

25 Right away she hurried back to the feast, went right up to the chief and said, "Give to me, here and now, the head of He Shows Goodwill (John) in a basket!"

26 The heart of Chief Looks Brave (Herod) fell to the ground, but because he had made a solemn promise in front of his guests, he could not refuse her request. 27 So right then he ordered a soldier to bring him the head of He Shows Goodwill (John). So he went to where he was in prison and cut off his head. 28 He brought his head to the young girl in a basket, and she gave it to her mother.

29 Now, when the followers of He Shows Goodwill (John) heard about his *tragic* death, they came for his body and buried it properly.

The Message Bearers Return

30 The message bearers returned from their journeys and with *full hearts* told Creator Sets Free (Jesus) about all that they had done and taught. 31 There were so many people coming and going all around them that they didn't even have time to eat.

So Creator Sets Free (Jesus) said to them, "Come with me, and we will find a quiet place in the wilderness to rest for a while."

32 Then they left in a canoe to go to an out-of-way place to be alone and rest. 33 But the people saw where they were going and ran ahead of them. They came from all the surrounding villages and

were waiting for them when they arrived.

34 As Creator Sets Free (Jesus) climbed out of the canoe, he saw the great crowd of people, and his heart went out to them again. He saw that they were like sheep with no shepherd to watch over them. He stayed there with them and began to teach and tell them stories *about Creator's Good Road.*

A Meal for Five Thousand

35 It was late in the day, so his followers said to him, "This is a deserted place and the day is almost over. 36 We should send the people away to the villages in the countryside so they can find food to eat."

Creator Sets Free (Jesus) looked around at the great crowd of people—over five thousand men and also women and children. Then he turned and looked right at his followers.

37 "You feed them!" he said to them.

They could not believe their ears! How could they feed so many people?

"It would take over eight moons' worth[h] of gathered food to feed all these," they answered him. "Do you want us to go and trade for that much?"

38 Then he said to them, "Go and see how many loaves of bread we have."

After looking around they said, "We have five loaves of bread and two fish."

39 Then Creator Sets Free (Jesus) instructed the people to sit down in groups on the green grass. 40 So the people *gathered up their traveling bundles and their children* and sat down, some in groups of one hundred and some in groups of fifty.

41 Then he took the five loaves and two fish *and held them up to the sky.* He looked up into the world above and spoke words of blessing over them. He then broke the bread into smaller pieces and gave them to his followers to give to the people. Then he did the same with the fish.

42 Everyone ate until they could eat no more. 43 When they gathered up the leftovers, there were twelve baskets full. 44 The number of men fed in this great gathering of people was about five thousand!

45 Right away Creator Sets Free (Jesus) urged his followers to get into their canoe and sent them ahead to the other side of the lake toward House of Fishing (Bethsaida), while he sent the crowd on their way. 46 He then left them and went up by himself into the mountainside to send his voice to the Great Spirit.

He Walks on Water

47 As the sun was setting, his followers were still in the canoe out in the middle of the lake, while Creator Sets Free (Jesus) was alone on the land. 48 He could see them paddling hard against the wind. Then, early in the morning, just before sunrise, he walked out on

---

h 6:37 Two hundred denarii. A denarius was about a single day's wages.

the lake and was going to pass right past them.

⁴⁹His followers looked out *in the dim light* and saw him walking on the lake. Thinking he was a ghost, ⁵⁰they wailed and cried out loud as fear took hold of them.

Right away Creator Sets Free (Jesus) called out to them, "Do not fear. Take heart. It is I!"

⁵¹He then came to them and climbed into the canoe as the wind calmed down. His followers were amazed beyond words, for their hearts were still too hard. ⁵²Even the miracle of the loaves and fishes did not open their eyes *to see who Creator Sets Free (Jesus) truly was.*

⁵³They came to shore at the village of Chief Garden (Gennesaret) and tied their canoe to a rock. ⁵⁴As soon as they got out of their canoe, the people recognized Creator Sets Free (Jesus). ⁵⁵So they ran to all the nearby villages, gathered up the sick on their sleeping bundles and brought them to Creator Sets Free (Jesus).

⁵⁶Wherever he would go— into villages, camps or in the countryside—they would take the sick, lay them in front of the trading posts and beg him to let them touch the fringes of his clothes. And all who touched him were healed.

Traditions Made by Men

7 The Separated Ones (Pharisees) and some of the scroll keepers had come from Village of Peace (Jerusalem). *Like hungry wolves* they gathered around Creator Sets Free (Jesus).

They were looking for ways to accuse him and make him look bad in the eyes of the people, for they were jealous of his reputation.

²They noticed that some of his followers had not ceremonially washed their hands before eating the food.

³The Separated Ones (Pharisees) and many of the tribal people will not eat until they ceremonially wash their hands, following the traditions of the elders. ⁴They will not eat the food offered at the trading posts unless it is first purified by washing. They also follow many other traditions, like the washing of drinking cups, bowls, and even the benches they sit on.

⁵So the Separated Ones (Pharisees) and the scroll keepers asked him, "Why do your followers not walk in the traditions of the elders and ceremonially wash their hands before eating?"

⁶"Your false faces do not fool me," he answered back, "The prophet Creator Will Help Us (Isaiah) was talking about you when he said in the Sacred Teachings: 'These people honor me with their lips, but their hearts are far away from me. ⁷Their prayers are empty words and their ceremonies are for show. Their teachings are nothing but rules made up by weak human beings.'ⁱ"

---

i 7:7 Isaiah 29:13

He paused to let these words sink into their ears.

8 Then he said to them, "You ignore the instructions given by the Great Spirit and use your traditions to make yourselves look good to others. 9 You are *as sly as coyote* in the way you set aside Creator's instructions and replace them with your traditions.

10 "The lawgiver Drawn From The Water (Moses) said, 'Give honor to your father and mother,'ʲ and 'The ones who dishonor them should be put to death.'ᵏ 11 But your tradition says, 'If someone says to their father or mother, "I have given to the Great Spirit the things that were meant to honor and take care of you," 12 then they no longer have to honor and care for their parents.' 13 This is only one of the many ways you use your traditions to do away with the words of the Great Spirit."

What Makes One Impure?

14 Creator Sets Free (Jesus) then gathered the people around him and said, "Listen with your hearts and understand what I tell you. 15 There is nothing you can take into your mouth that will make you impure. It is what comes out of your mouth that makes you impure."ˡ

17 Later when they entered a house away from the crowds, the ones who walked the road with him asked the meaning of his wise saying.

18-19 "Why do you also not understand?" he answered. "When food enters the mouth, it goes into the stomach, not the heart, and then out of the body."

In saying this, Creator Sets Free (Jesus) declared that nothing you eat can make you impure.

20 "It is what comes out of a person, from within, that makes one impure. 21 From people's bad hearts and broken ways come worthless plans, sexual impurity, stealing, killing, 22 unfaithfulness in marriage, greed, evil doings, forked tongues, uncontrolled desires, selfish ways, speaking evil of others, boastful talk, and foolish ways. 23 It is things like this that make a person impure, *not failing to wash one's hands.*"

He Heals the Daughter of an Outsider

24 From there Creator Sets free (Jesus) journeyed into the territory of Rock Land (Tyre) and Hunting Grounds (Sidon). He wanted to keep away from the crowds, so he found a house to stay out of sight, but was unable to stay hidden.

25-26 A woman came to him who had a daughter with an unclean spirit in her. As soon as she heard about Creator Sets Free (Jesus), she came to him and fell down at his feet. She was an Outsiderᵐ from the territory along the coastline of the Great Middle Sea (Mediterranean).ⁿ She begged Creator Sets Free (Jesus)

---

j 7:10 Exodus 20:12; Deuteronomy 5:16   k 7:10 Exodus 21:17; Leviticus 20:9   l 7:15 Some ancient manuscripts add verse 16: The ones with ears to hear should listen and understand.   m 7:25-26 Lit., a Greek   n 7:25-26 Lit., a Syrophoenician by birth

to force the evil spirit out of her daughter.

27 "The children should be fed first," he said. "It is not right to take the children's portion and throw it to the dogs."

28 "But Wisdomkeeper," she answered back, "even the dogs under the table can eat the children's crumbs."

29 "Because your words are well chosen," he replied, "you may return home. You will find that the evil spirit has left your daughter."

30 The woman went home and found her daughter resting on her sleeping mat—the evil spirit had left her.

A Powerful Healing

31 From the territory of Rock Land (Tyre) Creator Sets Free (Jesus) went through Hunting Grounds (Sidon) to the Lake of Circle of Nations (Sea of Galilee) in the territory of the Ten Villages (Decapolis).

32 The people who lived there brought a man who could not hear or speak right. They begged Creator Sets Free (Jesus) to lay his hands on him. 33 So he took the man away from the crowd. When he was alone with him, he put his fingers into the man's ears, and then spit and touched the man's tongue.

34 He then looked up into the world above, let out a deep breath and said in his native language, "Ephphatha!" which means, "Be opened."

35 Right then the man's ears were opened and his tongue was released. He could now hear and speak clearly! 36 Creator Sets Free (Jesus) then instructed the people to tell no one. But the more he told them not to, the more they told the story to others. 37 The people were amazed beyond belief and full of wonder.

"He does all things well!" they told everyone. "He even heals the ones who cannot hear or speak!"

Four Thousand Hungry People

8 On another one of those days a great crowd had gathered and, like the time before, they were hungry with nothing to eat.

Creator Sets Free (Jesus) called his followers to his side and said to them, 2 "I am concerned for all these people, for they have been with us for three days with no food. 3 Some of them have come from a great distance, and if I send them away hungry, they might lose their strength and faint."

4 "This is a desolate and out-of-the-way place," they answered him. "Where could we find enough food to feed all these people?"

5 "How much bread do we have?" he asked.

"We have seven loaves of bread," they answered.

6 Creator Sets Free (Jesus) instructed all the people to sit down on the ground. He then took the seven loaves, gave thanks and broke them into pieces. He gave them to his followers, and they gave them out to the people.

7 They also had a few small fish, so he prayed a blessing over them and told them to give them out as well.

8 Everyone ate as much as they wanted, and when they were done eating, his followers gathered up the leftovers—seven baskets full! 9 They had fed about four thousand men *and also women and children.* He then sent the crowd on their way.

10 Right away he climbed into the canoe with his twelve followers and went to the territory of Cold Springs (Dalmanutha).°

No Sign Will Be Given

11 While they were there, the Separated Ones (Pharisees) came to argue with him. They asked from him a sign from the world above to prove who he was.

12 "Why do the people of this generation need a sign?" he asked as he breathed out a sigh from his spirit. "I tell you from my heart, this generation will not be given a sign—*not today!*"

13 He then climbed back into his canoe and launched out toward the other side of the lake.

The Yeast of the Separated Ones

14 They had only one loaf of bread with them because his followers had forgotten to bring more.

15 "Be on the lookout for the yeast of the Separated Ones (Pharisees)," he told them firmly, "and also of the Friends of Looks Brave (Herodians)."

16 His followers tried to figure out why he said this. They said to each other, "Is it because we forgot to bring more bread?"

17 Creator Sets Free (Jesus) could hear what they were saying.

"Why are you thinking like this?" he said. "Why are you worried that you forgot to bring bread? How is it that you do not understand? Are your hearts still hard? 18 Have you no eyes to see with and no ears to hear with?"

His words were sharp, and frustration showed on his face as he tried to make things clear.

"Have you forgotten so soon?" he asked. 19 "When I broke the five loaves to feed five thousand, how many baskets of broken pieces were left over?"

"Twelve," they answered.

20 "When I broke the seven loaves to feed four thousand, how many baskets of broken pieces did you gather?"

"Seven," they said.

21 "So, do you still not understand?" he said.

He Heals a Man Born Blind

22 They walked on to the village of House of Fishing (Bethsaida). The people there brought a blind man to Creator Sets Free (Jesus) and begged him to touch him. 23 He took the blind man by the hand, and led

---

o 8:10 Some ancient manuscripts say 'Magdala' or 'Magadan.' See Matthew 15:39

him to the outside of the village. He rubbed some of his spit into the man's eyes and then laid his hands on him.

"What do you see?" Creator Sets Free (Jesus) asked the man.

24 He looked around and said, "I can see people, but they look like trees walking around."

25 Creator Sets Free (Jesus) put his hands over the man's eyes again. His sight returned and he could see everything clearly.

26 He then sent the man to his home and said to him, "Do not go back into the village."

You are the Chosen One

27 They journeyed on and came into the villages of the territory of Ruler of Horsemen (Caesarea Philippi).

"What are the people saying about me?" Creator Sets Free (Jesus) asked his followers as they walked along the road. "Who do they think I am?"

28 "Some say you are He Shows Goodwill (John) who performed the purification ceremony," they answered. "Others say you are Great Spirit Is Creator (Elijah) or one of the other prophets."

29 "But who do you say I am?" he asked.

"You are the Chosen One!" Stands On The Rock (Peter) answered.

30 Creator Sets Free (Jesus) then sternly warned them not to tell this to anyone.

The Road of Suffering Lies Ahead

31 Creator Sets Free (Jesus) then began to instruct his followers that he must suffer many things. The council of elders, the head holy men and the scroll keepers would turn their faces from him. He would then be killed, and after three days he would return from the world of the dead. He said this openly to all his followers.

32 Stands On The Rock (Peter) pulled him aside from the others and spoke sharply to him.

33 Creator Sets Free (Jesus) turned and looked to his followers and then spoke sharply to Stands On The Rock (Peter), "Out of my way, Accuser (Satan)! These are not the thoughts of the Great Spirit, but of a weak human being."

Carrying the Cross

34 He then gathered his followers and the crowd around him and said, "Any who want to walk the road with me must turn away from their own path and carry their own cross as they follow me *to the place of ultimate sacrifice.*

35 "The ones who hold on to their lives will not find life, but the ones who are willing to let go of their lives, for me and for the Good Story I bring, will find the true life. 36 How will it help you to get everything you want in this world, but lose the true life? 37 Is there anything in this world worth trading for it?

38 "There are bad-hearted and unfaithful people living today, in this generation, who are ashamed of me and my message. So, when the True Human Being comes to show the great power and glory of his Father along with his holy spirit-messengers, he will also be ashamed of these people."

9 "I speak to you from my heart," he said to his followers and the crowd who had gathered around him. "There are some of you standing here today who, before you cross over to death, will see the coming of Creator's Good Road and all its power!"

The Ancestors Speak With Him

2-3 Six days later Creator Sets Free (Jesus) took his three closest followers—Stands On The Rock (Peter), He Takes Over (James) and He Shows Goodwill (John)—and led them up a high mountain to be alone *and pray.*

Right before their eyes his appearance began to change. His clothes became shining white, whiter than anyone on earth could make them. 4 Two ancestors appeared before them also, the prophet Great Spirit is Creator (Elijah) and the ancient lawgiver Drawn From The Water (Moses). They were both talking with Creator Sets Free (Jesus).

His three followers rubbed their eyes and looked again. They were filled with wonder and trembled with fear and excitement!

5 Stands On The Rock (Peter) spoke out, "Wisdomkeeper, this is a good place to be! We should set up three tipis—one for you, one for Drawn From The Water (Moses) and one for Great Spirit Is Creator (Elijah)."

6 He said this without thinking because they were all afraid and didn't know what to say.

7 Then, from above, a bright cloud came down around them and a voice spoke out from the cloud, "This is my Son, my Much Loved One, *he is the one who speaks for me now.* Listen to him!"

8 Right then the cloud lifted. They looked around to see their ancestors, but they were gone, and standing alone before them was Creator Sets Free (Jesus).

Great Spirit Is Creator

9 As they walked down the mountainside, he instructed them to tell no one what they had seen until after the True Human Being had come back to life from the dead. 10 So they told no one, but wondered what this "coming back to life from the dead" meant.

11 *During the long walk down the mountain,* they asked him, "Why do the scroll keepers say that Great Spirit Is Creator (Elijah) must be the first to come?"

12-13 "It is true," he answered, "Great Spirit Is Creator (Elijah) comes first to prepare the way for all things to be restored. And I tell you that he has already come— but none recognized him—and they did whatever they wanted to him, just as the Sacred Teachings foretold. But do you know that it has also been foretold that the True Human Being will suffer many things and be treated with scorn and disrespect?"

His Followers Fail to Force Out a Spirit

14 When they had finished coming down the mountain to join with the other followers, they found a large crowd around them. The scroll keepers were there arguing with them *about something.* 15 As soon as the crowd saw Creator Sets Free (Jesus), they were filled with awe and ran to greet him.

Creator Sets Free (Jesus) made his way through the crowd and came to the scroll keepers, who were arguing with his followers.

16 "What are you arguing with my followers about?" he asked them.

17 *Before they could answer,* someone stepped out from the crowd and said to him, "Wisdomkeeper, I came and brought my son to you. He has a spirit that keeps him from speaking. 18 The evil spirit will take hold of him and throw him to the ground. He then becomes stiff, grinds his teeth together and foam comes from his mouth. I asked your followers to force out this spirit, and they tried but failed."

19 "This is a generation with no faith!" Creator Sets Free (Jesus) said to them all. "How much longer will I have to put up with you? Bring the boy to me."

20 So they brought the boy to him, and right when the spirit saw Creator

Sets Free (Jesus), it took hold of the boy, who then fell to the ground. He began to roll around on the ground and foam came from his mouth.

21 "How long has he been this way?" Creator Sets Free (Jesus) asked the father.

"From the time he was a child." the father answered. 22 "The evil spirit has many times thrown him into a fire to burn him or into water to drown him. If you are able to do anything, have pity and help us!"

23 "What do you mean 'If I am able?'" Creator Sets Free (Jesus) answered him. "Nothing is too hard for the one with faith!"

24 "I do believe!" the father cried out right away. "Help my weak faith!"

25 Creator Sets Free (Jesus) saw that the crowd was now pushing in closer to see, so he spoke sharply to the unclean spirit.

"Spirit that makes one unable to speak or hear," he said firmly, "I order you now, to leave this boy and never enter him again!"

26 The spirit cried out, and the boy began to twist and turn upon the ground. The spirit then came out, and the boy became so still it looked as if he were dead.

"He must be dead!" the people said out loud.

27 Then Creator Sets Free (Jesus) took hold of the boy's hand and stood him on his feet.

28 Later, when they were alone with him in the house, his followers asked him, "Why were we unable to force out the evil spirit?"

29 "This kind of spirit can only be forced out by prayer,*p*" was his answer to them.

He Again Foretells His Death

30 From there, Creator Sets Free (Jesus) took his followers on through Circle of Nations (Galilee) but stayed away from the crowds 31 so he could further instruct the ones who walked the road with him.

"The True Human Being will soon be taken and handed over to men who will kill him, but on the third day he will come back to life from the dead."

32 But his followers did not understand what he meant and were afraid to ask.

Who is the Greatest?

33 They returned again to Village of Comfort (Capernaum) and settled down into the house there.

"What were you talking about as we walked the road just now?" he asked them.

34 None of them would answer him, because they had been arguing about who among themselves was the greatest. 35 So Creator Sets Free (Jesus) sat down and gathered his twelve followers around him.

"The one who would be first must be the one who will serve all the others—and become last," he told them.

36 He then stood a small child in front of them.

"When you represent me and welcome a child like this one, you welcome me."

37 He then took the child into his arms and said, "When you welcome me, you do not welcome me alone, but also the one who sent me."

The Ones Not Against Us Are For Us

38 Then He Shows Goodwill (John) said to him, "Wisdomkeeper, we saw a man forcing out evil spirits using your name. We told him to stop, because he doesn't walk the road with us."

39 "Do not stop him," he answered. "No one who can do works of power using my name will suddenly turn against me. 40 The ones who are not against us are for us. 41 I speak from my heart, anyone who brings the gift of even a drink of water to the ones who represent me will never lose the honor that has been gained.

Stumbling Stones

42 "But, let no one cause one of these little ones who have put their trust in me to stumble away from the path. It would be better to have a great stone tied to his neck and be thrown into the great waters. 43 If what your hand does causes you to stumble off the path, then cut it off and throw it away! It would be better to live this life with only one hand than to go with two hands into the Valley of Smoldering Fire—a fire that cannot be put out. 45 If where your foot walks causes you to stumble from

---

p 9:29 Some ancient manuscripts add 'and fasting.'

the path, then cut it off and throw it away. It would be better to walk this life with only one foot than to walk with two feet right into the Valley of Smoldering Fire—a fire that cannot be put out.

Valley of Smoldering Fire

47 "The same thing goes for your eye. If what it sees makes you stumble from the path, then pluck it out and throw it away. It would be better to walk Creator's Good Road with only one eye than to see with two eyes and be thrown into the Valley of Smoldering Fire. 48 This Valley of Smoldering Fire is the place *spoken of in the Sacred Teachings:*q 'Where their worm does not die and the fire cannot be put out.'r

49 "All will be salted with fire,s for all ceremonial offerings are salted before they are burned with fire.t 50 Salt is a good thing, *for it purifies, heals and makes things taste better;* but if it becomes unsalty, what will make it salty again? So make sure that you, like salt, keep your true flavor by walking with each other in the way of peace."

10 Creator Sets Free (Jesus) then left that place and walked to the territory of the Land of Promise (Judea) beyond the river Flowing Down (Jordan). There, as he usually did, he began to teach the crowds that had once again gathered around him.

Tested About Divorce

2 *Like hungry wolves* the Separated Ones (Pharisees) came to test and accuse him.

"Does our Tribal Law permit a man to send his wife away?" they asked.

3 "What did the lawgiver Drawn From The Water (Moses) instruct the people about this?" he replied.

4 "He permitted a man to send her away by giving her divorce papers," they answered back.

5 "It is because of your hard hearts that he permitted this," he said to them. 6 "But this was not always so, for from the beginning of creation 'he made them to be male and female.'u 7 'This is why a man will leave his father and mother and be joined to his wife, 8 and together they make one flesh'v—no longer two—but the two braided together as one. 9 So no human being should tear apart what the Maker Of Life has joined together."

10 Later, back in the house, his followers asked him some more questions about this.

11 He then said to them, "Whoever sends his wife away, *without properly divorcing her,* and marries another is guilty of being unfaithful to his *first* wife. 12 If she then, after being sent away, marries another man, then she is also guilty of being unfaithful."

---

q 9:48 Isaiah 66:24; Jeremiah 7:31-32   r 9:48 Some ancient manuscripts include this sentence in verses 46 and 48 that are omitted in this translation, and in most other translations. s 9:49 Most manuscripts omit the end of this verse.   t 9:49 Leviticus 2:13   u 10:6 Genesis 1:27 v 10:8 Genesis 2:24

In those days men would sometimes send their wives away for any reason without giving them divorce papers, leaving them destitute and unable to properly remarry.

Little Children and the Good Road

¹³ The people were bringing their little children to Creator Sets Free (Jesus) so he would lay his hands on them and bless them, but his followers spoke harsh words to the ones bringing them.

¹⁴ When Creator Sets Free (Jesus) saw what his followers were doing, it made him angry, so he said to them, "Let the little children come to me! Do not turn them away. Creator's Good Road belongs to the ones who are like these children. ¹⁵ I speak from my heart, the only way onto the Good Road is to become as trusting as a little child."

¹⁶ He then took the children into his arms, laid his hands on them and blessed them.

Possessions and the Great Spirit

¹⁷ As Creator Sets Free (Jesus) set out walking from there, a man ran up to him and honored him.

"Good Wisdomkeeper," the man asked, "what path will lead me to the life of the world to come that never fades away?"

¹⁸ "Why do you call me good?" he asked the man. "There is only one who is good—the Great Spirit.

¹⁹ You must know the instructions *from the lawgiver Drawn From The Water (Moses).* 'You are not to take the life of another, or be unfaithful in marriage, or take what is not yours. Never lie about or cheat a fellow human being, and always give honor and respect to your father and mother.'"ʷ

²⁰ "Wisdomkeeper," the man answered, "from my youth I have followed all of these instructions."

²¹ Creator Sets Free (Jesus) looked at the man with love and said, "Only one thing remains. Take all your possessions, invite the poor of your village to come, and have a Giveaway. Then in the world above you will have many possessions waiting for you. Then leave everything behind, and come, walk the road with me."

²² The man's heart fell to the ground. He hung his head and walked away, for he had many possessions.

Possessions and the Good Road

²³ Creator Sets Free (Jesus) then looked around at the people and said to his followers, "Finding and walking the Good Road is a hard thing for the ones who have many possessions."

²⁴ His followers could not believe what they were hearing.

They thought having many possessions was a sign of blessing from the Great Spirit.

---

w 10:19 Exodus 20:12-16; Deuteronomy 5:16-20

25 Creator Sets Free (Jesus) spoke again to them. "Little children," he said, "the ones who trust in their many possessions will have a hard time finding their way onto the Good Road. It would be easier for a moose[x] to go through the eye of a needle."

26 They shook their heads in wonder, looked at each other and said, "How then can anyone walk the Good Road that sets all people free?"

27 He looked at them and said, "It is not possible for weak human beings, but with Creator's help all things are possible."

28 Stands On The Rock (Peter) spoke up, "We have left all our possessions, and our relatives, to walk the road with you! What will become of us?"

29 "I speak from my heart," he answered, "no one who has given up homes and families to follow me and walk my Good Road will go without. 30 In this present world they will become part of an even greater family, with many homes and lands. Even though they have been abused and mistreated, they will receive much more than they have lost.[y] Then, in the world to come, they will have the life of beauty and harmony that never fades away.

31 "But many who are first *in this present world* will be last *in the world to come,* and many who are last *in this present world* will be first *in the one to come.*"

He Foretells His Death and Rising

32 Creator Sets Free (Jesus) led the way as they walked the road toward Village of Peace (Jerusalem). As they followed behind him, they began to worry *about what would happen when they arrived,* and fear began to cover them like a blanket.

Creator Sets Free (Jesus) took the twelve aside and told them once again what would happen to him.

33 "This is what you must see and understand," he said to them. "We will soon arrive in Village of Peace (Jerusalem) where the True Human Being will be turned over to the head holy men and the scroll keepers. They will condemn him to death and then turn him over to the People of Iron (Romans). 34 They will mock him, spit on him, and whip him with cowhide strips. After that, they will kill him, but three days later he will come back to life again."

A Place of Honor?

35 After that, He Takes Over (James) and He Shows Goodwill (John), the sons of Gift of Creator (Zebedee), came up to Creator Sets Free (Jesus).

"Wisdomkeeper," they said, "We want to ask you to do something for us."

36 "What is it you want from me?" he replied.

37 "When your great power and glory is revealed," they said back to him, "permit us a place of honor

---

x 10:25 Lit., camel   y 10:30 Lit., one hundred times as much beside you—one on your right hand the other on your left."

³⁸ "You do not understand what you are asking," he answered. "Are you able to drink the cup of suffering that I will drink, or endure the purification ceremony that I will endure?"

³⁹ "We are able!" they answered.

"Yes," he said to them, "you will drink from my cup of suffering and endure my purification ceremony, ⁴⁰ but the place at my right and left hand is not mine to give. This honor belongs to the ones for whom it has already been prepared."

⁴¹ When the other ten message bearers heard this, they began to look down on He Takes Over (James) and He Shows Goodwill (John).

The Good Road is About Serving Others

⁴² So Creator Sets Free (Jesus) called them together and said, "Other nations have rulers, *like the People of Iron (Romans)*. They like to show their power over people and push them around. ⁴³ But this will not be the way of the ones, like you, who walk with me. ⁴⁴ The great ones among you will humble themselves and serve all the others. ⁴⁵ In the same way, the True Human Being did not come to be served by others, but to offer his life in the place of many lives, to set them free."

Moon Village Healing

⁴⁶ Creator Sets Free (Jesus) and his followers walked through Moon Village (Jericho), and a large crowd followed behind them as they left the village. As the crowd passed, a blind beggar, whose name was Son Of Honored One (Bartimaeus), was sitting on the side of the road.

⁴⁷ When he heard that Creator Sets Free (Jesus) from Seed Planter Village (Nazareth) was there, he cried out loudly, "Descendant of Much Loved One (David), have pity on me!"

⁴⁸ Many in the crowd scolded him, telling him to be quiet, but this only made him cry out even louder, "Descendant of Much Loved One (David), have pity on me!"

⁴⁹ Creator Sets Free (Jesus) stopped walking, *turned to the crowd* and said, "Tell him to come to me."

So they called out to the blind man, "Have courage! He is calling for you!"

⁵⁰ He jumped up, threw aside his outer garment, and walked *with the help of others* to Creator Sets Free (Jesus).

⁵¹ "What do you want from me?" Creator Sets Free (Jesus) said to him.

"Wisdomkeeper," he answered, "Make me see again!"

⁵² "Be on your way," he said to him, "Your faith in me has made you whole again."

Right then and there his eyes were opened! So he began to follow after Creator Sets Free (Jesus) as they continued on their way down the road.

Preparation for His Grand Entry

11 Creator Sets Free (Jesus) and his followers came to the foot of Olive Mountain at House of

Figs (Bethany) and House of Unripe Figs (Bethphage) near Village of Peace (Jerusalem). From there he sent out two of his followers.

2 "Go on into the village just ahead of us," he instructed them. "Right when you enter the village, you will see a donkey colt that no one has ever ridden. Untie it and bring it to me. 3 If anyone asks, 'What are you doing?' say to them, 'Our Wisdomkeeper is in need of this donkey and will soon return it.'"

4 His followers went where they were told, found a colt tied by a gate near the village pathway, and untied it. 5 Some of the people standing nearby said to them, "What are you doing untying that colt?"

6 They answered them just as their Wisdomkeeper had instructed, so they were permitted to go. 7 They brought the young donkey to Creator Sets Free (Jesus), laid their *deer skins and Pendleton* blankets on the colt, and then he sat down upon it.

Grand Entry

8 A crowd gathered around, and some of them laid their *buffalo* robes on the road, while others spread out branches with large leaves they had cut from the fields.

The people were hoping he would be a mighty warrior chief, like their ancestor Much Loved One (David), to set them free from the People of Iron (Romans). But he did not ride a warhorse on that day, as one might expect. Instead, he rode a small humble donkey colt. He came weeping over the Village of Peace (Jerusalem), but even this could not silence the hopes of the crowd.

9 The people encircled him, front and back.

"Hosanna!" z they shouted out *in their tribal language.* 10 "Blessed is the one who comes representing the Great Spirit! The Good Road of our ancestor Much Loved One (David) has arrived! Hosanna, to the One Above Us All!"

11 Creator Sets Free (Jesus) rode into Village of Peace (Jerusalem) until he came to the Sacred Lodge. He went into the Lodge and looked around at everything—then he left. It was time for the sun to set, so he returned to House of Figs (Bethany), along with his twelve followers, *to the place where they were lodging.*

The Fig Tree Without Fruit

12 The next day, as Creator Sets Free (Jesus) was returning *to Village of Peace (Jerusalem)* from House of Figs (Bethany), he became hungry. 13 He saw a fig tree with leaves on it in the distance and went to see if he might find some figs on it. But when he came to the tree, he found only leaves, for it was not the season for figs.

14 He responded by speaking to the tree, "No one will eat fruit from you ever again!" And his followers heard what he said.

Sacred Lodge Keeper

15 They went into Village of Peace (Jerusalem) *through the village gate, made their way through the crowded*

---

z 11:9 Lit., Help us or save us.

pathways, and went *straight* to Creator's Sacred Lodge.

He came to the area called Gathering Place for the Nations. It was here that other nations could come to learn about the Great Spirit and his ways.

Creator Sets Free (Jesus) entered the Lodge and began to force out the ones who were selling and buying the ceremonial animals. He turned over the benches and tables of those who were selling the doves [16] and blocked the way of the ones who were carrying trading goods through the Lodge.

[17] "It is written in the sacred teachings," he instructed them, "'My Lodge will be called a House of Prayer for all Nations.'[a] *Then his voice rose like the sound of thunder,* 'But you have turned it into a hideout for thieves!'"[b]

[18] The head holy men and the scroll keepers heard about what Creator Sets Free (Jesus) had said and done. They began to counsel together about how they could kill him, for they feared his reputation among the many people who respected his teachings.

[19] When the sun began to set, Creator Sets Free (Jesus) and his followers left the village *to return to where they were lodging.*

[20] In the morning, as they were walking on their way to Village of Peace (Jerusalem), they saw the fig tree dried up from the roots. [21] Stands On The Rock (Peter) remembered that it was the same tree Creator Sets Free (Jesus) had spoken against.

"Wisdomkeeper!" he said. "Look, the fig tree you spoke against has dried up from the roots!"

[22] "You must put all your trust in the Great Spirit," Creator Sets Free (Jesus) replied. [23] "I speak from my heart. Anyone who says to this mountain, 'Lift up and go into the great waters,' with a heart that believes and does not doubt that what he says will happen, then it will be done. [24] That is why I say that when you send your voice to the Great Spirit, believe that he has heard you and the answer will come.

[25] "In the same way, when you stand and pray and there remember you have something against another, release them from the wrong they have done, so that your Father from above will also release you from the wrongs you have done."[c]

Spiritual Leaders Challenge Him

[27] Creator Sets Free (Jesus) returned to Village of Peace (Jerusalem) and was walking about in the Sacred Lodge. The head holy men and the scroll keepers came to him, along with some of the tribal elders.

[28] "By what right do you do these things?" they challenged. "Who gave you this right?"

[29] "I will give you one question to answer. If you answer me, then I

---

a 11:17 Isaiah 56:7   b 11:17 Jeremiah 7:11   c 11:25 Some ancient manuscripts also add verse 26: "But if you fail to release others, then your Father from above will not release you."

will answer you. [30] The purification ceremony performed by He Shows Goodwill (John), was it from the world above, or did it come from human beings?"

The spiritual leaders looked at each other. They could not decide on how to answer him. Creator Sets Free (Jesus) stood before them and held his ground.

"Answer me!" he challenged back.

[31] So they put their heads together and talked it over. "We cannot say, 'From the world above,' for then he will say, 'Why did you not listen to him?' [32] But neither can we say, 'From human beings,' for the people honor He Shows Goodwill (John) as a prophet."

[33] They feared the people, so they said, "We do not know."

"So then, I will not answer your question," he said to them, "and tell you by what right I do these things."

12 *Once again* Creator Sets Free (Jesus) began to speak to them using stories:

Story About the Vineyard

[2] "A tribal member planted a *large* vineyard. He encircled it with a hedge, dug a hole for stomping the juice from the grapes, and built a tower for watching over it. He then rented it out to other tribal farmers *for a share of the grapes.* Then he traveled far away on a long journey to another land.

"When harvest time came, the tribal member who owned the vineyard sent a trusted messenger to gather his share of the grapes; [3] but the farmers beat him and sent him away empty-handed.

[4] "The vineyard owner sent another messenger; but they treated him shamefully, struck him on the head and sent him away also.

[5] "So he sent a third messenger, and this one they killed. The same thing was done to many others he sent; they beat some and killed others.

[6] "Finally, the vineyard owner had only one more that he could send—his much loved son. So, last of all, he sent his own son to them.

"'They will respect my son,' he said to himself.

[7] "But those tribal farmers said to themselves, 'This vineyard will one day belong to this son. If we kill him, the vineyard will be ours.'

[8] "So they killed him and threw his dead body out of the vineyard.

[9] "What do you think the owner of the vineyard will do?" Creator Sets Free (Jesus) asked *the people who were listening.*

He waited for an answer, but no one said a word.

Then he said, "He will return, put those *dishonorable* men to death and give the vineyard to others. [10] Have you not read in the Sacred Teachings where it is said, 'The tree the lodge builders threw away has become the Chief Pole. [11] This is what the Great Spirit will do, and when we see it, we will be filled with wonder.'"[d]

---

d 12:11 Psalm 118:22-23

¹² The spiritual leaders wanted to take him prisoner right then and there, for they knew the story was about them. But they were afraid of what the people might do, so they left him and went away.

They Set a Trap for Him

¹³ The spiritual leaders sent some of the Separated Ones (Pharisees) and the Friends of Looks Brave (Herodians) to trap Creator Sets Free (Jesus) in his words.

¹⁴ "Wisdomkeeper," they came and said to him, "we know you always speak the truth about the Great Spirit and represent him well, no matter what others may think or say. Tell us what is right," they asked. "Does our Tribal Law permit our people to pay taxes to the government of the People of Iron (Romans)? ¹⁵ Yes or no?"

Creator Sets Free (Jesus) could see right through their false faces!

"Why are you putting me to the test?" he said to them. "Bring to me one of their silver coins and I will look at it."

¹⁶ So they brought one to him.

He took a good long look at it, holding it up to the sky to see it clearly. Then he turned the face of the coin for them to see.

"Whose image and words are carved into this coin?" he asked.

"The Ruler of the People of Iron (Caesar)," they replied.

¹⁷ "Then give this ruler the things that are his," he told them, "but give to the Great Spirit the things that belong to the Great Spirit."

The spiritual leaders were amazed *at his words.*

They could not believe it. They had failed right in front of all the people and could not use his words against him, so they walked away in silence.

The Upright Ones Test Him

¹⁸ Then the Upright Ones (Sadducees), who say that there is no rising from the dead, also came to him *to test him.*

¹⁹ "Wisdomkeeper," they said to him, "Drawn From the Water (Moses) instructed us in the Sacred Teachings that if a Tribal Member should die before having children, then his brother should marry his widow and give her children. This way the man will have descendants.

²⁰ "What if, in a family of seven brothers, the oldest took a wife, but died without children. ²¹ Then the second brother married her, but he also died leaving no children. Then the third brother also married her and he, like the others, died with no children. ²² The same happened to all seven of them, and last of all the woman also crossed over to death. ²³ So then, when they all come back to life in the time when the dead rise, whose wife would she be, since all seven brothers married her?"

²⁴ "You are asking the wrong kind of question," Creator Sets Free (Jesus) answered back, "for you do not understand the Sacred Teachings or the power of the Great Spirit. ²⁵ When men or women rise again from the dead, they will not

marry, for they will be like the spirit-messengers from the world above."

And then he added, 26 "As for the dead rising again, do you not remember what was written in the Sacred Teachings about the time when the Great Spirit spoke to Drawn From The Water (Moses) from the burning bush? He said, 'I am the Great Spirit of Father Of Many Nations (Abraham), of He Made Us Laugh (Isaac), and of Heel Grabber (Jacob).'*e* 27 He is not the Great Spirit of the dead, but of the living! So in this matter you are greatly in the wrong."

The Greatest Instruction of All

28 One of the scroll keepers overheard Creator Sets Free (Jesus) opposing the Upright Ones. When he heard the good answer he had given, he asked him, "Which instruction in our Tribal Law stands first?"

29 "The first and greatest instruction is this," Creator Sets Free (Jesus) answered. "'Hear me, O tribes of Wrestles With Creator, there is only one Great Spirit and Maker of us all. 30 You must love the Great Spirit with your whole being—with the strength of your arms, the thoughts of your mind, and the courage of your heart.'*f*

31 "The second instruction is like the first," he added. "You must love your fellow human beings in the same way you love yourselves.

There is no other instruction greater than these.

32 "Wisdomkeeper," said the scroll keeper *with a smile,* "you have answered well and spoken the truth, for the Great Spirit is One and there is none other except him. 33 To love him with your whole being—with the strength of your arms, the thoughts of your mind, and the courage of your heart, and to love your fellow human beings in the same way you love yourselves— is far greater than all ceremonies and offerings we make to the Great Spirit."

34 When Creator Sets Free (Jesus) heard the scroll keeper's wise answer, he said, "You are not far from Creator's Good Road."

After that, no one dared to ask him any other questions.

A Question No One Could Answer

35 While Creator Sets Free (Jesus) was teaching at the Sacred Lodge, he asked, "How is it that the scroll keepers say the Chosen One is a descendant of Much Loved One (David), 36 when Much Loved One (David) himself, speaking with the voice of the Holy Spirit, said, 'The Honored Chief said to my Honored Chief, "Sit down beside me at my right hand, the place of greatest honor, until all your enemies come under my loving power.*g*'"*h*

37 "If Much Loved One (David) called the Chosen One 'My Honored

---

e 12:26 Exodus 3:6   f 12:30 Deuteronomy 6:4,5   g 12:36 Lit., under my feet   h 12:36 Psalm 110:1

Chief,' how then can the Chosen One be his descendant?"[i]

The large crowd of people listened with glad hearts, *because his wisdom was greater than the wisdom of the spiritual leaders.*

False Spiritual Leaders

[38] During his teachings he said, "Be on the lookout for the scroll keepers who like to show off by walking around in their fancy regalia, who want to be noticed at the trading posts, [39] who take the best seats at the gathering houses and the places of honor at the feasts. [40] With many words they make a big show of their prayers, and trick widows into giving them their homes and possessions; but they will come to a worse end than others."

A Sacrificial Gift

[41] Creator Sets Free (Jesus) found a place to sit across from the storehouse of the Sacred Lodge. He watched as people came to put their gifts on the offering blanket. The ones with many possessions were putting down more than others. [42] Then he saw a poor widow come to the blanket and place two small poorly-beaded earrings[j] on it, worth almost nothing.

[43] He gathered his followers around him, and told them about the widow's gift.

"I speak from my heart," he said, "this widow has given more than all the others. [44] What they gave

was only a small part of their many possessions, but this poor widow has given all she had left to live on."

Signs of the End of the Age

13 As they were walking away from the Sacred Lodge, one of his followers said to him, "Look, Wisdomkeeper, these buildings are made from such handsomely carved logs and great stones!"

Creator Sets Free (Jesus) stopped walking, and as he looked around at all the buildings of the Sacred Ceremonial Lodge, a look of sadness came over his face.

[2] "Do you see all these great buildings?" he replied. "They will all fall to the ground! Not one log or stone will be left standing against another."

[3] *Later that day* Creator Sets Free (Jesus) was sitting on Olive Mountain across from the Sacred Lodge.

From there he could look across the valley and see Village of Peace (Jerusalem) and the Sacred Lodge.

While he was there, *four of his followers*—Stands On The Rock (Peter), He Takes Over (James), He Shows Goodwill (John), and Stands With Courage (Andrew)—came to him in private.

[4] "Tell us when these things will happen," they said *with worried looks on their faces,* "What sign should we be looking for?"

Stay On the Lookout!

[5] "Stay alert or you may be led down a false path!" he told them. [6] "Many will come representing

me. 'I am the Chosen One,' they will claim, and many will listen to their lies.

The Sign of Warfare

7 "When you hear of wars and stories of war breaking out, do not fear, for all of this must happen before the end will come. 8 There will be tribal wars, and nations will make war against other nations. Food will be scarce, and the earth will shake in many places—but this is only the beginning of the time of sorrow, like a woman feeling the pains of birth.

The Sign of Tribal Betrayal

9 "You must stay ready and alert! Your own people will turn you over to the local tribal councils and beat you in their gathering houses. Because you are representing me, you will be brought before the governors and rulers *of the People of Iron (Romans)*. You will then tell them about Creator's Good Road,[k] 10 for before the end comes, the Good Story must first be told to all nations. 11 So when they put you on trial, do not worry ahead of time about what you will say. Speak what is given you at the time, for the Holy Spirit himself will give you the words to speak.

The Sign of Family Betrayal

12 "Brother will betray brother to death, and a father his child. Children will rise up against their parents and have them killed.

13 And because you represent me, all will look down on you and hate you; but the ones who stand strong to the end will be rescued and made whole.

The Sign of the Coming Destruction

14 "When you see the 'horrible thing that brings destruction' making its stand where it does not belong—the reader will know what this means[l]—the ones who live in the Land of Promise (Judea) should escape to the mountains. 15 The ones who are on their rooftop should not even go back into the house to take anything. 16 The ones working in the field should not go back to get their outer garments. 17 It will be a time of pain and sorrow for the women who are with child and the ones nursing their babies, 18 so pray that it will not happen in the winter. 19 A worse time of suffering and sorrow has not been seen since the Great Spirit created the world—and never will be seen again. 20 If those days were permitted to reach the end of the trail, then no one would survive; but, because of Creator's Chosen Ones, those days will be cut short.

False Chosen Ones and Prophets

21 "So, if in those days anyone would say to you, 'Look, the Chosen One is over here,' or 'Look, he is over there,' pay no attention. 22 For false Chosen Ones will rise up, and false prophets will appear.

---

k 13:9 Lit., bear witness to them   l 13:14 Matthew 24:15; Luke 21:20

They will provide great signs and omens to mislead, if possible, even Creator's Chosen Ones.

23 "I have told you all of this ahead of time, so stay on the lookout and be ready!

Signs in the World Above

24 "Then, right after that time of trouble and sorrow, 'the sun will no longer shine, the moon will go dark, 25 the stars will fall from the sky, and the powers in the world above will tremble.'m

Sign of the True Human Being

26 "This is when they will see the True Human Being, coming with power, riding the clouds and shining like the sun! 27 He will then send out his messengers to gather his Chosen Ones from the winds of the four directions—from the world above to the earth below.

A Wise Story About the Fig Tree

28 "Listen to this wise story and learn the lesson of the fig tree: When its branches get soft and leaves appear, you know that summer will soon be here. 29 In the same way, when you see all these things happening, you will know that the time is near—almost upon you. 30 I speak from my heart! All of this will happen in this generation. 31 You can be sure of what I am saying—for the earth and sky will fade away, but my words will not!

32 "But no one knows the day or hour when these things will take place—not the spirit-messengers from the world above, not even Creator's own Son—only the Father knows.

Always Be Ready

33 "So keep both eyes open and be ready at all times, for no one knows when this time will come. 34 Be ready, like a chief who goes away on a long journey. He appoints the young men to watch over the village while he is gone, giving each of them responsibilities. Then he sets his warriors to guard the village gate. 35 They must stay awake and be ready, doing what he says, for they do not know when the chief will return. It may be when the sun is setting, or late into the night, or when the rooster crows early in the morning. 36 When the chief comes, he better not find them sleeping!

37 "I am telling all of you the same thing—so be ready and stay alert!"

Plot to Kill Him

14 It was now only two days before the traditional yearly Passover and Bread Without Yeast festival would be celebrated. The head holy men and the scroll keepers were scheming together about ways to have him captured and killed.

2 "We should not do it during the festival," they decided, "for that might create an uprising among the people."

---

m **13:25** Isaiah 12:10

Preparing for His Burial

[3] Creator Sets Free (Jesus) was in the village of House of Figs (Bethany), in the home of He Hears (Simon) who had a skin disease. He was leaning back sitting on the floor at the table when a woman with a pottery jar full of costly sweet-smelling ointment came to Creator Sets Free (Jesus), broke the pottery jar, and poured the ointment over his head.

[4] Some of his followers, who saw this, became angry and said to each other, "Why waste this costly oil?[n] [5] It could have been traded for food and goods to give to the poor."

So they spoke harshly to her.

[6] "Let her be!" Creator Sets Free (Jesus) spoke up, "Why are you troubling her? She has done a good thing for me! [7] You can help the poor anytime, for they will always be among you, but I will not. [8] This is her gift to me, to prepare me for my burial. [9] I speak from my heart, when the Good Story is told all over the world, her story will also be told as a memorial."

The Betrayal Begins

[10] It was then that Speaks Well Of (Judas) *also known as* Village Man (Iscariot), who was one of the twelve, left there and went to the head holy men to betray Creator Sets Free (Jesus) into their hands. [11] When they heard this, it pleased them, so they promised to pay him well. So Speaks Well Of (Judas) began to look for the right time to betray him.

Preparation for the Ceremonial Meal

[12] It was now the first day of Bread Without Yeast. This was when the ceremonial lamb would be killed and eaten.

"Where do you want us to go to prepare the ceremonial meal?" his followers asked their Wisdomkeeper.

[13] "Go into the village," he instructed two of his followers, "and there you will meet a man carrying a water pouch. Follow him [14] into whatever lodging-house he enters, and say to the headman of the lodging-house, 'Our Wisdomkeeper asks: Where is the room where I can eat the ceremonial meal with my followers?' [15] He will then show you a large upper room that will be set up and ready for you. There you can prepare *the ceremonial meal* for us."

[16] They did as he said and found everything just as he told them, so they prepared the room for the ceremonial meal.

The Ceremonial Meal Begins

[17] When the sun was setting, Creator Sets Free (Jesus) and his twelve followers went to the room that had been prepared, [18] and they all sat down around the table.

"I speak from my heart," he said during the meal, "One of you, who eats with me now, will betray me."

[19] Their hearts fell to the ground, and one by one they said to him, "I am not the one, am I?"

---

n 14:4 Worth almost a year's wages

20 "It is one of the twelve, the one who has just dipped his bread into the bowl with me," he said to all. 21 "The True Human Being must walk the path chosen for him, as written in the Sacred Teachings; but it will not go well for the one who betrays him. It would be better if he had never been born."

A New Peace Treaty

22 During the meal Creator Sets Free (Jesus) took some of the bread and gave thanks to the Great Spirit. He then broke it into pieces and gave some to each of his followers.

"This is my body," he told them. "Take it *and eat it*."

23 He then took a cup *of wine,* gave thanks to the Great Spirit, and passed the cup to all, who then drank from it.

24 "This is my life-blood of the Peace Treaty, ° poured out on behalf of many people," he said to them. 25 "I speak from my heart, I will not drink from the fruit of the vine again until the day when I will drink it with you in a fresh and new way, as we walk together in the Land of Creator's Good Road."

All of You Will Turn Away

26 They all sang a traditional song and then left to walk to Olive Mountain.

27 "All of you will turn away from me," he told them as they walked along. "It was written in the Sacred Teachings, 'Attack the shepherd and the sheep will scatter.'ᵖ 28 But when I return from the world of the dead, I will go on ahead of you to Circle of Nations (Galilee)."

29 Then Stands On The Rock (Peter) spoke out, "Even if they all turn away from you, I will not!"

30 "I speak from my heart," he said back to him. "This very night, before the rooster crows twice, you will deny three times that you even know me."

31 "No!" Stands On The Rock (Peter) cried out fiercely, "Even if I must die with you, I will never turn away!"

And all the others said the same thing.

The Garden Where He Prayed

32 Creator Sets Free (Jesus) and his followers came to the place called Where the Olives are Crushed (Gethsemane), *a garden with many olive trees.*

"Sit here," he told his followers, "while I go over there and pray."

33 He then took with him Stands On The Rock (Peter), He Takes Over (James) and He Shows Goodwill (John) *to a place not far from the others.* There he became deeply troubled and full of sorrow.

34 "My heart is full of sorrow to the point of death," he said *to his three followers who were with him.* "Stay here and watch over me."

35 He went a little ways from them, dropped his face to the ground and prayed that, if possible, he

o 14:24 Covenant   p 14:27 Zechariah 13:7

would be spared from this time of suffering.

36 "Abba, Honored Father," he cried out, "nothing is too hard for you. Take this bitter cup of suffering away from me. But I want only your way, not mine."

37 He then returned and found his followers sleeping.

"One Who Hears (Simon)," he said *to Stands On The Rock (Peter) using his family name.* "Are you asleep? Could you not stay awake with me for even one hour? 38 Stay awake and pray so that you will be able to face the fiery trial ahead of you. The human body is weak, but the spirit is strong."

39 Once again he went from them and prayed the same words. 40 He returned and again found his followers sleeping, for their eyes were heavy, and they had no answer for him.

41 After praying again, he returned a third time, *and woke them up from their sleep.*

"Do you still sleep? Have you rested enough?" he said to them. "Wake up! The time is upon us! The True Human Being has been betrayed into the hands of the ones with bad hearts. 42 Rise up! We must go! Look! The one who has turned against me is here!"

Betrayed With a Kiss

43 Right then, while Creator Sets Free (Jesus) was speaking, a crowd of people stormed into the garden. Speaks Well Of (Judas), one of the twelve, was leading the way. Along with the betrayer came the large crowd, sent from the head holy men and elders of the tribal council, carrying clubs and long knives.

44 The betrayer had given them a sign, "Take hold of the one I greet with a kiss and arrest him, for he will be the one."

45 Speaks Well Of (Judas), *also know as* Village Man (Iscariot), when he arrived, walked right up to Creator Sets Free (Jesus). "Wisdomkeeper!" he said, and then kissed him.

46 They moved in and took hold of Creator Sets Free (Jesus) to arrest him. 47 But then one of his followers, who had drawn his long knife from its sheath, struck and cut off the ear of the servant of the chief holy man.

48 Creator Sets Free (Jesus) then turned to the ones who had come to take him and said, "Why do you treat me as if I were a thief by coming with clubs and long knives to take me away? 49 Did I not sit with you every day in the Sacred Lodge? Why did you not take me then? But now the words of the prophets have come true and found their full meaning."

50 Then all his followers left him and ran away. 51 A young man dressed only in an under cloth trailed from behind. The people tried to grab hold of him, 52 but his under garments tore away and the young man ran away naked into the night.

Questioned by the High Holy Man

53 The ones who had arrested Creator Sets Free (Jesus) dragged him away and brought him to the

chief holy man. The scroll keepers and elders of the Grand Council had gathered there *to question him.*

54 Stands On The Rock (Peter) followed from a safe distance and went right into the courtyard of the chief holy man. He then sat down next to the lodge guards and warmed himself by the fire.

55 The head priests and the Grand Council kept trying to find someone who would speak against Creator Sets Free (Jesus) so they could put him to death, 56 but found none who could agree, even though many came forward and spoke lies against him.

57 Then some false witnesses came forward and said, 58 "We heard him say, 'I will tear down this Sacred Lodge made with hands and in three days I will build another not made with hands.'"

59 But even about this they could not keep their stories straight.

60 The chief holy man stood before all in the center of the room.

"Have you nothing to say to these accusations?" he said to Creator Sets Free (Jesus).

61 But he just stood there silently and gave no answer.

"Are you the Chosen One," the chief holy man asked him, "the Son of the One Who Is Blessed?"

The room became silent, and when he spoke, every eye and ear was fixed on Creator Sets Free (Jesus).

62 "I am," he answered, "and you will see the True Human Being sitting at the right hand of the Power when he comes riding the clouds of the world above!"

63 The chief holy man tore his regalia *and turned to the council.*

"Why do we even need witnesses?" he said to them. 64 "You have heard him speak against the Great Spirit with your own ears! What does the council have to say?"

The decision was agreed on by all—death.

65 Some began to spit on him. They covered his face and struck him saying, "Prophesy!" Then the Lodge guards took him and struck him with the backs of their hands.

Stands On The Rock Denies Him

66 Below the house, outside in the courtyard, one of the servant women of the chief holy man 67 saw Stands On The Rock (Peter) warming himself by the fire.

She looked closely at him and said, "You were also with Creator Sets Free (Jesus) from Seed Planter Village (Nazareth)!"

68 "I do not know him or what you are saying!" he said to her, and as he moved away toward the outside of the courtyard, a rooster crowed.

69 The servant woman, seeing him walk away, said to some of the men there, "He is one of them!"

70 But again he denied it.

After a while, some others who were standing by said to him, "You must be one of his followers. You talk like someone from Circle of Nations (Galilee)."

71 Stands On The Rock (Peter) cursed, made a sacred oath and said, "I do not know this man you are talking about."

72 Right then a rooster crowed for the second time. Stands On The Rock (Peter) remembered what Creator Sets Free (Jesus) had told him, "Before the rooster crows twice, you will deny three times that you know me."

Then Stands On The Rock (Peter) broke down and wept.

Taken to the People of Iron

15 As the sun began to rise, the head holy men counseled together with the tribal elders, the scroll keepers and the Grand Council. Then with ropes they bound Creator Sets Free (Jesus) once again and took him to Spear Of The Great Waters (Pilate).

Spear Of The Great Waters (Pilate) was the local governor representing the People of Iron (Romans). He had the power to decide who would live and who would die.

2 "Are you the chief of the tribes of Wrestles With Creator (Israel)?" he asked Creator Sets Free (Jesus).

3 "You have said it," he answered as the head holy men kept accusing him.

4 "Why are you silent?" Spear Of the Great Waters (Pilate) said to him. "Do you not hear all their accusations?"

5 But, to the amazement of the governor, Creator Sets Free (Jesus) answered not one word.

Who Should Be Released?

6 It was a tradition during the Passover festival to release to the crowd one criminal, whomever they wanted. 7 At that time they were holding a man in prison, a killer who had been part of an uprising *against the People of Iron (Romans)*, whose name was Son Of His Father (Barabbas). 8 So the crowd began to ask Spear of the Great Waters (Pilate) to release a prisoner.

9 The governor *raised his voice and* asked the crowd, "Should I release to you the chief of your Tribal Nation?"

10 He said this because he knew the head holy men and elders had handed over Creator Sets Free (Jesus) because they were jealous of his reputation with the people. 11 But the head holy men and the elders stirred the crowd into asking for Son Of His Father (Barabbas) to be released instead.

12 "What then would you have me do with the one you call, chief of your Tribal Nation?" he asked them again.

13 "Nail him to the cross!" they shouted *with one voice.*

14 "Why? What wrong has he done to deserve this?" he said back to them.

But they only shouted louder and stronger, "Nail him to the cross!"

Condemned to Die

15 So Spear Of The Great Waters (Pilate), to satisfy the crowd, released *the man of violence*, Son Of His Father (Barabbas), to them. He then turned over the *man of*

peace, Creator Sets Free (Jesus), to the soldiers to be whipped with cowhide strips and then nailed to a cross.

> *The People of Iron (Romans) used a whip with many strips of leather, each braided together with bone and metal. The victim would be tied to a large rock, exposing his bare back, and then whipped. The pieces of bone and metal would rip and tear the skin from the body, leaving the victim almost lifeless.*

¹⁶ The soldiers took Creator Sets Free (Jesus) away into the great hall of the governor's headquarters, and all the soldiers gathered around him. ¹⁷ They wrapped a purple Chief Blanket around him and twisted together a headdress from a thorn bush and pressed it onto his head.

¹⁸ "Honor! Honor! To the chief of the tribes of Wrestles With Creator (Israel) they said mocking him ¹⁹ as they bowed to the ground in front of him. Then they spit on him and beat his head over and over again with a wooden staff."

His Trail of Tears

²⁰ When they were finished putting on their big show, they stripped him of the purple Chief Blanket and dressed him in his own clothes.

> *The soldiers forced Creator Sets Free (Jesus) to carry a heavy wooden crossbeam on his back. He stumbled under the weight, because he was weak from the beating he had endured, too weak to bear the burden.*

But they continued to march him down the road to the place where they would nail him to a cross.

²¹ On the way they came across a man who was just passing by, coming in from the countryside. The man's name was He Hears (Simon), the father of Man Fighter (Alexander) and Red Man (Rufus). The soldiers forced him to carry the *heavy* crossbeam for Creator Sets Free (Jesus).

Nailed to the Cross

The cross was an instrument of torture and terror, used by the People of Iron (Romans) to strike fear into the hearts of any who dared to rise up against their empire. The victim's hands and feet would be pierced with large iron nails, fastening them to the cross. The victims would hang there, sometimes for days, until they were dead. This was one of the most cruel and painful ways to die ever devised by human beings.

²² They brought Creator Sets Free (Jesus) to the Place of the Skull (Golgotha). ²³ There they gave him wine mixed with bitter herbs, but he would not drink it. ²⁴ Then they *stripped him of his clothes and* nailed him to a wooden cross and gambled for his clothes by drawing straws to see who would win.

²⁵ It was the third hour of the day when they nailed him to the cross. ²⁶ Carved above his head *onto a piece of wood* was the accusation against him:

CHIEF OF THE PEOPLE
OF THE LAND OF PROMISE

[27] They also nailed two thieves to their own crosses, one to his right, the other to his left. [28] And so this gave full meaning to the Sacred Teachings that said, "He will be counted among the outlaws."[q]

Mocked by His Own People

[29] The people passing by wagged their heads and heaped insults upon him.

"Aha!" *they laughed out loud.* "So you can destroy the Sacred Lodge and build it again in three days! Can you? [30] Why don't you come down from that cross now—and save yourself?"

[31] The head holy men along with the scroll keepers also mocked him.

"He set others free," they said, "but he cannot even set himself free! [32] Let the Chosen One, the Chief of the tribes of Wrestles With Creator (Israel), come down from the cross now—then we will believe."

The men on crosses to his left and right also heaped insults upon him.

[33] At the sixth hour of the day, *when the sun was high,* darkness covered the whole land like a blanket for three hours.

He Cries Out in Sorrow

[34] At the ninth hour Creator Sets Free (Jesus), speaking in his own language, cried out with a loud voice, "Eli, Eli lema sabachthani?"—which means, "O Great Spirit, my Creator, why have you left me alone?"

[35] Some of the people standing there heard him and said, "He is calling on *the prophet,* Great Spirit Is Creator (Elijah), to help him."

[36] Someone then ran and soaked a cloth with the bitter wine, put it on a staff, held it to his mouth and said, "Wait, let's see if Great Spirit Is Creator (Elijah) will come and take him down."

He Breaths His Last

[37] Then Creator Sets Free (Jesus), with his dying breath, lifted his voice and with a loud cry gave up his spirit.

[38] *At that very moment* in the Sacred Lodge the great heavy blanket that hung over the entry to the most holy place was torn from top to bottom.

For the first time the inner chamber, where only the chief holy man could go, was open to all.

[39] When the head soldier of the People of Iron (Romans), who was standing in front of Creator Sets Free (Jesus), saw how he died, he said, "This man must truly be the Son of the Great Spirit!"

The Women Who Walked With Him

[40] Watching from a distance were some of the women *who had walked the road with him.* Among them was Strong Tears (Mary) of the village of Creator's High Lodge (Magdala), Brooding Tears (Mary) the mother of He Takes Over (James) the Small

---

q 15:28 Some less ancient manuscripts omit verse 28. Isaiah 58:12

One and Creator Gets More (Joses), and Peaceful Woman (Salome). ⁴¹ These were some of the women who had served Creator Sets Free (Jesus) during the times when he was at Circle of Nations (Galilee). There were also many others who had made the journey with him to Village of Peace (Jerusalem).

Preparing for His Burial

⁴² The sun would soon set, ending the Day of Preparation, and marking the beginning of the Day of Resting. ⁴³ He Gives More (Joseph) from the tribal village of High Mountain (Arimathea), who was also looking for Creator's Good Road, was a respected member of the Grand Council. He found the courage to ask Spear Of The Great Waters (Pilate) for the body of Creator Sets Free (Jesus).

⁴⁴ Spear Of The Great Waters (Pilate) was surprised to hear that Creator Sets Free (Jesus) had already died, so he summoned the head soldier and asked how long he had been dead. ⁴⁵ Once he was assured that Creator Sets Free (Jesus) was truly dead, Spear of the Great Waters (Pilate) released his body to He Gives More (Joseph).

⁴⁶ He took the dead body down *from the cross and* wrapped it in a soft blanket *in the traditional way*. He laid the body of Creator Sets Free (Jesus) in a burial cave freshly cut from the rock hillside and then rolled a large stone in front of the cave.

⁴⁷ Strong Tears (Mary) of the village of Creator's High Lodge (Magdala) and Brooding Tears (Mary) the mother of Creator Gets More (Joses) were nearby watching closely where the body of Creator Sets Free (Jesus) had been laid.

The Burial Cave

16 After the Day of Resting was over, Strong Tears (Mary) of the village of Creator's High Lodge (Magdala) and Brooding Tears (Mary) the mother of He Takes Over (James), along with Peaceful Woman (Salome) brought herbal spices to rub into the body of Creator Sets Free (Jesus). ² So, on the first day of the week they came to the burial cave very early in the morning just as the sun was rising.

³ They were asking each other, "Who will roll the stone away from the opening to the burial cave?"

Spirit Messengers

⁴ But when they arrived, they saw that the stone, which was very large, had already been rolled away. ⁵ When they went inside the burial cave, they saw a young man, dressed in a pure white garment, sitting to the right side of the cave. This filled the women with fear *that covered them like a blanket.*

⁶ "Do not fear!" the young man said to them, "The one you are looking for is not here! Creator Sets Free (Jesus) from Seed Planter Village (Nazareth), who was killed on the cross, has returned to life. See for yourselves. Here is where they laid him. ⁷ Now go and tell his followers, and Stands On The Rock (Peter), that he is going ahead of them to Circle of Nations (Galilee). It is there that they will see him again—just as he told them."

[8] Terror and amazement came upon the women, and they ran as fast as they could from the burial cave.[r]

He Shows Himself

[9] When Creator Sets Free (Jesus) returned to life on the first day of the week, he showed himself first to *a woman*, Strong Tears (Mary) of the village of Creator's High Lodge (Magdala), the one he had set free from seven evil spirits. [10] She went to his followers, who were still grieving and weeping, and told them what she had seen and heard. [11] But when they heard that she had seen Creator Sets Free (Jesus) alive, they would not believe it.

[12] On the same day Creator Sets Free (Jesus) also appeared to two of his followers as they were walking in the countryside, but in a different form, *so they did not recognize him.* [13] But when they returned and told the others, no one believed them.

[14] Later, at another time, he showed himself to the eleven message bearers while they were sitting around a table *eating a meal.* He scolded them for their hard hearts and failure to believe the others who had seen him alive.

His Last Instructions

[15] "Go into all the world," he instructed them, "and tell the Good Story *about me* to all of creation. [16] The ones who trust in me will participate in the purification ceremony, setting them free from their broken ways *and initiating them into my Sacred Family.* But the ones who will not walk this road with me[s] will come to a bad end.

[17] "Powerful signs will follow the ones who follow me. Here are some of the things they will do in my name, representing who I am: They will force out evil spirits, [18] pick up and throw out snakes, and even if they drink deadly poison it will not harm them. They will speak in new languages and heal the sick by laying hands on them."

He Goes Back to the Father Above

[19] When he was finished speaking to them, Creator Sets Free (Jesus), our great Chief *and Wisdomkeeper,* was taken up into the world above to sit down at the right hand of the Great Spirit—*the place of greatest honor, dignity and power.* [20] His followers then went out from there, far and wide, telling everyone *the Story of Creator's Good Road.* The Holy Spirit[t] continued to walk with them, showing his approval of their message by powerful signs.

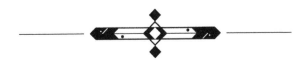

---

r **16:8** Most ancient manuscripts end at this verse. Some others include verses 9-20, as we have in this translation.   s **16:16** Lit., believe   t **16:20** Greek: Kyrios, often translated Lord or Master

*Come, let us sit down in the council house
together. Then face to face you can hear
what my heart is saying.
Your bad hearts and broken ways
have stained your spiritual garments,
A stain so deep, you cannot wash them clean.
But this is what I will do for you:
I will take your blood-red garments
and wash them until they are as white as
snow upon the branches of the cedars.
I will wash away the deepest stain
until you are as clean and white
as the tail feathers of an eagle.*

*From the Great Spirit
To the tribes of Wrestles With Creator*

Isaiah One Eighteen

Shining Light
Tells the Good Story

Gospel of Luke

FIRST NATIONS VERSION

FIRST NATIONS VERSION

Shining light
Tells the Good Story
(Gospel of Luke)

Eye Witnesses

1 ¹⁻³ O most honored Friend Of Creator (Theophilus), many have told this story, given to them from those who saw these things with their own eyes, the ones who first walked out this message to hand it down to us.

Having searched out this story from the first, it seemed like a good thing for me to retell it from beginning to end. ⁴ In this way you will know for yourself the truth about the things you were taught.

Creator Remembers His Promise

⁵ It was in the time of *the bad-hearted* Chief Looks Brave (Herod), who ruled the territory of the Land of Promise (Judea) that Creator chose to send a powerful spirit-messenger to Sacred Village of Peace (Jerusalem), to a holy man whose name was Creator Will Remember (Zechariah).

He and his wife, Creator Is My Promise (Elizabeth), were both descended from the tribe the ceremonial holy people are chosen from. ⁶ They were in good standing in the eyes of the Great Spirit, and with good and pure hearts they walked a straight path, staying true to the tribal ways and traditions given them by the Great Spirit.

They lived in the hill country in the Land of Promise (Judea) of the tribes of Wrestles With Creator (Israel).

⁷ But Creator Is My Promise (Elizabeth) was unable to have children, and both were growing old.

⁸ Creator Will Remember (Zechariah) belonged to the clan of He Is My Father (Abijah) that shared the responsibility of prayers and ceremonies in the Great Spirit's Ceremonial Lodge that was in Village of Peace (Jerusalem).

⁹ He was chosen in the traditional way to be the one to enter the Sacred Lodge and perform the sweet smelling smoke ceremony for the evening prayer.

*Most holy men could only hope
for this honor once in a lifetime.*

¹⁰ A large number of people gathered outside to pray while he went inside.

¹¹ As the smoke went up with his prayers, suddenly a spirit-messenger from the Great Spirit appeared to him, standing to the right of the altar of sweet smelling smoke. ¹² Creator Will Remember (Zechariah) was troubled when he saw the spirit-messenger. He trembled with fear that covered him like a blanket.

¹³ "Do not fear!" the messenger said to him. "Your prayers have been heard. The Maker of Life will give you and your wife a son. You will give him the name He Shows Goodwill (John). ¹⁴ He will bring great joy to you and many people will be glad that he has been born."

*The aroma of the sweet smelling
smoke filled the Sacred Lodge as
the spirit-messenger continued.*

¹⁵ "He will be great and honorable in Creator's sight and will not drink wine or any strong drink, but will drink deeply of the Holy Spirit even in his mother's womb. ¹⁶ Because of him many of the children of the tribes of Wrestles With Creator (Israel) will *find the Good Road and* return to the Great Spirit *and His ways.*"

*Creator Will Remember
(Zechariah) stood silently. His
whole being continued to tremble
as the messenger finished.*

¹⁷ "He will prepare the way for the Chosen One, walking in the same spiritual powers of the prophet Great Spirit Is Creator (Elijah). He will turn the hearts of many fathers back toward their children and many rebellious children will again honor the wisdom of their elders, so that people will be ready to participate in Creator's plan."[a]

*When the spirit-messenger
finished speaking, his words
echoed through the Lodge.
Still trembling, Creator Will
Remember (Zechariah) finally
found his voice.*

¹⁸ Then he questioned the messenger, "We are too old to have children. How can I believe you?"

¹⁹ The spirit-messenger answered, "My name is Creator's Mighty One (Gabriel), *his chief messenger.* I stand close to the Great Spirit! These good words I have spoken to you will come to pass, ²⁰ but since you did not believe my words, you will not be able to speak until they are fulfilled."

²¹ The people who were praying outside began to wonder why it was taking so long for Creator Will Remember (Zechariah) to come out of the Lodge. ²² When he finally came out, unable to speak and making signs with his hands, they understood that he had seen a vision.

²³ When his traditional ceremonies were finished, he returned to his home in the hill country. ²⁴ Soon afterward, Creator Is My Promise

---

a 1:17 Malachi 4:5-6

(Elizabeth) was with child. She stayed at home and for five moons did not show herself to anyone.

25 She said in her heart, "The Giver of Breath has looked upon me with kindness and has taken away my shame. Now I will have respect in the eyes of my people."

Bitter Tears

26 When six moons had passed, the Great Spirit sent the same spirit-messenger, Creator's Mighty One (Gabriel), to another small, out-of-the-way place in the hill country called Seed Planter Village (Nazareth). 27 There he appeared to a young virgin woman named Bitter Tears (Mary), who was promised in marriage to a man named He Gives Sons (Joseph), a descendant of the great chief Much Loved One (David).

28 Creator's Mighty One (Gabriel) said to her, "Greetings, highly favored one! You are close to the Great Spirit and greatly honored among women."

29 Bitter Tears (Mary) was deeply troubled by this greeting and wondered what the spirit-messenger would say.

30 "Do not fear," he comforted her, "for you have found goodwill in the eyes of the Great Mystery. 31 You will be with child and give birth to a son. You will name him Creator Sets Free (Jesus)."

It seemed like time stood still, and all creation stopped to listen as the messenger continued to speak.

32 "He will be greatly honored, the Son of the One Above Us All.

He will be a great chief like his ancestor Much Loved One (David) and will sit in his place of honor. 33 He will always be chief over the tribes of Wrestles With Creator (Israel). His chiefly guidance will never end."

Bitter Tears' (Mary's) voice trembled with emotion and her eyes grew wide as she looked into the face of the spirit-messenger.

34 She asked, "How will this be, since I have never been with a man?"

35 Creator's Mighty One (Gabriel) answered, "The Holy Spirit will spread his wings over you and his great power from above will overshadow you. This Holy Child born to you will be the Son of the One Above Us All."

Then, to encourage her, 36 he said, "Your cousin, Creator Is My Promise (Elizabeth), who was called barren one, is six moons with child. 37 See! There is nothing too hard for the Great Spirit."

She looked bravely into the face of the messenger.

38 "I am Creator's servant," she said with boldness. "Let it be for me just as you have said."

Then Creator's chief spirit-messenger left her.

Cousins

39 Bitter Tears (Mary) quickly put together a traveling bundle and went to visit her cousin, Creator Is My Promise (Elizabeth), who lived in a nearby village in the hill country of the Land of Promise (Judea)

40 When she entered the home of her relatives, she greeted her cousin.

41 When Creator Is My Promise (Elizabeth) heard Bitter Tears' (Mary's) greeting, she felt her child jump inside her. She was filled with the Holy Spirit, 42 and with a loud cry she lifted her voice and spoke these blessing words to Bitter Tears (Mary).

"The Most Holy One has honored you more than any other woman," she laughed. "The child you carry inside you will bring great blessings to all people. 43 Why is Creator being so kind to me, sending the mother of the Great Chief to visit my home? 44 As soon as I heard your greeting, my baby jumped for joy inside me! 45 You have been chosen by the Maker of Life for a great honor, because you believed his words to you."

When Bitter Tears (Mary) heard this, she was filled with gladness and her words flowed out like a song.

46-47 "From deep in my heart I dance with joy to honor the Great Spirit. 48 Even though I am small and weak, he noticed me. Now I will be looked up to by all. 49 The Mighty One has lifted me up! His name is sacred. He is the Great and Holy One."

Her face seemed to shine as she continued.

50 "He shows kindness and pity to both children and elders who respect him. 51 His strong arm has brought low the ones who think they are better than others. 52 He counts coup[b] with arrogant warrior chiefs, but puts a headdress of honor on the ones with humble hearts."

She smiled, looked up to the sky and shouted for joy!

53 "He prepares a great feast for the ones who are hungry, but sends the fat ones home with empty bellies. 54-55 He has been kind to the tribes of Wrestles With Creator (Israel) who walk in his ways, for he has remembered the ancient promises he made to our ancestors—to Father Of Many Nations (Abraham) and his descendants."

When she finished, they both laughed with joy. With hearts full of gladness they told each other their stories.

56 For three moons Bitter Tears (Mary) stayed in the home of her cousin and then returned home to her own village.

A Promise Fulfilled

57 When her time came, Creator Is My Promise (Elizabeth) gave birth to a son. 58 When her relatives and close friends heard the good news that the Great Spirit had been so kind to her, they were glad and rejoiced! 59 Then eight days later at his naming ceremony,[c] all the relatives wanted to name him after his father, Creator Will Remember (Zechariah).

---

b 1:52 'Counting Coup' was a Native American practice among the plains tribes of touching an enemy with a 'coup stick' as an act of courage during battle, to show he could have killed him, but chose to spare him instead. Each time it was used in battle, a mark would be placed on it. It 'counted' the number of victories won. c 1:59 According to Jewish Tribal Law all male children were circumcised (cutting of the flesh) on the eighth day. The child's name was also given at that time.

60 "No," she said to everyone's surprise. "His name will be He Shows Goodwill (John)!"

61 But they said to her, "No one in your family has that name." 62 They made signs with their hands to Creator Will Remember (Zechariah) to see what he wanted to name him.

63 He asked for a writing tablet and to their surprise wrote, "His name is He Shows Goodwill (John)." 64 Suddenly he could speak again, and when he opened his mouth, he began to give praise to the Great Spirit.

65 All the people who heard about this trembled with wonder. Throughout the hills and valleys of the Land of Promise (Judea) they began to tell others what they had seen and heard. 66 All who listened began to wonder and say to themselves, "This child must have been born for some great thing." For it was clear that the hand of the Great Spirit was upon him in a powerful and good way.

67 Then, with a glad heart, Creator Will Remember (Zechariah) spoke these words the Holy Spirit was giving him to say.

68 "All blessings to the Great Spirit of the tribes of Wrestles With Creator (Israel)! For he has come to rescue his people from a great captivity. 69-70 Just as the prophets foretold long ago in the land of our ancestor Much Loved One (David), he has lifted up his coup stick[d] to show his great power to help us, 71 to rescue us from the arrows of our enemies and all who look down upon us with hate."

He lifted trembling hands to the sky and cried out.

72-73 "He has given to us the same pity he has shown our ancestors, and remembered the promise he made in the Great Peace Treaty with Father Of Many Nations (Abraham). 74-75 He has come to free us from the fear of our enemies, so we can walk all our days in his sacred and right ways."

Then he turned to his newborn son, and from deep in his spirit he spoke these words of blessing to him.

76 "And you, my son, will be a prophet from the One Above Us All. You will make a clear path for the coming of the Great Chief, 77 to show his people that he will heal our broken ways by cleansing us from our bad hearts and releasing us from our wrongdoings. 78 Because Creator is kind and gentle, he will come to us as the sunrise from above, 79 to shine on the ones who sit in darkness and in the land of death's shadow, to guide our feet on the good path of peace."

80 He Shows Goodwill (John) grew strong in *body and* spirit and stayed in the desert, waiting until the time was right to show himself to the tribes of Wrestles With Creator (Israel).

Humble Birth

2 1-2 When the time drew close for Bitter Tears (Mary) to have her child, the government of the

---

d 1:69-70 The 'coup stick' was a stick with an eagle or hawk claw attached to its tip; used by many tribes of the Plains. A warrior in battle would scratch an enemy with it as an act of courage to show he could have killed him but chose to spare him instead.

People of Iron (Romans) ordered that the people be numbered and put on government rolls. This happened during the time that Powerful Protector (Quirinius) was the governor of Bright Sun (Syria). ³ All the Tribal Members were required to travel to their ancestral homeland to register.

⁴⁻⁵ He Gives Sons (Joseph) and Bitter Tears (Mary) set out on a long journey from Seed Planter Village (Nazareth) in Circle of Nations (Galilee), to House of Bread (Bethlehem) in the Land of Promise (Judea), the village of their ancestor, the great chief Much Loved One (David).

The journey took several long days and cold nights as they traveled over high hills and through the dry desert. When they arrived, tired and weary, they entered the crowded village.

⁶ The time for Bitter Tears (Mary) to have her child was upon her! ⁷ But no place could be found in the lodging house, *so He Gives Sons (Joseph) found a sheep cave where it was warm and dry.* There she gave birth to her son. They wrapped him in a warm soft blanket *and laid him on a baby board.* Then they placed him on a bed of straw in a feeding trough.

⁸ That night, in the fields nearby, shepherds were keeping watch over their sheep. ⁹ Suddenly a great light from above was shining all around them. A spirit-messenger from Creator appeared to them. They shook with fear and trembled ¹⁰ as the messenger said to them, "Do not fear; I bring you the Good Story that will be told to all nations.

¹¹ Today in the village of Much Loved One (David) an Honored Chief has been born who will set his people free. He is the Chosen One!"

¹² The spirit-messenger continued, "This is how you will know him— you will find the child wrapped in a blanket and lying in a feeding trough."

¹³ Suddenly, next to the messenger, a great number of spirit warriors from the world above appeared giving thanks to Creator saying,

¹⁴ "All honor to the One Above Us All, and let peace and good will follow all who walk upon the earth."

¹⁵ When the messengers returned to the world above, the shepherds said to each other, "Let us go and see this great thing the Creator has told to us." ¹⁶ So they hurried to the village of Chief Much Loved One (David) and found Bitter Tears (Mary), He Gives Sons (Joseph) and the child who, just as they were told, was lying in a feeding trough!

¹⁷ The shepherds began to tell everyone what they had seen and heard about this child, ¹⁸ and all who heard their story were amazed.

¹⁹ Bitter Tears (Mary) kept these things hidden in her heart and wondered what all this would mean. ²⁰ The shepherds returned to their fields, giving thanks to the Great Spirit for the wonders they had seen and heard.

Keeping the Traditions

²¹ Eight days after the birth of their son, in keeping with the traditional cutting of the flesh

ceremony, *e* they named him Creator Sets Free (Jesus), the name given them by the spirit-messenger before the child was born.

22-23 Then, about one moon later, the time came for them to present their child to the Great Spirit in the Sacred Village of Peace (Jerusalem). This was for their cleansing ceremony, an ancient tradition from the lawgiver Drawn From The Water (Moses), who said, "Every male child who is first to open the womb will be holy in the Great Spirit's sight. 24 Bring two turtledoves or two young pigeons*f* to be burned with fire as a sweet smelling smoke offering."

25 When they arrived at the Sacred Lodge in Village of Peace (Jerusalem), they were welcomed by Creator Hears (Simeon), a respected elder who did what was right in the Great Spirit's sight, and waited patiently for him to fulfill his promises to the tribes of Wrestles With Creator (Israel). 26 The Holy Spirit rested on him and told him he would not die until he saw Creator's Chosen One with his own eyes.

27 As Creator Hears (Simeon) followed the guidance of the Spirit, he arrived at the Sacred Lodge just in time to see He Gives Sons (Joseph) and Bitter Tears (Mary) bringing their child for the traditional ceremony given in their Tribal Law. 28 Creator Hears (Simeon) took the child into his arms and spoke words of blessing over him.

29-32 "O Great Father," he prayed, "I now see with my own eyes the one you have prepared for all Nations, the one who will heal our broken ways and set us free. He will make a clear path for all people to see and bring honor to the tribes of Wrestles With Creator (Israel). Now, just as you have said, I can cross over in peace."

33 The child's father and mother were amazed at what was being said. 34 So Creator Hears (Simeon) spoke blessing words over them also.

He then turned to Bitter Tears (Mary) and spoke softly in her ear.

"This child has been chosen for the fall and rising of many in the tribes of Wrestles With Creator (Israel). He will be a sign that will be spoken against, 35 exposing the thoughts of many."

His voice softened as she looked sadly into his eyes.

He said to her, "Even your own spirit will be pierced through like a sharp arrow."

36-37 As they pondered his words, a holy woman named Woman Of Goodwill (Anna) welcomed them. She was an elder from the tribe of Walks With A Glad Heart (Asher) and the daughter of Face Of Creator (Phanuel). She had married at a young age and lived with her husband for seven winters, but had now been a widow for eighty-four winters. She served the Great Spirit at his Sacred Lodge night and day with fasting

---

e 2:21 Circumcision   f 2:24 This shows they were poor, for this was the offering a poor family was permitted to bring according to the Law of Drawn From The Water (Moses).

and many prayers. 38 When she saw the child, she gave thanks to Creator and began telling about the child to all who were waiting for Creator to fulfill the promises he made to the Sacred Village of Peace (Jerusalem).

39 After they performed all the ceremonies which Creator's Law required, they returned to Circle of Nations (Galilee), to their home in Seed Planter Village (Nazareth). 40 In this village the Child grew strong in his spirit and was filled with wisdom, for the blessing of the Great Spirit was resting on him.

Coming of Age

41 By traditional Law it was a custom for all the families of the tribes of Wrestles With Creator (Israel) to journey to Village of Peace (Jerusalem) to participate in the ancient Passover festival.

This festival celebrated the time when the lawgiver, Drawn From The Water (Moses), had set them free from captivity to the powerful nation of Black Land (Egypt). He did this by using the great power Creator gave him to perform many signs and wonders.

42 When Creator Sets Free (Jesus) was twelve winters old, his family traveled together to celebrate this traditional feast.

43 When the festival was over, his parents began their journey home. Without telling his parents, Creator Sets Free (Jesus) stayed behind in Village of Peace (Jerusalem). 44 They thought he was with the other relatives and friends traveling with them. After a *long* day's journey,

they began to look for him, but were unable to find him, 45 so they returned to Village of Peace (Jerusalem) to look for him there.

46 After searching for three days, they found him at Creator's Ceremonial Lodge. He was sitting with the elders, listening to them and asking questions. 47 All who heard his answers were amazed at his wisdom and understanding of the spiritual ways.

48 His parents were surprised and at a loss for words, but then his mother scolded him, "Son, why have you treated us this way? Your father and I were worried and our hearts were heavy as we looked everywhere for you!"

49 "Why were you looking everywhere for me?" he asked. "I thought you would know to look for me here, in my Father's Lodge, doing what he sent me to do."

50 But they did not understand the meaning of what he was saying to them. 51 He then returned to Seed Planter Village (Nazareth) with them and continued to be a respectful son following the guidance of his parents. But his mother hid these words in her heart.

52 Creator Sets Free (Jesus), as a young man, grew in wisdom and strength, and had respect in the eyes of the people and the Great Spirit.

He Shows Goodwill Comes Forward

3 *Eighteen long winters had now come and gone. The People of Iron (Romans) had many new rulers and governors,* *and the tribes of Wrestles With Creator (Israel) had a new chief holy man for the Sacred Lodge.*

It was now the fifteenth year of the rule of Son Of The Great River (Tiberius Caesar). Under him was Spear Of The Great Waters (Pontius Pilate), the governor ruling over the Land of Promise (Judea).

The bad-hearted chief Looks Brave (Herod) had been chosen by the People of Iron (Romans) to rule over the territory of Circle of Nations (Galilee). His brother Friend Of Horses (Philip) ruled over the nearby territory of Guarded Mountains (Iturea) and Place of Stones (Trachonitis), and End Of Sorrow (Lysanias) ruled the territory of the Ten Villages from its chief village Many Meadows (Abilene).

2 Walks Humbly (Annas) was still the chief holy man, along with Hollow In The Rock (Caiaphas), *who would soon replace him.*

It was during this time that Creator's message came down from above *like a burden basket*g and rested on He Shows Goodwill (John), the son of Creator Will Remember (Zechariah), while he was *praying* in the desert wilderness.

The time had come for him to begin his work with the tribes of Wrestles With Creator (Israel) and prepare the way for the Chosen One.

3 He Shows Goodwill (John) began to walk the territory around the River Flowing Down (Jordan). His message was for all to return to Creator's right ways of thinking and come to the river to perform the purification ceremony to be released from their bad hearts and broken ways.

4 The prophet Creator Will Help Us (Isaiah) told about him long ago, *"He will be a* voice howling in the desert, 'Clear the pathways! Make a straight path for the coming of the Honored One! 5 The valleys will be filled in. The mountains and hills will be brought down low. The crooked places will be made straight and the rough road smooth. 6 Then all people will clearly see the Good Road that sets them free.'h"

Preparing the Way

7 Large crowds of people were coming out to hear his message and have him perform the purification ceremony. He noticed *some of the spiritual leaders in* the crowd and warned them, "You nest of poisonous snakes! Who warned you to run and hide from the coming storm? 8 Prove to others by the way you live that you have returned to the Good Road. Do you think you can say, 'Father Of Many Nations (Abraham) is our ancestor?' Don't you know the Great Spirit can make these stones into his children? 9 The tomahawk is at the root of the trees. The ones that have no good fruit will be cut down and tossed into the fire."

---

g 3:2 The Apache and a few other Southwestern tribes have burden baskets. They are often used in a coming of age ceremony, symbolizing the transition from the old generation to the new. We use it here for He Shows Goodwill (John), who is called by Creator to carry the burden of transition from the Old Peace Treaty to the New Peace Treaty. h 3:6 Isaiah 40:3-5

¹⁰ When the crowds heard his words, they *were afraid and* asked, "What should we do?"

¹¹ He answered, "If you have two blankets give one to someone who has none, and the one with food should share it."

¹² There were tribal tax collectors who came to participate in the ceremony who asked him, "Wisdomkeeper, what should we do?"

¹³ "Collect no more taxes than the People of Iron (Romans) permit," he answered. *"To take more is to steal from the people and dishonor the Great Spirit."*

¹⁴ When the Lodge soldiers heard this, they said, "What about us? What can we do?"

"Do not use fear or violence to force money from people or accuse them falsely," he answered, "and be satisfied with your pay."

¹⁵ When the people heard these words, they began to have hope. They were pondering in their hearts, "Could He Shows Goodwill (John) be the Chosen One?"

¹⁶ He gave them this answer, "I perform the purification ceremony with water, but there is one coming who is greater and more powerful than I."

He paused for a moment and softened his voice.

Then he said, "I am not even worthy to bend low and untie his moccasins."

Then he lifted his hands and cried out with a loud voice!

"He is the one who will perform the purification ceremony with the fire of the Holy Spirit! ¹⁷ He will separate the grain from the husks. His harvest basket is in his hands. He will store the good grain in his barn, but the husks he will burn away with a fire no one can put out."

¹⁸ With many more words He Shows Goodwill (John) warned and encouraged the people with the Good Story *of Creator's Good Road.*

¹⁹ He Shows Goodwill (John) warned Chief Looks Brave (Herod) about stealing his own brother's wife, and his many other bad-hearted ways; ²⁰ so Looks Brave (Herod) had him put in prison, adding this to his many evil deeds.

Creator Sets Free Comes Forward

The time had now come for Creator Sets Free (Jesus) to show himself to all the people. He was now a full grown man of about thirty winters. He came from Circle of Nations (Galilee) to the Flowing Down (Jordan) River to have He Shows Goodwill (John) perform the purification ceremony.

²¹ While the people were coming to He Shows Goodwill (John) for the ceremony, Creator Sets Free (Jesus) came also. Then the ceremony was performed on him, and while he was praying, the sky opened up ²² and the Holy Spirit came down in the form of a dove *and rested on him.* A voice from the world above spoke like distant thunder, "You are

my Much Loved Son who makes my heart glad!"

His Family Tree

23 Creator Sets Free (Jesus) was about thirty winters old when he began his great work. He was the son, so it was thought, of He Gives Sons (Joseph),

the son of One Above Us (Heli), 24 son of Gift Of Creator (Matthat), son of He Brings Together (Levi), son of My Chief (Melchi), son of He Grows Strong (Jannai), son of He Gives More (Joseph),

25 son of Gift From Above (Mattathias), son of Burden Bearer (Amos), son of He Gives Comfort (Nahum), son of Protected One (Esli), son of Light Bringer (Naggai),

26 son of Small One (Maath), son of Gift From Above (Mattathias), son of He Listens (Semein), son of Creator Gives More (Joseph), son of Gives Honor (Judah),

27 son of Shows Goodwill (Joanan), son of Walks Friendly (Rhesa), son of Born In Village of Confusion (Zerubbabel), son of Ask Creator (Shealtiel), son of Burning Light (Neri),

28 son of My Chief (Melchi), son of Clothed In Beauty (Addi), son of Talks To Spirits (Cosam), son of Love Beyond Measure (Elmadam), son of He Looks Around (Er),

29 son of He Sets Free (Joshua), son of He Helps Him (Eliezer), son of Honored By Creator (Jorim), son of Gift Of Creator (Matthat), son of He Brings Together (Levi),

30 son of Creator Hears (Simeon), son of Give Him Honor (Judah), son of He Gives More (Joseph), son of Creator Shows Goodwill (Jonam), son of He Builds Up (Eliakim),

31 son of He Makes Full (Melea), son of He Is Ready (Menna), son of Gift Giver (Mattatha), son of He Will Give (Nathan), son of Much Loved One (David),

32 son of Original Man (Jesse), son of He Works Hard (Obed), son of Moves With Strength (Boaz), son of He Makes Peace (Salmon), son of Talks With Snakes (Nahshon),

33 son of Noble Relative (Amminadab), son of He Is Lifted Up (Admin), son of Lifted Up High (Arni), son of Circle Of Teepees (Hezron), son of He Breaks Through (Perez), son of Give Him Honor (Judah),

34 son of Heel Grabber (Jacob), son of He Made Us Laugh (Isaac), son of Father Of Many Nations (Abraham), son of He Made Them Wait (Terah), son of Snorting Buffalo (Nahor),

35 son of Growing Stem (Serug), son of Faithful Friend (Reu), son of Where The Water Divides (Peleg), son of Over The River (Eber), son of Shooting Arrow (Shelah),

36 son of Made Straight (Cainan), son of Son Of His Mother (Arphaxad), son of His Name Is Known (Shem), son of One Who Rests (Noah), son of Strong Wild Man (Lamech),

37 son of Long Arrow (Methuselah), son of Walks With Creator (Enoch), son of He Came Down (Jared), son of Full Of Praise (Mahalaleel), son of Made Straight (Cainan),

38 son of Weak Human Being (Enos), son of Drinks Too Much (Seth), son of Red Clay (Adam), son of the Great Spirit.

Vision Quest

4 Creator Sets Free (Jesus) was now filled with *the power of* the Holy Spirit. From the River Flowing Down (Jordan), the Spirit guided him into the desert wilderness, *a dry and lonely place filled with wild animals and many other dangers.* 2 There, for forty days, he would be put to the test by Accuser (Satan), the evil trickster snake.

In the story of creation, the first man and woman lived in a Garden of Beauty and Harmony. The evil trickster snake came to them and twisted the words of the Great Spirit to deceive them. They listened to the snake, lost the life of beauty and harmony, and fell under the curse of death—both physical and spiritual. This snake is an evil spirit, sometimes called Accuser (Satan), who opposes the good things Creator wants for all two-leggeds.

For forty days and nights Creator Sets Free (Jesus) ate nothing. His body became weak and his hunger grew strong.

When the evil snake saw that Creator Sets Free (Jesus) was weak and hungry, he came to him and whispered in his ear.

3 "Are you the Son of the Great Spirit?" *he hissed.* "Prove it by turning these stones into bread."

4 "It is written in the Sacred Teachings," Creator Sets Free (Jesus) said, "'bread is not the only food for two-leggeds.'i"

5 Once more Accuser (Satan) took him up *to a high mountain* and, in a moment of time, showed him all the great nations of the world. 6 "All of their power and beauty can be yours!" the snake said smoothly. "They were given over to me and I can give them to anyone I choose. 7 If you will bow down to me and my ways, they will all be yours!"

8 "Go away from me, you evil trickster!" he answered. "For it also says in the Sacred Teachings, 'The Great Spirit is the only one to bow down to and walk in his ways.'j"

9 The evil snake took him to the Great Spirit's Sacred Lodge in Village of Peace (Jerusalem). He took him to the very top of the Lodge, high above the village. "Prove you are the Son of the Great Spirit and jump down from here!" the snake taunted him. 10 "Do not the Sacred Teachings also say, 'His spirit-messengers will watch over you to keep you from harm. 11 They won't even let your foot hit a stone.'k?"

12 "Yes," Creator Sets Free (Jesus) said back to him, "but they also say, 'Do not put the Great Spirit to a foolish test.'l"

---

i 4:4 Deuteronomy 8:3   j 4:8 Deuteronomy 6:13   k 4:11 Psalm 91:11-12   l 4:12 Deuteronomy 6:16

[13] Creator Sets Free (Jesus) had passed every test. The evil snake could think of nothing more, *so he slithered away to wait for another time.*

His Own Village Rejects Him

[14] The power of the Spirit was now resting on Creator Sets Free (Jesus), so he returned to the territory of Circle of Nations (Galilee). News about him began to spread like wildfire throughout the villages, [15] for he was teaching in their gathering houses, and the people gave him much honor.

In the Law, given by Drawn From The Water (Moses), all the tribes were instructed to keep a Day of Resting called the Sabbath. This was the seventh day of the week, to honor and remember the time when Creator rested on the seventh day after making all things. On that day no work was to be done, and how far one could walk was limited. The tribal people would meet together at their village gathering houses on this day.

[16] On one of these Days of Resting, Creator Sets Free (Jesus) returned to his boyhood home in Seed Planter Village (Nazareth). As was his tradition, he entered the gathering house, and stood up to read from the ancient Sacred Teachings. [17] The headman handed him the scroll with the words from the prophet Creator Will Help Us (Isaiah). He opened the Scroll and began to read.

He spoke with deep respect in his voice as he held the Scroll in a sacred manner. His words were strong and clear and his eyes were bright and full of life as he read.

[18] "The Spirit of Creator has come to rest on me. He has chosen me to tell the Good Story to the ones who are poor. He has sent me to mend broken hearts, to tell prisoners they have been set free, to make the blind see again, and to lift up the ones who have been pushed down— [19] to make it known that Creator's Year of Setting Free[m] has come at last!"[n]

[20] He rolled up the scroll, returned it to the headman and sat down. All eyes were fixed on him, wondering what he would say.

He looked around at them and spoke clearly with a strong voice,

[21] "Today these words you have heard have found their full meaning."

Then he began to teach and share his wisdom with them.

[22] At first they were amazed at the power and beauty of his words.

But soon the meaning of his words sank into their hearts, and the mood of the people began to change.

"Isn't this the son of *Bitter Tears (Mary)* and He Gives Sons (Joseph), the wood carver?"

[23] So he said to them, "I am sure you will tell me this wise saying,

---

m 4:19 Jubilee, see Leviticus 25:8-17.   n 4:19 Isaiah 61:1-2

'Healer, use your medicine on yourself.' And you will say, 'We want to see you do here in your own village the powerful signs you did in Village of Comfort (Capernaum).' ²⁴ But the truth is, a prophet is given much honor except in his own village, among his own clan, and in his own house."

Those who were listening continued to grumble out loud, shaking their heads and rolling their eyes.

²⁵ "I speak from my heart," he said to them. "There were many widows in the land of Wrestles With Creator (Israel) during the days of the prophet Great Spirit Is Creator (Elijah). It was a time of great hunger, and food was hard to find. It had not rained for more than three winters. ²⁶ But Great Spirit Is Creator (Elijah) was not sent to any of these widows; instead he was sent to Refining Fire Woman (Zarephath), a widow in the territory of Hunting Grounds (Sidon), *an Outside nation.* ᵒ ²⁷ And there were many with a skin disease in the days of the prophet Creator Saves Us (Elisha), but none were healed and cleansed except for Looks Handsome (Naaman), an outsider from Bright Sun (Syria), *the head soldier of the enemy's army.*ᵖ

²⁸ The people in the gathering house were insulted and furious at his words. ²⁹ Together they herded him out to the village hillside to throw him off the cliff, ³⁰ but he slipped through the crowd and went on his way.

Village of Comfort

³¹ From there he went to Village of Comfort (Capernaum) in the territory of Circle of Nations (Galilee). On the Day of Resting ³² he was teaching in their gathering house and the people were amazed at his manner of speaking, for he spoke boldly with authority, *not like the other spiritual leaders.*

³³ There was a man that day in this gathering house who had an unclean evil spirit. Suddenly, the man wailed out loud, ³⁴ "AAAIIIEEE! Creator Sets Free (Jesus) from Seed Planter Village (Nazareth). What are you doing here? Have you come to put an end to us? I know who you are! You are the Holy One from the Great Spirit!"

³⁵ Creator Sets Free (Jesus) spoke sharply to him, "Be silent! Leave this man now!" The evil spirit shook the man, threw him to the ground, and came out without hurting him.

³⁶ The people were in awe and began to ask each other, "What is he teaching? What new medicine is this? He even tells the unclean spirits what to do—and they do it!"

³⁷ Because of this, his reputation spread like wildfire throughout the Circle of Nations (Galilee) and to all the surrounding territories.

Home of One Who Hears

³⁸ After he left the gathering house, Creator Sets Free (Jesus) went to the home of One Who Hears (Simon). The wife of One

---

o 4:26 1 Kings 17:8-24   p 4:27 2 Kings 5:1-19

Who Hears (Simon) was there. Her mother was sick in bed with a bad fever, so they asked Creator Sets Free (Jesus) to help her. ³⁹He went and stood over her, told the fever to go, and it left! *With a glad heart she got up and went to prepare a meal for them.*

⁴⁰Later that day, when the sun was going down, many sick people were brought to him. He touched them all and healed them. ⁴¹Many were set free from evil spirits. As the spirits left them, they howled with loud voices saying, "You are the Chosen One, Creator's own Son!" But he spoke sharply to them, and didn't let them speak, for they knew who he was.

⁴²The next day, before the sunrise, he found a quiet, out-of-the-way place to be alone and pray. But the crowds found him again and would not let him go. ⁴³He said to them, "I was sent to tell you the Good Story about the Good Road. You must let me go to other villages, so they can also hear."

⁴⁴So he continued to teach and tell his stories in the gathering houses of the Land of Promise (Judea).

Fishing for Two-leggeds

5 As Creator Sets Free (Jesus) was teaching at Lake of Chief Garden (Gennesaret), a great number of people pressed in close to hear him speak the words of the Great Spirit. ²He was standing on the shore and saw two fishing canoes, but the fishermen had left their canoes and were washing their nets. ³He climbed into the canoe belonging to One Who Hears (Simon) and asked him to push out a little from the shore. He then sat in the canoe and taught the large gathering of people.

⁴When he had finished speaking, he said to One Who Hears (Simon), "Push out further into the deep water and throw in your nets for a catch."

⁵"Wisdomkeeper," he answered, "we have been fishing all night and caught nothing, but because it is you who ask, I will do it."

⁶They threw the net out into the water.

Before they knew what was happening, the net became heavy. They struggled with the weight of it and began to pull it in.

But the net was so full of fish it began to tear. ⁷They called out to the other canoe for help. The men came and began to pull in the nets. *Fish of every size poured into the two canoes until they were so full they began to sink.*

⁸⁻¹⁰When One Who Hears (Simon), along with his fishing partners— He Takes Over (James) and He Shows Goodwill (John), the sons of Gift Of Creator (Zebedee)— saw what happened, they were filled with wonder and awe at the great catch of fish.

One Who Hears (Simon) fell to his knees in front of Creator Sets Free (Jesus). "Wisdomkeeper!" he groaned. "Go away from me! For I am a bad-hearted and unholy man."

"Do not fear!" Creator Sets Free (Jesus) told him. "From now on your nets will catch two-leggeds."

[11] When they returned to the shore, they left everything and began to walk the road with him.

Skin Disease Cleansed

[12] While he was in one of these villages, a man with a skin disease all over his body came to Creator Sets Free (Jesus). He humbled himself, bowed down and pleaded with him. "Honored One!" he cried. "If you want to, you can heal and cleanse me."

[13] Creator Sets Free (Jesus), stirred with compassion, reached out and touched the man. "I want to!" he said. "Be cleansed!" And right away the disease left him and he was healed.

[14] Creator Sets Free (Jesus) sent him away at once. "Tell no one!" he said. "Go and show yourself to a holy man and have him perform the cleansing ceremony given to us by the lawgiver Drawn From The Water (Moses), to show the holy man what the Great Spirit has done for you."[q]

> Tribal Law instructed that a person healed of a skin disease must be pronounced ceremonially clean by a holy man.

[15] The reputation of Creator Sets Free (Jesus) began to grow among the people as word about him spread. The crowds came from everywhere to hear him speak and be healed of their sicknesses. [16] But he often left the crowds and went out into the desert wilderness to pray.

Spiritual Leaders Offended

[17] On another day he was teaching at a house in Village of Comfort (Capernaum). The Separated Ones (Pharisees) and the scroll keepers had come from the surrounding villages of Circle of Nations (Galilee) and from as far as the Land of Promise (Judea) and Village of Peace (Jerusalem) to hear him speak.

The healing power of the Great Spirit was there, resting on Creator Sets Free (Jesus).

[18] Several men came carrying a paralyzed man on a sleeping mat to bring him to Creator Sets Free (Jesus), [19] but they couldn't get past the crowd. In their desperation, they climbed up to the rooftop and broke through the roof tiles. They lowered the paralyzed man down, sleeping mat and all, right in front of Creator Sets Free (Jesus). [20] When he saw their faith in him, he said to the paralyzed man, "Young man, you are released from your broken ways and wrongdoings."

[21] The scroll keepers and the Separated Ones (Pharisees) began to grumble among themselves, "Who is this man to speak lies against the Great Spirit with such disrespect? Who but the Maker of Life can release a man from his wrongdoings?"

[22] In his spirit, Creator Sets Free (Jesus) knew what they were thinking and said to them, "Why are your hearts full of dark thoughts and questions? [23] Is it easier to tell a paralyzed man, 'Get up and walk,' or to say to him, 'You are released from your wrongdoings'?"

> The room became quiet as he waited for an answer. Then he said to them,

---

q 5:14 Leviticus 14:2-32

24 "This is how you will know the True Human Being has the right to forgive bad hearts and wrongdoings on this earth." He turned to the paralyzed man and said, "Get up, and when you have rolled up your sleeping bundle, walk to your home." 25 Right away the man stood up in front of them and did what he said, giving thanks to the Great Spirit for his healing.

26 Great respect and awe filled the hearts of all who were in the house. They gave honor to Creator, saying, "Today we have seen how mysterious the ways of the Great Spirit can be."

Eating With Outcasts

27 After this he taught again by the lake shore. As he walked by, he saw a tribal tax collector sitting at his tax booth.

Tribal tax collectors were often tribal members who were given the right to collect taxes for the People of Iron (Romans). They could force their own people, under the threat of violence, to pay them. To make a living they would take more than the People of Iron (Romans) required. But many of them became greedy and took even more than they were permitted. They were hated and looked down on by the people.

The name of this tribal tax collector was He Brings Together (Levi, later known as Matthew). Creator Sets Free (Jesus) went to him and said, "Come, walk the road with me." 28 He got up from his booth, left it all behind, and began to walk the road with him.

29 He Brings Together (Levi/Matthew) hosted a great feast for Creator Sets Free (Jesus). *He invited all his friends to come.* Tribal tax collectors, along with other outcasts, were all sitting around the table with Creator Sets Free (Jesus).

The Separated Ones (Pharisees) called certain people outcasts. They used their strict interpretation of their Tribal Law as a way to point them out. These outcasts were not permitted to enter the gathering houses. They were looked down on and despised by the Separated Ones (Pharisees). Outcasts included tribal tax collectors, prostitutes, people who ate and drank too much, the ones with diseases that made them ceremonially unclean, and anyone who was not a member of the tribes of Wrestles With Creator (Israel).

30 When the Separated Ones (Pharisees) and the scroll keepers saw Creator Sets Free (Jesus) eating with outcasts, they complained to his followers saying, "Why does your wisdomkeeper keep company with tribal tax collectors and outcasts?"

31 Creator Sets Free (Jesus) overheard them and said, "People who are well do not need medicine. 32 I have not come for the ones with good hearts. No! I have come to help the outcasts find the path back home again."

Fresh Skins for New Wine

33 Then they asked Creator Sets Free (Jesus) another question, "The followers of He Shows Goodwill

(John), often go without eating to pray, and so do the followers of the Separated Ones (Pharisees). So why do your followers feast and eat so much?"

A gentle smile came across the face of Creator Sets Free (Jesus), and with a sigh he responded.

34 "Do you expect wedding guests to be sad and go without eating when the groom is hosting a feast?" he asked. 35 "The time will come when he is gone; then they will be sad and go without eating."

They still didn't understand, 36 so he told them this wise saying, "No one uses a new piece of cloth to patch an old garment; it would shrink and make the tear worse. 37 No one puts new wine into an old wineskin, for the new wine would burst the skins. 38-39 New and fresh wineskins are what is needed, but the ones who have a taste for the old do not want the new."

He said this to show that the old ways of the spiritual leaders did not reflect the beauty of the new way he was bringing.

Chief of the Day of Resting

6 On another Day of Resting, Creator Sets Free (Jesus) and his followers were walking through a field of grain. The men were hungry, so they plucked some grain, rubbed the husks off in their hands and began to eat. 2 When the Separated Ones (Pharisees) saw what they were doing, they said to him, "Why do your followers do what is not permitted on the Day of Resting?"

3-4 He answered them, "Have you not heard about the time long ago when the great chief, Much Loved One (David), was hungry? How he and his followers went into Creator's Sacred Lodge and ate the ceremonial bread? Only the holy men are permitted to eat this bread."

He paused to let them think about his words.

5 And then he added, "The True Human Being is Chief over the Day of Resting!"

Healing on the Day of Resting

6 On another Day of Resting Creator Sets Free (Jesus) went into a gathering house and began to teach the people. A man was there with a shriveled and useless hand. 7 The scroll keepers and the Separated Ones (Pharisees) kept a close eye on Creator Sets Free (Jesus) to see if he would heal the man, so they could accuse him of not honoring the Day of Resting.

8 Creator Sets Free (Jesus) knew what they were scheming, so he said to the man, "Come, stand here, where everyone can see you." So the man did what he said. 9 Then Creator Sets Free (Jesus) asked them, "On the Day of Resting, is it permitted to help or to harm, to rescue or destroy?"

They just looked at him and said nothing. At first there was fire in his eyes! But his anger turned to sorrow when he saw their hearts of stone.

10 He looked around the room and then turned to the man and

said, "Stretch out your hand." He stretched it out, and it was the same as his good hand!

11 The Separated Ones (Pharisees) stormed out in a fit of rage and began to council together about what could be done with Creator Sets Free (Jesus).

Twelve Message Bearers

The crowds were growing larger. The task of healing and helping this great number of people was too much for Creator Sets Free (Jesus) to do alone. He knew that he needed help from the ones who were walking the road with him.

12 He went by himself to a mountain where he prayed all night to the Great Spirit. 13 In the morning, on the mountain side, he gathered the ones who had been walking the road with him. He chose twelve of them to be his message bearers.r

Here are the names of the ones he chose:

14 First there was One Who Hears (Simon), whom he named Stands On The Rock (Peter), and his brother Stands With Courage (Andrew). Then he chose two brothers that he called Sons of Thunder—He Takes Over (James) and He Shows Goodwill (John).

Next there was Friend Of Horses (Philip) and Son Of Ground Digger (Bartholomew) 15 along with He Brings Together (Levi/ Matthew) and Looks Like His Brother (Thomas).

Then he chose He Takes Over (James), son of First To Change (Alphaeus), along with One Who Listens (Simon) the Man On Fire (Zealot) 16 and Speaks Well Of (Judas) the son of He Takes Over (James). And last of all he chose Speaks Well Of (Judas), who later betrayed him.

17 Creator Sets Free (Jesus), along with his twelve message bearers and a large number of his followers, went down from the mountain to where the ground is flat. A great number of people came to hear him speak and to be healed. They came from all over the Land of Promise (Judea), from Village of Peace (Jerusalem), and from the coast of Rock Land (Tyre) and Hunting Grounds (Sidon).

18 The ones tormented by unclean spirits were being set free. 19 All the people were trying to touch him, for great power was flowing out from him to heal them all!

Ways of Blessing or Sorrow

20 Creator Sets Free (Jesus) looked out over the crowd of his followers and began to teach them about the ways of Creator's Good Road.

"Creator's blessing rests on you who are poor and in need; the Good Road is yours to walk.

21 "Creator's blessing rests on you who hunger now, for you will be filled to the full.

"Creator's blessing rests on the ones who weep now, for your sorrow will turn into laughter.

---

r 6:13 Apostles, meaning 'sent ones'

²² "Creator's blessing rests on you when you are hated and rejected, looked down on and treated as worthless, all because you have chosen to walk the good road with the True Human Being.

²³ "When this happens, let your hearts be glad and jump for joy; the world above will honor you, for this is the same way your ancestors treated the prophets of their day. *You are walking in their moccasins now!"*

Here is what he said to the privileged among the people:

²⁴ "Sorrow and trouble will be the end of you who store up possessions for yourselves, for you have already had a life of ease.

²⁵ "Sorrow and trouble will be the end of you who eat your fill now; you will go hungry later.

"Sorrow and trouble will be the end of you who are laughing about this now, for your own trail of tears is coming.

²⁶ "Sorrow and trouble will be your end, when others say only good things about you, for that is what our ancestors said about the prophets who told lies.

The Way to Treat Your Enemies

²⁷ "Hear me, you who are listening now, I am telling you to show love to your enemies, do good to the ones who look down on you, ²⁸ return blessing for cursing, and send up good prayers for the ones who give you trouble and pain.

²⁹ "If someone slaps you on the side of your face, show the strength of your heart and offer the other side. In the same way, if a thief takes your coat, offer your shirt also.

³⁰ "When someone in need asks, do not hold back—do what you can to help. If someone takes what is yours, let them keep it."

"Here is another way to see what I am saying: ³¹ Help others in the same way you would want them to help you.

³²⁻³⁴ "Where is the honor in only showing love to the ones who do the same for you? Why should you be given respect for doing good to the ones who do you good, or for lending only to the ones who can repay you? Even tribal tax collectors and outcasts do these things.

³⁵ "Instead, show love and respect to your enemies, help them when they are in need without asking them to repay you. This will show that you are children of your Father from above, for he is kind and has pity on the ones with bad hearts, even when they do not thank him for it. ³⁶ So then, show kindness to others in the same way.

Blind Guides

³⁷ "Do not judge others, and you will not be judged. When you release others from their wrongdoings, you will be released from yours. ³⁸ The amount you measure out to others is the amount that comes back, like a basket that has been filled to the top, shaken down and packed together, until it overflows. What you give out will come back to you—full circle."

39 He gave them a wise saying, "How can a blind person guide another who is blind? Will they not both stumble and fall? 40 The one guided cannot rise above his guide, but will be just like him—*blind.*

"Think of it this way, 41 how can you see the speck of wood in someone else's eye when you can't even see the log in your own eye? 42 How can you say, 'Here, let me help you,' when you can't see that you are the one who needs help? Stop pretending to be something you are not!

Good and Bad Trees

43 "Healthy trees give good fruit and rotten trees give bad fruit. 44 Do grapes come from a thorn bush or figs from thistles?

45 *"The human heart is like a medicine pouch.* Good hearted people speak from the good medicine stored in their hearts. Bad-hearted people speak from the bad medicine stored in their hearts. For the mouth will speak what the heart is filled with.

46 "How is it that you call me 'Great Chief' but do not walk in my ways? 47 The ones who listen to me and walk in these ways are like a man who built a lodge. 48 He dug deep to find solid ground to build on. When a flood came, the waters beat against the lodge, but it stood strong. Nothing could shake it, for it was built on solid ground.

49 "The ones who hear my words but do not walk in these ways are like another man, who built his lodge on soft ground. When the flood came against it, the lodge crashed to the ground, and all that was in it was lost."

A Soldier From the People of Iron

7 When Creator Sets Free (Jesus) was finished speaking to the people, he went to Village of Comfort (Capernaum).

2 A head soldier[s] of the People of Iron (Romans) had a servant he cared deeply about, who was sick and near death. 3 When the head soldier heard about Creator Sets Free (Jesus), he asked some elders from the tribes of Wrestles With Creator (Israel) to go to him and ask him to heal the servant.

4-5 The elders found Creator Sets Free (Jesus), and begged him to help the head soldier. "He is a man of honor who loves our nation and has built a gathering house for us. He is worth helping."

6 So Creator Sets Free (Jesus) followed them. They were not far from the house when the head soldier sent some messengers to say to him, "Honored one, I do not want you to bring trouble on yourself by coming into my house. 7 That's why I didn't think it wise to come to you myself. If you will only speak a word, my servant will be healed. 8 I too am a man under orders and have many soldiers under me. I say to this one 'go' and he goes, and to another 'come' and he comes. My servants do what I say."

---

s 7:2 Centurion, an officer of the People of Iron (Romans)

⁹Creator Sets Free (Jesus) was amazed at this answer. He turned to the large crowd that was with him and said, "I have never seen such great faith, not even among the tribes of Wrestles With Creator (Israel)."

¹⁰When the elders returned to the head soldier, they found the servant well.

The Son of a Widow

¹¹Not long after this, Creator Sets Free (Jesus) and the ones who walked the road with him went to Village of Harmony (Nain). A large crowd of people trailed behind him. ¹²As he came near the village gate, a man who had crossed over was being carried, wrapped in a blanket, to a burial site. He was the only son of his mother, a widow. A crowd of people from the village were walking with her. ¹³When Creator Sets Free (Jesus) saw her, he felt pity for her and said, "Don't weep. *The Great Spirit has seen your tears.*"

¹⁴He walked up, opened the blanket, and laid his hands on the young man. The ones carrying it stopped and *waited to see what he would do.* "Young man," he said out loud, "rise up!" ¹⁵To the amazement of all, he sat up and began to talk. Creator Sets Free (Jesus) then gave him back to his mother.

Her weeping turned to joy as she threw her arms around her son and kept kissing his face.

¹⁶Great fear and trembling fell on the crowd. They gave honor to the Great Spirit, and said, "A great prophet has been sent to us! The Giver Of Breath has come to visit his people!" ¹⁷News about this traveled far and wide throughout the Land of Promise (Judea) and into the surrounding villages and territories.

Are You the One?

¹⁸Followers of He Shows Goodwill (John), who performed the purification ceremony, told him what Creator Sets Free (Jesus) had done. ¹⁹He sent two of his followers to ask the Wisdomkeeper a question. ²⁰When they found Creator Sets Free (Jesus), they asked him the question from He Shows Goodwill (John), "Are you the one who is to come, or should we look for someone else?"

²¹The messengers watched as he healed many who were sick and tormented by evil spirits, and gave sight to the ones who were blind.

²²He told them, "Go back to He Shows Goodwill (John), and tell him about the things you have seen with your own eyes and heard with your own ears. The blind can see again, the lame can walk, the ones with skin disease have been healed and ceremonially cleansed! Ears that cannot hear have been opened and the poor have been told the Good Story! Even the dead have come back to life again!"

Creator Sets Free (Jesus) sent them back to him with these last words:

²³"Creator's goodwill rests on the ones who do not stumble and leave the path because of me."

A True Prophet

24 When the messengers left, Creator Sets Free (Jesus) spoke to the people about He Shows Goodwill (John), "What were you looking for in the desert wilderness? A frail reed blowing in the wind? 25 Did you see a man in costly garments? No! The ones who wear costly clothes and buy whatever they want live in grand houses. 26 Were you looking for a true prophet? Yes! He is a true prophet but also much more! 27 He is the one spoken of in the Sacred Teachings, 'Look! I am sending my messenger ahead of you. He will make a clear path.'t

28 "Listen closely, no one born of a woman has ever been greater, but now the smallest one who walks Creator's Good Road is greater than he is."

29 When the people and tribal tax collectors heard this, they agreed that the ways of the Great Spirit are true and right, for they had received the purification ceremony of He Shows Goodwill (John). 30 But the scroll keepers and Separated Ones (Pharisees) turned away from the Great Spirit's plan for them, for they had refused the ceremony of He Shows Goodwill (John).

31 "This generation, what can I compare them to?" Creator Sets Free (Jesus) told the crowd, 32 "They are like children at a trading post, teasing each other, saying, 'You didn't dance when we played the drum! You didn't cry when we played a sad flute song.'

33 "He Shows Goodwill (John) did not feast or drink wine, but you say, 'He has an evil spirit.' 34 The True Human Being comes feasting and drinking and you say, 'He eats too much and is a drunk, a friend of tribal tax collectors and outcasts with broken ways!' 35 But wisdom is proved right through the behavior of her children."

A Meal With A Spiritual Leader

36 A spiritual leader from the Separated Ones (Pharisees), named One Who Hears (Simon), invited Creator Sets Free (Jesus) to a meal. So he went to his house and joined the guests at the table.

37 There was a woman in the village, an outcast with broken ways, who heard that Creator Sets Free (Jesus) was eating with the spiritual leader. So she went to the house and brought with her a small pottery jar of sweet smelling oil. 38 She came up behind Creator Sets Free (Jesus) and began to weep at his feet. Her tears fell on his feet and she wiped them with her hair. Then she kissed his feet and rubbed the oil on them.

39 When the spiritual leader saw this, he thought to himself, "If this man were a true prophet he would know who is touching him. He would see what kind of woman this is—an outcast!"

40 Creator Sets Free (Jesus) knew what he was thinking and said to him, "He Hears (Simon), I have something to say to you."

t 7:27 Malachi 3:1

"Wisdomkeeper," he answered, "say what you will."

⁴¹ "Two men were in debt to the same person. One owed him five-hundred horses, the other two buffalo hides. ⁴² Neither of them had enough to pay him back, so he released them from their debt. Which one do you think will love him the most?"

⁴³ "I suppose it would be the one who owed him the most."

"You have answered well," Creator Sets Free (Jesus) told him.

⁴⁴ Then he turned to the woman and said to He Hears (Simon), "Do you see this woman? When I entered your house, you did not offer me water to wash the dust from my feet; but she washed them with her tears and wiped them with her hair. ⁴⁵ You did not welcome me with a kiss, but this woman is still kissing my feet. ⁴⁶ You did not put oil on my head, but she has rubbed sweet smelling oil on my feet. ⁴⁷ I tell you, she is forgiven and set free from her broken ways because of her great love. But small is the love of one who has been forgiven only for small things."

Creator Sets Free (Jesus) looked at her with kindness in his eyes.

⁴⁸ "You are forgiven!" he said to her.

⁴⁹ The other guests at the table began to grumble to each other and say, "Who is this man who thinks he can forgive wrongdoings?"

⁵⁰ Creator Sets Free (Jesus) *ignored them and* said to the woman, "Your faith has healed your broken ways. Go in peace."

Women of Honor

8 After this, Creator Sets Free (Jesus) began to walk from one village to another telling stories about Creator's Good Road. The twelve he had chosen were with him ² and also some women who had been healed and set free from evil spirits. One was Strong Tears (Mary) from the village of Creator's High Lodge (Magdala), who had been set free from seven evil spirits. ³ Another was Woman Of His Goodwill (Joanna), the wife of Vision Seer (Chuza), the headman of the household of Chief Looks Brave (Herod). And then there was Water Flower (Susanna). These women and many others helped out with their own goods.

Four Kinds of Soil

⁴ The people began to gather in crowds as they came from village after village to Creator Sets Free (Jesus). As the crowds gathered he told them a story.

"Listen!" he said, ⁵ "A seed planter went to plant some seeds and began to scatter them about on the ground.

"Some seeds fell on the village pathway, but people walked on them, and the winged-ones pecked at the seeds and ate them all.

⁶ "Some of the seeds fell on the rocks where there was only a little dirt. The plants grew, but they dried up because they had no water.

7 "Other seeds fell into the weeds, and thistles sprouted around the seeds and choked the life out of them.

8 "But some seeds fell on good ground, grew strong, and gave a harvest of one-hundred times what was planted. If you have ears to hear, you will understand this story."

Blind Eyes and Deaf Ears

9 But his followers didn't understand, so they asked him for the meaning of the story.

10 He answered them, "To you the honor has been given to understand the mysterious ways of Creator's Good Road. *This honor is not given to those who are not ready for it.* I speak to them in stories because 'even though they have eyes to see, they do not see, and even though they have ears to hear, they fail to understand.'u

Meaning of Four Kinds of Soil

11 "This is what the story means," he told them. "The seed in this story is the teaching from the Great Spirit *about his Good Road.*

12 "The village pathway represents the ones who hear, but then Accuser (Satan), the evil snake, sneaks up and steals the words out of their hearts to keep them from believing the teaching and being set free.

13 "The rocky ground represents the ones who hear and receive

the teaching with glad hearts, but because they have no roots, their faith is shallow and does not last. As soon as the teaching brings them trouble or opposition, they stumble and fall away.

14 "The weeds and thistles represent the ones who have heard the teaching, but they are too busy worrying about their earthly possessions, so the teaching is choked and their faith stops growing good fruit.

15 "The good ground represents the ones who hear the teaching with good and pure hearts, hold on tightly to it, and never let go until it grows good fruit in their lives.

16 "No one after lighting a lamp hangs a blanket in front of it. Instead, they would put it on a table so everyone can see. 17 The ones who have ears to hear will understand this teaching.

18 "But they must listen carefully, for the ones who understand will gain wisdom and be ready for more—much more. But the ones who do not listen wisely will lose even the little they think they understand."

All My Relatives

19 The mother of Creator Sets Free (Jesus) and his brothers came to see him. They were unable to get to him because of the great number of people gathered there. 20 Someone told him, "Your relatives are here, waiting to see you."

u 8:10 Isaiah 6:9

²¹Creator Sets Free (Jesus) *smiled and* told the messenger, "The ones who listen to the teachings of the Great Spirit, and walk in his ways, are all my relatives—my mother, aunts and uncles, brothers and sisters."

Power Over Violent Storms

²²On another day Creator Sets Free (Jesus) said to his followers, "Let's cross over to the other side of the lake." They climbed into a large canoe and pushed off from the shore.

Tired from a long day, ²³Creator Sets Free (Jesus) fell into a deep sleep.

> *His followers let him sleep and continued to paddle across the lake. A windstorm came up suddenly and began to move over the waters. They paddled harder, trying to get to shore before the storm hit.*

Soon the storm overtook them and threatened to sink the canoes. ²⁴In *desperation* they woke him from his sleep and cried out, "Wisdomkeeper! Wisdomkeeper! We are all going to drown."

He woke up from his sleep, *stood up* and spoke sharply to the wind and the raging water. At his words the wind stopped blowing and the waves calmed down. Great peace fell upon the surface of the waters. ²⁵He turned to his followers and said to them, "Where is your faith?"

Amazed and afraid, they *shook their heads and* whispered to each other, "Who is this man? Even the wind and the waves listen to him!"

Power Over Evil Spirits

²⁶When they finished crossing, they came to the territory of Walled In Ones (Gadarenes), across the Lake of Circle of Nations (Sea of Galilee). ²⁷As soon as he stepped from the canoe, a man from the village was there. This man had been tormented with evil spirits for a long time. His clothes had worn off him, and he had no house, so he lived in the local burial grounds.

²⁸When the man saw Creator Sets Free (Jesus), he fell to the ground in front of him. The evil spirit cried out through the man, "Creator Sets Free (Jesus), Son of the Great Spirit, what do you want with me? I beg you not to torment me!" ²⁹He said this because Creator Sets Free (Jesus) had ordered the evil spirit to leave the man.

In the past this evil spirit had often taken hold of the man, so the villagers had kept the man bound with chains and under close watch. But the man had broken the chains, and the spirit had forced him out into the desert.

³⁰Creator Sets Free (Jesus) asked, "What is your name?"

"Many Soldiers,"ᵛ he answered, because thousands of spirits had entered into him. ³¹They begged him not to send them into the deep dark pit of the world below.ʷ

³²There was a large herd of pigs feeding on a nearby mountainside,

v 8:30 Lit., 'legion' a segment of the occupying army of the People of Iron (Romans) of about 5,000 soldiers   w 8:31 Abyss or underworld

so the spirits begged him to permit them to enter the pigs. 33 When he gave them permission, the evil spirits left the man and entered into the herd of pigs. Then the whole herd stampeded down the mountainside headlong into the lake and drowned.

34 The ones who were watching over the pigs were scared to death and ran away. They went to the nearby village and told them everything that had happened. 35 As word spread, people came from the villages and the countryside to see for themselves. There they found the man whom the evil spirits had come out of, sitting quietly at the feet of Creator Sets Free (Jesus). He was clothed and in his right mind. This filled the hearts of the people there with awe and fear.

36 The ones who had seen what happened told the people how the man with evil spirits had been set free. 37 Then the people from the territory of the Walled In Ones (Gadarenes) begged Creator Sets Free (Jesus) to go away from their land.

38 As Creator Sets Free (Jesus) entered the canoe to return to the other side, the man who had been set free from the evil spirits begged him to take him along. Creator Sets Free (Jesus) would not permit it and said to the man, 39 "Return home to your family and friends," he told the man. "Tell them all the powerful things the Great Spirit has done for you."

The man went his way and told his story in the villages, telling everyone the great things Creator Sets Free (Jesus) had done for him.

A Desperate Request

40 Creator Sets Free (Jesus) canoed back to the other side of the lake. A great crowd, waiting for him at the lakeshore, welcomed him with glad hearts. 41 A man named He Gives Light (Jairus), the headman of the local gathering house, pushed his way through the crowd and fell down on his knees in front of Creator Sets Free (Jesus) and begged him to come to his house. 42 For he had an only daughter, about twelve winters old, who was dying.

As Creator Sets Free (Jesus) went with the man, the crowd also trailed along, pressing in around him from all sides.

Who Touched Me?

43 There was a woman in the crowd who had been bleeding in an unusual way for more than twelve winters. *This would have made her ceremonially unclean and untouchable.* She spent all she had on medicine men who were not able to heal her. 44 She came up close behind him, *reached out her hand and* touched the fringe of his outfit, and right away the blood stopped flowing.

Creator Sets Free (Jesus) stopped, turned and looked around the crowd.

45 "Who touched me?" he asked.

The ones who heard him shrugged their shoulders and began to look around also.

When no one came forward, Stands On The Rock (Peter) said to him, "Wisdomkeeper, the crowds are pushing, shoving and touching you, what do you mean?"

⁴⁶ "Someone touched me," he said again. "I felt power go out from my body."

⁴⁷ The woman knew she could hide no longer. She came forward, trembling with fear, and fell down at his feet. In front of all the people she told the story of why she touched him and how she was healed right then.

⁴⁸ Creator Sets Free (Jesus) looked at her with kindness in his eyes and said, "Daughter, your faith has made you well. Go in peace."

Power Over Death

⁴⁹ As they continued on, a messenger from the home of the headman of the gathering house came. *With sadness on his face* he said to He Gives Light (Jairus), "There is no need to trouble the Wisdomkeeper any longer, your little girl has died."

The man's heart fell to the ground and grief began to creep over him.

⁵⁰ Creator Sets Free (Jesus) overheard *and quickly* said to him, "Do not fear, simply trust me and all will be well."

⁵¹ When they came to the house, Creator Sets Free (Jesus) did not permit anyone to go in with him except the child's parents and his most trusted followers—Stands On The Rock (Peter), He Shows Goodwill (John), and He Takes Over (James).

⁵² All the people there were crying for the little girl. Creator Sets Free (Jesus) said to them, "Don't cry. The child is not dead; she only sleeps."

⁵³ They mocked him and laughed, for they knew she was dead. ⁵⁴ So he sent them outside, and then, taking the little girl by the hand, he said, "Little girl, stand up!" *She drew in a deep breath as* ⁵⁵ her spirit returned to her body, and she stood up. Creator Sets Free (Jesus) had them give her some food.

⁵⁶ Her father and mother stood there, amazed beyond words, *weeping for joy. Their little girl was alive!* Then he firmly told them not to tell anyone what had happened.

Message Bearers Sent Out

9 He then gathered his twelve message bearers together. He gave them the authority over all evil spirits and the power to heal all kinds of sickness and disease. ² Then he sent them out to present the message of Creator's Good Road and heal the sick.

³ "Take nothing with you," he instructed them, "not even walking sticks for your journey. Take no coins for your money pouches, no food for your traveling bundle, and only one outer garment for warmth.

⁴ "When people welcome you into their home, stay there until you move on. ⁵ If no one in that village welcomes you, when you go from there, shake the dust from your moccasins to warn them that you have done all that you can do."

⁶ The twelve went out to represent Creator Sets Free (Jesus) to all the villages, telling all who would listen about the Good Story and healing the sick everywhere they went.

His Reputation Grows

[7] The reputation of Creator Sets Free (Jesus) *had spread far and wide, until it finally* reached Chief Looks Brave (Herod). He was troubled because some were saying that He Shows Goodwill (John) had come back to life from the dead. [8] Others were saying that the ancient prophet, Great Spirit Is Creator (Elijah), had been seen again, and some said that one of the prophets of old had come back to life from the dead.

[9] Chief Looks Brave (Herod) wondered about this, and said, "I cut off the head of He Shows Goodwill (John), but who is this one I am hearing about?" So he began to look for Creator Sets Free (Jesus) to see for himself who he was.

[10] The twelve message bearers returned from their journeys and told Creator Sets Free (Jesus) all the things they had done. He then took them to a deserted place near House of Fishing (Bethsaida) to be alone. [11] The crowd of people saw where they were going and followed him.

When Creator Sets Free (Jesus) saw the great crowd of people, his heart went out to them again. He welcomed them and took the time to tell stories and help them understand many things about Creator's Good Road. He also healed the ones among them who were sick.

He Feeds Five Thousand

[12] It was becoming late in the day, so his message bearers said to him, "This is a deserted place, let us send the people away to the villages in the countryside so they can find food to eat."

[13] "You feed them!" he said *with a smile on his face.*

"We have only five loaves of bread and two small fish—unless you want us to go and buy food for this many people. [14] For there were about five thousand men there, *and also women and children.*"

Creator Sets Free (Jesus) said to them, "Have the people gather together in groups of fifty and sit down on the grass." [15] So they did what he asked.

The people began to scoop up their children and belongings and gather together. Creator Sets Free (Jesus) waited patiently for them to finish. When they were all settled down, he had his message bearers bring baskets and stand in a circle around him.

[16] He took the five loaves of bread with the two fishes *and held them up to the sky.* He looked up, spoke words of blessing over them, broke them into pieces, and gave them to his message bearers to give to the people. [17] Everyone ate until they were full!

When they gathered up the leftovers, it took twelve baskets to hold them all.

Who Do the People Say I Am?

One morning, [18] after praying alone with his followers, he asked them, "Who do all the crowds say that I am?"

They *looked around at each other and* said, [19] "Some say you are He Shows Goodwill (John) who performed the purification ceremony. Others say you might be Great Spirit Is Creator (Elijah), or one of the prophets of old come back to life from the dead."

Creator Sets Free (Jesus) lowered his voice and spoke with a more serious tone.

[20] "So tell me," he asked them. "Who do you say I am?"

Silent faces stared back at him. They began to look at each other and some looked down to the ground. The moment of truth had come, but no one dared to speak. Then suddenly a voice pierced through the silence.

"You are Creator's Chosen One!" Stands On The Rock (Peter) answered.

[21] He then warned them all not to tell anyone that he was the Chosen One, [22] and said to them, "The True Human Being must enter a time of much suffering. The elders, the head holy men, and the scroll keepers will turn their faces from me. They will have me killed, but I will come back to life on the third day.

[23] "If you want to walk the road with me, each day you must also be ready to give up your own life and carry your own crossbeam with me [24] *to the place of ultimate sacrifice.* The ones who hold on to their lives will lose them, but the ones who are willing to lay down their lives for me and my message will live. [25] How will it help you to get everything you want, but lose what

it means to be who Creator made you to be? Is there anything in this world worth trading for that?

[26] "If anyone is ashamed of me and my teaching, then the True Human Being will be ashamed of them when he comes in his glory, to be honored by the Father above and all of his holy spirit-messengers.

[27] "I speak from my heart, there are some of you standing here with me today who, before you cross over, will see Creator's Good Road."

The Mountain Where He Shined

[28] About eight days later Creator Sets Free (Jesus) took Stands On The Rock (Peter), He Takes Over (James), and He Shows Goodwill (John) up on a mountain to be alone and pray. [29] As he was sending his voice to the Great Spirit, the appearance of his face began to change and his clothes turned white as snow.

[30] Two men appeared and began to talk with him. One was the prophet of old, Great Spirit Is Creator (Elijah), and the other, the ancient lawgiver Drawn From The Water (Moses). [31] They were shining like the sun and were talking to him about his crossing over from this life to the next, that would take place in Village of Peace (Jerusalem).

[32] Stands On The Rock (Peter) and the others were deep asleep, but they woke up and shook the sleep from their eyes. They saw Creator Sets Free (Jesus) with his face and clothes shining. They also saw the two men standing with him. [33] As the men with him turned to go, Stands On

The Rock (Peter) spoke *without thinking,* "Wisdomkeeper!" he said. "This is a good place to stay. Let's make three tipis—one for you, one for Drawn From The Water (Moses), and one for Great Spirit Is Creator (Elijah)."

34 While he was saying this, a bright cloud from above began to fall on them. Their knees shook as the cloud surrounded them. 35 A voice spoke from the cloud, saying, "This is my Son, the one I have chosen—listen to him!"

36 When the voice finished speaking, they saw Creator Sets Free (Jesus) standing there alone in front of them. After this they kept silent and told no one at that time what they had seen.

A Generation With No Faith

37 The next day when Creator Sets Free (Jesus) finished coming down from the mountain, a large crowd was there. 38 A man called out from the crowd, "Wisdomkeeper!" he said *with desperation in his voice.* "I beg you, have pity on my son, my only child! 39 A spirit takes hold of him making him scream out loud, then foam comes from his mouth. It seldom stops tormenting him— leaving him beaten and bruised. 40 I asked your followers to force this spirit to go from him, and they tried but failed."

41 "Your generation is bent and twisted—with no faith," Creator Sets Free (Jesus) said. "How much longer will I have to be with you and put up with you? Bring your son to me."

42 As they were bringing the boy to him, the evil spirit took hold of him and threw the boy to the ground. But Creator Sets Free (Jesus) spoke sharply to the evil spirit, healed the boy and gave him back to his father. 43 Everyone there stood in awe at Creator's great power.

While the crowd stood there in amazement, Creator Sets Free (Jesus) turned to his followers and said to them, 44 "Let these words sink deep into your ears: The True Human Being will soon be betrayed and turned over to others."

45 But still they did not understand. The meaning was hidden from them. Their hearts would not let them believe what they heard with their ears. His words filled them with sorrow and dread, and they were afraid to ask him what it all meant.

Who is the Greatest?

46 The ones who walked the road with Creator Sets Free (Jesus) began to argue with each other over which one of them was the most important. When they got back to the house, Creator Sets Free (Jesus) asked them, "What were you arguing about as we walked on the road?"

But they just looked around at each other, not wanting to answer him.

47 Creator Sets Free (Jesus) knew the thoughts of their hearts, so he had a small child come and sit next to him. 48 "The ones representing me who welcome this little child are welcoming me. When you

welcome me, you are not only welcoming me, but also the one who sent me. That is what I meant when I said, 'The smallest among you will become the greatest of all.'"

⁴⁹ He Shows Goodwill (John) came close to him and said, "Wisdomkeeper, we saw a man forcing out evil spirits using your name. We told him to stop because he doesn't walk the road with us."

⁵⁰ "Do not stop him," Creator Sets Free (Jesus) told them. "The ones who are not against us are for us."

The Wrong Spirit to Follow

⁵¹ His work on earth was coming to an end, and Creator Sets Free (Jesus) would soon be returning to the world above. So he *drew strength from deep within and* made up his mind to go to the Sacred Village of Peace (Jerusalem) *and finish what his Father sent him to do.*

⁵² He sent some other messengers ahead to High Place (Samaria) to find lodging, ⁵³ but the people of High Place (Samaria) would not welcome him, for they knew he was on his way to Village of Peace (Jerusalem) *and they wanted nothing to do with the people there.*

⁵⁴ When He Takes Over (James) and He Shows Goodwill (John) found out he was not welcome there, they said, "Wisdomkeeper, do you want us to call down fire from the world above to burn them up, like the prophet Great Spirit Is Creator (Elijah) did?"

⁵⁵ Creator Sets Free (Jesus) spoke sharply to them, "You do not know what spirit you are listening to,

⁵⁶ for the True Human Being came to help people, not hurt them."

After that, they walked *silently* with him toward another village.

Walk the Road With Me

⁵⁷ As they traveled on, a man walked up to Creator Sets Free (Jesus). *"Honored One,"* he said, "I will follow you wherever you go."

⁵⁸ He answered the man, "The foxes live in their holes, the winged-ones who fly above us live in their nests, but the True Human Being has no place to lay his head."

⁵⁹ Creator Sets Free (Jesus) turned to another man and said, "Come, walk the road with me."

"Honored One," he said, "let me first go home to my father *until it is time* to bury him."

⁶⁰ "Let the ones who are dead bury their own dead," he said to the man. *"You are alive,* go and tell others about Creator's Good Road."

⁶¹ Another said to him, "Honored One, I will walk the road with you, but first let me go home and prepare my family."

⁶² Creator Sets Free (Jesus) told him, "No one who begins a journey and then turns back is ready to walk Creator's Good Road."

The Great Harvest

10 After this, Creator Sets Free (Jesus) chose seventy men from the ones who walked the road with him. He sent them out, two by two, to prepare the way for him in the villages he was about to visit *on his way to the Sacred Village of Peace (Jerusalem).*

²He said to them, "There is a great harvest before us, but there aren't enough helpers. Pray to the Harvest Chief, so he will send more helpers. Go and represent me. ³You will be like lambs walking among wolves. ⁴Take no money pouch or traveling bundle with you—not even a second pair of moccasins. Waste no time greeting others on the way.

⁵"When you lodge with someone, say to them first, 'Peace be to this house.' ⁶If people of peace live there, you will be welcomed; if not, your blessing of peace will return to you as you leave. ⁷Stay with the ones who welcome you; there is no need to move around from house to house. Share their food and drink with them, for the ones who work hard are worth feeding.

⁸"In any village that welcomes you, eat whatever they set before you. ⁹Offer healing prayers for any who are sick and say to them, 'Creator's Good Road has come close to you.'

¹⁰"If you enter a village and no one welcomes you, go into the village pathways and say, ¹¹'We must wipe the dust of your village from our *clothes* as a sign against you, for Creator's Good Road has come close to you, *but you would not welcome it.*' ¹²I speak from my heart, that village will face a worse end than Village of Bad Spirits (Sodom)."

Creator Sets Free (Jesus) began to warn about what would happen to the villages that saw his greatest signs and wonders but did not believe his message.

¹³"Sorrow and trouble will come to you, Village of Secrets (Chorazin), and the same for you, House of Fishing (Bethsaida). If the ancient villages of Rock Land (Tyre) and Hunting Grounds (Sidon) had seen the powerful signs you have seen, they would have thrown dirt and ashes on their heads and turned their hearts back to Creator's ways. ¹⁴It will be worse for you in the day when you face your end.

¹⁵"As for you, Village of Comfort (Capernaum), do you think you will be lifted up to the world above? No! You will be brought down low, to the Dark Underworld of Death."

Then he turned to his followers and said, ¹⁶"The ones who welcome you, welcome me. The ones who send you away are sending me away. The ones who send me away send away the One who sent me."

So, after he said these things, the seventy went out, two by two, to all the villages.

The Harvesters Report Back

¹⁷The seventy that were sent out by Creator Sets Free (Jesus) returned. Their hearts were overflowing with joy as they reported back to him. "Wisdomkeeper!" they said. "Even the evil spirits did what we said when we spoke to them in your name, representing you."

Creator Sets Free (Jesus) looked up to the sky and back down at them.

¹⁸Then he said to them, "With my own eyes I have seen Accuser (Satan) fall down like lightning from the world above. ¹⁹Look and see! I have given you authority over snakes

and spiders and over all the power of this enemy. Nothing will be able to harm you."

But then he gave them some words of wisdom.

²⁰ "Yes, the spirits must listen to you, but do not be too happy about this. Instead, let your hearts be glad that your names are carved into the rock cliffs of the world above."

²¹ The Holy Spirit filled the heart of Creator Sets Free (Jesus) with joy. "O Great Father, maker of the earth and sky," he prayed, "you have hidden these things from the ones who are wise in their own eyes but have shown them to the humble of heart. Yes, my Father, it has made your heart glad to see this day come."

²² He then turned to the seventy who walked the road with him, and said, "My Father has put everything into my hands. Only the Father knows the Son and only the Son knows the Father. No one can truly know the Father *in his fullness* unless the Son makes him known."

²³ Then he turned to his twelve *message bearers and whispered to them*, "You have been given a great honor to see these things. ²⁴ There were many prophets and chiefs who wanted to see and hear the things you have, but did not."

A Sly Scroll Keeper
Sets a Trap

²⁵ A scroll keeper, *one who was skilled in his knowledge of Tribal Law*, came to Creator Sets Free (Jesus) to test him and trap him in his words.

"Wisdomkeeper," he said. "What path must I walk to have the life of the world to come that never fades— full of beauty and harmony?"

²⁶ He answered him, "What is written in the Law about this? Tell me, how do you see it?"

²⁷ The scroll keeper spoke from the words of the Law, "You must love the Great Spirit from deep within, with the strength of your arms, the thoughts of your mind, and the courage of your heart,ˣ and you must love your fellow human beings in the same way you love yourselves."ʸ

²⁸ "You have answered well," Creator Sets Free (Jesus) said back to him. "If you walk this path you will live."

²⁹ But the scroll keeper, wanting to look good to others, asked him, "Who are my fellow human beings?"

He Turns the Trap
with a Story

³⁰ Creator Sets Free (Jesus) answered him with a story.

"There was a man walking on the road from Village of Peace (Jerusalem) to Moon Village (Jericho). On the way he was attacked by thieves who beat him, stripped him of his clothes and left him bleeding to death.

³¹ "Now it happened that a holy man was on the same road, not far behind. When he saw the man, he

---

x 10:27 Deuteronomy 6:5   y 10:27 Leviticus 19:18

went around him on the other side of the road. 32 Not far behind him was another man, also from the tribe holy men are chosen from. When he saw the wounded man, he did the same thing as the holy man.

33 "Then a man from High Place (Samaria),ᶻ who was also walking the road, saw the wounded man. *Even though he was not a Tribal Member but a mixed blood despised by the tribal people,* he felt pity for the man. 34 He helped him by pouring good medicine on his wounds and wrapping them in a cloth. He put the man on his own animal and took him to a lodging house to care for him.

35 "The next day, when the man of High Place (Samaria) was leaving, he gave from his own money pouch to the keeper of the lodging house, 'Use this to care for him,' he said, 'and when I return, I will give you anything more that is needed.'"

36 Creator Sets Free (Jesus) then *looked at the scroll keeper* and said, "Which one of these three acted as a fellow human being to the man who was attacked by the thieves?"

37 The scroll keeper answered, "The one who had pity on him."

"Go," Creator Sets Free (Jesus) said, "and walk in the same way."

Choosing the Best Part

38 As they journeyed on, they went to a village where a woman named Head Woman (Martha) gave them lodging at her house. 39 Her sister Healing Tears (Mary), who lived with her, sat next to Creator Sets Free (Jesus) on the floor, listening to his teaching.

As their Wisdomkeeper, Creator Sets Free (Jesus) would teach the men who gathered around him, but this would not have been proper for a woman of that culture.

40 Head Woman (Martha) was distracted, trying to get the meal ready for the honored guests. When she saw Healing Tears (Mary) sitting down, she walked up to Creator Sets Free (Jesus) and said, "Wisdomkeeper, don't you care that my sister has left me to work alone? Tell her to help me."

41 "Head Woman (Martha), O Head Woman (Martha)," he said, "I know many things worry and trouble you. 42 But you must set your heart on the one thing that matters. That is what Healing Tears (Mary) has done, and I will not take it from her."

He Gives His Followers a Prayer

11 Another time, after Creator Sets Free (Jesus) had finished praying, one of his followers said to him, "Wisdomkeeper, teach us how to pray in the same way He Shows Goodwill (John) taught his followers."

2 Creator Sets Free (Jesus) *smiled and* said to them, *"When you send your voice to the Great Spirit,* here is how you should pray:

"O Great Father, the one who lives above us all, your name is sacred and holy.

---

z **10:33** The people of High Place (Samaria) were mixed bloods who had changed the traditional ceremonial ways and were despised by the Tribal People (Jews).

"Bring your Good Road to us, where the beauty of your ways in the world above is reflected in the earth below.

3 "Provide for us day by day—the elk, the buffalo, and the salmon; the corn, the squash, and the wild rice; all the good things we need every day *to feed our families.*

4 "Release us from the things we have done wrong in the same way we release others for the things done wrong to us.

And guide us away from the things that tempt us to stray from your Good Road."

More Wisdom About Praying

5 *Then he added,* "Suppose you went to a friend in the middle of the night and said, 'I need three loaves of bread! 6 A relative of mine has come from a long way to see me, and I have nothing for him to eat.' 7 But he says to you, 'Quit bothering me! I can't help you; my children and I are all in bed.' 8 Don't give up! If your friendship isn't enough, then he will do it just because you won't give up asking.

9 "So, keep dancing your prayers, and the way will open before you. Search *for the ancient pathways,* and you will find *them.* Keep sending up your prayers, and they will be heard.

10 "Answers will come to the ones who ask, good things will be found by the ones who search for them, and the way will open before

the ones who keep dancing their prayers.

11 "What kind of father, if his son wanted a fish, would give him a rattlesnake, 12 or, if he asked for an egg, would give him a deadly spider? 13 If even fathers with bad hearts will give good gifts to their children, how much more will the Creator, who is your Father from the world above, give the Holy Spirit to all who ask!"

Spiritual Leaders Accuse Him

14 One day Creator Sets Free (Jesus) was setting a man free from a spirit that kept him from speaking. When the spirit left the man, he could speak again and the crowd was amazed. 15 But some of them said, "His power over evil spirits comes from the Worthless Ruler (Beelzebul),[a] the one who rules over all evil spirits."

16 And others were putting him to a test, asking him for a sign from the world above.

17 Creator Sets Free (Jesus) knew what they were thinking and said, "Any nation warring against itself comes to a bad end. 18 A village or clan warring against each other will not survive. If Accuser (Satan) is against himself, how will he continue to rule? I say this because you have accused me of forcing out evil spirits by the power of the Worthless Ruler (Beelzebul).

19 "If my power over evil spirits comes from the Worthless Ruler

---

a 11:15 Beelzebul, another name for Accuser (Satan)

(Beelzebul), then by what power do your children do these things? They are the ones who will decide against you. 20 If I force out evil spirits by the finger of the Great Spirit, then Creator's Good Road has come close to you.

21 "When a strong warrior, who is dressed for war, guards his own belongings, they are safe. 22 But when someone who is stronger attacks and defeats him, he will strip him of his war garments that he trusted in, take away all his goods, and give them away to others.

23 *"In this spiritual battle there is no unclaimed territory. The one who is not fighting with me, fights against me. The one who does not help me gather, scatters and makes things worse."*

24 "When an evil spirit goes out of someone, it wanders through dry wastelands, looking for a place to rest. When it finds none, it says, 'I will go back to the house I left.' 25 It returns to find the house empty, swept clean and put in order. 26 The spirit then finds seven other spirits, more evil than itself, who all go in and live there, making the person worse than before."

27 As Creator Sets Free (Jesus) was speaking, a woman from the crowd raised her voice and said to him, "Creator's blessing is on the womb that birthed you and the breasts that nursed you!"

"That may be," 28 he answered her, "but a greater blessing belongs to the ones who listen to the words of the Great Spirit and walk in His ways."

The Sign of Wings Of Dove

29 More and more people came to hear Creator Sets Free (Jesus), so he said to them, "This is a generation of bad-hearted people, looking only for powerful signs. The only sign you will be given is the sign of Wings Of Dove (Jonah)." 30 In the same way he was a sign to the people of Village of Changed Minds (Nineveh), the True Human Being will be to the people living today.

31 The reputation of the female chief of the South *b* will speak against the people of today. What she did will show your guilt, for she journeyed from a land far away to listen to the wisdom of the great chief Stands In Peace (Solomon). Look! A greater one is standing right in front of you.

32 When Creator decides the fate of the people living today, the reputation of people of Village of Changed Minds (Nineveh) will speak against them. What they did will show your guilt, because they changed their minds when they heard the message of Wings Of Dove (Jonah). Look! One who is greater than he stands before you now.

The Way to See Possessions

33-34 "No one, after lighting a lamp, hides it or puts it under a basket; instead it would be lifted up high on a pole so all who enter can see it."

Among the tribes of Wrestles With Creator (Israel) a greedy person

---

b 11:31 Queen of Sheba

was said to have a bad eye and unable to see the Good Road. A generous person was said to have a good eye, full of light and able to clearly see the Good Road.

So he said to them, 35 "Light shines into the body through the eyes. If your eyes are clear, your whole being is full of light. 36 But, if your eyes are bad, then your whole being is full of darkness. Make sure your eyes are full of light and not darkness, then you will clearly see the path you walk, like a torch in the night."

He Confronts the Spiritual Leaders

37 When Creator Sets Free (Jesus) finished speaking, one of the Separated Ones (Pharisees) invited him to a meal, so Creator Sets Free (Jesus) sat with him at his table; 38 but the Separated One (Pharisee) was upset that he did not ceremonially wash his hands before eating.

39 "You Separated Ones (Pharisees) always wash the outside of your cups and bowls, but on the inside your hearts are full of greed and worthless ways. 40 How can you be so foolish? The one who made the outside also made the inside! 41 If you will give food to the hungry from the inside of you, *from the pity in your heart,* then all things will be clean for you.

42 "Sorrow and trouble await you Separated Ones (Pharisees)! For you are careful to do what Tribal Law says by giving a tenth of each little herb in your garden, as you should, without ignoring the more important instructions, like treating others equally and walking in the love of the Great Spirit.

43 "Sorrow and trouble await you Separated Ones (Pharisees)! For you love to sit in the seats of honor at the gathering houses and to be noticed at the trading posts.

44 "Sorrow and trouble will be waiting at the end of the trail for you, for you are like unmarked burial grounds that others walk over without even noticing."

45 A scroll keeper, one who was an expert in Tribal Law, spoke up. "Wisdomkeeper," he complained, "when you say these things, you insult us also."

46 Creator Sets Free (Jesus) did not hold back. "Sorrow and trouble is coming your way," he warned the scroll keeper, "for you put heavy spiritual loads on the backs of others, too much for them to carry, but will not lift even one finger to help them.

47 "Sorrow and trouble are waiting for you, for you carve statues on the burial grounds of the prophets of old to honor them, but it was your ancestors who murdered them. 48 Your actions show you are walking in their moccasins, for they killed the prophets, and you decorate their burial grounds.

49 "But here is what the Great Spirit in his wisdom says to you, 'I will send to you prophets and message bearers. Some you will murder, and others you will track down and torture.'

50 "The people living today will have to give an answer for shedding the blood of all the prophets who have lived since the beginning of the world, 51 from the blood of His Breath Goes Up (Abel) to the blood of Creator Will Remember (Zechariah), who was murdered in the courtyard of the Sacred Lodge.

52 "Sorrow and trouble await you experts in Tribal Law, for you have taken for yourselves the secrets of wisdom and understanding. You have failed to walk in them, and *even worse,* you have stood in the way of others who were trying to get in."

53 As Creator Sets Free (Jesus) began to leave, the scroll keepers and Separated Ones (Pharisees) grew fierce in their anger toward him. 54 They began to attack him with sharp questions, trying to trap him in his words.

Creator Sees All

12 Many thousands of people were now crowding around Creator Sets Free (Jesus), so many that they were trampling on each other. Before he spoke to the crowd, he first said to his followers, "Be on the lookout for the teachings[c] of the Separated Ones (Pharisees) who put on a false face. 2 *Remember,* nothing can be hidden from Creator's eyes; he will uncover all secrets. 3 What is spoken in darkness will be heard in the light, and what is whispered in secret will be shouted from the rooftops.

4 "Hear me, my friends, do not fear the ones who can kill only the body. 5 The one who should be respected and feared is the one who has the right to bring an end to your entire being and throw you into the Valley of Smoldering Fire. This is what should make you tremble.

6 "Five small winged-ones could be traded for two stones, yet Creator cares for each of them. 7 He even knows the number of hairs on your head. Do not fear; are you not worth more to him than many small winged-ones?

8 "Listen! When you represent me before others, the True Human Being will represent you before Creator's spirit-messengers. 9 But the ones who disown me will be disowned before them.

10 "Anyone who speaks against the True Human Being can be forgiven, but speaking evil of the Holy Spirit will not be forgiven.

11 "When they drag you into their gathering houses and before government rulers, do not worry how to defend yourselves or what to say. 12 When that time comes, the Holy Spirit will give you the words to speak."

Look Out for Greed

13 Someone from the crowd pushed forward and said to him, "Wisdomkeeper, tell my brother to give me my part of what our father left to us."

14 Creator Sets Free (Jesus) said to him, "Who made me the one to decide this between you and your brother?

c 12:1 Lit., yeast

15 Watch your step, or greed will make you stumble. Remember, one's life is not made up of many possessions."

There were many people in the crowd who heard what he said about possessions, 16 so he told this story to help them see more clearly.

"A man with many possessions had a field that was growing a great harvest of food. 17 'What will I do with all this food?' he said to himself. 'I don't have room in my storage barns for this great harvest.'

"The man thought about it and then said to himself again. 18 'I know what I will do, I will tear down my old storage barns and build larger ones. 19 I will have enough to last me many winters; then I will take my rest, eat, drink and celebrate.'

20 "But the Great Spirit said to him, 'Why are you being so foolish? This is the day you will cross over and give an answer for your life. Now who will get the goods you have stored up for yourself?'"

Creator Sets Free (Jesus) let the people think about the story, and then he said, 21 "This is how it will be for the ones who make themselves rich but forget about Creator's true riches."

Fear Not Little Flock

22 Then he said to the ones who walked the road with him, "This is why I am telling you not to be troubled about getting enough to eat or drink, or what to wear. Is eating, drinking and clothing yourself all there is? 23 Does your life not have more meaning than this?

24 "Look to the ravens, the winged-ones who fly above us. Do they plant seeds and gather the harvest into a storehouse? No! But the Great Spirit gives them plenty to eat. Do you not know he cares even more for you? 25 Will worrying about these things help you live one hour longer? 26 If you cannot do such a small thing, why worry about other things?

27 "Have you seen how the wildflowers grow in the plains and meadows? Do you think they work hard and long to clothe themselves? No! I tell you, not even the great chieftain Stands In Peace (Solomon), wearing his finest regalia, was dressed as well as even one of these.

28 "If the Great Spirit covers the wild grass in the plains with such beauty, which is here today and gathered for tomorrow's fire, will he not take even better care of you? Why is your faith so small? 29 Why worry so much about what to eat or drink. 30 This is what the Nations of the world, *who have lost their way,* have given their hearts to, but your Father from above knows you need these things.

31 "If you will make Creator's Good Road your first aim, he will make sure you have all you need for each day. 32 Do not fear, for even though you are a small flock, it makes your Father's heart glad to give you the Good Road!

33 "Share your possessions with the ones in need, and you will have money pouches that never, filled wear out with possessions from the world above. 34 For where you

store your possessions is where your heart will be.

35 "Be ready at all times, with your torches burning bright. 36 Be like the ones who, waiting for their chief to return from a distant wedding feast, were watching and ready to welcome him. 37 When he returns and finds them ready, he will take off his chiefly garments, dress himself in servant's clothes, sit them at his own table, and serve them a great feast, 38 whether he returns late in the night or early in the morning.

39 "Here is another way to see what I am saying. If the elder of a family had known what night the thieves were coming, he would not have let them break in. 40 In the same way you must always be ready, for the True Human Being will return at a time you do not expect."

Who is This Story For?

41 Hearing this, Stands On The Rock (Peter) said to him, "Wisdomkeeper, is this story for us, or for all people?"

42 "You tell me," Creator Sets Free (Jesus) answered, "who is the wise one, worthy of trust? The uncle who feeds and cares for the family while the elder is away? 43-44 Yes!— and when the elder returns, he will honor that uncle, take him into his home and share everything with him.

45 "But what if the uncle says to himself, 'It will be a long time before he returns,' then begins to abuse the family, eat all the best food, and get drunk on the wine? 46 I will tell you what will happen," Creator Sets Free (Jesus) continued. "The elder will return at an unexpected time and find the uncle abusing his family. He will then put him out of the family and send him away to live with the other outcasts.

"Who is the story for?" Creator Sets Free (Jesus) asked his followers. 47 "Like the bad-hearted uncle, it is for the ones who know Creator's right ways but fail to walk in them. They will be given the greatest punishment, 48 for more is required from the ones who are given and trusted with more. As for the ones who do not know but still fail to do what is right, their punishment will not be as great."

My Message Will Bring Division

Creator Sets Free (Jesus). He knew that his followers were not prepared for the effect his message would have on their nation and what would soon happen to him in the Sacred Village of Peace (Jerusalem).

49 "I came down from above to ignite a fire on this land, and how I long for it to burn!" he said to his followers. 50 "I have a purification ceremony *with fire* to accomplish— and I am desperate to finish it!

51 "Do you look for me to bring peace to this land? No! I tell you. First there will be great conflict. 52 The message I bring will pierce like the blade of a long knife. It will even separate family members. A family of five will take sides, three against two and two against three.

53 Fathers and sons, mothers and daughters, uncles and nephews, aunties and nieces—will all fight like enemies—*because of me and my message."*d

54 Creator Sets Free (Jesus) then said to the crowd, "When a cloud rises in the west, you say, 'It will rain soon,' and so it does. 55 The wind blows from the south and you say, 'It will be a hot day,' and so it is."

Then he spoke to the spiritual leaders, 56 "You who wear false faces! You understand what the earth, wind and sky are saying, but you are blind to the message of the season you live in.

57-58 "If someone has a complaint against you, why not work things out on the way to tribal council? Can't you decide on your own what is right and come to an agreement? The council may decide against you, and turn you over to ones who have the power to banish you 59 where there is no way back until honor is restored."

Take A New Path

13 Then some of the people there told Creator Sets Free (Jesus) about the people from Circle of Nations (Galilee) whom Spear Of The Great Waters (Pilate) had put to death and mixed their blood with their own ceremonial offerings.

2 He said to them, "Do you think it was because of their bad hearts and wrongdoings that they suffered? Do you think their hearts were worse than all the others in Circle of Nations (Galilee)? 3 No! I say to you! But if you, *the people of Village of Peace (Jerusalem),* do not change your ways of thinking and take a new path, you will all die in the same way.

4 "What about the eighteen people on whom the tower in Sending Village (Siloam) fell? Do you think they were worse than all others living in Village of Peace (Jerusalem)? 5 No, I say to you! But if you, *the people of the Sacred Village of Peace (Jerusalem),* do not change your ways of thinking and take a new path, you will all die in the same way."

6 So he told them this story, "There was a man who planted a fig tree in his garden, but when he came to find fruit, there was none. 7 He said to the keeper of the garden, 'I have been looking for fruit on this tree for three seasons and have found none. Cut the tree down! Why waste good dirt on it?'

8 "But the garden keeper answered the man, 'Give me another season. I will dig around the tree and fertilize it. 9 If it has no fruit after that, then cut it down.'"

Conflict About the Day of Resting

10 On another Day of Resting, Creator Sets Free (Jesus) was teaching at a gathering house. 11 There was a woman there who had a spirit of weakness for eighteen winters. Her

---

d 12:53 Micah 7:6

back was bent and twisted, so she could not stand up straight.

[12] When Creator Sets Free (Jesus) saw her, he told her to come to him and said, "Honored woman you are set free from your weakness." [13] He put his hands on her and right away she stood up straight and gave thanks to the Great Spirit.

[14] The headman of the gathering house was offended because Creator Sets Free (Jesus) had healed on the Day of Resting. He stood up and told the people, "Are there not six other days to do your work? Come on one of those days to be healed, not on the Day of Resting."

Creator Sets Free (Jesus) helped the woman back to her seat. He then turned to the headman with a look of sorrow mixed with anger on his face.

[15] "You who wear false faces!" he said to the headman. "Is there anyone who would not untie his horse on the Day of Resting and take it to a watering hole? [16] This woman is a daughter of Father Of Many Nations (Abraham). Accuser (Satan), that evil trickster, has kept her this way for eighteen winters. Why should she not be set free on the Day of Resting?"

[17] The enemies of Creator Sets Free (Jesus) were put to shame by his words, but the hearts of the people jumped for joy because of the wonderful things he was doing.

The Good Road Will Cover the Earth

[18] "What is Creator's Good Road like? What can I compare it to?" Creator Sets Free (Jesus) asked. [19] "It is like a man who planted in his garden a single grain of mustard seed,[e] where it grew into a great tree, large enough for the winged-ones who soar in the sky to find lodging in its branches.

[20] "Again, think of the Good Road [21] like the yeast a grandmother uses when she makes bread dough. When she mixes a little yeast into a large amount of flour, then the yeast spreads throughout all of the dough."

Will Only A Few Find the Good Road?

[22] Creator Sets Free (Jesus) continued to travel on to Village of Peace (Jerusalem). As he passed through the villages on the way, he would stop and teach the people. [23] At one of these villages a man asked him, "Wisdomkeeper, will only a few find their way onto the Good Road and be set free?"

[24] "Yes," Creator Sets Free (Jesus) said to the man, "so make it your aim to enter in by the narrow way *that I have taught you.* There will be many who try to enter some other way but will not be able.

[25] "Once the elder of a home has closed the door, others will come *pound on the door and* say to him, 'Elder! Elder! Open the door for us!'

---

e 13:19 The mustard plant was used as an herbal medicine.

"But the elder will tell them, 'I don't know who you are.'

26 "'But didn't we eat and drink with you?' they will argue. 'Didn't you teach on our village pathways?'

27 "'No!' he will say to them, 'I don't know where you are from. Go away from me, you bad-hearted trouble makers!'

28 "For there will be much weeping and grinding of teeth in anger when you see Father Of Many Nations (Abraham), He Made Us Laugh (Isaac), Heel Grabber (Jacob) and all the prophets of old, feasting in the Land of Creator's Good Road; but you are on the outside looking in! 29 People will come from many Nations—from the East, South, West and North—and sit down to join in the feast.

"So you see," Creator Sets Free (Jesus) said to the man, 30 "some who are last will be first, and some who are first will be last."

The man's face became pale as the meaning of the words of Creator Sets Free (Jesus) sank into his heart.

No Peace in Village of Peace

31 At that time some of the Separated Ones (Pharisees) came to him and said, "You should leave this place! Looks Brave (Herod) is looking for you—to put you to death."

32 He answered them, "You can tell that sly coyote, 'look out! I am forcing out the evil spirits and healing the sick today and tomorrow. On the third day I will finish the work I came to do.' 33 That is why I will go from this place today, tomorrow and the day after. For a prophet cannot be put to death this far from Village of Peace (Jerusalem)!

34 "O Village of Peace (Jerusalem), you who kill the prophets and stone to death the ones sent to you! How I have longed to gather your children together, like the eagle gathers her young under her wings, but you would not have it. 35 Look! Your house has fallen and will be left in ruins!

"I speak from my heart, you will not see me again until you say, 'Blessed is the one who comes representing the Great Spirit!'"*f*

Healing Again on the Day of Resting

14 On a Day of Resting, Creator Sets Free (Jesus) was invited to the house of a headman of the Separated Ones (Pharisees) for a meal. All were keeping their eyes on him.

2 A man with a sickness that made parts of his body swell up, came and stood in front of him. 3 Creator Sets Free (Jesus) asked the Separated Ones (Pharisees) and the scroll keepers, who are experts in Tribal Law, "Is it permitted to heal on the Day of Resting? Yes or no?"

4 The spiritual leaders glared at him in silence. 5 So he took hold of the man, healed him, and sent him on his way.

He then turned to the spiritual leaders and said, "If your child, or

f 13:35 Psalm 118:26

even a horse, fell into a watering hole, would you not pull it out on the Day of Resting?"

6 The spiritual leaders had no answer for him.

Humility Instead of Self Importance

7 He noticed how the invited guests had chosen the best seats at the table, so he gave them some wise counsel.

8 "If you are invited to a wedding feast, do not sit in the best seats, for someone with greater honor may be invited. 9 Then the host will come to you and say, 'Give your seat to this person.' Then, hanging your head, you will have to take the lowest seat.

10 "Instead, take the lowest seat and the host may say to you 'Friend, come and sit in the seat of honor.' You will then be honored in the eyes of all the guests."

Creator Sets Free (Jesus) looked around the table at all the guests and said,

11 "The ones who put themselves above others will be brought down, but all who humble themselves will be lifted up."

12 Creator Sets Free (Jesus) then turned to the headman who had invited him and said, "When you have a feast, do not invite only your friends, relatives and the ones with many possessions, who can repay you. 13 Instead, invite the poor, the blind and the crippled, who cannot repay you. 14 Then you will

be honored when the ones who are upright in heart are brought back to life again."

15 One of the guests at the feast said to Creator Sets Free (Jesus), "Creator's blessing rests on the ones who will feast at the table in the Land of Creator's Good Road!"

Story of the Great Feast

Creator Sets Free (Jesus) could see they still did not understand, so he told them another story.

16 "There was a man who prepared a great feast and invited many people. 17 When the feast was ready, he sent a messenger to tell the ones he had invited, 'Come to the table, the feast is ready!' 18 But one by one they all began to make excuses.

"One said, 'I must go and tend to my new field. Please excuse me.'

19 "Another said, 'Please excuse me also, for I must try out the horses[g] I just traded for.'

20 "And another, 'I cannot come, for I have just been married.'

21 "When the messenger told the man their answer, he became angry and said, 'Waste no time! Go out into the village pathways and invite the ones who are poor, crippled, blind and lame.'

22 "When the messenger returned, he told the man, 'I have done what you said, but there is still room for more.'

23 "So he told the messenger, 'Go out to the mountain trails, look

g 14:19 Lit., oxen

behind all the bushes and urge them to come, so that my house may be filled with people. ²⁴None of the ones I first invited will even taste of this feast!'"

Counting the Cost

Creator Sets Free (Jesus) was coming near to Jerusalem.

²⁵Large crowds were following him, so he turned to them and said, ²⁶*"The ones who come to me must put me first, above all others.* To walk the road with me, they must love and respect me above their own fathers and mothers, wives and children, and aunties and uncles—even more than their own lives. ²⁷Only the ones who are willing to follow me and carry their own crossbeam are ready to walk the road with me and learn my ways.

²⁸"Who would build a great lodge without first making sure he had enough trees to finish it? ²⁹If he only built the floor and then ran out of trees, others would laugh at him and say, ³⁰'How will you finish what you started?'

³¹"Would a chief go to war against another chief if he only had half as many warriors? ³²No! He would send messengers ahead to make a peace treaty!

³³"You must count the cost of following me, for all who are not willing to give up all they have are not ready to walk the road with me and learn my ways."

³⁴Then he added, "Salt is a good thing, but if it loses its saltiness, how will it get its flavor back? ³⁵That kind of salt is thrown away— it is no good for the garden or the manure pile.

"Let the ones who have ears, hear what I am saying!"

The Worth of the Lost Ones

15 Tribal tax collectors and other outcasts would often gather around Creator Sets Free (Jesus) to listen to him tell his stories. ²But the Separated Ones (Pharisees) and the scroll keepers would complain about this. They would say things like, "This man welcomes outcasts to join him at the table and eat with him."

³On one of those occasions Creator Sets Free (Jesus) answered them with this story:

⁴"Who among you, if you were caring for one-hundred sheep, and one of the lambs wandered away, would not leave the ninety-nine and search for that lost lamb until you found it? ⁵Would you not then put that lamb on your shoulders, hurry home ⁶and invite your friends to a celebration, saying to them, 'Rejoice with me for I have found my lost lamb!'?

⁷"In the same way, the world above will celebrate even more over one outcast who finds the way back home than for ninety-nine who are already safely there."

⁸*"Let me say it another way,"* he explained. "What man who has ten eagle feathers,ʰ and loses one, would not light a torch, sweep the

---

h 15:8 Lit., woman who has ten silver coins

house clean and look everywhere until he found it? ⁹Then, after he finds it, wouldn't he gather his friends together for a celebration? ¹⁰In the same way, Creator's spirit-messengers will celebrate when even one outcast finds the way back home."

Story About Two Sons

Creator Sets Free (Jesus) then told this story to help them see even more clearly:

¹¹"There was a man with two sons. ¹²The younger son said to his father, 'Father, give me now my share of what is coming to me.'"

This was a great insult to the father, for this would not have been done until the father had crossed over to death.

"But the Father, *who was good hearted and loved his sons,* divided all he had with his two sons anyway.

¹³"Not many days later the younger son took his share and went far away to another land. He began to spend it all on wild living and soon had nothing left. ¹⁴The time came when there was not enough food in the land for everyone, and he found himself poor and hungry. ¹⁵So he went to work for a rancher, who sent him out to feed the pigs. ¹⁶He became so hungry that he wanted to eat the husks he was feeding the pigs, but no one would even give him a meal.

¹⁷"Soon the younger son came back to his right mind and said to himself, 'Look, here I am naked and starving, but the servants who work for my father are well fed! ¹⁸I am going back to humble myself to my father. I will tell him that I have dishonored both him and the world above, ¹⁹and I am no longer worthy to be called his son. I will ask him just to let me be a hired servant to work in his fields.'

²⁰"He then made up his mind and began to go home. While he was still far away, his father saw him walking. The father's heart opened wide, he ran to his son, threw his arms around him and kissed him.

²¹"The son said, 'Father, I have failed the world above and you, I am not worthy to be called your son.'

²²"But the father ignored his son's words, turned to his servants and said, 'Go! Find my best regalia and put it on him. Give him a headdress of feathers for his head and new moccasins for his feet! ²³Go get the fattest calf and prepare a great feast for a celebration. ²⁴This is my son! He was lost, but I have found him. He was dead to me, but now he is alive!' Then they all began to feast, sing and dance.

²⁵"Now, the older son was just returning from a hard day's work in the field. He heard the music and dancing, ²⁶so he asked one of the servants what was going on. ²⁷The servant told him, 'Your brother has come home and your father has prepared a great feast for him, because he is alive and well.'

²⁸"Hearing this, the older brother became very angry and refused to go into the lodge. The father saw him *brooding outside,* so he went to him and urged him to come in.

29 "The older son said to his father, 'Why can't you see? I have worked hard for you all my life, and done all that you have asked of me, but you have not even given me one small goat to have a feast with my friends. 30 But when this son of yours, who wasted all you gave him on sexual favors with women, comes home, you kill the fattest calf for him.'

"The father looked kindly into his older son's face.

31 "'My son,' he said to him, 'you are always close to my heart and everything I have is yours. 32 But it is a good thing for us to celebrate with glad hearts, for your brother was dead but now is alive. He was lost, but now we have found him!'"

Possessions and the Good Road

16 He then told the ones who walked the road with him another story:

"There was a man with so many possessions, he had to have someone to oversee them all. The rich man was told that his overseer was mishandling his possessions. 2 He sent for the man and said to him, 'Why am I hearing these things about you? Give me an account of all I possess, for I can no longer trust you to oversee my belongings.'

3 "The man said to himself, 'What will I do? I am too old to dig ditches and too proud to beg from others.'

"Then an idea came to his mind. 4 'I know what to do so that others will help me and give me a place to live.' 5 He went to each person who was in debt to the rich man.

"He said to the first one, 'How much do you owe?' 6 'One hundred containers of oil,' the man answered. 'Make it to be fifty,' the overseer told him.

7 "He then said to another, 'How much do you owe?' 'One hundred baskets of wheat,' he answered. 'Make it to be eighty,' the overseer said back to him.

8 "When the rich man found out what the dishonest overseer had done, he *shook his head but* admired the man's craftiness.

"Do you see what this means?" Creator Sets Free (Jesus) asked. "The children of darkness are *sometimes* wiser in the ways of this world than the children of light are in the ways of the world above.

9 "So then, use the possessions of this world to help others in need, who will become your friends. Then when possessions run out, these new friends *of Creator's Good Road* will always welcome you into their homes.

10-12 "If Creator cannot trust you with the possessions of this world, then how will he trust you with the treasures of the world above? But if you do well with the small things *of this world,* you will do well with the great things *of the world above.*

13 "No one can be loyal to two rival chiefs. He will have to choose between them, for either he will hate one chief and love the other or he will honor one and resent the

other. You cannot be loyal to the Great Provider and to possessions at the same time."

14 When the Separated Ones (Pharisees) heard him, they shrugged their shoulders and rolled their eyes, for they loved their many possessions.

15 Creator Sets Free (Jesus) said to them, "You always make yourselves look good to others, but the Great Spirit sees your heart. What many see as valuable he sees as worthless.

Nothing in Tribal Law Will Fail

16 "Tribal Law and the Prophets spoke until He Shows Goodwill (John) came. From his time until now, the Good Story about Creator's Good Road has been told, but people are trying to force their way upon it. 17 Not one thing the Law or the Prophets have said will fail; it is as sure as the sky above and the earth below."

About Divorce

In those days men would sometimes send their wives away for no good reason without giving them divorce papers, leaving them destitute and unable to properly remarry. Drawn From The Water (Moses), in the Law, said they must give a woman divorce papers before sending her away.[i] *To protect the honor and dignity of women, Creator Sets Free (Jesus) set them straight about how to apply this law.*

18 "Whoever sends his wife away, *without properly divorcing her,* and marries another is guilty of being unfaithful to his first wife. Anyone who then marries her is guilty of marrying another mans wife."

The Rich Man and the Beggar

19 "There was once a man with many possessions who always dressed in the best clothes, had more than enough to eat, and lived a life of ease. 20 Every day a beggar named Creator Helps Him (Lazarus) was laid at the gate of his lodge. 21 Dogs would come and lick the sores that covered his body as he begged for crumbs from the rich man's table.

22 "When the time came for the beggar to cross over to the world of the dead, spirit-messengers carried him into the welcoming arms of his ancestor, Father Of Many Nations (Abraham).

"At the same time the rich man also crossed over to death and his body was buried. 23 In the Dark Underworld of the Dead he was suffering and in pain. He looked up and saw his ancestor, Father Of Many Nations (Abraham), far off in the distance. He could see Creator Helps Him (Lazarus) being comforted in his arms.

24 "He cried out in his pain, 'Father Of Many Nations (Abraham), my ancestor, have pity on me. Send Creator Helps Him (Lazarus) to dip the tip of his finger in water and

---

i **16:18** Deuteronomy 24:1; Matthew 5:31

cool my thirsty tongue. Help me, for I am suffering in this flame.'

25 "Father Of Many Nations (Abraham) said to him, 'My son, do you not remember? All your days were filled with good things, but the days of Creator Helps Him (Lazarus) were filled with sorrow and pain. It is now his time for comfort, but it is your time for sorrow and pain. 26 Look! There is a great canyon between us, so wide that none can make the journey from here to there.'

27 "The rich man *hung his head* and said, 'Please, my ancestor, send him back to the lodge 28 of my father and my five brothers. He can warn them of this place of suffering and pain, so they won't have to come here also.'

29 "Father Of Many Nations (Abraham) said to him, 'They have the words of Drawn From The Water (Moses) and the words of the prophets. Let your family listen to them.'

30 "'No!' the rich man cried out. 'If someone goes back to them from the world of the dead, they will turn their hearts back to Creator.'

31 "Father Of Many Nations (Abraham) *shook his head and* said, 'If your family will not listen to Drawn From The Water (Moses) and the prophets, then they will not listen even to one who comes back to life from the dead.'"

Trouble Will Come

17 Creator Sets Free (Jesus) said to the ones who walked the road with him, "This world of sorrow and pain will make many stumble, but how terrible it will be for the ones who go along with it. 2 It would be better to be thrown into the deep waters with a great stone tied to your neck than to cause even one of these little ones, who trust in me, to stumble on the path.

"When you are wronged, 3-4 look first at what is in your own heart. If one of your brothers or sisters *in the Sacred Family* has wronged you, then tell them face to face; if they turn around and ask forgiveness, then release them—even if they do this seven times in one day."

5 "Wisdomkeeper," his message bearers said, "help our weak faith!" 6 "If you had faith as small as a mustard seed," he replied, "you could also say to this mulberry tree, 'Come out by the roots and be planted in the sea,' and it would do what you say.

Doing Only What is Expected

7 "Would an elder who sent a young man out to hunt for a deer, when the young man returned, say to him, 'Sit down while I skin the deer and cook the meal for you?' 8 No, but he would say, 'Now skin the deer, then clean up and cook for me, then when I am finished, you can eat.'

9 "The young man is only doing what is expected and deserves no special thanks. 10 In the same way, when you have done everything the Great Spirit expects of you, serve him as you would an elder,

and do not expect to be rewarded for doing only what you should do."

Honor from an Outsider

¹¹ On His way to Village of Peace (Jerusalem), Creator Sets Free (Jesus) took the path following the border between High Place (Samaria) and Circle of Nations (Galilee). ¹² He went into a small village where ten men with a skin disease came across his path. ¹³ They *kept a respectful distance from him and* called loudly, "Creator Sets Free (Jesus)! Honored One!" they pleaded, "have pity on us!"

¹⁴ Creator Sets Free (Jesus) looked at them and said, "Go to the holy men and show yourselves to them."ʲ

Tribal Law instructed that a person healed of a skin disease must be pronounced ceremonially clean by a holy man.

They did what he said, and as they were on the way, they were healed. ¹⁵ One of the ten men, when he saw he was healed, returned to Creator Sets Free (Jesus) giving loud praise to the Great Spirit. ¹⁶ He then bowed down to honor Creator Sets Free (Jesus) and offered him thanks. This man was from High Place (Samaria).

All the people from there were despised and looked down on by the tribes of Wrestles With Creator (Israel).

¹⁷ Creator Sets Free (Jesus) said *to those who were watching,* "Were not ten men healed? Where then are the other nine? ¹⁸ Was the only one who returned to give thanks

and honor to the Great Spirit an outsider from High Place (Samaria)?"

¹⁹ Then he said to the man, "Stand up and be on your way. Your trust in me has healed you."

The Good Road Has Come

²⁰ Another time the Separated Ones (Pharisees) asked him, "When will we see the Land of Creator's Good Road?"

He said to them, *"Creator's Good Road is not what you expect.* It does not come with the outward signs you are looking for. *You will need new eyes to see it.* ²¹ No one will say, 'Here it is! I found it!' or 'Look! It is over there!' For Creator's Good Road is already here—in me, as I walk among you."

Signs of Troubled Times

²² He then said to his message bearers, "In the time of trouble ahead, you will long for the days when the True Human Being walked among you. Those days will be no more. ²³ People will say, 'Look! He is over there or over here!' Don't listen to them, ²⁴ for when the day of the True Human Being comes, it will be like lightning when it flashes and lights the whole sky. ²⁵ But first he will suffer many terrible things and be turned away by the people living today.

²⁶ "The days of the True Human Being will be the same as it was in the days of One Who Rests (Noah), before the great flood. ²⁷ The people were eating and

---

ʲ **17:14** Leviticus 14:2-32

drinking and getting married until the day that One Who Rests (Noah) entered the great wooden canoe. No one believed what was coming until the flood waters came, washed them away and drowned them all.

²⁸ "It will be the same as it was in the days of Covers His Head (Lot). The people were eating and drinking, trading goods, planting seeds, and building their lodges ²⁹ until the day came that Covers His Head (Lot) left Village of Bad Spirits (Sodom). Then rocks burning with fire fell from the sky and destroyed them all. ³⁰ This is how it will be when the True Human Being is revealed.

³¹ "When that day comes, the ones on their rooftops should flee, not even taking the time to get their belongings from inside their house. The ones who are working in the field should not take time to go home. ³² Remember what happened to the wife of Covers His Head (Lot)."

In the days of Covers His Head (Lot), the ancient Village of Bad Spirits (Sodom) was destroyed by fire-rocks that fell from the sky. He and his wife had to flee, leaving all behind. But his wife held back, and the ashes from the fire covered her, turning her into a mound of salt.

³³ "The ones who cling to their life's *belongings* will lose their own lives, but whoever is willing to leave everything behind will survive.

³⁴ "During that night two people will be asleep in bed, one will be taken away and the other left. ³⁵ Two women will be husking grain, one will be taken away and the other left.

³⁶⁻³⁷ "Taken where?" his followers asked him.

"To the place where the dead bodies lie and the eagles^k gather over them," he answered.

Never Give Up Praying

18 Creator Sets Free (Jesus) told them a story to show that they should pray at all times and never lose heart.

² *"Listen!"* he said. "There was a village that had a tribal council-chief that did not fear the Great Spirit or respect his fellow human beings. ³ A woman of that village, who had lost her husband, kept bothering him. She would say to him, 'Stand up for me against the one who has done me wrong!'

⁴⁻⁵ "The tribal council-chief ignored her at first, but the woman kept demanding that he help her. The council-chief grew weary, changed his thinking and said, 'This woman really troubles me. If I don't help her and right this wrong, she will never stop bothering me! I will see that she gets justice, not because I respect her or even fear the Great Spirit, but only because she won't give up until I help her.'"

⁶ Creator Sets Free (Jesus) then said, "Can you hear the words of this bad-hearted tribal council-

---

k 17:36-37 The same word for eagle can also be translated vulture.

chief? [7] If a council-chief like that will do what is right, how much more will the Great Spirit right the wrongs done to the ones who cry out to him day and night? Will he ignore their cries? No! [8] I tell you, he will not be slow to bring justice to them. But when the True Human Being comes, will he find this kind of faith anywhere in this land?"

Arrogance and Humility

[9] He then told this story to warn the ones who trusted in themselves and thought they were better than others:

[10] "Two men, a Separated One (Pharisee) and a tribal tax collector, went to the Great Spirit's Sacred Lodge to send up their prayers.

[11] "The Separated One (Pharisee) kept his distance from the tribal tax collector and prayed out loud, 'Creator, I thank you that I am not like the rest of mankind—like the ones who use force to get from others what they want, or who are not faithful in marriage, or who have no understanding of right or wrong. I thank you also that I am not like this tribal tax collector standing here! [12] I go without food twice a week for spiritual reasons and I give a tenth of all my gain.'

[13] "Now the tribal tax collector hung his head down and would not even lift his face to the world above. He beat his hands against his chest and cried out, 'Creator! Be kind and have pity on me. I am a pitiful man, full of bad thoughts and wrongdoings!'

[14] "Can you not see?" Creator Sets Free (Jesus) said. "The tribal tax collector returned home in good standing with Creator, but the Separated One (Pharisee) did not! The ones who think too highly of themselves will be brought down low; the ones who humble themselves will be lifted up."

Little Children and the Good Road

[15] The people were bringing their little children to Creator Sets Free (Jesus) so he would lay his hands on them *and bless them,* but his followers spoke harsh words to the ones bringing them.

[16] So Creator Sets Free (Jesus) said to them, "Let the little children come to me! Do not turn them away. Creator's Good Road belongs to the ones who are like these children. [17] I speak from my heart, unless you welcome Creator's Good Road in the way a little child does you will never walk on it."

Possessions or the Great Spirit?

[18] A spiritual leader came to Creator Sets Free (Jesus). "Good Wisdomkeeper," he asked, "what must I do to have the life of the world to come, that never fades— full of beauty and harmony?"

[19] "Why do you call me good?" he asked the man. "Only the Great Spirit is good. [20] You know the sacred instructions from Tribal Law: Do not be unfaithful in marriage, do not take the life of another, or take anything that is not yours. Do not lie about others,

and always give honor and respect to your parents."[l]

21 *"Wisdomkeeper,"* the man answered, "from my youth I have followed all of these instructions."

22 "Then only one thing remains," Creator Sets Free (Jesus) told him, "Take all of your possessions and give them to the ones who have none; then you will have great possessions in the world above. And then come, walk the good road with me."

23 The young man's heart fell to the ground and he hung his head, for he had many possessions.

24-25 A great sadness came to the face of Creator Sets Free (Jesus) as he looked at the man. And then he said, "Walking the Good Road is a hard thing for the ones who have many possessions. It would be easier for a moose[m] to squeeze through the eye of a beading needle."

26 After hearing this, they asked him, "How then can anyone walk the Good Road that sets all people free?"

27 Creator Sets Free (Jesus) *looked at them* and said, "This is only possible with the help of the Great Spirit."

28 Stands On The Rock (Peter) spoke up, "Can you see that we have left all our possessions, *and our relatives,* to walk the road with you?"

29 "I speak from my heart," he said to them, "No one who has left homes and families to walk the Good Road will go without. 30 For in this world they will gain an even greater family with many homes, and in the world to come, the life of beauty and harmony will be theirs."

The Road Ahead

31 Creator Sets Free (Jesus) took the twelve aside and told them again about what was coming on the road ahead.

"Consider closely what I am telling you," he reminded them. "We are on our way to the Sacred Village of Peace (Jerusalem), where all the words of the prophets about the True Human Being will come to pass. 32 He will be handed over to the People of Iron (Romans).[n] They will treat him shamefully, spit on him, 33 and put him to death, but on the third day he will come back to life."

34 But his twelve message bearers did not understand what he was saying. The meaning was hidden from their eyes.

A Blind Man Healed

35 As they walked the road toward Village of Peace (Jerusalem), they came to Moon Village (Jericho). A blind man was sitting by the road begging for food. 36 When he heard the sound of the passing crowd, he asked what was happening. 37 He was told that Creator Sets Free (Jesus), from Seed Planter Village (Nazareth), was passing by.

38 The blind man cried out in a loud voice, "Creator Sets Free (Jesus), descendant of Much Loved One (David), have pity on me!"

---

l 18:20 Deuteronomy 5:16-20   m 18:24-25 Lit., camel   n 18:32 Lit., Gentiles

39 The people in the front of the crowd scolded him and said, "Be quiet!"

That only made him cry out louder, "Descendant of Much Loved One (David), have pity on me!"

40 Creator Sets Free (Jesus) stopped walking and told them to bring the man to him. When the man was close, Creator Sets Free (Jesus) asked him, 41 "What do you want from me?"

"Wisdomkeeper," he said, "heal my eyes, so I can see again."

42 "Open your eyes and look around," he told the man. "Your trust in me has healed you."

43 As soon as he said this, the man could see!

The people laughed with joy as the man blinked his eyes and looked into their faces.

Right then the man began to walk the road with Creator Sets Free (Jesus), giving honor to the Great Spirit. And all the people who saw this also sang songs to thank the Great Spirit.

Restoring Pure Of Heart

19 Creator Sets Free (Jesus) was walking through Moon Village (Jericho). 2 There, a man named Pure Of Heart (Zacchaeus), who was a head tribal tax collector with many possessions, 3 was trying to see who was coming, but was too short to see over the crowd. 4 So he ran ahead and climbed up a tall tree to get a better view.

5 When Creator Sets Free (Jesus) came to the tree, he looked up and said, "Pure Of Heart (Zacchaeus),

come down from there and take me to your house, for I need a place to rest."

6 He quickly climbed down the tree and with a glad heart welcomed him into his house. 7 But when the people saw this, *they shook their heads.* "What is he doing?" they grumbled out loud. "Why would he go into the house of an outcast?"

8 Pure Of Heart (Zacchaeus) stood up to the crowd and said to Creator Sets Free (Jesus), "Hear me, Wisdomkeeper. I will give half my possessions to the ones who have none. If I have cheated anyone, I will give them back four times as much."

9 Creator Sets Free (Jesus) smiled and said, "This a good day, because this man and his family have finally been set free; for he also is a descendent of Father Of Many Nations (Abraham), *who had lost his way.* 10 The True Human Being has come to find the ones who have lost their way and guide them back again to the Good Road."

Rejecting the New Chief

11 Since they were now close to Village of Peace (Jerusalem), and his followers thought the Land of Creator's Good Road would appear as soon as they arrived, he decided it was time to tell them this story:

12 "There was a man who was born to be chief of a large tribal nation. The time had come for him to take his place as chief. But first he had to take a long journey to another land, *to meet with a council of many nations,* to be approved.

13 "Before he left, he called together ten trusted tribal members who worked for him. He gave them each one woven blanket of great value. 'Go,' he told them, 'and trade well until I return.'

"He then left on his journey to meet with the council.

14 "But many of his own people despised him, so they sent some messengers ahead of him to speak with the council. 'We do not want this man to be our chief,' they said.

"But the council did not listen to them.

15 *"Much later,* after being appointed as chief, he returned to his own tribal nation. He called together the trusted tribal members to whom he had given the woven blankets, to see how well they had traded.

16 "The first to come to him said, 'Honored chief, look, I now have ten blankets to return to you.'

17 "'You have done well!' the chief replied, 'Since you did well with this small thing, you will now represent me in ten villages.'

18 "The second man came to him, and said, 'Look, my chief, your one blanket is now five.'

19 "'Well done. You will now represent me in five villages,' the chief told him.

20 "Another came to him and said, 'See, my chief, I have returned to you the blanket you gave me. I folded it and hid it safely away. 21 I dared not trade with it, for I know you to be a harsh man and I was afraid. You take from others what is not yours and harvest food you did not plant.'

22 "'You have betrayed my trust,' he said to the man. 'Your own words will decide your fate! If you thought I was this way, 23 why did you not give your blanket to the trading post, and at least have something to show for it when I returned?'

24 "Then the newly appointed chief turned to the ones who stood close by and said, 'Take the blanket from him and give it to the one who has ten.'

25 "They were confused by this. 'But honored chief,' they said, 'he already has ten blankets!'

26 "The chief said to them, 'The ones who do well with what they have will be given more. But for the ones who do nothing, even what they have will be taken away.'"

Then the chief turned to the tribal members who had opposed his appointment.

27 "'Now bring to me the ones who opposed me before the council,' he said with authority. 'They will now have to die, while I watch, because they have made themselves my enemies.'"

He told them this so they would see that the Good Road would not come in the way they expected.

His Grand Entry

28 After he told this story, Creator Sets Free (Jesus) walked on ahead of his followers to Village of Peace (Jerusalem). 29-30 When he came to House of Figs (Bethany) at the foot

of Olive Mountain, he said to two of his followers, "Go to House of Unripe Figs (Bethphage) on the other side of the mountain. When you come into the village, you will see a young pony tied there that no one has ever ridden. Untie it and bring it to me. 31 If anyone asks what you are doing, say this to them, 'Our Wisdomkeeper is in need of it.'"

32 His followers did as they were told. When they arrived at the village, they found everything just as he had said. 33 When they started untying the pony, the owners asked them, "What are you doing?" 34 They answered the owners just as they had been instructed, so they were permitted to go.

35 They brought the young pony to Creator Sets Free (Jesus) and laid their *deer skins and pendleton* blankets on the pony. He then mounted the pony and began his ride.

Creator Sets Free (Jesus) came riding into the Sacred Village of Peace (Jerusalem) down Olive Mountain toward the Eastern entry into Village of Peace (Jerusalem) that is called Beautiful Gate. His twelve followers encircled him and led the pony forward.

He did not fit the powerful image of a conquering ruler, for he was not riding a warhorse; instead he rode a small, humble pony. No mighty warriors rode next to him. No dignitaries came out to meet him. It was mostly the common people who welcomed him that day.

36 As he rode forward, some of the people began to spread their *buffalo* robes on the road in front of Creator Sets Free (Jesus). 37 When he reached the foot of Olive Mountain, the whole village was in an uproar. His followers began to sing to Creator and shout out loud, praising him for the powerful signs they had seen.

38 "Blessed is the Grand Chief who comes representing the Great Spirit! Peace to the world above and honor and glory to the One Above Us All!" o

39 Some of the Separated Ones (Pharisees) who were in the crowd spoke up. "Wisdomkeeper!" they cried out, "Warn your followers to watch what they are saying."

It was a dangerous thing to call anyone a chief or ruler in front of the soldiers of the People of Iron (Romans) who were guarding the area.

40 "I will tell you this," he said to them. "If they were silenced, the very stones and rocks *we are walking on* would lift their voices and cry out!"

The Trail Where He Cried

41 As he rode forward, he could see the Sacred Village of Peace (Jerusalem), and tears began to flow down his face.

He could taste the salt from his tears as he opened his mouth in anguish.

42 "Jerusalem, O Jerusalem, you are the Sacred Village of Peace," he wept out loud. "Of all people, you should

o 19:38 Psalm 118:26

be the ones who would know the way of peace; but on this *sacred* day, the way of peace is hidden from your eyes.

⁴³ "In the days ahead your enemies will encircle you and close in on you from every side. You will be crushed and trampled down, along with all your children. ⁴⁴ Every lodge will fall, and not even one pole, log or stone will be left standing against another. All of this, because you did not know it was your time for the Great Spirit to visit you."

⁴⁵ Then he rode through the Beautiful Gate, into the village and up to the Sacred Lodge.

> *He entered the Lodge and came into the area called Gathering Place for the Nations. It was here that other nations could come to learn about the Great Spirit and his ways. The holy men were using this place to buy and sell the ceremonial animals. But it was so crowded that there was not enough room for the people from other nations who wanted to learn about Creator's ways. They were not honoring the purpose of this holy place.*

He entered the Lodge and began to force out the ones who were buying and selling the ceremonial animals. ⁴⁶ "It is written in the Sacred Teachings," he cried out, "'my Lodge will be a house of prayer; but you have turned it into a hideout for thieves!'ᵖ"

⁴⁷ In the days that followed, Creator Sets Free (Jesus) came each day to the Sacred Lodge to teach and tell his stories. The head holy men, the scroll keepers and the spiritual leaders took counsel together to plan new ways to have him killed; ⁴⁸ but they could not figure out what to do, for the people had great respect for him, and held on to every word he said.

The Spiritual Leaders Challenge Him

20 One day that week when Creator Sets Free (Jesus) was telling the Good Story at the Sacred Lodge, the head holy men and the scroll keepers came to him, along with the elders. ² "By what right do you do these things?" they challenged. "Who gave you this right?"

³ "I will answer your question," he said to them, "but first you must answer mine:

⁴ "The purification ceremony performed by He Shows Goodwill (John), was it from the world above, or did it come from human beings?"

> *The spiritual leaders looked at each other. They didn't know how to answer him. All the people there kept their ears wide open to hear what the spiritual leaders would say. Creator Sets Free (Jesus) stood before them and quietly held his ground.*

⁵ They put their heads together and talked it over. "If we say it is from the world above, he will ask us why we didn't listen to him. ⁶ If we say it is from human beings, the people would stone us to death, for they think He Shows Goodwill (John) is a great prophet."

---

p 19:46 Isaiah 56:7 and Jeremiah 7:11

7 So they said to him, "We do not know."

8 Creator Sets Free (Jesus) looked straight at them and said, "Then I will not answer your question either."

Story of the Vineyard

9 Then he turned again to the people and began to tell them this story:

"A tribal member planted a large vineyard, and rented it out to other tribal members for a share of the grapes. Then he traveled far away to another land to stay for a long time.

10 "When harvest time came, the tribal member who owned the vineyard sent a trusted messenger to gather his share of the grapes; but the farmers beat him and sent him away empty handed. 11 The vineyard owner sent another messenger; but they treated him shamefully, beat him, and sent him away also. 12 So he sent a third messenger, but they did the same things to him.

"The tribal member who owned the vineyard was at the end of his rope.

13 "'What can I do?' he wondered. 'I know,' he said to himself, 'I will send my much loved son. They will have to respect him.'

14 "When they saw that he had sent his son, they put their heads together and came up with an evil plan. 'This vineyard will one day belong to this son,' they schemed.

'If we kill him, the vineyard will be ours.'

15 "So they dragged him out to the edge of the vineyard, murdered him, and left his dead body there."

Creator Sets Free (Jesus) turned to the spiritual leaders.

"What will the owner of the vineyard do?" he asked.

He waited for an answer, but no one said a word.

16 Then he said, "He will return, put those dishonorable men to death and give the vineyard to others."

The spiritual leaders were insulted by this story.

"That must never happen!" they said.

17 Creator Sets Free (Jesus) looked at the spiritual leaders and said, "Then what do the Sacred Teachings mean when they say, 'The tree the lodge builders threw away has become the Chief Pole'? 18 The ones who stumble over this pole will be broken into pieces; and when it falls on them, they will be crushed *and scattered like dust in the wind.*"q

The Separated Ones Attack

19 When the head holy men and the scroll keepers realized that this story was about them, they looked for a way to arrest him; but they could not, for they were afraid of what the people might do. 20 So they kept an eye on him and sent spies who pretended to be good hearted to trap him in his words, so they would have a reason to turn him

q 20:18 Psalm 118:22

over to the power of the governor of People of Iron (Romans).

21 "Wisdomkeeper," the spies said to him. "We know you always speak the truth about the Great Spirit and represent him well. 22 Tell us what is permitted, should our tribal members pay taxes to the Ruler of the People of Iron (Caesar)? Yes or no?"

23 Creator Sets Free (Jesus) could see right through them. 24 "Show me one of their silver coins."

They found a silver coin and handed it to him. He took a good long look, holding it up to the sky to see it clearly. Then he turned the face of the coin toward them.

"Whose image and words are carved into this coin?" he asked.

"The Ruler of the People of Iron (Caesar)," they answered.

He handed the coin back to them.

25 "Then give to this ruler the things that are his," he said, "and give to the Great Spirit the things that belong to the Great Spirit."

26 The spiritual leaders had failed, right in front of the people, and could not use his words against him. They were amazed at his wisdom, and hung their heads in silence.

The Upright Ones Attack

27 Then some of the Upright Ones (Sadducees), who say there is no rising again from death, came to Creator Sets Free (Jesus) 28 to question him also.

"Wisdomkeeper," they said, "in the Law Drawn From The Water

(Moses) gave us these instructions: 'If a Tribal Member should die before having children, then his brother should marry his widow and give her children. This way the man will have descendants.'r

29 "In a family of seven brothers, the oldest took a wife, but died without children. 30 The next brother married her, but he also died with no children. 31 A third brother married her, and, like his other brothers, he died with no children. The same happened to all seven of them, 32 and, last of all, the woman also crossed over to death. 33 When they all come back to life in the new world, whose wife would she be, since all seven men married her?"

34 "Marriage belongs to this present world and to the ones who live in it," he answered, 35 "The ones who are chosen to rise to life in that world will not marry, for they will be like the spirit-messengers. 36 They will never die, for they are the children of the Great Spirit who raises them again to new life."

37 *And then he added,* "As to the dead rising again, listen to what the Sacred Teachings tell us that Drawn From The Water (Moses) said when he saw the burning bush. He calls Creator the 'Great Spirit of Father Of Many Nations (Abraham), He Made Us Laugh (Isaac), and Heel Grabber (Jacob).'s

38 "He is not the Great Spirit of the dead, but of the living—for to him all are alive."

---

r 20:28 Deuteronomy 25:5-6   s 20:37 Exodus 3:6

³⁹ Hearing this, some of the scroll keepers said to him, "Wisdomkeeper, you have answered well."

⁴⁰ After that none of the Upright Ones (Sadducees) dared to ask him any more questions.

⁴¹ So Creator Sets Free (Jesus) asked them a question: "How is it that you call the Chosen One the descendant of Much Loved One (David), ⁴² when Much Loved One (David) in the Sacred Songs says, 'The Great Chief said to my Great Chief, Sit down beside me at my right hand, my place of greatest honor, ⁴³ until I defeat your enemies by humbling them'?"^t

He paused to let his words sink in.

⁴⁴ "If Much Loved One (David) calls the Chosen One, 'My Great Chief,'" he asked them, "then how can the Chosen One be his descendant?"

The Upright Ones (Sadducees) had no answer for him.

⁴⁵ Then Creator Sets Free (Jesus) said to his followers, loud enough for all to hear, ⁴⁶ "Beware of the scroll keepers, who walk about dressed up in fancy regalia, who love to be noticed at the trading posts, who take the seats of honor at the gathering houses, and the best seats at the feasts. ⁴⁷ With many words they make long, empty prayers to trick widows into giving them their homes and possessions; but they will all come to a worse end than others."

A Sacrificial Gift

21 Creator Sets Free (Jesus) looked up and saw people with many possessions bringing their gifts to the Giveaway at the Sacred Lodge. ² He then saw a poor widow walk up and place two poorly beaded earrings on the blanket, worth almost nothing.

³ "I speak from my heart," he said to his followers, "this widow's gift is better than all the others. ⁴ When they put their gifts on the blanket, they gave only a small part of their many possessions; but this poor widow has given all she had."

Signs and Warnings

⁵ Some of his followers began to point out to him the beauty of the Great Lodge with its handsomely carved logs, its large stones, and ceremonial gifts.

A look of sadness came over the face of Creator Sets Free (Jesus).

⁶ "Take a good long look," he said, "for in the days ahead, all of this will fall to the ground. Not one log will be left standing against another."

They looked at him with worried faces.

⁷ "Wisdomkeeper, when will this happen?" they asked. "What will be the sign?"

⁸ "Make sure no one leads you down the wrong path," he warned them, "for many will falsely represent me and say, 'I am the

---

t **20:43** Psalm 110:1

Chosen One, *follow me*, there is no time left!' Do not follow after them.

9 "When you hear of wars and uprisings, do not fear, for these things will come first—but the end is not yet. 10 Tribal wars will break out, and nations will war against nations. 11 There will be great earthquakes, food will be scarce, sickness will spread everywhere, and bad signs will appear in the sky.

12 "Before all of this happens, you will be betrayed by your own people. They will hunt you down, drag you into their gathering houses, and put you in jail. They will hand you over to the government and officials *of the People of Iron (Romans)*. All of this they will do to you because of me and my name. 13 But remember, this will be your chance to represent me and tell them the Good Story. 14 Do not worry about what to say ahead of time to defend yourselves, 15 for I will give you the mouth of a wisdomkeeper, and no enemy will be able to answer you or prove you wrong.

16 "You will be betrayed by your own family members and friends. They will even have some of you killed. 17 They will all hate you because you are representing me and my teachings.

18 "But none of these things can truly harm you, *u* 19 so you must stand up strong and never give up trusting in me, for my life inside you will help you walk with firm steps."

The Day of Sorrow and Destruction

20 "When you see Village of Peace (Jerusalem) surrounded and encamped about by the armies *of the People of Iron (Romans)*, you will know that the time of her destruction has come. *v* 21 The people of the Land of Promise (Judea) should run to the mountains for safety, and the ones who are inside the walls of Village of Peace (Jerusalem) must get out, and the ones outside should not go in. 22 For this is the time when Creator will let justice have its way, to bring the bad end spoken of in the Sacred Teachings.

23 "It will be a bad time for women who are pregnant or nursing their babies, for great sorrow and trouble will come like an angry storm upon the land and against this people. 24 The great Village of Peace (Jerusalem) will be cut down by the long knives; the people will be taken captive and scattered into all the nations. The Sacred Village of Peace (Jerusalem) will then be trampled down by the Outside Nations until their time has come to an end.

25 "There will also be signs in the sun, moon and stars, and on the earth the nations will tremble with fear. Panic and confusion will grow strong when they hear the sea roar and see the waves swell. 26 The people will shake with fear, and hearts will fall to the ground when they see what is happening to the world around them. Even the powers of the world above will tremble and shake.

---

u 21:18 Lit., Not one hair on your head will perish.   v 21:20 Matthew 24:15; Mark 13:14

²⁷"Then they will look up and see the True Human Being coming with power, riding on the clouds, and showing his great beauty!^w

²⁸"When you see all these things begin to happen, stand strong, my followers, and lift up your heads; for the time of your captivity will soon come to an end!"

Story About the Fig Tree

²⁹Then he told them this wisdom-story: "Look at this fig tree or any tree, and see what it is saying to you. ³⁰When the branches of a tree grow soft and buds appear, you know that it is nearly summer. ³¹In the same way when you see these things happening, you will know that Creator's Good Road is about to come into full bloom.

³²"I speak from my heart! All of this will happen to this generation, during the lifetime of the people who live today. ³³What I have told you is sure, for my words will last longer than the sky above and the earth below.

³⁴"So keep your eyes straight, do not let your hearts fall to the ground giving yourselves to drinking, or worrying about your life's possessions; or that day will take you by surprise. ³⁵For it will come without warning, to all who live on the land, like a beaver that is snared in a trap. ³⁶So stay on guard, praying that you will find a safe path through this time, and stand strong before the True Human Being."

³⁷During the day Creator Sets Free (Jesus) would teach and tell his stories at the Sacred Lodge. Then at night he would go to where he was lodging on Olive Mountain. ³⁸Then, in the morning, all the people would gather again at the Lodge to listen to him.

The Betrayer Makes His Move

22 It was time once again for the traditional feast of Bread Without Yeast, called Passover. ²The head holy men and the scroll keepers were looking for a way to capture Creator Sets Free (Jesus) and have him put to death, for they feared his influence over the people.

³During that time, Accuser (Satan) wrapped himself around the heart of Speaks Well Of (Judas), *also called* Village Man (Iscariot), who was one of the twelve followers of Creator Sets Free (Jesus).

⁴He went to the head holy men and the Lodge guards, and told them of his plan to turn against Creator Sets Free (Jesus). ⁵With glad hearts they agreed to pay him. ⁶He agreed to the amount and began to wait for the right time to betray Creator Sets Free (Jesus) when there were no crowds around him.

Preparing for the Ceremonial Meal

⁷It was now the day of Bread Without Yeast, when the ceremonial Passover lamb would be sacrificed *and eaten.*

---

w 21:27 Daniel 7:13

⁸ Creator Sets Free (Jesus) chose Stands On The Rock (Peter) and He Shows Goodwill (John), "Go and prepare a place for us to eat the ceremonial meal," he instructed them.

⁹ "Where should we go?" they asked him.

¹⁰ "Go into the village," he instructed them, "and look for a man carrying a pouch of water. He will take you to a lodge. Go in with him ¹¹ and say to the headman of the house, 'Our Wisdomkeeper wants to know where the room is to eat the Passover meal with his followers.' ¹² He will then take you to a large upper room that will be ready for you, there you can prepare the meal."

¹³ They did as he said and found everything was just as he told them, so they prepared the ceremonial meal.

The Ceremonial Meal Begins

¹⁴ When it was time for the ceremonial meal to begin, Creator Sets Free (Jesus) and his twelve message bearers sat down *around a table.*

Creator Sets Free (Jesus) looked into the faces of his followers.

¹⁵ "How I have longed to sit and eat this Passover meal with you before I suffer," he said.

¹⁶⁻¹⁸ He then lifted up a cup of wine, gave thanks for it, and said, "Take this and share it with one another."

The cup was then passed from Creator Sets Free (Jesus) to each of them, and one by one they all drank from it.

Creator Sets Free (Jesus) said to them, "Listen to me closely, I will not drink from the fruit of this vine again until it finds its full meaning in the Land of Creator's Good Road."

During the meal ¹⁹ Creator Sets Free (Jesus) took some of the bread, *lifted it up* and gave thanks. He broke it into pieces, gave some to each of his followers and said, "This is my body, my gift to you, take it and eat it. Do this to remember me."

They all passed the bread around the table and ate it with wondering hearts, because this was something new. Creator Sets Free (Jesus) was showing his followers that this ancient ceremony was finding its full meaning in him.

²⁰ In the same way, after the meal was over, he took a cup *of wine,* lifted it up *and gave thanks.* He gave it to his followers and said, "This cup *of wine* is for the New Peace Treaty.ˣ It is my life-blood poured out for you."

²¹ "But look and see!" he said to the surprise of all. "The one who has turned against me is sitting at this table. ²² The True Human Being will walk the path that has been chosen for him, but it will not go well for the one who betrays him."

²³ His message bearers looked around at one another, asking who among them would do such a thing.

---

x 22:20 New Covenant

Who Is the Greatest?

²⁴ This led to an argument about which one of them was to be seen as the first and greatest among them.

²⁵ So Creator Sets Free (Jesus) reminded them, "Rulers from the Nations show their power by forcing people around, and then call it 'helping them.' ²⁶ This will not be the way of the ones who walk my road. The greatest among you will be least, like a child, and the rulers will be like household servants."

He let his words sink into their hearts.

²⁷ "Who is the greater one?" he asked. "The one who is being served or the one who serves?"

They all hung their heads and would not look him in the eye.

"Is it not the one being served?" he responded. "But here I am serving you."

The voice of Creator Sets Free (Jesus) became full of compassion and love. His followers lifted their heads up and looked at their Wisdomkeeper.

²⁸ "You have stood with me even in my time of sorrow and testing. ²⁹ My Father has made me the Chief of the Good Road. As Chief, I give you the right to walk this Road with me ³⁰ and share my table. There you will sit in twelve council seats and decide all things for the tribes of Wrestles With Creator (Israel)."

All Of You Will Turn Away

The Passover meal was coming to an end. It was time to close the ceremony and face the dark night ahead. Turning to Stands On The Rock (Peter), Creator Sets Free (Jesus) spoke to him using his family name.

³¹ "One Who Hears (Simon), hear me!" he said. "Accuser (Satan) has asked to put you all to the test, like one who separates the grain from the husks. ³² But I have prayed for you that your failure will not turn you from the Good Road. When you turn back once again, then help the others to do the same."

³³ But One Who Hears (Simon) *could not hear, so he* said, "Wisdomkeeper, I am ready to go with you to both prison and death!"

³⁴ Creator Sets Free (Jesus) *looked at him with sad eyes and* said, "Stands On The Rock (Peter), listen to me! Before the rooster crows, this very night, you will deny that you know who I am. *Not once, not twice, but* three times."

Trouble Ahead

Creator Sets Free (Jesus) knew that trouble was coming, ³⁵ so he said, "When I sent you out *to tell the Good Story to the villages,* you took no money pouch, no traveling bundle, not even extra moccasins. Did you need anything?"

"Nothing," they answered.

³⁶ *"That is good,"* he said, "but now take your money pouch and your traveling bundle with you."

Then he spoke of what they would need to face that very night.

"Also, if you have no long knife, then trade your outer garment for one, ³⁷ for there is another prophecy in the Sacred Teachings that tells what will happen to me, that says, 'He was numbered with the rebels.'ʸ This also must find its full meaning and come to an end in me."

³⁸ "Wisdomkeeper!" they said, "Look, here are two long knives."

"That will be enough," he answered.

Prayer of Suffering

³⁹ Creator Sets Free (Jesus) and his followers left from there and went to the place where he often prayed at Olive Mountain. ⁴⁰ When they arrived, he said to them, "Pray that you will have the strength to face this time of testing ahead of you."

⁴¹⁻⁴² He went from them about as far as one can throw a stone. He lowered himself to the ground, fell on his face and sent his voice to Creator, "If you want, my Father, you can take this bitter road of pain and sorrow away from me, but even so I want to walk your path, not my own."

The night was silent and cold as Creator Sets Free (Jesus) trembled and prayed. The powers of darkness were pressing in hard.

⁴³ While he prayed, a spirit-messenger from the world above appeared, giving him strength. ⁴⁴ In great agony he prayed with renewed strength, until his sweat began to fall like great drops of blood watering the ground.

⁴⁵ When he had finished sending his voice to the Great Spirit, he got up and found his followers sleeping. ⁴⁶ "Why are you sleeping?" he asked.

"Wake up and pray for strength to face this time of testing!"

The Fiery Trial Begins

⁴⁷ While Creator Sets Free (Jesus) was speaking, suddenly a crowd stormed in led by Speaks Well Of (Judas), one of the twelve. He walked up to Creator Sets Free (Jesus) to greet him.

⁴⁸ "Will you betray the True Human Being with a kiss?" he said to him.

⁴⁹ When his followers saw what was happening, they said, "Wisdomkeeper, should we strike with our long knives?"

⁵⁰ Before he could answer them, one of them drew his long knife from its sheath and cut off the right ear of the servant of the chief holy man.

⁵¹ "Stop! No more fighting!" Creator Sets Free (Jesus) cried out. Then he touched the man's ear and healed it. ⁵² He then turned to the head holy men, the Lodge soldiers, and the council elders, who had come to take him.

"Why do you come at me with clubs and long knives as if I were a thief?" he asked them. ⁵³ "Did I not sit with you every day in the Sacred Lodge? Why didn't you take me then? This is your time, and you have given the powers of darkness their day."

⁵⁴ The Lodge soldiers grabbed hold of him, dragged him away, and took him to the house of the chief holy man. Watching from

---

y 22:37 Isaiah 53:12

a distance, Stands On The Rock (Peter) followed them.

Stands On The Rock Denies Him

55 Some of the men built a fire in the courtyard and sat down to warm themselves. Stands On The Rock (Peter) sat down with them. 56 When a servant girl noticed him sitting by the fire, she looked closely into his face and said, "This man was with Creator Sets Free (Jesus)!"

57 "Woman," he denied, "I do not know the man."

58 A short time later someone else noticed him, and said, "You are one of his followers."

"I am not!" he argued back.

59 About one hour later another man accused him, "He must be one of his followers, for he is also from Circle of Nations (Galilee)."

60 "Man!" Stands On The Rock (Peter) defended himself, "I do not know what you are talking about."

Before he could get the words out of his mouth, a rooster crowed. 61 Then Creator Sets Free (Jesus) turned and looked at him *from a distance.*

Stands On The Rock (Peter) remembered what he had been told earlier, "Before the rooster crows today, you will deny three times that you know me."

62 Then Stands On The Rock (Peter) ran out of the gate, *at the first light of dawn,* and wept bitter tears *as he stumbled down the road.*

The Grand Council Questions Him

63 The soldiers who were guarding Creator Sets Free (Jesus) began to mock and beat him with their fists. 64 They put a blindfold over his eyes. "Prophesy to us! Tell us who struck you!" 65 they laughed, insulting him *with cruel words and twisted faces.*

66 As the sun began to rise, the Grand Council[z] of elders, along with the head holy men and the scroll keepers, all came together. They brought Creator Sets Free (Jesus) into the council house.

67 "If you are the Chosen One, then tell us!" they demanded.

"If I say that I am, you will not believe me, 68 and if I ask for your answer, you will not tell me." 69 And then he said, "But from now on the True Human Being will be seated at the right hand of the Great Power."[a]

70 Then with one voice they asked, "Are you then the Son of the Great Spirit?"

"You have said it," he answered them. "I am."

71 "Why question any more witnesses?" the council ruled. "We have heard it ourselves from his own mouth."

Questioned by the People of Iron

23 When they were done, they tied ropes around him again. All the ones who had gathered there got up and followed as they took Creator Sets Free (Jesus)

---

z 22:66 The Sanhedrin, the council of seventy that served as supreme court for the tribes of Wrestles With Creator (Israel).   a 22:69 Psalm 110:1

to Spear Of The Great Waters (Pilate), the governor of the People of Iron (Romans).

Spear Of The Great Waters (Pilate) represented the People of Iron (Romans). His job was to keep the "peace" and make sure there were no uprisings among the tribes. He came out of his headquarters to hear the charges against Creator Sets Free (Jesus).

2 So they began to accuse him, "We caught this man misleading our nation and telling people not to pay taxes to the government of the People of Iron (Romans). He tells the people that he is the Chosen One, a Great Chief."

3 Spear Of The Great Waters (Pilate) turned to Creator Sets Free (Jesus) and asked him, "Do you say that you are chief of the tribes of Wrestles With Creator (Israel)?"

"It is you who have said it," he replied.

4 Spear Of The Great Waters (Pilate) turned to the head holy men and said in front of all the people, "I see no reason to find this man guilty."

5 But they kept accusing him and saying, "He is making trouble with the people of the Land of Promise (Judea), spreading his teachings from Circle of Nations (Galilee) to Jerusalem."

6 After hearing this and finding out Creator Sets Free (Jesus) was from Circle of Nations (Galilee), 7 he decided to send him to Looks Brave (Herod), who was in Village of Peace (Jerusalem) for the festival; for Looks Brave (Herod) was chief of the territory of Circle of Nations (Galilee).

Questioned by Chief Looks Brave

8 Chief Looks Brave (Herod) was happy to see him. He had waited a long time for this, for he had heard much about Creator Sets Free (Jesus). He was hoping to see some powerful medicine come from him.

9-10 The head holy men and scroll keepers made strong accusations against him, so Looks Brave (Herod) dug deep with many questions.

But Creator Sets Free (Jesus) stood silent and gave no answer.

11 Chief Looks Brave (Herod) mocked him along with his soldiers. They dressed him in a fancy robe and sent him back to the People of Iron (Romans). 12 Looks Brave (Herod) and Spear Of The Great Waters (Pilate) had been enemies, but on that day they became friends.

Back to the People of Iron

13 When they brought Creator Sets Free (Jesus) back to Spear Of The Great Waters (Pilate), he then gathered the head holy men, the spiritual leaders, and the people together 14 and said to them, "You told me this man was a troublemaker, but I questioned him and found him not guilty of your accusations. 15 Looks Brave (Herod), one of your own people, also questioned him and found nothing wrong with him. Can't you see that this man has done nothing that deserves death? 16 I will have him whipped and release him."

¹⁷By tradition the People of Iron (Romans) would release one criminal during the festival. ¹⁸But they all shouted, "No! Not Creator Sets Free (Jesus)! Instead release Son Of His Father (Barabbas)!" ¹⁹Now this man was a troublemaker who had caused an uprising and had been imprisoned for murder.

²⁰Spear Of The Great Waters (Pilate) wanted to release Creator Sets Free (Jesus), so he asked again what they wanted to do with Creator Sets Free (Jesus). ²¹The crowd began to roar, "Death! Death on the cross!"

²²Spear Of The Great Waters (Pilate) *quieted the crowd and* a third time said, "Why! What evil has he done? I have not found him guilty or worthy of death. I will have him beaten and then set him free."

²³The crowd would not back down. Louder and louder they demanded his death on the cross again and again, ²⁴until Spear Of The Great Waters (Pilate) finally gave them what they wanted. He made his official decision, ²⁵released Son Of His Father (Barabbas) a man of violence, guilty of uprising and murder; and he turned Creator Sets Free (Jesus), *the man of peace,* over to what the people wanted.

The cross was used by the People of Iron (Romans) as an instrument of torture to strike fear into criminals or anyone who dared to rise up against their empire. Iron nails would be used to pierce the hands and feet of the victims, fastening them to the tree-pole and its crossbeam. They would then hang there until dead. It was one of the most painful and cruel ways to die ever created by human beings. Often the victim was forced to carry the large wooden crossbeam to the place where they would be executed.

Nailed to the Cross

²⁶The soldiers then marched Creator Sets Free (Jesus) away. A man named He Hears (Simon), from Strong Wall (Cyrene) *in northern Africa,* was just entering Village of Peace (Jerusalem). The soldiers forced him to walk behind Creator Sets Free (Jesus) and carry the crossbeam for him.

²⁷A large crowd of people trailed behind. Some of the women were wailing and crying out loud. ²⁸Creator Sets Free (Jesus) turned to them and said, "Daughters of Village of Peace (Jerusalem), weep not for me but for yourselves and your children.

²⁹"The time is coming soon when people will say, 'It is better for the women who have borne no children, *for they will not have to watch them die.*' ³⁰People will say to the mountains and the hills, 'Fall on us and cover us over.'*ᵇ*

³¹"If they do this to a green tree, what will they do to the trees that are dead and dry?"

³²Two other men, both of them criminals, were also walking the road with him to be put to death.

³³When they came to the place called "The Skull," they nailed the

---

b 23:30 Hosea 10:8

hands and feet of Creator Sets Free (Jesus) to the cross. They did the same for the two criminals, putting one on each side of him.

34 "Father, forgive them!" Creator Sets Free (Jesus) cried out. "They do not know what they are doing."

The soldiers divided up his garments and gambled for them by drawing straws.c

35 The people watched as the spiritual leaders mocked him. "He set others free," they said, "why can't he free himself if he is Creator's Chosen One?"

36 The soldiers offered Creator Sets Free (Jesus) wine mixed with bitter herbs 37 and mocked him. "If you are the Great Chief of the tribes," they laughed, "then set yourself free."

38 Above his head, carved above the crossbeam, were these words in three languages:

THIS IS THE CHIEF
OF THE TRIBES
OF WRESTLES WITH CREATOR

39 One of the thieves next to him spewed out angry words, "If you are the Chosen One, then save yourself and us!"

40 Then the other thief spoke up and said, "Have you no fear or respect for the Great Spirit? 41 We are guilty and suffering for our own wrongdoings, but this man has done nothing wrong!"

42 The man turned to Creator Sets Free (Jesus) and said to him, "Honored One, remember me when you come into the power of your Good Road."

43 Creator Sets Free (Jesus) looked at the man and said, "Listen closely, before the sun sets today, you will walk with me in the beautiful garden."d

44 It was now midday, for the sun had reached the center of the sky.e A great shadow of darkness covered the land like a blanket; the sky remained dark until mid-afternoon.f 45 The light of the sun grew dim, and the great heavy blanket that hung over the entry to the Most Holy Place in the Sacred Lodge was torn in two down the middle.

46 At the same time Creator Sets Free (Jesus) cried out with his last breath, "O Great Father, my spirit is in your hands!"g

Creator Sets Free (Jesus) was dead.

47 One of the head soldiers of the People of Iron (Romans), who saw all these things, honored the Great Spirit by saying, "He must have been an upright man, not deserving death."

48 When the large crowd that had gathered to watch saw and heard all that was happening, they began to wail and beat their fists against their chests as they walked home.

49 Many friends of Creator Sets Free (Jesus) stood watching from a distance, along with the women who had walked the road with him from Circle of Nations (Galilee).

---

c 23:34 Psalm 22:18   d 23:43 Paradise   e 23:44 Lit., the sixth hour   f 23:44 Lit., the ninth hour
g 23:46 Psalm 31:5

Preparation for His Burial

50-51 A man named He Gives More (Joseph), sat on the Grand Council of elders, but had not agreed with the decision to put Creator Sets Free (Jesus) to death. He was a good hearted and upright man from the tribal village of High Mountain (Arimathea), one who looked for Creator's Good Road.

52 He went to Spear Of The Great Waters (Pilate) and asked for the body of Creator Sets Free (Jesus). 53 He then took it down from the cross and ceremonially wrapped his body with soft cloths. Then he laid the body in a newly carved burial cave that had never been used.

54 It was still the Day of Preparation for the Passover, and a Day of Resting would soon begin. 55 After the women who had walked the road with him from Circle of Nations (Galilee) saw where they put his body, 56 they left and went to prepare herbal spices and sweet smelling ointments. Then they settled into their homes and followed the instructions for Day of Resting.

Death Defeated

24 It was now sunrise on the first day of the week. The women who had prepared the spices and oils were on their way to the burial cave. 2 When they arrived, they saw that the large stone in front of the cave had been rolled away. 3 They went inside, only to find the body of Creator Sets Free (Jesus) was gone!

4 They were standing there in amazement and wonder when suddenly two men appeared beside them dressed in shining white outfits. 5 The women, trembling with fear, fell down to the ground on their faces.

The men said, "Why do you look for the living in the place of the dead? 6 He is not here, he has returned to life. Do you not remember what he told you in Circle of Nations (Galilee)? 7 That the True Human Being would be turned over to the ones with bad hearts. They would put him to death on the cross, but he would come back to life on the third day."

8 Then the women remembered what he had said. 9 They hurried back to tell the eleven message bearers and the others what they had seen and heard. 10 There was Strong Tears (Mary) of the village of Creator's High Lodge (Magdala), Woman Of His Goodwill (Joanna) and Brooding Tears (Mary) the mother of He Takes Over (James), and other women with them.

These women told the message bearers and the others what they saw with their own eyes. 11 But the men did not believe the women, thinking it was only empty talk.

12 But Stands On The Rock (Peter) ran to the burial cave. He bent down to look inside and saw strips of cloth lying there, *but no sign of the body of Creator Sets Free (Jesus)*. He then walked away wondering what had happened.

The Road to Warm Springs

13 On the same day, two of the followers of Creator Sets Free

(Jesus) were walking to the Village of Warm Springs (Emmaus), seven miles out from Village of Peace (Jerusalem). [14] As they walked along, they were talking about all that had happened. [15] Creator Sets Free (Jesus) came alongside them as they walked, [16] but their eyes were kept from seeing who he was.

[17] He said to them, "What are you talking about?"

They stopped walking and a look of sadness fell over their faces. [18] One of the men, Honored By His Father (Cleopas), answered him, "How can you not know about the things that have happened in Village of Peace (Jerusalem)? You must be coming from far away."

[19] "What things are you talking about?" he asked.

"About Creator Sets Free (Jesus) from Seed Planter Village (Nazareth). He was a prophet from the Great Spirit, with powerful medicine, who did many good things among all the people. [20] The head holy men and other leaders handed him over to the People of Iron (Romans) to be put to death on the cross. [21] We had hoped that he would free the tribes of Wrestles With Creator (Israel) *from the People of Iron (Romans)*. It is now the third day since they killed him on the cross, [22-23] but today some women told us an amazing story.

Early this morning they went to his burial cave and found that his body was not there. They told us about visions of spirit-messengers who told them he was alive! [24] Some of our men went to see with their own eyes and found the empty cave,

but they did not see Creator Sets Free (Jesus)."

[25] "Why are your hearts so slow to believe the words of the prophets?" he said. [26] "It should be clear to you that the Chosen One would suffer first before he would be lifted up and honored above all."

[27] So Creator Sets Free (Jesus) told them his story, beginning with Drawn From The Water (Moses) and all the prophets. He showed them how all the ancient Sacred Teachings were written about the Chosen One and pointed the way to him.

They still didn't know it was Creator Sets Free (Jesus) talking to them.

[28] As they entered the village, he walked on as if to go further. [29] They said to him, "Please, stay with us. It is late and the sun will soon set."

So he went into the lodging house with them. [30] When they sat down to eat a meal together, Creator Sets Free (Jesus) took some bread into his hands. He gave thanks and broke it, giving each of them a piece. [31] Suddenly, their eyes were opened and they knew who he was, but he vanished right in front of them.

[32] The men looked at each other in wide-eyed wonder and said, "It felt like our hearts were on fire when he was talking with us on the road, showing us the meaning of the Sacred Teachings!"

[33] They got up without finishing their meal and walked back to Village of Peace (Jerusalem) as fast as they could, for the sun was setting.

They found where the eleven had gathered together with the others.

³⁴ They were saying, "Our Wisdomkeeper is alive! He has shown himself to One Who Hears (Simon)."

³⁵ So the two men told them what happened on the road and how their eyes were opened when Creator Sets Free (Jesus) broke the bread into pieces.

The Message Bearers See Him

³⁶ Before the men finished speaking, suddenly Creator Sets Free (Jesus) himself was standing there among them. "Peace be with you!" he said to them.

³⁷ Filled with fear, they all moved back from him, thinking he was a ghost. ³⁸ "Why are you trembling?" he asked. "Why do you doubt what your eyes see? ³⁹ Look at my hands and feet. Touch me. A ghost does not have flesh and bone, as I have."

⁴⁰ Then he showed them his hands and feet. ⁴¹ They still could not believe their eyes, and with glad but fearful hearts they could only stare at him.

Then he said to them, "Give me something to eat." ⁴² They gave him some cooked fish ⁴³ and he ate it in front of them. ⁴⁴ As he ate, he said this to them, "When I was with you before, I told you that all the words of Drawn From The Water (Moses), the Prophets, and the Sacred Book of Songs must find their full meaning in me."

⁴⁵ He then opened their minds so they could see the full meaning of the Sacred Teachings, ⁴⁶ and said to them, "The Sacred Teachings foretold long ago that the Chosen One would walk a path of suffering. He would then die and rise to life on the third day.

⁴⁷ "It was also foretold that, beginning in the Sacred Village of Peace (Jerusalem), the Good Story would be told to all nations. This story will change hearts and minds and release people from their bad hearts and broken ways.

⁴⁸ "You, my message bearers, have seen these things with your own eyes so that you can go and tell others. ⁴⁹ But first you must wait in Village of Peace (Jerusalem) until I send to you the Holy Spirit, just as my Father promised. He will dress you in my regalia, with power coming down from the world above."

He Returns to the World Above

⁵⁰ Creator Sets Free (Jesus) then walked with them to House of Figs (Bethany). He lifted his hands and spoke blessing words over them; ⁵¹ and as he spoke, he was taken up into the world above.

⁵² As he went up, his followers bowed down to honor him, and then with glad hearts they returned to the Sacred Village of Peace (Jerusalem). ⁵³ Day by day they gathered at the Sacred Lodge, praying and giving thanks to the Great Spirit.

Long ago, in the time before all days, at the beginning of all things...

The Great Spirit created the world above and the earth below. At that time, our mother earth was an empty wasteland with no form or beauty, and great darkness was over the face of the ancient deep waters. The Breath of the Great Spirit moved over the surface of the waters like an eagle brooding over her nest. Then Creator sounded his voice. "Let light be!" he said. And light was! The Great Spirit could see that light was good, so he separated the light from the darkness. Creator gifted the light with the name 'day' and to the darkness he gave the name 'night.' Then the night faded and morning came. The first day.

Genesis Chapter One
Verses One to Five

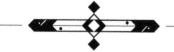

He Shows Goodwill

Tells the Good Story

Gospel of John

FIRST NATIONS VERSION

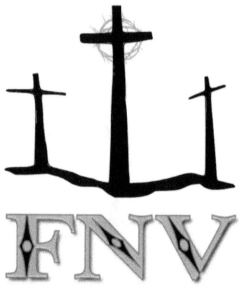

He Shows Goodwill
Tells the Good Story
(Gospel of John)

Creator's Word
Comes Down

1 ¹⁻²Long ago, in the time before all days, before the creation of all things, the Word was there face to face with the Great Spirit. This Word fully represents Creator and shows us who he is and what he is like. He has always been there from the beginning, for the Word and Creator are one and the same. ³Through the Word all things came into being, and not one thing exists that he did not create.

⁴Creator's life shined out from the Word, giving light to all human beings. This is the true Light that comes to all the peoples of the world and shines on everyone. ⁵The Light shines into the darkness, and the darkness cannot overcome it or put it out.

⁶⁻⁷Into the wilderness of the Land of Promise (Judea) came a man named He Shows Goodwill (John). He was sent by the Great Spirit to tell what he knew about the Light so everyone could believe. ⁸He was not the Light but came to speak the truth about the Light. ⁹The true Light that shines on all people was coming into the darkness of this world.

¹⁰He came down into this world, and even though he made all things, the world did not recognize him. ¹¹Even his own tribe did not welcome or honor him. ¹²But all who welcome and trust him receive their birthright as children of the Great Spirit. ¹³They are born in a new way, not from a human father's plans or desires, but born from above—by the Great Spirit.

¹⁴Creator's Word became a flesh and blood human being and pitched his sacred tent among us, living as one of us. We looked upon his great beauty and saw how honorable he was, the kind of honor held only by this one Son who fully represents his Father—full of his great kindness and truth.

¹⁵He Shows Goodwill (John) told what he knew about him, and cried out with a loud voice, "The one I have told you about is here!

He comes after me, but is much greater—*my Elder! He has more honor, for even though he is thought to be younger,* he existed before I was born."

[16] From the fullness of his being we have all had many gifts of kindness poured out on us. [17] Drawn From The Water (Moses) gave us our Tribal Laws, but great kindness and truth came from Creator Sets Free (Jesus)—the Chosen One.

[18] No one has ever seen the Great Spirit; but the one Son, who is himself the Great Spirit, has shown us what he is like.

Questions from the Tribal Leaders

[19] Some of the holy men and Tribal Leaders[a] from the tribes of Wrestles With Creator (Israel) were sent from Village of Peace (Jerusalem).

They came to question He Shows Goodwill (John). This is how he answered them.

"Who are you?" they asked.

[20] He knew what they were asking, so he hid nothing, and said plainly, "I am not the Chosen One."

[21] "Who are you then?" they demanded. "The prophet from long ago, Great Spirit Is Creator (Elijah)?"

"No," he answered, "I am not."

"Are you The Prophet[b] *who is to come?*" they asked.

"No," was his answer again.

[22] So they said to him, "Tell us who you are, so we will have an answer for the ones who sent us. What do you have to say about yourself?"

He Shows Goodwill (John) looked at the spiritual leaders straight in the eyes and spoke with authority as he announced the full meaning of the ancient prophecy.

[23] "I am saying the same thing the prophet Creator Will Help Us (Isaiah) said. I am a voice howling in the desert, 'Make a straight pathway for our Honored Chief.'"

[24] These tribal leaders were sent by the Separated Ones (Pharisees), [25] so they asked He Shows Goodwill (John), "Why do you perform the purification ceremony if you are not the Chosen One, or Great Spirit Is Creator (Elijah), or The Prophet *who is to come?*"

[26] "I perform the purification ceremony with water," he answered, "but there is one you do not know, who is walking among you. [27] He is the one who comes after me, but he has greater honor. I am not even worthy to untie his moccasins."

[28] These things took place in House of Figs (Bethany) on the far side of the river Flowing Down (Jordan).

Creator's Lamb

The tribes of Wrestles With Creator (Israel) performed a ceremony every year, where a lamb was killed and then ceremonially eaten. This was to remind them of the time when the Great Spirit set them free from

---

a 1:19 Levites   b 1:21 Deuteronomy 18:15

their slavery to the ruler of Black Land (Egypt) and took them to a new land.[c]

29 The next day He Shows Goodwill (John) saw Creator Sets Free (Jesus) walking toward him from a distance. "Behold! Take a good long look," he said to the ones gathered with him. "There is Creator's Lamb, the one who carries away and heals the bad hearts and broken ways of the world!"

The crowd of people looked to see the one He Shows Goodwill (John) was talking about.

30 "He is the one I said is greater than I, for he was there before I was born. 31 The reason I perform the purification ceremony with water is to make him known to the tribes of Wrestles With Creator (Israel). 32 With my own eyes I saw the Holy Spirit come down from above like a dove and rest on him. 33 I now know he is the one, because the Father above who sent me said, 'The man you see the Spirit come down and rest on will perform the purification ceremony with the Holy Spirit.'"

The people could only stare in amazement at Creator Sets Free (Jesus) as they listened to the words that they had longed to hear for many generations.

34 He Shows Goodwill (John) finished, by saying, "With my own eyes I have seen the one chosen by the Great Spirit."

Come and See

35 The next day, He Shows Goodwill (John) was standing with two of his followers. 36 They saw Creator Sets Free (Jesus) walking nearby.

He said to them, "Look! There is Creator's Lamb!"

37 So they went after Creator Sets Free (Jesus).

38 When they caught up to him, he saw them and asked, "What are you looking for?"

"Wisdomkeeper," they asked, "where are you staying?"

39 "Come," he said, "and you will see."

So they went with him, saw where he was staying and spent the rest of the day with him, for the day was almost over.

40 One of the two men, Stands With Courage (Andrew), went to find his brother, One Who Hears (Simon), also named Stands On The Rock (Peter). 41 When he found him, he ran up to him and said, "My brother! We have found the Messiah" (which means 'the Chosen One'[d]). 42 So he took his brother to meet Creator Sets Free (Jesus).

Creator Sets Free (Jesus) *looked deep into his eyes and* said, "You are One Who Hears (Simon), son of He Shows Goodwill (John). I will give you the name Stands On The Rock (Peter)."

The Great Ladder

43 The next morning Creator Sets Free (Jesus) walked to the territory of Circle of Nations (Galilee). There he found a man named Friend Of Horses (Philip) and said to him,

---

c 1:28 See Exodus 12 for the story.   d 1:41 Lit., Anointed One

"Come, and from now on walk the road with me."

[44] Friend Of Horses (Philip) was from House of Fishing (Bethsaida), the same village where Stands With Courage (Andrew) and Stands On The Rock (Peter) also lived. [45] Friend of Horses (Philip) looked for his friend Creator Gives (Nathanael) *and found him sitting under a fig tree.*

"We have found him!" he said *as he ran up to him.* "The one the lawgiver Drawn From The Water (Moses) told us about, the one foretold by the prophets of old. He is Creator Sets Free (Jesus), son of He Gives Sons (Joseph), from Seed Planter Village (Nazareth)."

[46] Creator Gives (Nathanael) *crossed his arms and, shaking his head,* said to him, "How can anything good come from Seed Planter Village (Nazareth)?"

"Come," he said, "and you will see!"

[47] When Creator Sets Free (Jesus) saw Creator Gives (Nathanael) walking toward him, he said, "Look, a true descendant of Wrestles With Creator (Israel)! There is nothing false in him."

[48] Creator Gives (Nathanael) asked him, "How do you know me?"

Creator Sets Free (Jesus) *smiled and* said, "Before Friend Of Horses (Philip) found you, I saw you under a fig tree."

[49] "Wisdomkeeper!" Creator Gives (Nathanael) answered. "You are the Son of the Great Spirit and the Chieftain of the tribes of Wrestles With Creator (Israel)!"

[50] "You believe me because I said I saw you under the fig tree?" he said to him. "I speak truth from my heart. You will see much more than this! [51] You will see the sky open wide and the spirit-messengers from Creator climbing up and down a great ladder.[e] On the True Human Being they will climb from the spirit world above to the earth below and back again."

His First Sign

2 Three days later there was a wedding in Reed Village (Cana), in the territory of Circle of Nations (Galilee). Bitter Tears (Mary), the mother of Creator Sets Free (Jesus), was there. [2] Creator Sets Free (Jesus) and the ones who walked the road with him were invited as guests to the wedding.

[3] During the celebration, they ran out of wine.

This would have been a great embarrassment to the groom and his family.

So the mother of Creator Sets Free (Jesus) said to him, *"Son, they have no more wine."*

[4] "*Honored* woman," he said to her. "Why are you telling me? Is this our concern? It is not yet my time to show who I am."

[5] But his mother turned to the helpers and said, "Do whatever he says."

They looked to him and waited for his instructions.

---

6 There were six *traditional* stone water pots, used for purification ceremonies, that could hold large amounts of water.

7-8 "Fill them to the top," Creator Sets Free (Jesus) told them, "and take some to the headman of the feast."

They filled the pots until they could hold no more and did what he said.

9-10 The water had turned into wine. The headman didn't know where it had come from, but the helpers who were serving the wine knew.

The headman took a drink and called to the groom, "Everyone serves the best wine first, and after the guests have had enough to drink, they bring out the watered down wine. But *even though you served good wine at first,* you have saved the best wine for last."

11 This was the first of the signs through which Creator Sets Free (Jesus) displayed his power. When his *new* followers saw this, their trust in him grew stronger. All of this happened in the territory of Circle of Nations (Galilee) at Reed Village (Cana). 12 After this he went with his mother, his brothers and his followers to Village of Comfort (Capernaum), where he stayed for a few days.

Passover Festival

It was a custom for all the families of the tribes of Wrestles With Creator (Israel) to journey to Village of Peace (Jerusalem) to participate an ancient festival called Passover. This festival celebrated the time when the lawgiver, Drawn From The Water (Moses), had set them free from captivity to the powerful nation of Black Land (Egypt). He did this by using the great power Creator gave him to perform many signs and wonders.

13 The time of the year had come for the ancient Passover Festival. Creator Sets Free (Jesus) made his way to the Great Spirit's Lodge in Village of Peace (Jerusalem).

This was the custom for all the families of the tribes of Wrestles With Creator (Israel).

He came into the area in the Lodge called Gathering Place for the Nations. It was here that other nations could come to learn about the Great Spirit and his ways.

14 As Creator Sets Free (Jesus) entered the Lodge, he saw people sitting at money tables. There were also others who were trading, buying and selling the cattle, sheep and doves for the ceremonies— inside the Lodge!

Sacred Lodge Keeper

It was so crowded that there was no room for the people from other nations who had come to learn about the Great Spirit. They were not honoring the purpose of this holy place.

15 So Creator Sets Free (Jesus) took some leather straps and made a whip. He cracked the whip *to startle and move the animals, and to drive all the people from the*

lodge. He tipped over the tables, which scattered their money on the floor. ¹⁶ He then turned to speak to the ones who were selling the ceremonial doves.

"Go!" he roared at them. "Take these things out from here. Do not make my Father's Sacred Lodge into a trading post!"

¹⁷ The ones who walked the road with him listened and remembered the ancient prophecy, "My desire to honor your Sacred Lodge burns like a fire in my belly."*f*

¹⁸ "What gives you the right to do these things?" the Tribal Leaders said to him. "Prove yourself and show us a sign!"

¹⁹ "Tear down this Sacred Lodge," he answered, "and in three days I will raise it up again."

²⁰ The people *shook their heads and* said to him, "It took forty-six winters to build this Great Lodge. How could you raise it up in three days?"

²¹ They did not understand that he was speaking about the Lodge of his own body. ²² After he was raised up from the dead, his followers remembered what he said, and then believed the ancient Sacred Teachings and the words he spoke to them.

²³ During the Passover festival many people began to believe in him because they saw the powerful miracles he was performing. ²⁴ But he didn't trust himself to them, for he could see right through them.

²⁵ He didn't need anyone to tell him about human beings, for he knew the hearts of mankind.

Born from Above

3 ¹⁻² A man named Conquers The People (Nicodemus) came to Creator Sets Free (Jesus) *in secret* at night. He was one of the Separated Ones (Pharisees) and a headman of the tribes of Wrestles With Creator (Israel) who sat in the Great Council.

Out of the shadows he whispered, "Wisdomkeeper, we know the Great Spirit sent you to teach us. No one can perform powerful signs like these unless the Maker of Life walks with him."

³ "I speak from my heart," Creator Sets Free (Jesus) answered, "Only one who has been born from above can see Creator's Good Road."

⁴ Conquers The People (Nicodemus) *was surprised by this strange answer, so he* asked, "Can a man be born when he is old? Can he enter his mother's womb to be born a second time?"

⁵ "Listen closely," Creator Sets Free (Jesus) answered. "One must be born of both water and spirit to walk on Creator's Good Road. ⁶ The human body only gives birth to natural life, but it takes the Spirit of Creator to give birth to spiritual life.*g* ⁷ Do not be surprised that I said to you, 'You must be born from above'? ⁸ Everyone born in this way is like the wind that blows wherever it wants. You can hear its sound, but no one knows

---

f **2:17** Psalm 69:9   g **3:6** Or more literally: Flesh gives birth to flesh, and spirit to spirit.

where it comes from or where it goes."

9 "How can these things be?" Conquers The People (Nicodemus) asked.

Creator Sets Free (Jesus) looked gently but firmly into his eyes and continued.

10 "How can it be that a wisdomkeeper and spiritual leader of the tribes of Wrestles With Creator (Israel) does not understand these things? 11-12 Listen closely, for you fail to hear what we are talking about. We are speaking about things we know to be true, but if you do not believe me when I talk about things on earth, how will you believe me when I talk about the things from the world above? 13 For there is only one who has gone up and come down from the world above—the True Human Being.

14-15 *Do you not remember when* Drawn From The Water (Moses) lifted up a pole with a snake on it in the desert wilderness?*h* This is what will happen to the True Human Being, so people will put their trust in him and have the life of the world to come that never fades—full of beauty and harmony."

Long ago, when the tribes of Wrestles With Creator (Israel) were wandering in the desert, they did not listen to the Great Spirit. Poisonous snakes came and bit them and many were dying. Drawn From The Water (Moses) prayed for them, so

Creator told him to put a snake on a pole and lift it up so the people could see it. When they looked at it, they were healed and did not die.

Conquers The People (Nicodemus) remained silent listening to the words of Creator Sets Free (Jesus).

16 "The Great Spirit loves this world *of human beings* so deeply he gave us his only Son—the one who receives everything from his Father. All who trust in him *and his way* will not come to a bad end, but will have the life of the world to come that never fades—full of beauty and harmony. 17 Creator did not send his Son to decide against the *people of this* world, but to set them free from *the worthless ways of* the world.

18 "The ones who trust in him are released from their guilt; but, for the ones who turn away from him *to follow the ways of this world,* their guilt remains, because they are turning away from the life of beauty and harmony the Great Spirit offers through his Son.

19 "This is what decides for or against them. My light has shined into this dark world, but because of their worthless ways people loved the dark path more than the light. 20 When they choose the dark path, they don't want others to see, so they hide in the darkness and hate the light. 21 But the ones who are true and do what is right are walking in the daylight so others can clearly see they are walking with Creator."

h 3:14-15 Exodus 21:9

He Shows Goodwill
Steps Back

[22] Creator Sets Free (Jesus) and the ones who walked the road with him went to the nearby countryside in the Land of Promise (Judea). They stayed there and began to perform the purification ceremony as the people came to the river.

[23] *About a two day walk to the north,* He Shows Goodwill (John) was also performing the purification ceremony, at Spring of Water (Aenon), near Peaceful Village (Salem), where there was much water. [24] This was before He Shows Goodwill (John) had been put in prison.

[25] Some of the followers of He Shows Goodwill (John) began to argue with a local Tribal Member about the purification ceremony. [26] They took their argument to He Shows Goodwill (John).

"Wisdomkeeper," they said to him, "the one you told us about at the river Flowing Down (Jordan) is performing the purification ceremony. All of the people are going to him now."

[27] "No one has anything," He Shows Goodwill (John) answered, "unless it is gifted from the world above. [28] You heard me say, 'I am not the Chosen One.' I was sent to clear the way for him. [29] The bride at a wedding belongs to the groom, and like the best man, a friend who stands with the groom, I am glad to hear his voice. [30] But it is time for me to step back and for him to come forward into his place of honor. My part is fading away.

[31-32] "The one who is greater than all speaks from the world above. The one who is from the earth speaks only about earthly things. The one from above speaks about the things he has seen and heard, but who believes him? [33] But I am one who receives his words, and I know for sure that the Great Spirit approves of all he says and does.

[34] "The one whom Creator sent is the one who has all the fullness of Creator's Spirit and clearly speaks his words. [35] The Father above loves his Son and gives him all things.

[36] "The ones who trust in his Son have the life of the world to come, that does not fade away; but the ones who do not walk in his ways will not have this life. Instead, they will remain *under the power of death,* which reveals Creator's great anger."

Living Water

4 *Many people were now coming to Creator Sets Free (Jesus) at the river Flowing Down (Jordan) for the purification ceremony.*

[1-3] Creator Sets Free (Jesus) was gathering more followers for the purification ceremony than He Shows Goodwill (John), although it wasn't he but his followers who were performing the ceremony. When Creator Sets Free (Jesus) found out that the Separated Ones (Pharisees) knew of this, [4] he left the Land of Promise (Judea) to return to Circle of Nations (Galilee); but on the way he had to journey through the territory of High Place (Samaria).

Many of the people from High Place (Samaria) were mixed bloods and despised by the tribes of Wrestles With Creator (Israel). They had their own Sacred Lodge and ceremonies and didn't respect the Tribal Members or consider Village of Peace (Jerusalem) to be a holy place. Both of them would go out of their way to keep from having contact with the other.

The sun was beating down from high above the head of Creator Sets Free (Jesus) as he journeyed through High Place (Samaria).

⁵ There he came to a place called Burial Site (Sychar), which was near a piece of land Heel Grabber (Jacob) had passed down to his son, He Gives More (Joseph).

⁶⁻⁸ Weary from his journey, about the sixth hour of the day, Creator Sets Free (Jesus) sat down to rest at the ancient watering hole of Heel Grabber (Jacob), while the ones who walked the road with him went to the nearby village to find some food.

A Woman from High Place

The sun had reached midpoint in the sky, it was now the time of day when no one would normally come to the watering hole.

A woman from High Place (Samaria) came to the well to draw water. Creator Sets Free (Jesus) saw the woman and said to her, "Would you give me some water to drink?"

This surprised the woman, because a traditional man would never speak to a woman in public.

⁹ She *found her voice and* asked, "Why would you, a man from the tribes of Wrestles With Creator (Israel), ask me for a drink, seeing I am a woman from High Place (Samaria)?"

She said this because the tribes of Wrestles With Creator (Israel) have no dealings with the people from High Place (Samaria).

¹⁰ "If you only knew about Creator's good gift," he answered, "and who it is that asks you for a drink, you would ask him for living water and he would give it to you."

¹¹ She said to him, "Honored One, this watering hole is deep, and you have no way to draw out the water. Where will you get this living water? ¹² Are you greater than our ancestor Heel Grabber (Jacob), who gave us this well and was first to drink from it with his children and animals?"

¹³ "The ones who drink from this well will thirst again," Creator Sets Free (Jesus) answered. ¹⁴ "But the ones who drink the water I give, will never thirst, for this water will become a river flowing from inside them, giving them the life of the world to come, that does not fade— full of beauty and harmony."

¹⁵ "Honored One, please give me this water," she said to him, "so I will never thirst again or need to walk this long path to get a drink."

¹⁶ He said to her, "Go to your husband and bring him here."

¹⁷ "I have no husband," she answered.

"Yes, that is true," Creator Sets Free (Jesus) said. [18] "You have had five husbands, and the man you are with now is not your husband."

Her eyes grew wide as she lifted a trembling hand to her mouth.

[19] "Oh! I see. You are a prophet!" she said back to him. [20] "Our ancestors honored and served the Great Spirit on this mountain. But your people say the only place to make our prayers and perform our ceremonies is in Village of Peace (Jerusalem)."

This was a very old argument between the people of High Place (Samaria) and the tribes of Wrestles With Creator (Israel).

[21-23] "Honored woman, trust my words," Creator Sets Free (Jesus) said to her. "Your people honor and serve him, but in ways they do not fully understand. We honor and serve him with understanding, for the Good Road[i] has been entrusted to the tribes of Wrestles With Creator (Israel).

Spirit and Truth

"But the time is coming when all who honor and serve the Great Mystery will not need to do so in this mountain nor in Village of Peace (Jerusalem). The Father is looking for the ones who will honor him in spirit and truth—and the day for this has now come. [24] The One Above Us All is spirit, and all who honor and serve him must do so in spirit and truth."

[25] "I know the Chosen One will come," she said, "and when he comes, he will make all things clear to us."

[26] Creator Sets Free (Jesus) said to her, "I am the Chosen One, the one who is speaking to you now."

[27] Just then his followers returned. They wondered why he was talking to a woman, but no one said to her, "What do you want?" or to him, "Why are you talking to her?"

The Harvest is Now

[28] The woman left her water pouch, went to the village and told the people, [29] "Come and see this man who knows everything about me. Could he be the Chosen One?"

[30] The people of the village went out to find him. [31] Meanwhile, the ones who walked the road with him said, "Wisdomkeeper, here is some food to eat!"

[32] "I have food to eat you know nothing about," he said.

[33] His followers whispered to each other, "None of us brought him anything to eat."

[34] *He knew what they were saying, so* he said to them, "What feeds me is to do the will of the one who sent me and to finish his work. [35] It has been said, 'Is it not four moons until the harvest?' No! Open your eyes! The harvest is upon you now! [36] The ones who reap the harvest are rewarded because they are gathering grain for the life of the world to come, that does not fade

---

i 4:21-23 Lit., salvation

away. Both the ones who plant the seed and the ones who harvest will celebrate together. ³⁷This is a true saying, 'One plants and another reaps.' ³⁸I send you to reap where others have done the work of planting, and now it is you who will gather."

Many Believe

³⁹Soon many people from the woman's village in High Place (Samaria) arrived. Many believed in him because the woman had said, "He knows everything about me." ⁴⁰They asked him to stay, so he remained there for two more days. ⁴¹When they heard him speak, many more believed in him.

⁴²They said to the woman, "We believe now, not just because of your words, but because we have heard him ourselves. We now see that this is the one who will restore the world and set all people free."

He Continues His Journey

⁴³After the two days he continued on his journey to Circle of Nations (Galilee), the territory near his boyhood home. ⁴⁴Creator Sets Free (Jesus) had said that a prophet is given much honor except in his own village, among his own clan, and in his own house. ⁴⁵But even so, the people there welcomed him, because they had seen with their own eyes the powerful things he had done at the Passover festival.

Second Sign

⁴⁶He returned to Reed Village (Cana), where he had turned the water into wine. At Village of Comfort (Capernaum) *almost a day's walk away,* the son of a government official was sick and near death. ⁴⁷When the man heard that Creator Sets Free (Jesus) had come to Circle of Nations (Galilee) from the Land of Promise (Judea), he came to him and asked him to come and heal his son.

⁴⁸Creator Sets Free (Jesus) *looked around at the crowd and* said, "Why do you need to see signs and wonders before you will believe?"

⁴⁹"Honored one," the man spoke *with desperation in his voice.* "Please come before my child dies!"

⁵⁰"Go home!" Creator Sets Free (Jesus) instructed him. "Your son will live."

The man believed him and left to go home. ⁵¹On the way his servants met him and told him his son was getting stronger. ⁵²He asked them the hour when this occurred.

"Yesterday, at the seventh hour, the fever left him," they answered.

⁵³The father knew it was the same time that he was told, "Your son will live," so he and his family believed.

⁵⁴This was the second powerful sign Creator Sets Free (Jesus) performed in Reed Village (Cana), having come from the southern territory of the Land of Promise (Judea) to Circle of Nations (Galilee).

Working on the Day of Resting

5 A short time later Creator Sets Free (Jesus) went *again* to Village of Peace (Jerusalem) to another traditional feast for all

the tribes of Wrestles With Creator (Israel).

2 In Village of Peace (Jerusalem) near the Sheep Gate there is a water hole with five covered porches called House of Kindness (Bethesda) in our tribal language. Under these porches 3 lay a great number of people who were sick, blind, or could not walk or stand. They were waiting for the swirling of the water, 4 because from time to time a spirit-messenger would go down into the water hole and make the water swirl. Then the first one to get into the water would be healed.

5 A man was there who had been ill for thirty-eight winters. 6 Creator Sets Free (Jesus) saw him lying there and knew that he had been sick for a long time.

He asked him, "Do you want to be healed?"

7 "Honored One," the man answered. "When the water swirls, there is no one to help me into the water, and someone else gets there first."

8 "Get up!" Creator Sets Free (Jesus) said to the man. "Roll up your sleeping bundle and walk."

The man felt his body begin to change. Strength rushed into his legs and arms.

9 Right then the man was healed! He got up, rolled up his bundle and walked.

Creator Sets Free (Jesus) healed this man on the Day of Resting. 10 The strict traditional Tribal Members saw the healed man carrying his bundle.

"It is the Day of Resting," they said to him. "Tribal Law forbids you to carry your sleeping bundle."

11 He said to them, "The one who healed me instructed me to take up my bundle and walk."

12 "Who is the man who told you this?" they asked.

13 But the man who was healed didn't know who he was. Creator Sets Free (Jesus) had left because too many people were there.

14 Later on, Creator Sets Free (Jesus) saw the man in the Sacred Lodge.

"Look! You are healed," he said to him. "Now that you have been set free, do not use your freedom to walk a path that leads to broken ways, or something worse may come to you."

15 The man went back to the strict traditional people and told them it was Creator Sets Free (Jesus) who had made him well again. 16 Because of this the Tribal Leaders were giving Creator Sets Free (Jesus) trouble and wanted to put him to death, because he was doing this on the Day of Resting.

17 Creator Sets Free (Jesus) made it clear to them, "My Father has been working, so I am working also."

18 This made them want to kill him all the more; for he not only showed no regard for the Day of Resting, he also was making himself out to be equal with the Great Spirit—calling him his own Father.

Equal Honor Belongs to the Son

19 "I speak from my heart," he said to them, "the Son only does what he sees the Father doing, for the Father and the Son do the same things. 20 The Father loves the Son and shows him everything he does. He will show him great and powerful medicine, things that will fill you with wonder. 21 You will see the Son give life to whoever he wants and bring the dead back to life again—just like the Father does.

22 "The Father doesn't make the final decision about anyone. He has given that decision to the Son. 23 He did this so all will honor the Son in the same way they honor the Father. The ones who do not honor the Son do not honor the Father who sent him.

24 "I speak from my heart. The ones who listen to me and trust the one who sent me have the life of the world to come, that does not fade away. The final decision about their end has been made, for they have already crossed over from death to life. 25 The time has now come when the ones who are *spiritually* dead will hear the voice of Creator's own Son—and all who hear it will live. 26 Just as all life comes from the Father, in the same way he has made all life come from the Son.

27 "I speak from my heart. The final decision about everyone has been given to the Son, it is his right, because he is the True Human Being.

28 "Don't look so surprised! For the day is dawning when the dead and buried will hear his voice and come out of their graves. 29 The ones who have done good will rise to a new life, but the ones who do what has no worth will rise to face the final decision about their end.

Father and Son

30 "I do nothing on my own, I listen *to my Father* before I decide about anyone. What I decide is right because I am not seeking my own way but the way of the one who sent me. 31 If I am the only one who speaks for myself, then my words are empty; 32 but there is another who speaks for me, and what he says is true.

33 "You sent messengers to He Shows Goodwill (John) and he told you the truth about me, 34-35 but I do not need a human being to speak for me. He Shows Goodwill (John) shined like a burning torch, and for a short time you were glad to walk in his light. Now, to be set free from your broken ways, you must listen to me. 36 My words carry more weight than his and are proven by the things I do. I have done the things the Father sent me to do. That is all the proof that is needed.

37 "The Father is the one who sent me, and he is the one who speaks for me. But, since you have never seen his form or heard his voice, 38 you do not trust the one he sent, so his words take no root in you.

39 "You search the Sacred Teachings, for you think they will give you the

life of the world to come—but they tell my story. ⁴⁰Why do you refuse to come to me for this life?"

The Tribal Leaders had heard enough! They just shook their heads and started to walk away.

⁴¹*Creator Sets Free (Jesus) said to them,* "I came representing my Father, yet you show me no respect. But I am not looking for honor or respect from you, ⁴²for I know you are empty inside, and the love of the Great Spirit has no place in you. ⁴³But you will honor the one who comes representing himself. ⁴⁴If you only look for honor from each other, and not from the only Creator, how will you believe?

⁴⁵"I have not come to tell the Father how wrong you are. It is Drawn From The Water (Moses), the one you have put your hope in, who will do this. ⁴⁶If you trust him, then you should trust me, for he told my story. ⁴⁷But if you do not believe his words, how will you ever believe mine?"

He Feeds Five Thousand

6 After this Creator Sets Free (Jesus) went over to the other side of Lake of Circle of Nations (Sea of Galilee), also called Sea of Rolling Water (Sea of Tiberias). ²A great crowd of people followed him because they saw the powerful signs he performed, healing the sick. ³Creator Sets Free (Jesus) walked up to the mountainside and sat down with his followers. ⁴Soon it would be time again for the yearly Passover festival for the tribes of Wrestles With Creator (Israel).

⁵From the mountain side Creator Sets Free (Jesus) could see how large the crowd following behind him had become—*over five thousand!*

He then looked at Friend of Horses (Philip) and said, "Where will we find enough food to feed all these people?"

⁶He said this to test him, for he already knew what he would do.

Friend of Horses (Philip) took a step back and looked at him with wide eyes. He wasn't sure if Creator Sets Free (Jesus) was serious or not.

⁷Friend Of Horses (Philip) answered, "'Eight moons' worth of gathered food would only give them enough for one small bite apiece!"

⁸Stands With Courage (Andrew), one of the twelve, the brother of Stands On The Rock (Peter), *tried to be helpful and* said, ⁹"Here is a boy with five loaves of bread and two small fish, but how would that possibly be enough?"

¹⁰Creator Sets Free (Jesus) said to them, "Have the people sit down on the grass."

There was much grass there, so they all began to sit down—five thousand men *along with women and children.*

Creator Sets Free (Jesus) waited patiently for them to finish. When they were all settled down, he had the ones who walked the road with him bring baskets and stand in a circle around him.

¹¹He took the five loaves of bread, given by the little boy, *and held them*

up to the sky. He gave thanks to the Great Spirit and began to break the bread into smaller pieces and gave them to his followers to give to the people. In the same manner he also divided the two fish, and they were given out to the people. 12 Everyone ate until they were full!

When they were done eating, he instructed them to gather the leftovers of fish and bread, so nothing would go to waste. 13 It took twelve baskets to hold it all.

He Must Be The Prophet

14 The people began to realize what had happened. This was a powerful sign that Creator Sets Free (Jesus) had just performed.

They began to wonder who this man was who could do such amazing things. Like wildfire, the hopes and dreams of generations began to rise in their hearts and minds.

They were saying to one another, "This must be The Prophet, spoken of long ago, who would come into the world!"

15 Creator Sets Free (Jesus) knew in his spirit that the people were about to take him by force to make him their Chief, so he left the crowd and went to a quiet place on the mountainside to be alone *and pray.*

Water Walker

16 Later, as the sun began to set, his followers climbed into a canoe to go to Village of Comfort (Capernaum) on the other side. 17 Darkness was beginning to creep across the water with no sign of Creator Sets Free (Jesus), so they pushed off from shore.

As they continued to row, lightning flashed in the distance, and the sound of thunder rolled across the sky.

18-19 A strong wind blew in over the waters. The waves grew large and pounded against them, *threatening to overturn the canoe.* They were pulling hard on the paddles, trying to make headway, but had only traveled part way across^j the great lake *and were still a long way from land.*

They looked out through the storm *and their eyes grew wide* with fear, for they saw Creator Sets Free (Jesus) coming toward them, walking on the water!

20 Creator Sets Free (Jesus) *saw the fear in their faces and* called out to them, "Do not fear, *take heart,* it is I!"

21 When they knew it was Creator Sets Free (Jesus), they were glad to bring him into the canoe, and suddenly they were at the shoreline on the other side of the great lake.

Looking for the Wrong Food

22 It was now morning, and the crowd of people on the other side of Lake of Circle of Nations (Sea of Galilee) began to look for Creator Sets Free (Jesus); for they knew there was only one canoe, and that he did not go with his followers. 23 Just then some canoes arrived from

---

j 6:18-19 About three and a half miles

Rolling Water (Tiberias) at the same place where Creator Sets Free (Jesus) had given thanks for the bread and fed them all. 24 When they couldn't find Creator Sets Free (Jesus) or his followers, they climbed into the canoes to go to Village of Comfort (Capernaum) to find him.

25 When they arrived on the other side and found Creator Sets Free (Jesus), they asked, "Wisdomkeeper, when did you get here?"

26 Creator Sets Free (Jesus) *ignored their question and* said to them, "Listen closely to my words, you are not looking for me because of the powerful sign you saw, but only because you filled your bellies with food. 27 Why are you working so hard for food that fades away? You should work for the food that gives you the life of the world to come, that never fades. The True Human Being will give you this food, for he has the Father's full approval."

28 "What does Great Spirit require from us," they asked, "so we can do what he wants *and have his approval also?*"

29 "Here is what he wants you to do," he answered, "put your trust in the one he has sent."

Bread From the World Above

30 "What powerful sign will you show us, that we should trust in you?" they asked. "What sign will you perform? 31 When our ancestors were wandering in the desert they ate bread, just as the Sacred Teachings tell us, 'From the world above he gave them bread to eat.'*k*"

32 "Listen closely," Creator Sets Free (Jesus) answered. "Drawn From the Water (Moses) did not give you the bread from the world above. It is my Father who gives you the true bread that comes down from the world above. 33 This bread gives the life of beauty and harmony to the world."

34 "Honored One," they said, "from now on give us this bread."

35 Creator Sets Free (Jesus) *smiled, held out his arms to them and* said, "I am the bread of life that came down from the world above. The ones who come to me will hunger no more; the ones who trust me will thirst no more."

36 *He lowered his arms and with heavy heart he continued,* "But even as I told you before, you have seen me but you still do not trust me. 37 The ones my Father has given to me will come to me. They are a gift from my Father that I will always keep.

38 "I came down from the world above, from the one who sent me, to walk his path, not to walk my own. 39 He wants me to keep safe the ones he has given me, and bring them back to life again at the end of all days. 40 The ones who see who the Son truly is will put their trust and hope in him, and have the life of the world to come, that never fades. Yes! I will bring them back to life again at the end of all days, for this is what the one who sent me wants."

k 6:31 Exodus 16:15

[41] Upon hearing this, the Tribal Members complained, "Who is this 'Bread from the world above'? [42] Is this not the son of He Gives Sons (Joseph)? We know who his mother and father are. How can he say 'I came down from the world above'?"

[43] "Stop grumbling to each other," he answered. [44] "The only ones who come to me have been drawn by my Father. These are the ones I will bring back to life at the end of all days. [45] The Sacred Teachings from the prophets of old tell us, 'There will come a time when the Great Spirit will instruct everyone.'[l] That is why the ones who hear and listen to the Father come to me.

[46] "The only one who has seen the Father is the one sent from the Great Spirit. This one has clearly seen the Father. [47] I speak the truth from my heart, the ones who trust in me have the life of the world to come, full of beauty and harmony.

[48] "I am the bread that gives this life. [49] Your ancestors ate bread in the desert wilderness, and they died. [50] Here, standing before you, is the bread that comes down from above. The ones who eat this bread will not die. [51] I am the living bread from above; the ones who eat this bread will live beyond the end of all days. And this is the bread that I will give as a gift to *all the people of the world*—my human body."

[52] His words caused a great division among the Tribal Members, and they began to argue with one another.

"How can this be?" they asked. "Will he give us his flesh to eat?"

[53] "I speak from my heart," he answered. "The only way to have my life in you is to eat the body of the True Human Being and drink his blood. [54] Then, the life of the world to come will be yours, and at the end of all days I will bring your body back to life. [55] My body is true food; my blood is pure drink. [56] The ones who eat and drink my body and blood live in me, and I live in them. [57] In the same way the living Father sent me, and gave me his life, the ones who feed on me will have my life. [58] The bread from above is not like the bread our ancestors ate—and then died. This bread gives the life of the world to come, that never fades away."

[59] These are the words he spoke to the people at the gathering house in Village of Comfort (Capernaum).

Many Followers Walk Away

[60] When the ones who walked the road with Creator Sets Free (Jesus) heard this, many of them said, "These words are too hard to hear. Who can even listen to them?"

[61] Creator Sets Free (Jesus) knew in his spirit what was troubling them, so he said, "Do these words make you stumble from the path? [62] What will you do when you see the True Human Being going back up to where he came from?

[63] "Life comes from the spirit, not from the human body.[m] My words

---

l 6:45 Isaiah 54:13   m 6:63 Lit., flesh

have spirit and life in them— [64] but some of you have no faith *in who I am.*"

He said this because he knew, from the beginning, the ones who did not believe, and who would betray him.

[65] He then finished by saying, "That is why I said no one can come to me on their own, but only as a gift from my Father."

[66] When they heard this, many who followed him turned and walked away. [67] Creator Sets Free (Jesus) looked at the twelve and said, "Do you also want to walk away?"

[68] "Wisdomkeeper," One Who Hears (Simon), also named Stands On The Rock (Peter), answered him, "who else would we walk the road with? You have the words that give the life of the world to come, full of beauty and harmony. [69] We have come to know and trust in you as the Holy One from the Great Spirit."

[70] Creator Sets Free (Jesus) said to them, "Even though I chose all twelve of you, one of you is an enemy."[n]

[71] He was talking about Speaks Well Of (Judas), one of the twelve, who would later turn on him and betray him.

Festival of Shelters

7 Creator Sets Free (Jesus) left the Land of Promise (Judea) because the Tribal Members there wanted to put him to death. To avoid conflict with them, he had been staying in the territory of Circle of Nations (Galilee), going from village to village. [2] But now it was almost time for the Festival of Shelters in Village of Peace (Jerusalem), which all the tribes participated in.

This festival was celebrated at the end of the harvest. The tribes were instructed to make temporary shelters made from tree branches. In this way they remembered the time after they had been set free from their captivity in Black Land (Egypt), when their ancestors migrated in the desert wilderness under the care of the lawgiver, Drawn From The Water (Moses).

[3] The brothers from the family of Creator Sets Free (Jesus) came to him and said, "You should leave here and go back to the Land of Promise (Judea) for the Festival. This way more of your followers will see the powerful signs you can do. [4] Why don't you show everyone who you are? The ones who want to be well known do not hide in secret. You should show all the world who you are."

[5] Even his own brothers did not believe *that he was the Chosen One.*

[6-7] Creator Sets Free (Jesus) answered them, "You are free to go anytime you want, for the people there do not hate you. But they do hate me, because I show them their bent and crooked ways. [8] You can go to the festival, but I am not going now—it is not my time yet."

[9] After he said this, he stayed behind in Circle of Nations (Galilee)

---

n 6:70 Lit., devil or adversary

[10] until his family left. Then he went to the festival, not openly, but in secret.

Looking for Him at the Festival

Tribal members from all the directions came to the Festival. Village of Peace (Jerusalem) was crowded and overflowing with thousands of people walking, donkeys pulling carts and merchants selling their crafts.

[11] Many were looking for Creator Sets Free (Jesus) at the festival. The people who had gathered there were whispering and wondering about him.

"Where is he?" they asked.

[12] Some of them said, "He is a true human being with a good heart."

But others were saying, "No! He is leading the crowds down a false path."

[13] No one was saying these things out in the open, because they feared what the Tribal Leaders might do to them.

Why Do You Want to Kill Me?

[14] Creator Sets Free (Jesus) *came secretly to the Festival and stayed away from the crowds.* He waited until the midpoint of the Festival, went to the Sacred Lodge, and began to teach.

[15] The tribal leaders were amazed at his teaching.

"Where did he get this wisdom and understanding?" they asked.

"He has not studied *under our wisdomkeepers or attended our learning houses.*"

[16] Creator Sets Free (Jesus) answered them, "The wisdom I share is not my own, but comes from the one who sent me. [17] The ones who desire to walk in the ways of the Great Spirit will understand my wisdom comes from him. [18] The one who represents himself is seeking his own honor. The one who represents the one who sent him is true and upright and there is nothing false in him.

[19] "Drawn From The Water (Moses) gave you the Law, but none of you keep it. *You did not try to kill him.* Why do you want to kill me?"

[20] "You must have an evil spirit!" they answered back. "Why else would you think we are trying to kill you?"

[21] He answered them, "I did one work—I healed a man. You were amazed to see such power, but you were offended because this was done on the Day of Resting.

[22] *"Do you not see?* Drawn From The Water (Moses) gave you the cutting of the flesh [o] ceremony, handed down to him from the ancestors. Sometimes this ceremony is performed for a baby boy on the Day of Resting. [23] If this is permitted on the Day of Resting, then why are you angry with me for healing a man's whole body on that day? [24] Do not decide things by their outward appearance. Instead,

---

o 7:22 Lit., circumcision, identifying the men as belonging to the tribes of Wrestles With Creator (Israel)

make your decisions in a good way, looking beyond what you see with your eyes."

How Could He be the Chosen One?

25 Some of the people who lived in Village of Peace (Jerusalem) began to say, "Isn't this the one they are seeking to put to death? 26 Look, he speaks boldly to all and they have nothing to say to him. Does our tribal council think he truly is the Chosen One? 27 But how could this be? When the Chosen One comes, no one will know where he comes from; but we know where this man is from."

28-29 Creator Sets Free (Jesus) then lifted up his voice in the Sacred Lodge and cried out, "You may think you know me and where I am from, but I know where I am truly from—the Father. He is the one who sent me. You do not know who I am or where I am from, because you do not know him."

Soldiers Sent to Arrest Him

30 The Tribal Leaders were looking for a way to arrest him, but no one could even lay a hand on him, for it was not yet his time. 31 Many of the people chose to trust in him.

They said, "When the Chosen One comes, will he do more powerful signs than this man has done?"

32 When the Separated Ones (Pharisees) and the head holy men heard what the crowds were saying about him, they sent the lodge soldiers to arrest him.

33 "I will be gone soon," he said to them. "I am returning to the one who sent me. 34 You will look for me, but you will not find me. Where I am going you cannot follow."

35 The Tribal Members began to grumble, "Where will he go that we can't find him? Will he go to where the Tribal Members live among the Wisdom Seekers (Greeks)? 36 Will he teach them there? What does he mean by saying, 'You will look for me, but will not find me,' and, 'Where I am going you cannot follow'?"

Source of Living Water

37 It was now the last and greatest day of the Festival of Shelters.

It has been said that on this day, by ancient tradition, a holy man would be chosen to take a golden pot to the Waters of Sending Village (Pool of Siloam) and fill it with water. He would then bring the water to the Sacred Lodge for a special ceremony and celebration. The holy man would take the water to the great altar, then at the sound of the ram's horn, called the shofar, he would pour out the water on the altar. They would recite the words of the prophet Creator Will Help Us (Isaiah), "With glad hearts we will draw from the wells, water that will set us free."ᵖ

After the ceremony Creator Sets Free (Jesus) stood before the people and cried out with a loud voice, "The ones who thirst must come to me and drink! 38 Put your hope and trust in me. I am the one the Sacred

---

p 7:37 Isaiah 12:3

Teachings spoke of when they said, 'Rivers of living water will flow out from inside him.'q"

39 He was saying this about the Spirit, who would soon be given to the ones who believed in him. The Spirit had not yet been poured out, for Creator Sets Free (Jesus) had not yet risen to his place of honor, power and beauty.

Conflict About Who He Is

40 When they heard these words, some of the people gathered there were saying, "This must be The Prophet, the one of whom it was foretold would come?"

41 Others were saying, "*No!* He is the Chosen One."

Still others did not agree and said, "How can this be? Will the Chosen One come from Circle of Nations (Galilee)? 42 Don't the Sacred Teachings tell us that the Chosen One will be a descendant of Chief Much Loved One (David) and come from House of Bread (Bethlehem), the village where he was born?"

43 So the people could not agree about him. 44 The Lodge soldiers were amazed by his words and could not bring themselves to arrest him. 45 They returned to the head holy men and the Separated Ones (Pharisees), who asked them, "Where is he? Why didn't you arrest him?"

46 The soldiers answered, "No one has ever spoken like this man!"

47 "Has he turned you from the path also?" they said. 48 "Does even one tribal leader or Separated One (Pharisee) believe in him? 49 These people are ignorant of the Sacred Teachings given by Drawn From The Water (Moses). They are under a curse!"

50 Conquers The People (Nicodemus), the same one who came to Creator Sets Free (Jesus) in secret at night, was one of the Separated Ones (Pharisees). 51 He *boldly* said to the other Tribal Leaders, "Our Tribal Law does not permit us to decide against a man without giving him a chance to stand before the council and give an answer for what he does."

52 The other Tribal Leaders *scorned him and* said, "Are you also from Circle of Nations (Galilee)? Look into the Sacred Teachings for yourself. You will see that no prophet comes from Circle of Nations (Galilee)."

53 *The Festival of Shelters was over and* the people all returned to *the peace and safety of* their own homes.

Conflict Between Law and Kindness

8 But Creator Sets Free (Jesus) went to Olive Mountain *to find lodging there.* 2 Early in the morning at the sunrise, he returned again to the Sacred Lodge. All the people began to gather around him, so he sat down and *once again* began to teach *and tell his stories.*

Across the plaza a cloud of dust was rising from a group of people who were walking toward Creator Sets Free (Jesus) as he was teaching. They were forcefully

q 7:38 Jeremiah 2:13

dragging a woman along with them. He could see her tears and the look of terror on her face.

3 It was the scroll keepers and the Separated Ones (Pharisees). They brought the woman to Creator Sets Free (Jesus) and forced her down on the ground in front of him and all the people.

4 "Wisdomkeeper," they said, "we found this woman in the very act of being unfaithful to her husband. 5 Drawn From The Water (Moses) instructed us in the Law to throw stones at her until she dies. What do you have to say about this?"

6 They were putting him to a test, so they could have a way to accuse him.

The crowd was silent and waited to see what he would say, but he said nothing.

He bent over and with his finger wrote something in the dirt.

When he didn't answer right away, the Separated Ones (Pharisees) *became angry and* kept questioning him.

7 Creator Sets Free (Jesus) looked up at them and said, "The one who has done no wrong should be the first to throw a stone at her."

8 He then bent over and again began to write in the dirt with his finger.

9 When they heard his words, they all stood there silently. Then, beginning with the elders, one at a time they dropped their stones and walked away. Soon all were gone except for Creator Sets Free (Jesus)

and the woman. 10 He stood up and looked at her.

"Honored woman," he said. "Where are the ones who were accusing you? Is there no one who finds fault with you?"

11 The woman *looked up timidly into his eyes and* said, "No one, Wisdomkeeper."

"Then I also find no fault with you," he said to her. "You may go your way, but take care not to return to this broken path you have been walking."

Conflict Between Light and Darkness

After the woman left, the people began to gather around him again, waiting to hear what he would say.

12 Creator Sets Free (Jesus) *lifted up his voice and* said to them, "I am the light shining on this dark world. The ones who walk with me will not stumble in the darkness, but will have the light that gives them life."

13 When they heard this, the Separated Ones (Pharisees) said to him, "When you say these things about yourself, you are the only one who says they are true. If no one else speaks for you, then we cannot receive your words."

14 Creator Sets Free (Jesus) answered them, "If I am the only one who speaks for myself, my words are still true. I know where I came from and where I am going. You are the ones who do not know where I came from or where I am

going. [15] You are deciding about me with weak human minds.[r] I am not deciding about anyone, [16] but even if I did, my decisions would be true, for I do not stand alone. My Father who sent me is the one who stands with me. [17] Your Tribal Law tells you it takes the word of two people to know the truth. [18] So then, I speak for myself and the Father speaks for me also."

Who is Your Father?

[19] "Who[s] is your Father?" they said back to him.

"You do not know me or my Father," he told them. "If you knew me, you would know who my Father is."

[20] Creator Sets Free (Jesus) said these things at the Sacred Lodge, where he was teaching, near the storehouse where they keep the ceremonial gifts. No one laid a hand on him, for his time had not yet come.

The people began to argue among themselves about him.

[21] So he *lifted up his voice again and* said, "You are not able to go where I am going. When I am gone, you will *wander in the darkness* looking for the Chosen One,[t] and your bad hearts will lead you down the path of death *and destruction.*"

[22] The people said to each other, "Is he going to kill himself, since he says he is going where we cannot follow?"

[23] So he said to them, "You are from below and belong to *the ways of* this world. I am from above and this world *and its ways* has no place in me. [24] This is why I said that your bad hearts and broken ways will lead you down a path of death. Unless you put your trust in who I am *and follow my ways,* your end will be death."

Who Do You Think You Are?

[25] When they heard this, they said to him *in anger,* "Who do you think you are?"

He answered, "From the beginning I have been telling you who I am. [26] I have many more things I could say and decide about you. The words I speak to the *people of this* world come from the one who sent me, and he is the Truth."

[27] But no one could see that he was talking about the Father, *who is the Great Spirit.*

[28] So Creator Sets Free (Jesus) said to them, "When you lift up the True Human Being *upon the cross,* then you will know that I am who I say I am. For I only do and say the things taught to me by my Father. [29] The one who sent me is with me now. He has never left me alone, for I always walk in the ways that make his heart glad."

Conflict About Freedom

[30] Many began to trust in him as they listened to his words, [31] so Creator Sets Free (Jesus) said to the Tribal Members who believed in him, "If you walk in my footsteps and follow my teachings, you will

---

r 8:15 Lit., the flesh   s 8:19 Lit., where   t 8:21 Lit., me truly be my followers. 32 Then you will see and understand the truth that sets all people free."

33 But they questioned him, "We are the descendants of Father Of Many Nations (Abraham) and have never been anyone's slave. How can you say, 'You will be set free'?"

34 "I speak truth from my heart," he answered them. "All who walk in the broken ways of this world become slaves to their bad hearts. 35 A slave is not a member of the family and will not always live with the family. But a son of the family always has a home. 36 The freedom the Son gives you is the way of true freedom.

Conflict Over Fatherhood

37 "I know you are the descendants of Father Of Many Nations (Abraham), but you still want to kill me 38 because my message has no home in you. I am telling you the things my Father has shown me, but you are doing the things you have heard from your father."

39 "Father Of Many Nations (Abraham) is our father," they said back to him in anger.

Creator Sets Free (Jesus) said to them, "If you were truly the children of Father Of Many Nations (Abraham), you would do the same things he did. 40 Instead, you want to put to death the one who has told you truth from the Great Spirit. This is not what Father Of Many Nations (Abraham) did. 41 You are doing the same things your father does."

"We were not born from an unmarried woman," they said. "We have but one Father—the Great Spirit."

The Battle Lines Are Drawn

42 Creator Sets Free (Jesus) told them, "If the Great Spirit was truly your Father, you would love me and show respect, for I came from him. I did not send myself; he is the one who sent me.

43 "Why can you not hear what I am saying to you? Are my words not clear? Then I will speak more clearly. 44 Your father is Accuser (Satan), the evil trickster. You are doing what he wants, for he was the first to take the life of another. He stands outside of the truth, because truth has no home in him. He speaks with a forked tongue and twists his words. His lies show who he truly is. He is a liar and the father of all that is false.

45-46 "Even though I am telling you the truth, you do not believe me. Which one of you can show that I have done anything wrong? 47 The ones who come from the Great Spirit can hear his words. The reason you do not hear me is because you are not from him."

Accused of Having an Evil Spirit

48 "Now we have the right to call you a mixed blood from High Place (Samaria) and one who has an evil spirit," they said to him in anger.

49 He answered them back, "I have no evil spirit. I honor my Father,

but you dishonor me. ⁵⁰ I am not trying to honor myself, but there is one who honors me, and he has the final decision. ⁵¹ I speak from my heart, death will not have the final word for the ones who walk in my message."

⁵² "Now we are sure you have an evil spirit," they said. "Father Of Many Nations (Abraham) and all the prophets crossed over to death. How can you say that the ones who walk in your word will not taste of death? ⁵³ Do you think you are greater than Father Of Many Nations (Abraham) and the prophets? Who are you making yourself out to be?"

My Father Honors Me

⁵⁴ Creator Sets Free (Jesus) answered them, "If I honor myself, then I have no honor. The one who honors me is my Father, the one of whom you say, 'He is our Great Spirit.' ⁵⁵ You do not truly know him, but I do. If I were to say, 'I do not know him,' I would be a liar, like you! But I know him deeply and walk in all his ways. ⁵⁶ Father Of Many Nations (Abraham) looked ahead to my day. He saw it, and it made his heart glad!"

⁵⁷ "How could you have seen Father Of Many Nations (Abraham)?" they asked, *shaking their heads.* "You have not even seen fifty winters."

⁵⁸ "I speak from my heart," he answered. "I was there before Father Of Many Nations (Abraham) was born—for I AM."ᵘ

The Tribal Leaders had heard enough! ⁵⁹ They picked up stones to throw at him; but he hid himself *in the crowd,* passed them by, and walked out of the Sacred Lodge.

Who Is Blind and Why?

9 After walking *safely away from the Lodge,* Creator Sets Free (Jesus) saw a man blind from birth *sitting by the pathway. They stopped near the man and* ² the ones who walked the road with him asked, "Wisdomkeeper, why was this man born blind? Was it his wrongdoings or his parents' that caused this?"

³ "The wrongdoings of neither he nor his parents caused this," he told them, "but that the healing power of the Great Spirit would be seen in him; ⁴ for while the sun still shines, we must be doing what he wants. A time of darkness is coming when no one will do what he wants. ⁵ But as long as I am in the world, I will be its light."

He Heals a Man Born Blind

⁶⁻⁷ After saying this, he spit on the ground. Then he made mud from his spit and rubbed it on the man's eyes and instructed him to go and wash in the Waters of Sending Village (Pool of Siloam). *With the help of others,* the man went and washed *the mud out of his eyes* and returned with his sight restored.

⁸ The people who lived near him, and others who knew he was a blind beggar, saw him and said *in amazement,* "Could this be the blind man who sat and asked for handouts?"

---

u **8:58** A possible reference to the name of the Great Spirit. See Isaiah 3:14.

⁹Some were saying it was he, others said he only looked like him, but he kept saying, "I am the one!"

¹⁰So they asked him, "How did your sight return to you?"

¹¹He said, "A man named Creator Sets Free (Jesus)ᵛ made some mud and rubbed it on my eyes. He told me to go to the Waters of Sending Village (Pool of Siloam) and wash. So I did what he said, and now I can see."

¹²"Where is he?" they asked.

"I don't know where he is," the man answered.

How Were You Healed?

¹³⁻¹⁴Since it was on the Day of Resting that Creator Sets Free (Jesus) had healed the man, they decided to take him to the Separated Ones (Pharisees) *to see what they would say.* ¹⁵The Separated Ones (Pharisees) asked the man how he was healed.

He said to them, "He rubbed mud on my eyes, I washed off the mud and now I can see."

¹⁶Then some of the Separated Ones (Pharisees) said, "This man, who does not honor the Day of Resting, cannot be from the Great Spirit."

But others were saying, "How can someone with a bad heart perform powerful signs like these?"

¹⁷The Tribal Leaders could not agree, so they said to the blind man, "You are the one he healed, what do you have to say about him?"

The man answered them, "He must be a prophet from the Great Spirit."

¹⁸The Tribal Leaders could not believe the man had been blind. So they found his parents ¹⁹and asked them, "Is this your son who you say was born blind? How does he now see?"

²⁰⁻²²His parents were afraid of the Tribal Leaders who had said that anyone who says Creator Sets Free (Jesus) is the Chosen One would be put out of the gathering house.

²³"Yes, this is our son and he was born blind," they answered, "but we do not know how he sees, or who opened his eyes. He is a full grown man, ask him. He will tell you for himself."

The Tribal Leaders did not want the people to think that Creator Sets Free (Jesus) had done a true miracle.

I Was Blind But Now I see

²⁴They went back to the man who was blind and said to him, "Give honor to the Great Spirit for healing you, not to Creator Sets Free (Jesus), for we know he is an outcast with a bad heart."

²⁵"I do not know if this man has a bad heart," he answered them. "But this I do know—I was blind but now I see."

²⁶They asked the man again, "What did he do to open your eyes?"

²⁷He said to them, "You didn't listen the first time I told you. Why

v 9:11 Creator Sets Free (Jesus) was a common name among the tribes of Wrestles With Creator (Israel) in that day.

do you want to hear it again? Do you also want to become one of his followers?"

This made the leaders angry, so they tried to insult the man.

28 "You are his follower!" they said with disrespect in their voices. "We follow Drawn From The Water (Moses), 29 for we know the Great Spirit has spoken to him, but we do not know where this man is from."

30 The man answered them, "This is a strange thing! You, who are Tribal Leaders, do not know where this man comes from, yet he is the one who opened my eyes. 31 The Great Spirit does not listen to people with bad hearts; he listens to the ones who humbly serve him and do what is right. 32 From the creation of the world no one has ever seen a man healed who was born blind. 33 If he is not from the Great Spirit, he could not have done this."

Banned from the Gathering House

The Separated Ones (Pharisees) were furious! How could this outcast talk back to them like this?

34 They *puffed up their chests and* said, "You were born an outcast and you think you can teach us?"

Then they threw him out *and banned him from his gathering house.*

35 When Creator Sets Free (Jesus) heard that they had put the man out of the gathering house, he went to him and said, "Will you put your trust in the True Human Being?"

36 "Honored One, tell me who he is," the man answered, "and I will put my trust in him."

37 "Look at me and see the True Human Being," Creator Sets Free (Jesus) said, "—he is talking with you now."

38 The man bowed down to him and said, "Honored One, I believe!"

39 Creator Sets Free (Jesus) said, "I came to show what is right and wrong about the ways of this world, so that the blind will see—and that the ones who see may become blind."

Blind Guides

40 Some of the Separated Ones (Pharisees) overheard what he said to the man. "Are you saying that we are blind?" they asked.

41 "If you were truly blind, you would have no guilt," he answered them. "But since you claim to see, your guilt remains."

The Good Shepherd

10 *Creator Sets Free (Jesus) told this story to the Separated Ones (Pharisees), for they were blind guides, leading the tribes of Wrestles With Creator (Israel) down a false path to a bad end.*

"I speak from my heart," Creator Sets Free (Jesus) said *to the blind Tribal Leaders.* "Thieves and outlaws do not use the gate to the sheep pen, but sneak in some other way. 2 But the *Good* Shepherd uses the gate to enter, 3-4 and the gatekeeper opens the way. The sheep know their Shepherd's voice, for he calls each one of them by name, and they follow him as he leads them *in and out of the sheep pen.*

5 "The sheep will not follow the voice of a stranger; they will run away, for they do not recognize a stranger's voice."

6 Because he was using a story to teach them, Creator Sets Free (Jesus) could see that they did not understand, 7 so he told them the meaning of the story.

The Gate for the Sheep

"I speak again from my heart," he said. "I am the gate for the sheep. 8 All who put themselves before me are thieves and outlaws—*false shepherds*. My sheep do not listen to them.

9 "I am the gate for the sheep. The ones who enter by me will be safe *and well cared for.* Following the Shepherd, they will go in and out and find good food to eat.

10 "But thieves enter only to take away life, to steal what is not theirs, and to bring to ruin all they cannot have. But I have come to give the good life, a life that overflows with beauty and harmony.

Good Shepherd

11 "I am the Good Shepherd, *the one who watches over the sheep.* I will lay down my life for them. 12 The ones who watch the sheep only for pay will run away when a wolf comes, because the sheep are not theirs. Then the wolf preys upon the sheep and scatters the flock. 13 The ones

who do it only for pay are not true shepherds, for they do not care for the sheep *but only for themselves.*

14-15 "I am the Good Shepherd, the one who lays down his life for the sheep. The Father knows me and I know him. In the same way, I also know each one of my sheep and they know me. 16 I have other sheep who are not from this flock. I will go and find them, and they will *also* hear my voice. Then there will be only one flock, with one Shepherd.

17 "My Father has a great love for me, for I lay my life down to take it back again. 18 No one takes my life from me, for I lay it down on my own. I have the right to lay my life down and the right to take it back. It is my Father who gives me this right."

Disagreement

19 This story brought much disagreement among the Tribal Members, and they began to argue about him.

20 Many were saying, "He has lost his mind and has an evil spirit. Why do we even listen to him?"

21 At the same time others were saying, "These are not the words of someone with an evil spirit. Can an evil spirit open blind eyes?"

Sacred Lodge Purification Festival

Two moons had passed since the Festival of Shelters, and 22 it was now time for the people to celebrate the Feast of Dedication w in Village of Peace (Jerusalem).

---

w 10:22 Also called Hanukkah and Festival of Lights

This festival was to remember the time when the Great Spirit's Lodge was cleansed after it had been made ceremonially unclean by an evil ruler.

²³ It was winter and Creator Sets Free (Jesus) was walking near the Sacred Lodge under the entryway named after the great chief, Stands In Peace (Solomon).

²⁴ The tribal leaders came to him and said, "How long will you make us wait? If you are the Chosen One, then tell us!"

²⁵ "I already told you who I am," he said to them, "but you did not believe me. The things I do, representing my Father, speak the truth about me. ²⁶ *As I told you before,* you do not trust me because you are not my sheep. ²⁷ I know who my sheep are, for they know my voice and go where I lead them. ²⁸ My gift to them is the life of the world to come, full of beauty and harmony, and they will never fade away or come to a bad end. ²⁹ My Father gave them to me and no one can take them from me, because no one is greater than my Father. My sheep are safe in his hands, ³⁰ for I and my Father are one."

Tribal Leaders Reject Him

³¹ The Tribal Leaders *became furious and* picked up stones to kill him.

³² Creator Sets Free (Jesus) *stood his ground and* said to them, "I have done many good things,

representing my Father. For which of these do you mean to stone me?"

³³ They answered, "Not for any good thing you have done, but for speaking lies against the Great Spirit. How can you, a weak human being, represent yourself as the Great Spirit."

³⁴ Creator Sets Free (Jesus) answered them, "In your Tribal Law it says, 'You are powerful spiritual beings.'ˣ ³⁵ If Creator's word, which came to you, says you are 'powerful spiritual beings,' and the Sacred Teachings are clear and cannot be changed, ³⁶ then how can you say that the one the Father has set apart and sent into the world is speaking against the Great Spirit when he says, 'I am the Son of the Great Spirit'?"

³⁷ "If I am not doing what my Father does, then do not believe me. ³⁸ But even if you do not believe me, then at least believe in the powerful things I do. Then you will see clearly that I am in the Father and he is in me."

³⁹ The Tribal Leaders moved toward him to take him by force, but he slipped through their hands and walked away.

Creator Sets Free Retreats

Creator Sets Free (Jesus) decided it was time to leave Village of Peace (Jerusalem) again.

⁴⁰ He went to the place on the east side of the river Flowing Down (Jordan) where He Shows Goodwill (John) first performed the

---

x 10:34 Lit., 'You are gods.' Psalm 82:6

purification ceremony. He *and his followers* remained there *for a time.*

[41] Many people from the area came *to hear him* and, *after seeing Creator Sets Free (Jesus) teach, tell his stories, heal the sick and force out evil spirits,* the people were saying, "He Shows Goodwill (John) never performed a miracle or did any powerful signs, but what he told us about this man is true."

[42] And so, many of the people there believed in him *that he was the Chosen One.*

A Friend Crosses Over

11 [1-2] In House of Figs (Bethany), near Village of Peace (Jerusalem), a man named Creator Helps Him (Lazarus) was very sick. He was the brother of Healing Tears (Mary) and Head Woman (Martha). Healing Tears (Mary) is the one who poured ointment over *the head and feet of* Creator Sets Free (Jesus) and wiped his feet with her hair.[y]

[3] The sisters sent a messenger to Creator Sets Free (Jesus), who said to him, *"Our brother, Creator Helps Him (Lazarus), the one you care deeply about, is sick."*

[4] When Creator Sets Free (Jesus) heard the message, he said, "This sickness will not end in death. Instead, this will bring honor to the Great Spirit and shine a light on his Son."

His Light Shines Brighter

[5] Even though Creator Sets Free (Jesus) loved this family dearly, [6] he stayed where he was for two more days. [7] Then he said to his followers, "Let us go back to the Land of Promise (Judea)."

[8] But his followers said to him, "Wisdomkeeper, the Tribal Members there tried to throw stones at you to kill you! Why would you want to go back there?"

[9] He answered them, "Does not the sun give us a full day of light? The ones who walk during the day never stumble, because they see the light that shines on this world. [10] But the ones who walk at night stumble in the darkness, because there is no light for them to see."

He was telling them that he was the light shining in this dark world, and that it was time to let his light shine even brighter.

[11] Creator Sets Free (Jesus) explained to them, "Our good friend, Creator Helps Him (Lazarus), has fallen asleep and I am going to wake him."

[12] They said to him, "Wisdomkeeper, if he is only sleeping, he will get well."

[13] They didn't understand that Creator Sets Free (Jesus) meant that Creator Helps Him (Lazarus) had died. [14] They thought he was sleeping naturally.

He then told them plainly, "Creator Helps Him (Lazarus) has crossed over to death. [15] It is a good thing that I was not there, so you will believe. But we must go to him now."

[16] Looks Like His Brother (Thomas) said to the others, "Yes, we should go and die with him."

---

y 11:1-2 See Mark 14:3.

Four Days Dead

17 When Creator Sets Free (Jesus) came to House of Figs (Bethany), he found out that Creator Helps Him (Lazarus) had died four days earlier and was laid in a burial cave. 18 House of Figs (Bethany) was a close walk z from Village of Peace (Jerusalem). 19 Many of the local Tribal Members had gathered, along with the women, to give comfort to Head Woman (Martha) and Healing Tears (Mary) for the loss of their brother.

I Am the Rising
From the Dead

20 When Head Woman (Martha) heard that Creator Sets Free (Jesus) was coming, she went out to greet him, but Healing Tears (Mary) stayed home.

21 When she found Creator Sets Free (Jesus), she said to him, "Wisdomkeeper, if you had been here, my brother would still be with us. 22 Even so, I know if you ask anything of the Great Spirit, he will give it to you."

23 "Your brother will live again," he answered.

24 "I know he will live again," she said, "when the dead rise up at the end of all days."

25-26 "I am the rising up from the dead and the life that follows," he told her. "The ones who trust me will live again, even after death. Death will never be the end of the ones who are alive and trust in me. Do you believe what I am saying to you?"

27 "Yes, Wisdomkeeper!" she *smiled and* said. "I believe you are the Chosen One, the Son of the Great Spirit—the one who came *down* into this world *from above*."

He Weeps With
Those Who Weep

28 After she said this, she left him and went in private to her sister Healing Tears (Mary) and said to her, "The Wisdomkeeper is nearby and wants you to come to him."

29-30 Creator Sets Free (Jesus) was still waiting outside of the village where Head Woman (Martha) had met him. When Healing Tears (Mary) heard this, she got up right away and went to see him. 31 The Tribal Members who were comforting Healing Tears (Mary) saw her get up and leave quickly, so they went with her, thinking she was going to the burial cave to weep.

32 When Healing Tears (Mary) found Creator Sets Free (Jesus), she crumpled at his feet and wept.

"Wisdomkeeper!" she said *as tears ran down her face.* "If only you had been here, my brother would still be alive."

33 Creator Sets Free (Jesus) stood there watching Healing Tears (Mary) weeping at his feet. He looked around and saw all the Tribal Members who came with her also weeping. A deep anguish began to well up inside him and he was troubled in his spirit.

He cried out, 34 "Where did they bury him?"

---

z **11:18** About 2 miles

"Wisdomkeeper, come with us," they said to him. "We will show you."

³⁵ Tears began to flow down the face of Creator Sets Free (Jesus).

³⁶ When the Tribal Members saw his tears, some said, "See how deeply he cared for him!"

³⁷ But others said, "If this man could open the eyes of a blind man, why couldn't he have kept this man from dying?"

Power Over Death

³⁸ Creator Sets Free (Jesus), still deep in anguish, found his way to the family burial place. It was a cave, and a large stone blocked the entrance.

³⁹ Creator Sets Free (Jesus) cried out, "Take away the stone!"

Head Woman (Martha) whispered to him, "Wisdomkeeper, he has been dead four days; there will be a terrible smell."

⁴⁰ He *looked at her and* said, "Do you not remember what I told you? If you believed, you would see the Great Spirit show his mighty power and great beauty."

Head Woman (Martha) could say nothing. She watched as ⁴¹ they rolled the stone away from the burial cave.

Creator Sets Free (Jesus) turned his eyes upward toward the sky and said, "I thank you, Father, that you have already heard my prayers and always listen to me. ⁴² The reason I say this out loud is so that all who are standing around me can hear and believe that you sent me."

The men and women gathered there stood silently, listening to his prayer.

⁴³ *Then the voice of* Creator Sets Free (Jesus) *pierced the silence as he* cried out with a loud voice, "Creator Helps Him (Lazarus), come out of there!"

The sound of his voice echoed from out of the burial cave and then faded into the distance. The people looked at Creator Sets Free (Jesus) and then back to the cave. No one dared say anything, so they all waited. Then suddenly, gasps could be heard from the crowd. There was movement in the cave!

⁴⁴ Creator Helps Him (Lazarus) came *stumbling* out of the burial cave with his ceremonial wrappings still clinging to his head, hands and feet.

He was alive!

Creator Sets Free (Jesus) told the people, "Take off his wrappings and set him free."

Head Woman (Martha) and Healing Tears (Mary) wept for joy as they tore the ceremonial wrappings from their brother. They couldn't stop hugging and kissing him! All the people were full of joy and began to celebrate.

⁴⁵ When many of the local Tribal Members saw what Creator Sets Free (Jesus) had done, they put their trust in him. ⁴⁶ But some of them went to find the Separated Ones (Pharisees) to tell them what had happened.

A War Council is Called

47 When the Separated Ones (Pharisees) and the head holy men heard about this great miracle, they called the Grand Council together.

"What are we going to do?" they asked each other. "This man has powerful medicine and performs many signs and wonders. 48 If we do not stop him, all the people will believe in him. Then the People of Iron (Romans) will come and take away our Sacred Lodge and, with it, our *power to rule this* nation."

49 Hollow In The Rock (Caiaphas), the chief holy man for that year, said to the council, "Is it too hard for you to see? 50 It would be better for us if one man were to die for the people than for our whole nation to be destroyed."

51 Hollow In The Rock (Caiaphas) was not aware that, as the chief holy man for that year, he prophesied that Creator Sets Free (Jesus) would die for their nation. *Little did he know that* 52 he would not only die for their nation but also to gather together all of Creator's scattered children *from every nation* and make them into one people.

53 From that day forward the Grand Council set in motion a plan to have him killed.

54 Knowing this, Creator Sets Free (Jesus) no longer walked openly among the people. He went into the countryside near the desert wilderness to the Village of Fruitful Place (Ephraim). There he stayed *for a time* with his close followers.

On the Lookout for Creator Sets Free

55 It was time again for the traditional festival of bread without yeast, called Passover. Tribal members would travel from their homelands to Village of Peace (Jerusalem). Many would arrive early to perform a purification ceremony *to prepare for the festival.*

56 The tribal leaders were all looking for Creator Sets Free (Jesus). As they stood in the *courtyard* of the Sacred Lodge, they asked each other, "What do think? Surely he will not come here to the festival?"

57 For the head holy men and the Separated Ones (Pharisees) had given instruction that anyone who saw Creator Sets Free (Jesus) should report back to them so they could arrest him.

Preparation for His Burial

12 It was now six days before the Passover festival. Creator Sets Free (Jesus) returned to House of Figs (Bethany) to lodge at the home of Creator Helps Him (Lazarus), whom he had brought back to life from the dead. 2 That night, they had a meal to honor Creator Sets Free (Jesus). Head Woman (Martha) was preparing the meal, and her brother, Creator Helps Him (Lazarus), was sitting with the Wisdomkeeper and the other guests.

3 Healing Tears (Mary), *the sister of Head Woman (Martha),* took a small pottery jar which held some costly ointment, broke it and poured the sweet smelling oil on the feet of Creator Sets Free (Jesus). She then

wiped his feet with her hair, and the scent of the sweet smelling oil filled the whole house.

4 When Speaks Well Of (Judas), *also known as* Village Man (Iscariot), the one who would soon betray Creator Sets Free (Jesus), saw this, he said, 5 "This could have been traded for a year's wages and given to the poor."

6 He said this, not because he cared for the poor, but because he was a thief, and, as the keeper of the money pouch, he would take what he wanted.

7 "Let her be!" Creator Sets Free (Jesus) said to all, "She has done a good thing, saving this for the day of my burial. 8 You can help the poor any time, for they will always be with you, but I will not."

9 Word got out that Creator Sets Free (Jesus) was there. Many people came from all around to see him, and not only him but also Creator Helps Him (Lazarus), the one he had brought back from the dead. 10 So the head holy men were also making a plan to kill Creator Helps Him (Lazarus), 11 for because of him many of the Tribal Members believed in Creator Sets Free (Jesus), *that he was the Chosen One.*

His Grand Entry

12 The following day, when the people who had come to the Passover festival heard that Creator Sets Free (Jesus) was entering Village of Peace (Jerusalem), 13 a great crowd of them took branches from palm trees and went out to greet him.

Waving palm branches in their hands, they began to shout, "Hosanna!" meaning "Help us!" They cried out with glad hearts. "We honor you as the one who is to come representing the Great Spirit. You are the Great Chief of the tribes of Wrestles With Creator (Israel)!"

14 Creator Sets Free (Jesus) was riding on the colt of a donkey to give full meaning to the ancient prophecy, 15 "Do not fear, O daughter of Strong Mountain (Zion). Your Great Chief is coming to you, in a humble way, riding upon a young donkey."a

16 At the time his followers did not understand these things. It was not until some time later, when he had entered his place of honor and glory, that they remembered how the things done to him had first been written down by the ancient prophets long ago.

17-18 Among this crowd were the ones who had seen Creator Sets Free (Jesus) bring Creator Helps Him (Lazarus) back from the dead. They were telling everyone about this great miracle, and that is why the crowd was so large that day.

Creator Sets Free (Jesus) came riding down Olive Mountian and went into Village of Peace (Jerusalem). His twelve followers encircled him and led the donkey forward.

He did not fit the powerful image of a conquering ruler, for he was

---

a 12:15 Zechariah 9:9-10

not riding a warhorse; instead, he rode a small humble colt of a donkey. No mighty warriors rode next to him. No dignitaries from Village of Peace (Jerusalem) came out to meet him. It was mostly the common people who welcomed him that day.

19 The Separated Ones (Pharisees) *huddled together near the crowd.*

"Nothing we have done to stop him has worked," they complained. "Look! The whole world is now following him."

Wisdom Seekers Seek Him

Along with the tribal members of Wrestles With Creator (Israel) who came to participate in the Passover festival, there were also many outsiders from other nations who would come.

20 There were people from these nations who came to celebrate the Festival from the Land of Wisdom Seekers (Greece).

These were people who often prided themselves in their study of wisdom and knowledge.

21 They went up to Friend of Horses (Philip), who was from House of Fishing (Bethsaida) in Circle of Nations (Galilee), *and, knowing him to be one who walked with Creator Sets Free (Jesus),* they said to him, "Honored friend, we would like to see Creator Sets Free (Jesus), your Wisdomkeeper."

22 Friend of Horses (Philip) *didn't know what to do, so he* found Stands With Courage (Andrew) and asked him what he thought. Then together they both went to see Creator Sets Free (Jesus) and told him that the Wisdom Seekers (Greeks) wished to see him.

23 He answered them, "It is time for the True Human Being to be lifted up to his place of honor. 24 I speak from my heart. If a seed is unplanted, it remains only one seed; but if it dies, falls to the earth and enters the ground, it will then grow and become many seeds.

25 "The ones who love the kind of life this world gives will lose the life they seek, but the ones who let go of their life *in this world and follow my ways* will find the life of the world to come, full of beauty and harmony.

"Tell these Wisdom Seekers (Greeks) to walk the road with me. 26 Anyone who wants to serve me will walk in my footsteps, and I will take them to the same place I am going. If they give up their lives to serve me in this way, my Father will honor them."

The Time of Honor Has Come

A look of sorrow came over the face of Creator Sets Free (Jesus).

27 "But now I am deeply troubled and in anguish!" he said. "Should I ask my Father to rescue me from this hour that has now come? No! I came into the world for this time and for this purpose."

He then lifted his face, looked up to the sky and sent his words to the Great Spirit.

28 "Father," he prayed, "honor your name and show the world the beauty of it."

Suddenly, a voice from above spoke out of the sky, "I have honored my name, *for it represents who I am,* and I will once again honor and show the beauty of it."

29 Some of the people standing nearby heard the voice and said, "Was that thunder?"

Others said, "No, a spirit-messenger has spoken to him."

30 Creator Sets Free (Jesus) said to them, "This voice you heard was not for my sake, but for yours. 31 It is a sign to you that it is now time for the Great Spirit to make his final decision about this world. The evil one who now rules this world will be defeated and thrown down. 32 But I, the True Human Being, will be lifted up from the ground *and nailed to a cross.* This is the way I will bring all things, *in the world above and the earth below,*b to myself."

33 Creator Sets Free (Jesus) said this to show the kind of death he would die *and what his death would accomplish.*

34 The people who heard him said, "How can this be? We have been told from our Sacred Teachings that the Chosen One, when he comes, will remain beyond the end of all days. How can you say the True Human Being will be lifted up like this? Who are you talking about?"

35 Creator Sets Free (Jesus) spoke to them *with sadness in his voice.* "My light will shine on you for only a little while longer, so walk in my light before the darkness comes, for the ones who walk in darkness cannot see the path. 36 Put your trust in the one who gives you light, and then you will become children of light."

He looked around at the people, knowing that these were nearly the last public words he would speak.

He then went away to hide himself from the crowds.

Blind Eyes and Hard Hearts

37 Even though Creator Sets Free (Jesus) had *healed the sick, brought the dead back to life, and* shown the people powerful medicine from the Great Spirit, his own tribal nation still did not believe in him or trust him.

38-39 This showed the full meaning of the ancient prophecy, "Who will believe such a thing? Who will see that Creator's great power *would be shown in weakness?*"c 40 and, "His great light has blinded their eyes and his great love has hardened their hearts. If only they would open their hearts to him, then they would see clearly and he would make them whole."d

41 The prophet Creator Will Help Us (Isaiah) saw the true beauty of Creator Sets Free (Jesus) long ago and prophesied the reasons the people could not believe. 42 But even so, many Tribal Leaders did believe in him, but would not tell anyone because they feared the Separated Ones (Pharisees). They knew if they openly confessed their faith in him they would be

---

b **12:32** Colossians 1:19-20   c **12:38-39** Isaiah 53:1   d **12:40** Isaiah 6:10

put out of the gathering houses. [43] In the end, their reputation with the people was more important to them than bringing honor to the Maker of Life.

My Message Will Decide

As he was leaving, [44] Creator Sets Free (Jesus) *turned around, lifted his voice, and* cried out to the people *one last time,* "If you trust me, you are not only trusting me, but the one who sent me. [45] When you see me, you see the one who sent me. [46] I came into this dark world as a shining light, so the ones who trust me will no longer have to stumble in the darkness.

[47] "I have not come to decide against the ones who have heard my words but fail to walk in them. Instead, I have come to rescue them from the *worthless ways of this* world and set them free. [48] But a day is coming when the ones who have turned away from me and my words will be decided against. In the end, it will be the message I have spoken that will decide for or against them.

[49] "The message I have spoken is not from myself, it is from the one who sent me. I have spoken only what my Father gave me to speak, nothing more. [50] The instructions he gave me lead to the life of the world to come, that never fades— full of beauty and harmony."

The Ceremonial Meal Begins

13 The Passover festival was drawing near. Creator Sets Free (Jesus) knew it was time to leave this world and go back to his Father. His love for the ones who walked the road with him had always been great, and now, at the end, his love for them remained strong.

[2] The evil snake had already twisted the heart of Speaks Well Of (Judas), *also know as* Village Man (Iscariot), son of He Hears (Simon), to betray Creator Sets Free (Jesus).

[3] Creator Sets Free (Jesus) knew that his Father had put all things in his hands and that he had come from the Great Spirit and was returning to him.

Foot Washing Ceremony

[4] Knowing all of this, during the meal Creator Sets Free (Jesus) got up from the table, took off his outer garments, and wrapped a cloth around himself like a sash. [5] He poured water into a vessel and, one by one, he began to wash the feet of his followers and dry them with the cloth.

This was a task reserved for only the lowest servant of the household.

[6] He came to Stands On The Rock (Peter), who said to him, "Wisdomkeeper, are you going to wash my feet?"

[7] "You do not understand now what I am doing, but later you will," he answered.

[8] "No!" Stands On The Rock (Peter) lifted his voice, "This can never be!"

Creator Sets Free (Jesus) *looked deep into his eyes and* said, "If you refuse this, then you have no part in who I am."

⁹"Wisdomkeeper," he answered back, "*if this is so,* then wash my hands and head also!"

¹⁰Creator Sets Free (Jesus) replied, "If you have already had a bath, only your feet need washing, and then you will be clean all over. Now, you are all clean—except for one."

¹¹He said this because he knew who would betray him.

After he had finished washing all their feet, ¹²he put his outer garment back on and sat down again at the table.

"Do you see what I have done?" he said to them. ¹³"You are right to call me Wisdomkeeper and Chief—because I am. ¹⁴If I, your Wisdomkeeper and Chief, have washed your feet, then you should wash each others' feet. ¹⁵So follow my footsteps and do for each other what I have done for you.

¹⁶"I speak from my heart, the one who serves is not greater than the one who is served. A message bearer is not greater than the one who sent him. ¹⁷If you walk in this way of blessing, you will do well and it will return to you— full circle.

One of You Will Betray Me

¹⁸"I am not talking about all of you, for I know *the hearts of* the ones I have chosen. Now you will see the full meaning of the Sacred Teachings that said, 'The one who ate with me has turned against me.'*ᵉ* ¹⁹I am telling you this ahead

of time, so when it happens you will believe that I am *the Chosen One.*

²⁰"I speak from my heart, the one who welcomes the one I send welcomes me. The one who welcomes me, welcomes the one who sent me."

²¹When he finished saying this, Creator Sets Free (Jesus) became deeply troubled in his spirit. *As sorrow moved over his face,* he said to all, "From my heart I tell you, one of you will turn against me."

²²His followers' *hearts fell to the ground. They* looked around at each other, wondering who would do such a thing. ²³The follower*ᶠ* for whom Creator Sets Free (Jesus) had a special love was sitting next to him. ²⁴Stands On The Rock (Peter) motioned him to ask Creator Sets Free (Jesus) who it was. So he leaned back on his chest and whispered into his ear, "Wisdomkeeper, who is it?"

²⁵"When I dip my bread into the dish," he whispered back, "I will give it to the one who will turn against me."

He did as he said and handed the bread to Speaks Well Of (Judas), *also known as Village Man (Iscariot),* the son of He Hears (Simon). ²⁶When Speaks Well Of (Judas) took the bread, the evil snake took hold of his heart.

²⁷"Go now!" Creator Sets Free (Jesus) said to him, "and do what you have planned."

---

e 13:18 Psalm 41:9   f 13:23 He Shows Goodwill (John), the one who is telling the story, is speaking of himself.

28 None of the others understood what Creator Sets Free (Jesus) was saying to him. 29 Since he was the keeper of the money pouch, they thought he was going to pay for the ceremonial meal or give something to the poor. 30 As soon as he had taken the bread, Speaks Well Of (Judas) got up from the table and went out into the night.

A New Road

31 After he left, Creator Sets Free (Jesus) said to them all, "The time has now come for the True Human Being to honor the Great Spirit and to be honored by him. 32 As soon as the Son gives him honor, it will come back again—full circle."

The Passover meal was coming to an end. It was time to close the ceremony and face the dark night ahead. The heart of Creator Sets Free (Jesus) was full of compassion and love for the ones who had walked the road with him for over three winters.

33 "My little children," he said to them, "my time with you is almost gone. You will look for me, but where I am going you cannot follow. This is the same thing I said to the other Tribal Members and I now say to you."

His followers lifted their heads up and looked into the face of their Wisdomkeeper.

34 "I am giving you a new road to walk," he said. "In the same way I have loved you, you are to love each other. 35 This kind of love will be the sign for all people that you are walking the road with me."

Where Are You Going?

36 Stands On The Rock (Peter) spoke up and asked, "Wisdomkeeper, where are you going?"

"The path I walk tonight you cannot walk with me," he answered, "but you will walk it later."

37 "Wisdomkeeper!" he replied. "Why can't I walk with you now? I am ready to give my life for you!"

38 "Will you truly lay down your life for me?" Creator Sets Free (Jesus) asked. Then he said, "Before the rooster crows in the morning, you will deny three times that you know who I am!"

No Other Guide

14 *His followers hung their heads as his words sank deep into their hearts. Creator Sets Free (Jesus) gathered them together and had them sit down in a circle, like an eagle gathering her young under her wings. He spoke softly but clearly to them.*

"Don't let your hearts fall to the ground," he encouraged them. "Trust in the Great Spirit, and trust in me. 2 My Father's Lodge has room for everyone. If this were not so, then why would I tell you that I am going to prepare a place for you? 3 When I am finished, I will come back to you, so that you will always be with me. 4 You already know the path to where I am going."

5 Looks Like His Brother (Thomas) interrupted and said, "Wisdomkeeper, if we do not know where you are going, how can we know the path?"

6 "I am the *Great Spirit's* pathway, the truth *about who he really is*, and the life *of beauty and harmony he offers to all.* There is no other guide who can take you to the Father. 7 To know me is to know my Father, so from now on you know him and have seen him."

Show Us The Father

8 Friend Of Horses (Philip) said to him, "Wisdomkeeper, show us the Father and that will be enough."

9 "Friend Of Horses (Philip)," Creator Sets Free (Jesus) said, "how long have you walked with me, and still you do not know me? How can you say, 'Show us the Father'? The ones who have seen me have seen the Father. 10 Do you not believe that the Father is in me and I am in the Father?

"The words I speak to you are not my own; it is the Father speaking in me. 11 Trust in me, for I am in the Father and he is in me; or at least trust in the works my Father does through me.

12 "I speak from my heart. The ones who trust in me will do the same things I do, and even greater things, for I am going away to my Father. 13-14 When you ask the Father for anything, ask it in my name, representing who I am. When you ask for anything in this way, I will do it to bring honor to my Father.

Promise Of The Holy Spirit

15 "If you love me, you will walk in my ways. 16 I will ask the Father to send one who will always walk beside you and guide you *on the Good Road.* 17 He is the Spirit of Truth, the one this world is not able to accept because it does not see or know him. But you know him, for he is with you now and will soon be in you.

18 "I will not leave you like a child with no parents—I will come back to you. 19 Soon this world will no longer see me, but you will see me. Because I will live again, you will also live. 20 When that day comes, you will know that I am in the Father, that you are in me and I am in you. 21 The ones who walk in my ways and stay true to my message love me. They will be loved by my Father, and I will love them and show them my true self."

22 Speaks Well Of (Judas), not the one who betrayed him, asked, "Wisdomkeeper, how will you show yourself to us and not to the rest of the world?"

23 "I will show myself to the ones who love me and are staying true to my teachings. They will be loved by my Father, and we will come and make our home in and among them. 24 The ones who do not *return my* love will not walk in my message. This message is not only mine. It is from the one who sent me—my Father.

25 "I have told you these things while I am still with you, 26 but there is one whom the Father is sending to represent me. He will walk beside you and be your Spirit Guide. He is the Holy Spirit, who will be your Wisdomkeeper, and will help you to remember all that I have told you.

Great Peace

27 "I leave you now with my great peace—it is my gift to you. It is not the kind of peace the world gives. Do not let the troubles of this world fill you with fear and make your hearts fall to the ground and do not let fear hold you back. 28 I told you I am going away and that I will come back. This should make your hearts glad if you truly love me, for I am going to the one who is greater than I am—to my Father, *the One Above Us All.*

29 "I have told you all these things beforehand, so when you see them happen you will believe. 30 There is only a little time left for me to talk with you. The dark ruler of this world is coming. His power over me is nothing; 31 but I must walk the path the Father has for me, so the world will know the great love I have for him.

"Get up!" he said to them, "It is time for us to go from here."

The True Vine

15 "I am the true grapevine. My Father is the Vine Keeper. 2 He cuts off the branches in me that have no fruit. He carefully trims back the branches with fruit, so they will grow more fruit.

3 "My teachings have purified you, 4 but you must stay joined to me in the same way a branch is joined to the vine. A branch cannot grow fruit unless it is joined to the vine. It is the same with you and me.

5 "I am the vine and you are the branches. The ones who stay joined to me will grow much fruit, for without me nothing grows. 6 The ones who do not stay joined to me are broken off and dry up, then they are gathered up and used to make a fire.

7 "If you are joined to me and my words remain in you, you can ask me for anything and it will be done. 8 When you grow a harvest of fruit, this will show that you are walking my road. You will then bring great honor to my Father.

The Road of Love

9 "In the same way the Father loves me, I have loved you; so never stop walking this road of love. 10 By doing what the Father has told me, I have remained in his love. 11 As you walk in my ways, my love will remain in you. I am saying this so your hearts will be filled with the same joy I have.

12 "To walk the road with me, you must love each other in the same way I have loved you. 13 There is no greater way to show love to friends than to die in their place. 14 You are my friends if you walk in my ways and do what I say. 15 I no longer see you as my servants but as friends. Masters do not share their hearts and plans with their servants, but I have shown you everything I have heard from my Father.

16 "You may think you chose me, but I am the one who chose you. You are my new garden where I will grow a great harvest of my love— the fruit that remains. When you bear this fruit, you represent who I am—my name. Then the Father will give you whatever you ask for.

[17] I am telling you this so you will walk the road of love with each other.

The World Will Hate You

[18] "If you are hated by the world, remember, it hated me first. [19] The ones who walk in the ways of this world love the ones who do the same but look down on and hate the ones who do not. I have chosen you to walk away from the ways of this world, on a different path, and that is why the world will hate you. [20] Remember, I told you a servant is not greater than the one he serves. If I was hunted down, it will be the same for you. If they walk in my message, they will walk in yours.

[21] "The *people who walk in the ways of this* world will do this to you because you walk in my ways, representing me. This shows they do not know the one who sent me.

[22] "If I had not come to them and represented the truth, they would not be guilty of this, but now their guilt remains. [23-24] If I had not done the things no one else has done, they would have no guilt; but now they have seen with their own eyes and hated me and my Father. [25] The full meaning of their own Sacred Teachings have become clear, 'They hated me for no reason.'[g]

Spirit of Truth

[26] "I am sending you the Spirit of Truth, the one who is coming from the Father. He will walk close by your side, representing me, and telling the truth about me. [27] You will also represent me as truth-tellers, for you have walked with me from the first and have seen these things with your own eyes.

It Is Better If I Go Away

16 "I am telling you these things to keep you from stumbling away from the path. [2] The Tribal Leaders will force you out of their gathering houses, and the time will come when they will put you to death thinking they are doing what the Great Spirit wants, [3] all because they do not know me or my Father. [4] I am telling you this so when the time comes you will remember I told you ahead of time. I did not tell these things from the first because I was with you— [5] but now I am going away.

"I am returning to the one who sent me, but none of you are asking, 'Where are you going?' *You are thinking only of yourselves* [6] because my words have made your hearts fall to the ground. [7] But I speak from my heart, it is better for you that I go away. If I remain, the one who will guide you will not come; but if I go, I will send him to you.

The Holy Spirit's Work

[8] "When the Holy Spirit comes, he will clearly show the wrong ways of this world, the right ways of the world above, and the answer that will be required of them in the end. [9] He will show them that the answer to their broken ways is to trust in me. [10] The right ways of the world above will come when I

---

g 15:25 Psalm 69:4

return to the Father, and they no longer see me. [11] The final decision *about this world* will come because *Accuser (Satan)*—the ruler of this world—has been found guilty.

[12] "There are many more things I want to say to you, but your hearts are not strong enough to hear them now. [13] When the Spirit of Truth comes, he will be the one to tell you. He will be your *one true* Spirit Guide and will lead you down the path of truth. He will fully represent me and will tell you only what I have told him. The Spirit will show you what is coming on the road ahead. [14] He will honor me by making known to you everything I have shown him. [15] All that I am and all that I have comes from the Father. He has not held back one thing from me, and the Spirit will not hold back anything from you.

A Little While

[16] "Soon I will be gone and you will not be able to see me, and then after a little while you will see me again."

[17-18] His followers began to whisper to each other, "What is he saying? We don't know what he means by 'a little while' and 'not seeing him and then seeing him again.' What does he mean by 'I go to the Father'?"

[19] Creator Sets Free (Jesus) knew what they wanted to ask him, so he said, "You want to know what I meant when I said 'soon you will not see me, but then you will see me again.'

[20] "I speak from my heart. Your tears will be many and your hearts will fall to the ground, because of what will happen to me, but the world around you will have glad hearts. [21] All of you will be filled with sorrow, but your sorrow will turn into dancing!

"When a woman is giving birth, she has sorrow, for her time of pain has come. But when she gives birth to her child, she forgets her pain, for a new human being has been born into the world. [22] It will be the same for you. You will have sorrow for now; but when I see you again, you will dance for joy—and no one will be able to take your joy from you.

A New Way of Asking

[23-24] "When that time comes, your questions will be answered—not by asking me, but by asking the Father himself. You will then ask the Father in my name, fully representing me. I know you have never asked in this way before, but it is now time. I speak from my heart, when you ask in this new way, the Father will answer, and your hearts will know the full meaning of joy.

The End of Stories

[25] "I have told you truths from the world above, using earthly stories. The time is coming when I will not have to use stories, but will tell you plainly about the Father. When that time comes, you will not need me to ask the Father for you, because you will ask him yourself. [26] When you ask in my name, you

are representing me, 27and your love and trust in me will bring the Father's love to you—full circle. 28You now believe that I came from the Great Spirit. Yes, I came into this world from the Father, and now I am leaving this world and returning to the Father."

29His followers said to him, "Now you are speaking plainly to us instead of using stories! 30We now see that you know all things and can answer a question before it is asked. This helps us to believe that you came from the Great Spirit."

I Have Defeated the World

31"You say you believe now," Creator Sets Free (Jesus) said to them, 32"but soon you will all be scattered and return to your families. You will leave me alone, but I will not be alone, for my Father is with me.

33"I have told you all these things so you will have my peace. This world is full of sorrow, pain and trouble; but have strong hearts, for I have defeated the world."

He Prays for His Followers

17 When Creator Sets Free (Jesus) was finished speaking to his followers, he lifted his eyes to the world above and sent his voice to the Great Spirit.

"O Great Father," he prayed, "it is time for you to bring honor to your Son, so he may bring honor to you. 2You have put all human beings under the care of your Son, so he can give them the life of the world to come, that never fades—full of beauty and harmony. 3This life comes from knowing you, the only true and Great Spirit, and from knowing the Chosen One, Creator Sets Free (Jesus), the one you have sent into this world.

4"I have brought you honor on earth by finishing the work you sent me to do. 5It is now time, my Father, for you to honor me with the beauty I shared at your side before you created all things."

6"I have shown who you truly are to the ones you gave me from this world. They were always yours and you trusted me with them, and they have walked in your ways. 7They now know that everything I have comes from you. 8The message you gave to me I have given to them. They have welcomed the truth about who I am and trust that you sent me. 9These are the ones I now pray for. I am not praying for the ones who walk in the ways of the world, but for the ones you gave to me, for they belong to you. 10My followers bring honor to me; they are a gift from you, a gift we share together.

11*"Since I am returning to you,* I will no longer be in the world, but my followers will still be here. O Father of all that is holy, watch over them with the loving care that we share with one another. In this way they will also share the love that makes us one.

12"During my time on earth representing you, I kept them safe in your loving care. Not one of them has been lost, except for the one foretold in the Sacred Teachings, the one doomed to a bad end.

13 "I am returning to you now; but while I am still here, I pray for my followers, so they may share in my joy. 14 Your message, that I gave them, has taken root in their hearts. Like me, they have chosen not to walk in the ways of this world, and so the world hates them. 15 I am not asking you to remove them from the world, but that you keep them safe from the evil one and his ways. 16 They no longer belong to *the ways* of this world, any more than I do. 17 Make them holy through the beautiful message of your truth.

18 "You sent me into the world, and now, in the same way, I send them into the world. 19 I set my life apart for them in a sacred manner, so they may also set their lives apart to walk in the beauty of your truth.

20 "My prayers are not only for them, but for all who will trust in me through their message. 21 I pray that all who walk with me will be joined together as one, in the same way that you, Father, are in me and I am in you—that they may be one in us. This is how the world will believe that you have sent me.

22 "The beauty you gave to me I have given to them; this will join them together with us. 23 In the same way you are in me, I will be in them, beautifully joined together as one. This is the reason you sent me into this world, to show that you love them just as you love me.

24 "O Great Father, I want the ones you have given to me to share this place of beauty that I have so they can see the power of your love for me, a love that we shared before you created all things.

25 "O Father of all that is good and right, the world does not know you; but I know you, and my followers know you sent me. 26 I have represented, and will always represent, who you truly are, so that the love you have for me will be in them and I will live in them also."

Betrayal

18 When he finished sending up his prayers, he and the ones who walked the road with him walked across the Valley of Darkness (Kidron) and entered a garden with many olive trees.

2 Speaks Well Of (Judas), the betrayer, knew about this place because Creator Sets Free (Jesus) would often go there with his followers. 3 The betrayer came into the garden, and with him came a band of lodge soldiers sent from the scroll keepers, head holy men and Separated Ones (Pharisees), *representing the elders of the Grand Council.* The air was filled with the smell of burning torches as they entered the garden carrying clubs and long knives.

4 Creator Sets Free (Jesus) knew all this would happen, yet he turned to the soldiers and asked, "Who have you come for?"

5 *With one voice* they answered back, "Creator Sets Free (Jesus) from Seed Planter Village (Nazareth)!"

The betrayer, Speaks Well Of (Judas), was standing there with the lodge soldiers when Creator Sets Free (Jesus) answered, "I am he!"

⁶At the sound of his voice they all moved back and fell to the ground.

⁷He asked them again, "Who have you come for?"

They answered, "Creator Sets Free (Jesus) from Seed Planter Village (Nazareth)."

⁸"I told you already, I am the one you are looking for," he said. "Let these other men go."

⁹He said this to fulfill his promise, "None of the ones you gave to me have been lost."ʰ

¹⁰Right then, Stands On The Rock (Peter) drew his long knife from its sheath and cut off the right ear of the servant of the chief holy man. The servant's name was Chieftain (Malchus).

¹¹Creator Sets Free (Jesus) turned to Stands On The Rock (Peter) and cried out, *"Enough of this!* Put your long knife back into its sheath. Shall I not drink the cup of suffering my Father has asked of me?"

Creator Sets Free
Is Arrested

¹²The lodge soldiers, along with their head soldier and the Grand Council representatives, took hold of Creator Sets Free (Jesus), tied him securely with cowhide strips, ¹³and took him first to Walks Humbly (Annas), one of the high holy men. He was the father of the wife of Hollow In The Rock (Caiaphas), the chief holy man ¹⁴who had advised the Grand Council by saying, "It will be better if one man dies for all the people."ⁱ

First Denial

¹⁵Stands On The Rock (Peter) and one other followerʲ had been watching from a distance. Since this follower was known by the chief holy man, he entered the courtyard of the house; ¹⁶but Stands On The Rock (Peter) stood outside the gate. This follower spoke to the gatekeeper, a young woman, who then let Stands On The Rock (Peter) in.

¹⁷She said to him, "Aren't you one of his followers?"

"No!" he told her, "I am not."

¹⁸The night was growing cold, so some of the men, along with the soldier guards from the Lodge, built a fire in the courtyard to keep warm. Stands On The Rock (Peter) stood there with them, trying to stay warm.

Creator Sets Free Questioned

¹⁹Back inside, the chief holy man began to question Creator Sets Free (Jesus) about his followers and his teachings. ²⁰Creator Sets Free (Jesus) said to him, "I have spoken openly to all, in the gathering houses and the Sacred Lodge. I said nothing in secret. ²¹Why ask me? Ask the ones who heard me—they will know."

²²One of the head soldiers struck him in the face and said, "Is that how you answer a chief holy man?"

²³Creator Sets Free (Jesus) answered him back, "If I have spoken wrongly, tell me what I said wrong. If I spoke what is true, then by what right do you strike me?"

---

h 18:9 John 6:39   i 18:14 John 11:49-50   j 18:15 He Shows Goodwill (John)

²⁴ Walks Humbly (Annas) decided to send Creator Sets Free (Jesus) to Hollow In The Rock (Caiaphas), the chief holy man. So they took him, still bound by ropes, to Hollow In The Rock (Caiaphas).

The Rooster Crows

²⁵ Outside in the courtyard Stands On The Rock (Peter) was still warming himself by the fire. The others asked him, "You are not one of his followers, are you?"

"No!" Stands On The Rock (Peter) denied. "I am not!"

²⁶ One of the servants of the chief holy man, a relative of the man whose ear had been cut off, looked at him, and said, "Yes, you are! I saw you in the garden with him!"

²⁷ Stands On The Rock (Peter) shook his head in denial—and right then a rooster began to crow.

To the People Of Iron

²⁸ Creator Sets Free (Jesus) was taken from the house of Hollow In The Rock (Caiaphas) to the headquarters of the governor of the People of Iron (Romans). The Tribal Leaders stayed outside, for they did not want to become ceremonially unclean by going inside. It was early in the morning and many of them had not yet eaten the ceremonial meal of Passover.

²⁹ Spear Of The Great Waters (Pilate) came outside to meet them.

They took Creator Sets Free (Jesus) and stood him before Spear Of The Great Waters (Pilate). He took a good long look at him, then turned to back to the crowd.

"What has this man done wrong?" he asked them?

³⁰ "If he was not a criminal, would we have brought him to you?" they answered.

"Take him away!" ³¹ Spear Of The Great Waters (Pilate) said to them, "and use your own law to decide what to do."

"Our Tribal Law will not permit us to put him to death," they answered.

³² This proved that Creator Sets Free (Jesus) was right when he told them how he would die—*by being nailed to a cross.*

Are You Their Chief?

³³ Spear Of The Great Waters (Pilate) went back into his headquarters and had Creator Sets Free (Jesus) brought to him, *so he could question him in private.*

Once inside, he said to him, "Are you the chief of the tribes of Wrestles With Creator (Israel)?"

³⁴ "Is this your question," Creator Sets Free (Jesus) asked, "or are you listening to others?"

³⁵ "I am not from your tribes," Spear Of The Great Waters (Pilate) answered. "It is your own people and their head holy men who have turned you over to me. What have you done?"

³⁶ "My way of ruling is a Good Road, it is not in the ways of this world. If it were, my followers would have fought to keep me from being captured."

³⁷ "So then, you are a chief," he said back to him.

"It is you who have said it," Creator Sets Free (Jesus) answered. "I was born for this and have come into the world for this purpose—to tell about the truth. The ones who belong to the truth will listen to my voice."

³⁸ Spear Of The Great Waters (Pilate) *shook his head* and said, "What is truth?"

I Find No Guilt In Him

³⁹ Then Spear Of The Great Waters (Pilate) went outside to the Tribal Leaders and said to them, "I find no guilt in this man. By your own tradition we set free one criminal during your Passover festival. Do you want me to release Creator Sets Free (Jesus), your chief?"

⁴⁰ "No! Not him," the crowd roared back. "Release Son Of His Father (Barabbas)!"

Son of His Father (Barabbas) was a troublemaker who had caused an uprising.

Crown of Thorns

19 Spear Of The Great Waters (Pilate) turned Creator Sets Free (Jesus) over to his soldiers to have him beaten. ² The soldiers twisted together a headdress from a thorn bush, pressed the thorns into his head and wrapped a purple Chief Blanket around him. ³ They bowed down before him, making a big show of it, and kept mocking him saying, "Honor! Honor to the Great Chief of the tribes of Wrestles With Creator (Israel)."

They took turns hitting him on his face *until he was bruised and bloodied.*

⁴ Spear Of The Great Waters (Pilate) stood before the crowd again and said, "I bring to you the one in whom I have found no guilt."

Creator Sets Free (Jesus) was brought forward, *blood flowing down his bruised face.* ⁵ He was wearing the headdress of thorns and the purple Chief Blanket that was wrapped around him.

"Behold the man!" Spear Of The Great Waters (Pilate) said to them. ⁶ "Take a good long look at him!"

The crowd stared at him in stunned silence.

But then the head holy men and the Lodge guards began to shout, "Death! Death on the cross!"

"Then take him and kill him yourselves," Spear Of The Great Waters (Pilate) said to them. "I find no guilt in him!"

⁷ They answered him back, "Our Law tells us he must die, for he has represented himself as the Son of the Great Spirit."

Power of Life and Death

⁸ When Spear Of The Great Waters (Pilate) heard this, his fear grew stronger, ⁹ so he took Creator Sets Free (Jesus) back inside his headquarters.

"Who are you, and where are you from?" he questioned him.

Creator Sets Free (Jesus) *stood there and* remained silent.

¹⁰ "Speak to me! Do you not know I have the power of life and death over you? I can have you killed or set you free," he warned him. "Have you nothing to say?"

11 "The only power you have is what has been given you from above," he answered. "The ones who turned you over to me carry the greater guilt."

12 Spear Of The Great Waters (Pilate) tried harder to have Creator Sets Free (Jesus) released, but the people would not have it.

They stood their ground, saying, "If you release a man who says he is a chief, you are not honoring the ruler of your people, for anyone who claims to be a chief challenges his power."

Stone of Deciding

13 When Spear Of The Great Waters (Pilate) heard this, he took Creator Sets Free (Jesus) and went to the Stone of Deciding, called Gabbatha in the tribal language, and sat down. 14 It was now midday on the Day of Preparation for the Passover festival.

He brought Creator Sets Free (Jesus) before the people and said, "Here is your chief."

15 "Take him away! Take him away!" the crowd shouted with one voice. "Nail him to the cross!"

"Would you have me nail your chief to the cross?" he asked them.

This time the head holy men answered back, "We have no other chief than the Ruler of the People of Iron (Caesar)."

16 Spear Of The Great Waters (Pilate) then turned Creator Sets Free (Jesus) over to the soldiers to have him put to death on the cross, so they took him away.

The cross was an instrument of torture and terror used by the People of Iron (Romans) to strike fear into the hearts of any who dared to rise up against their empire. The victim's hands and feet would be pierced with large iron nails, fastening them to the cross. The victims would hang there, sometimes for days, until they were dead. This was one of the most cruel and painful ways to die ever devised by human beings.

Ultimate Sacrifice

The soldiers placed a wooden crossbeam on his back and forced him to carry it to the place where he would be executed.

17 Creator Sets Free (Jesus) carried the crossbeam to the Place of the Skull, which is called Golgotha in the tribal language. 18 There they nailed his hands and feet to the cross, along with the two others, and placed his cross between the two of them.

19 Spear Of The Great Waters (Pilate) fastened a sign to the top of the cross where they attached the crossbeam with these words written on it:

CREATOR SETS FREE
FROM SEED PLANTERS VILLAGE
CHIEF OF THE TRIBES
OF WRESTLES WITH CREATOR

20 This was near Village of Peace (Jerusalem). *So that many of the Tribal Members could read it,* the sign was written in Aramaic, their tribal language, but also in Latin and

Greek, *the languages of the People of Iron (Romans).*

21 The chief head holy men and the Tribal Leaders said to Spear Of The Great Waters (Pilate), "Don't write 'chief of the tribes.' Instead write, 'He said he is chief.'"

22 But he answered, "What I have written will stand."

23 The soldiers stripped his clothes from him when they nailed his hands and feet to the cross. They tore one of his garments into four pieces, one for each guard. His long outer garment was woven together into one piece, 24 so they said, "Let's not tear this, we can draw straws for it."

This gave full meaning to the Sacred Teachings that said, "They divided my clothes between them and gambled for my garment." [k] This is what the soldiers did *as they kept watch over Creator Sets Free (Jesus).*

25-26 Standing near the cross was Bitter Tears (Mary), the mother of Creator Sets Free (Jesus), who had come to see him, along with her sister. Two other women also came with her—Brooding Tears (Mary) the wife of Trader (Clopas), and Strong Tears (Mary) from Creator's High Lodge (Magdala). The much loved follower[l] of Creator Sets Free (Jesus) was also there with them.

When Creator Sets Free (Jesus) looked down and saw them, he said to his mother, *"Honored woman, look to your son."* 27 Then he said to his follower, "Look to your mother."

From that time the follower took Bitter Tears (Mary) into his family and cared for her.

28 Creator Sets Free (Jesus), knowing he had done all the ancient Sacred Teachings had foretold, said, "I thirst."

29 There was a vessel of sour and bitter wine standing nearby. One of the soldiers dipped a cloth in it to soak up some wine. He wrapped the cloth around the tip of a hyssop branch and held it up to the mouth of Creator Sets Free (Jesus).

30 He then tasted the bitter wine, *turned his head to the sky* and cried out loud, "It is done!"

He then lowered his head to his chest, and *with his last breath,* gave up his spirit.

Creator Sets Free (Jesus) was dead.

Not One Bone Broken

31 Soon the sun would set and a special Day of Resting would begin, *when no work could be done.* It was time to prepare for this day, so the Tribal Members asked Spear Of The Great Waters (Pilate) to have the legs of the men on the crosses broken, *which would make them die sooner.* Then they could take the bodies down and prepare them for burial.

32 The soldiers came and broke the legs of the two men on each side of Creator Sets Free (Jesus), 33 but when they came to him, they saw he was already dead. Instead of breaking his legs, 34 one of the soldiers took a spear and pierced

---

k **19:24** Psalm 22:18   l **19:25-26** He Shows Goodwill (John)

his side. Blood and water flowed out from the wound.

35 The one who saw these things with his own eyes is telling the truth about this—so that all will believe. 36 This was foretold in the ancient Sacred Teachings that say, "Not one of his bones was broken,"[m] 37 and, "They will look upon the one they have pierced."[n]

Traditional Burial

38 He Gives More (Joseph) from High Mountain (Arimathea), *a man with many possessions,* was a follower of Creator Sets Free (Jesus), but in secret, because he feared the Tribal Leaders. *Since it would soon be sunset when the Day of Resting would begin,* he went to Spear Of The Great Waters (Pilate) and asked permission to remove the body of Creator Sets Free (Jesus) from the cross.

Spear Of The Great Waters (Pilate) released the body to him. So he and another man, 39 Conquers The People (Nicodemus), who had come to Creator Sets Free (Jesus) in secret at night, took his body away *to prepare it ceremonially for burial.* Conquers The People (Nicodemus) had brought a mixture of myrrh and oils weighing about seventy five pounds. 40 Together they ceremonially wrapped his body for burial in the traditional way, using strips of cloth and herbal spices and oils.

41-42 So because it was the Day of Preparation for the Passover festival, *and the day of resting was about to begin,* they laid the body of Creator Sets Free (Jesus) in a nearby burial cave that had never been used *and then returned to their homes.*

His Body is Gone

20 Early on the first day of the week, Strong Tears (Mary) from Tower of Creator's High Lodge (Magdala) came to the burial cave early in the morning while it was still dark. When she saw the stone had been removed from the burial cave, 2 she ran to find Stands On The Rock (Peter) and the much loved follower[o] of Creator Sets Free (Jesus).

She found them, and *catching her breath she* said to them, "They have taken the body of our Wisdomkeeper away, and we don't know where he is!"

3-4 Stands On The Rock (Peter) raced to the burial cave, but the other follower outran him and came there first. 5-7 He stooped low to look inside but did not go in all the way. He saw strips of cloth lying there, but the cloth that had been wrapped around the head of Creator Sets Free (Jesus) was rolled into a bundle, lying by itself. Stands On The Rock (Peter) arrived behind him and came to the cave. When he went inside, he saw the same things.

8 The other follower, who arrived first, now found the courage to go inside all the way. He saw the burial cave was empty—and believed. 9 But they still didn't understand from the Sacred Teachings that he would return from death. 10 Then

---

m 19:36 Psalm 34:20   n 19:37 Zechariah 12:10   o 20:2 He Shows Goodwill (John)

they went back to the place where they were staying.

A Woman Sees Him First

After the men left, Strong Tears (Mary) from Creator's High Lodge (Magdala) went back to the garden.

11 Her heart was on the ground as she stood outside the cave weeping. As the tears ran down her face, she looked inside. 12 There she saw two spirit-messengers dressed in white. They were sitting, one at the head, the other at the feet, of where the body of Creator Sets Free (Jesus) had once lain.

13 They looked at her and said, *"Honored woman,* why do you weep?"

"My Wisdomkeeper is gone," she answered, "and I don't know where they have taken him."

14 She turned around to see a man standing behind her. It was Creator Sets Free (Jesus), but she didn't recognize him.

15 *"Honored* woman, why the tears?" he said to her. "Who are you looking for?"

She thought he was the keeper of the garden, so she said, "If you have carried him away, tell me where, and I will find him."

16 "Strong Tears (Mary)," he said to her *in a soft and kind voice.*

She looked closer at him and her eyes grew wide. Then she hugged him close and whispered in his ear in her native language.

"Rabboni!" she said—meaning Wisdomkeeper.

17 "You must let me go," he said back to her. "I have not yet gone up to the Father. Go to my brothers who walked the road with me and say to them, 'I am going up to my Father and your Father, to the one who is the Great Spirit and Father of us all.'"

Creator Sets Free (Jesus) had chosen to show himself first to a woman, Strong Tears (Mary) from Creator's High Lodge (Magdala), the one he had set free from seven evil spirits.

18 Strong Tears (Mary) then went and found the followers of Creator Sets Free (Jesus) and said, "I have seen our Wisdomkeeper!"

She then told them everything she had heard from him.

His Followers See Him

19 It was now late in the same day, the first day of the week. His followers were all hiding behind locked doors in fear of being captured by the Tribal Leaders.

Suddenly, Creator Sets Free (Jesus) himself was standing in front of them, and said, "Peace be with you!"

20 He then showed them where the iron nails had pierced his hands and where the spear had cut into his side.

When they saw their Wisdomkeeper, the hearts of his followers were filled with joy, 21 so he said to them again, "Peace be with you! In the same way the Father above has sent me, I am now sending you."

22 He blew his breath on them and said, *"You will breathe in and receive the Holy Spirit. With his wisdom and*

guidance, 23 if you release others from their bad hearts and broken ways, they are released. If you do not release them, they are not released."

Put Away Your Doubts

24 Looks Like His Brother (Thomas), one of the original twelve followers, was not there when Creator Sets Free (Jesus) showed himself to the others. 25 They told him, "We have seen the Wisdomkeeper with our own eyes."

But he said to them, "Unless I see the nail marks in his hands, and put my finger into them, and put my hand into the hole in his side, I will not believe."

26 Eight days later his followers were gathered together again, and Looks Like His Brother (Thomas) was with them. The doors were all locked, but Creator Sets Free (Jesus) came in and stood before them all.

"Peace be with you," he said. 27 Then he turned to Looks Like His Brother (Thomas) and said, "Look closely at my hands, and touch my scars with your finger. Put your hand into the wound in my side. Then put away your doubts and trust in me."

28 "You are my Honored Chief and my Creator," he said.

29 "Now you believe, because you have seen me?" he said to him. "A greater blessing will rest on the ones who have not seen but still believe."

30 Creator Sets Free (Jesus) did many more powerful signs before the eyes of his followers that have not been written down in this book. 31 But, I have told this much so you will believe that Creator Sets Free (Jesus) is the Chosen One, the Son of the Great Spirit; and when you put your trust in all that his name represents, then the life of beauty and harmony he has promised to all will be yours.

Back to Fishing

21 A while later, Creator Sets Free (Jesus) showed himself again to his followers by Lake of Circle of Nations (Sea of Galilee), *also called Sea of Rolling Water (Sea of Tiberias).*

2 Stands On The Rock (Peter) along with other followers of Creator Sets Free (Jesus) had gathered there. With him were Looks Like His Brother (Thomas), Creator Gives (Nathanael) from Reed Village (Cana) in Circle of Nations (Galilee), the two sons of Gift Of Creator (Zebedee), and two other followers.

3 Stands On The Rock (Peter) said to them, "I'm going fishing."

They all agreed and said, "Take us with you."

So they took a canoe out onto the lake. *Under the light of the moon and stars* they worked hard all night. Again and again they threw out their nets and drew them back in—empty.

4 Just as the first light of day was dawning, Creator Sets Free (Jesus) came and stood on the shore; but they didn't know it was he.

5 "Friends!" he called out to them, "have you netted any fish?"

"No!" they answered.

⁶ "Throw out your nets to the right of your canoe," he shouted to them. "You will find some fish there."

They did as he said, and the net was filled with so many fish they could not pull it into the canoe. ⁷*He Shows Goodwill (John),* the much loved follower of Creator Sets Free (Jesus), said to Stands On The Rock (Peter), "It is our Wisdomkeeper!"

Stands On The Rock (Peter) had taken off his outer garment to fish. He put it back on and jumped into the water. ⁸ The shore was not far, so the others made their way in, dragging the net full of fish behind the canoe.

They came to the shore and stepped out of the canoe. ⁹ They saw a warm fire with fish cooking over the coals and some bread to eat.

He Feed His Followers

¹⁰ Creator Sets Free (Jesus) *looked up from cooking and* said, "Bring me some of the fish you caught."

¹¹ Stands On The Rock (Peter) climbed into the canoe and pulled the net to shore. The fish were large, and they counted them—one hundred and fifty three in all! But even with so many fish the net did not tear.

¹² Creator Sets Free (Jesus) said, "Let's eat."

They all sat down to eat, but no one dared ask, "Who are you?" They knew it must be their Wisdomkeeper.

¹³ He took the bread and gave some to each of them, along with a piece of fish. ¹⁴ This was the third time he had shown himself to them after coming back to life from the dead.

Stands On The Rock Restored

¹⁵ When they had finished eating, Creator Sets Free (Jesus) took Stands On The Rock (Peter) *and sat down with him by the lake.*

He spoke to him, *using the name his family gave him,* "One Who Hears (Simon), son of He Shows Goodwill (John), do you love me more than the others love me?"

"Yes, Wisdomkeeper," he answered, "you know I am your friend."

"Then feed my lambs," he said.

They sat looking out over the water and listening to the sound of the waves coming in to the shore.

¹⁶ Then a second time Creator Sets Free (Jesus) asked, "One Who Hears (Simon), son of He Shows Goodwill (John), do you love me?"

"Yes, Wisdomkeeper," he answered him again, "you know how deeply I care for you."

"Then watch over my sheep," he said.

The sound of the water birds could be heard in the distance and the sun felt warm as it rose higher in the sky.

¹⁷ Creator Sets Free (Jesus) asked him a third time, "One Who Hears (Simon), Son of He Shows Goodwill (John), do you love me as a friend?"

Stands On The Rock (Peter) felt his heart sink because he asked the third time, "Do you love me as a friend?"

"Wisdomkeeper!" he said, "you know all things, you must know how deeply I care for you—I am your friend!"

Creator Sets Free (Jesus) said to him again, "Feed my sheep."

18 Creator Sets Free (Jesus) then said to him, "I tell you from my heart, when you were a young man, you dressed yourself and walked wherever you wanted. But when you grow old, you will stretch out your hands and someone else will dress you and take you to a place you do not want to go."

19 He was telling him the kind of death he would die, to bring honor to Creator.

Then he said to Stands On The Rock (Peter), "Come, walk the road with me."

This was the same invitation he had given years earlier to Stands On The Rock (Peter) in Circle of Nations (Galilee) after the canoes had been filled with fish.

Walk the Road I Have Chosen

20 Stands On The Rock (Peter) looked over at *He Shows Goodwill (John),* the much loved follower of Creator Sets Free (Jesus)—the same one who, during the ceremonial meal, had leaned back and asked, "Wisdomkeeper, who will betray you?"

21 When Stands On The Rock (Peter) saw him, he said to Creator Sets Free (Jesus), "Wisdomkeeper, what about this man, *how will he die?"*

22 Creator Sets Free (Jesus) answered him, "If I want him to remain alive until I return, why would it matter? You must walk the road I have chosen for you."

23 When the others heard what Creator Sets Free (Jesus) had said about He Shows Goodwill (John), talk began to go around that he would never die. But Creator Sets Free (Jesus) did not say he would not die. He said, "If I want him to remain alive until I return, why would it matter to you?"

The Purpose of This Story

24 The one telling you this story has seen and heard these things with his own eyes, and all can agree he is telling the truth. 25 Many more things could be told about Creator Sets Free (Jesus), the message of his Good Road, and the people his life touched. This story has been written down in a book, but not everything; for he did so many things, if they were all written down in books, the whole world would not have room for them.

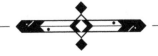

*In the last days I will rain down my Spirit
upon all human beings from every nation.
Your sons and daughters will prophesy.
Young braves will see visions and elders will
have dreams. In those days, my Spirit will rain
down on all who serve me, both men
and women. There will be powerful signs
and omens in the world above and on the earth
below—blood and fire with tall clouds of
smoke. The sun will grow dark and the moon
will turn red like blood, before the great and
dreadful Day of Creator comes. Then the
ones who cry out to the Great Spirit
will be made whole and set free."*

*From the Great Spirit
To the tribes of Wrestles With Creator*

*Joel Chapter Two
Verses Twenty-Eight to Thirty-Two*

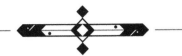

The Good Story Continues

Continues

Acts

FIRST NATIONS VERSION

FIRST NATIONS VERSION

The Good Story Continues
(The Book of Acts)

The Story Continues

1 *O most honored* Friend Of Creator (Theophilus), I have already told you the story of Creator Sets Free (Jesus), about the many things he did and taught among the people ²*from his birth* until the day he returned to the world above. ³ After he had suffered by being put to death on the cross, he returned to life, and then appeared to his message bearers, giving them many proofs that he was truly alive again.

Forty Days of Instruction

For forty days he continued to appear to them, and through the Holy Spirit he instructed them further about Creator's Good Road. ⁴ Once, during a meal with his followers, he said to them, "Wait here in the Sacred Village of Peace (Jerusalem), for the gift from my Father that I already told you about—the Holy Spirit. ⁵ He Shows Goodwill (John) performed the purification ceremony with water, but not many days from now, you will participate in the purification ceremony with the Holy Spirit."

They were all full of wonder about what was taking place. Was this the beginning of the new world the prophets of old had promised to the tribes of Wrestles With Creator (Israel)?

⁶ They crowded around Creator Sets Free (Jesus). "Wisdomkeeper," they asked him, "will you now give the Good Road back to the tribes of Wrestles With Creator (Israel)?

⁷ "Times and seasons are in the Father's hands," he answered. "These things are not for you to know. ⁸ Instead, set your hearts and minds on the Holy Spirit, who will give you strong medicine when he comes. You will then tell my story in Village of Peace (Jerusalem), in all the Land of Promise (Judea) and High Place (Samaria), and then to the furthest parts of the earth—*to all languages, tribes and nations.*"

⁹ As he spoke these words, he was taken up, and went into a cloud where they could no longer see him.

His followers bowed down low to honor him and then, full of wonder and awe, they stood there looking up into the sky.

¹⁰ As they watched him go up into the world above, two men appeared before them in pure white garments.

[11] "Men of Circle of Nations (Galilee)!" they said. "Why are you looking up into the sky? This same Creator Sets Free (Jesus), whom you saw going up into the world above, will return in the same manner you have seen him go."

They Gather in an Upper Room

[12] Village of Peace (Jerusalem) was nearby, about as far as one is permitted to walk on a Day of Resting. [13] So the followers of Creator Sets Free (Jesus) walked down Olive Mountain and returned to the village and to the place where they were staying, at a lodging house in an upstairs room.

Here are the names of the followers of Creator Sets Free (Jesus) who were gathering together to pray:

Stands On The Rock (Peter), He Shows Goodwill (John), He Takes Over (James), Stands With Courage (Andrew); Friend of Horses (Philip), Looks Like His Brother (Thomas), Son Of Ground Digger (Bartholomew), Gift From Creator (Matthew); He Takes Over (James) son of First To Change (Alphaeus), One Who Listens (Simon) the Man On Fire (Zealot), and Speaks Well Of (Judas),[a] the son of He Takes Over (James).

[14] Bitter Tears (Mary), the mother of Creator Sets Free (Jesus), was there along with some of his brothers. Also many of the honored women were welcomed among them. They were all gathering together, night and day, to send their voices to the Great Spirit.

[15] This group had grown into *one big family*, about a hundred and twenty of them, who all believed *in Creator Sets Free (Jesus), that he is* the Chosen One.

A New Message Bearer Chosen

There were now only eleven message bearers. Speaks Well Of (Judas), the one who betrayed Creator Sets Free (Jesus), was no longer among them. Since Creators Sets Free (Jesus) chose twelve message bearers to represent the twelve tribes of Wrestles With Creator (Israel),[b] someone must be chosen to replace him.

So during this time Stands On The Rock (Peter) stood up to speak.

[16] "Friends and family," he said to all, "Much Loved One (David), guided by the Holy Spirit, foretold in the Sacred Teachings the things that found their full meaning in Speaks Well Of (Judas) who betrayed Creator Sets Free (Jesus) into the hands of the ones who arrested him.

[17] "From the first, Speaks Well Of (Judas) was one *of the twelve* chosen to walk with us as one of his followers.

[18] "*After he betrayed him,* the 'blood money' paid to him was used to buy the field where Speaks Well Of (Judas), *after hanging himself on a tree[c],* fell to the ground, where his body broke open and his

---

a 1:13 John 14:22   b 1:15 Matthew 12:28   c 1:18 Matthew 27:5

insides spilled out. [19] News about this spread throughout Village of Peace (Jerusalem), and so that place became known *in our native language* as Akeldama, meaning Field of Blood."

[20] *Stands On The Rock (Peter) continued,* "This gives full meaning to the words of the Sacred Book of Songs (Psalms), 'Let his land become deserted, a place where no one will live;'[d] and it also says, 'Let another take his place in the council.'[e]

[21] *"We must now choose another to replace Speaks Well Of (Judas).* He must be one who was with us the whole time while we were walking the road with our Wisdomkeeper, [22] from the time he participated in the purification ceremony with He Shows Goodwill (John) until the day Creator Sets Free (Jesus) was taken up from us to the world above. Then, along with us, he will be able to tell what his own eyes have seen, about the rising from the dead of Creator Sets Free (Jesus)."

The Council of Twelve is Restored

[23] Two men were selected who met the requirements: He Gives More (Joseph), who was called Son Of Resting (Barsabbas), also known as Stands Upright (Justus), and Gifted From Creator (Matthias).

[24] They *stood the men before the council and* prayed over them, "O Great Chief, Knower Of Hearts, show to us the one you have chosen [25] to be your message bearer in the place of Speaks Well Of (Judas), who left the path given him and chose his own path."

[26] They decided to choose by drawing straws. The straw was in favor of Gifted From Creator (Matthias), and so he was added to the eleven message bearers *to form a council of twelve—representing the twelve tribes of Wrestles With Creator (Israel).*

Festival of Weeks

2 *The tribes of Wrestles with Creator (Israel) celebrated another great feast called the Festival of Weeks or Pentecost, meaning fifty, because it was celebrated seven weeks after the Passover festival, on the fiftieth day. This was a harvest festival when the people would bring the firstfruits of the harvest to Creator's Lodge in the Sacred Village of Peace (Jerusalem) and give thanks for his provision. Creator was about to send the Holy Spirit, promised by Creator Sets Free (Jesus), to begin the time of the great harvest, and gather people from all nations who would represent the Great Spirit.*

The time for *the full meaning of* the ancient festival had now arrived.

The followers of Creator Sets Free (Jesus), numbering about one hundred and twenty, were waiting and praying in the upstairs room where they were lodging. It had now been fifty days since the Passover festival— when Creator Sets Free (Jesus) returned to life from the dead.

d 1:20 Psalm 69:25   e 1:20 Psalm 109:8

Wind and Flames of Fire

They had all gathered together in one place, ² when suddenly the sound of a great windstorm came from the world above and could be heard throughout the house where they were sitting. ³ They saw flames of fire coming down from above, separating and resting on each of their heads. ⁴ The Holy Spirit had come down upon them, and began to fill them *with his life and power.* New languages began to flow out from their mouths, languages they had never learned, given from the Holy Spirit.

⁵ The Sacred Village of Peace (Jerusalem) was filled with devoted members of the tribes of Wrestles With Creator (Israel), *who had come for the festival* from every nation under the sun. ⁶ A crowd began to gather when they heard the loud noise.

⁷ In wonder and amazement the crowd began to ask, "How is it that these people from Circle of Nations (Galilee) are speaking in our many languages? ⁸ For we all can understand them in the languages of the places we have come from! ⁹⁻¹¹ There are people here from nations and places close by and far away who are members of the tribes of Wrestles With Creator (Israel), and outsiders who have been taken into the tribes.ᶠ We can hear them, in the languages of these nations, telling about the great and powerful things done by the Great Spirit!"

¹² Many were amazed and confused and began to ask each other, "What can this mean?"

¹³ But others in the crowd just laughed and said, "They are drunk on new wine!"

Stands On The Rock Speaks Out

¹⁴ Stands On The Rock (Peter), along with the other eleven message bearers, stood up to the crowd, and with a loud voice said, "Tribal members from far away and all who live in Village of Peace (Jerusalem), listen closely to me. I will tell you what this means!"

The crowd became quiet and turned to hear Stands On The Rock (Peter).

¹⁵ "No one among us is drunk on wine, for it is still the middle of the morning. No! This is not what you think it is. ¹⁶ This is what the prophet Creator Is The Great Spirit (Joel) spoke of long ago when he said, ¹⁷ "In the last days" says Creator, "I will rain down my Spirit upon all human beings *from every nation.* Your sons and daughters will prophesy. Young warriors will see visions and elders will have dreams.

¹⁸ When that time comes, my Spirit will rain down on all who serve me, both men and women, and they will boldly speak my words. ¹⁹ There will be powerful signs and omens in the world above and on the earth below—blood and fire with clouds of smoke. ²⁰ The sun will grow dark and the moon will be red like blood, as the great *and dreadful* day of Creator shines like the sun. ²¹ Then the ones who

---

f 2:9-11 These Gentiles were called Proselytes.

cry out to the Great Spirit will be made whole and set free.'"'"*g*

22 *Stands On The Rock (Peter) cried out,* "Listen to me, you men of the tribes of Wrestles With Creator (Israel)! You already know about Creator Sets Free (Jesus) from Seed Planter Village (Nazareth) and about the powerful signs and the wonders he performed among the people that proved Creator was with him. 23-24 Creator knew, before it happened, that the tribes would use the power of the People of Iron (Romans)*h* to have him killed by nailing him to the cross. But the Maker Of Life let you have your way with him, because he had made a plan, long ago, to bring him back to life. Creator Sets Free (Jesus) was released from the birth pains of death, for even death itself could not hold him captive.

Ancient Prophecies Fulfilled

25 "When the great chief Much Loved One (David) spoke these words long ago, he was telling us about Creator Sets Free (Jesus). Listen to what he said, 'The Great Spirit will never leave me. I will not tremble with fear, for he is close by my side, *and guides me on the pathways of life.* 26 My heart is glad and my mouth sings! I have hope that 27 *even after my body is dead,* I will not be left alone in the ground to return to dust. You will not leave your Holy One in the dark underworld of death. No! 28 For you have given me a clear path to your life of beauty and harmony. When I stand before you face to face, my heart will leap for joy!'"'*i*

Stands On The Rock (Peter) waited while the crowd thought about his words, and then he said:

29 "My fellow Tribal Members, there is no doubt that our ancestor, Much Loved One (David), died and was buried long ago. His burial cave is with us to this very day. 30-31 The Great Spirit gave him a sacred promise that one of his descendants would be a Great Chief to rule over all the tribes. Much Loved One was a prophet and saw, ahead of time, that the Chosen One would rise from the dead, and that he would not be left alone in the dark underworld of death, nor would his body return to the dust of the earth.

32 "Creator Sets Free (Jesus) is this Chosen One who has been raised to life from death! We have seen him with our own eyes. 33 He has now returned to his place of honor in the world above to sit at the right hand of the Great Spirit. The Father above has gifted him with the Holy Spirit that he promised to send. This Spirit has now been poured out upon us like the rain from above. This is the meaning of what you see and hear happening to us.

34 "Much Loved One (David) did not go up into the world above, so when he says, 'The Great Chief said to my Great Chief, "Sit down beside me at my right hand, my place of

---

g **2:21** Joel 2:28-32   h **2:23-24** Lit., those outside of the Law   i **2:28** Psalm 16:8-11

greatest honor, [35] until I bring your enemies under my loving power,"[j] *he was not talking about himself. He was talking about the Chosen One.*

[36] "So let all the tribes of Wrestles With Creator (Israel) have no doubt about what the Great Spirit has done. He has made Creator Sets Free (Jesus), the one you put to death on the cross, to be both Chief *of all the tribes* and the Chosen One, *the one he promised to send long ago.*"

The Crowd Responds

[37] When they heard this, the words pierced their hearts *like a long knife.* With troubled hearts they lifted their voices to Stands On The Rock (Peter) and all the message bearers.

"Fellow Tribal Members," they said, "tell us what we must do."

[38] "Change your thinking," Stands On The Rock (Peter) instructed them, "and participate in the purification ceremony that is done in the name of Creator Sets Free (Jesus), the Chosen One, representing him *and initiating you into his right ways.* You will then be healed from your bad hearts, released from your broken ways and gifted with the Holy Spirit *who will give you the strength to walk the Good Road with him.* [39] He has promised this to all generations of the tribes of Wrestles With Creator (Israel), and to all *the Nations* who live far away. For the Great Spirit, our Creator, is calling out to all who will, to share in this life of beauty and harmony."

[40] Stands On The Rock (Peter) said many more things to the ones who were listening. With strong words he kept telling them, "This is how you will be set free and rescued from the bent and twisted ways of this generation."

[41] The ones who believed the words of Stands On The Rock (Peter) became a part of Creator's new Sacred Family and participated in the purification ceremony. About three thousand people were added on that day!

A New Family is Formed

[42] This newly formed family continued daily to learn from the twelve message bearers. They lived together in harmony, ate ceremonial meals and prayed with one another. [43] Great respect and awe came down upon all, and the message bearers performed many powerful signs. [44] As these new followers lived together in peace, their harmony grew stronger and they shared all things. [45] Many of them had a give-away to provide for all who were in need.

[46] Each day they gathered at the Sacred Lodge. With good and pure hearts they feasted together in their homes and shared the ceremonial meal of bread and wine given to them by Creator Sets Free (Jesus). [47] They gave honor and thanks to the Great Spirit and were respected by the people. Each day Creator sent more people, who were being set free, to join with them.

---

j **2:35** Lit., a resting place for my feet

Rise Up and Walk

3 In the middle of the afternoon[k] the people would gather at the Sacred Lodge for a time of prayer. Stands On The Rock (Peter) and He Shows Goodwill (John) were walking together on their way to the lodge. ²Some people were carrying a man who had been unable to walk from his birth. Each day they would lay him down by the entrance to the lodge called the Beautiful Gate, so he could ask for handouts from the ones who were going into the Lodge.

³When the man saw Stands On The Rock (Peter) and He Shows Goodwill (John) passing by, he asked them for a gift of money. ⁴They stopped right in front of the man, looked straight at him, and said, "Look at us!"

⁵The man did as they said, hoping they would give him something.

⁶⁻⁷Stands On The Rock (Peter) said to him, "I have no silver or gold to give to you, but I have a gift for you *that is worth much more.*"

He reached his hand out to the man and said, "I represent the Chosen One, Creator Sets Free (Jesus) from Seed Planter Village (Nazareth). In his name I tell you now—stand up and walk!"

Stands On The Rock (Peter) took hold of his hand and began to pull him up. ⁸The man felt strength returning to his legs and feet and pushed himself up on his own feet and began to walk! He danced through the Beautiful Gate and went into the Lodge, walking and leaping and giving praise to the Great Spirit.

⁹All the people looked at the man ¹⁰and saw that he was the same one who sat and asked for handouts at the gate. Wonder and amazement swept through the crowd *like a wildfire* when they saw him healed and strong.

¹¹The man threw his arms around Stands On The Rock (Peter) and He Shows Goodwill (John) and would not let go of them. A great crowd of people ran up and began to circle around them under the covered walkway named after the great chief, Stands In Peace (Solomon). They looked at Stands On The Rock (Peter) and He Shows Goodwill (John) with wonder and amazement on their faces.

Stands On The Rock Speaks Out Again

¹²When Stands On The Rock (Peter) saw all the people, he lifted up his voice to give the people an answer for the healing of the crippled man.

"Fellow Tribal Members," he said to them, "You should not be amazed at us, or think that we are holy enough to make a crippled man walk. ¹³It was the one who walked with Father Of Many Nations (Abraham), He Made Us Laugh (Isaac), and Heel Grabber (Jacob)—the Great Spirit of our ancestors, who has done this.

"The Giver Of Life has honored Creator Sets Free (Jesus), the one

---

k 3:1 Lit., the ninth hour, about 3:00 p.m.

who served him and did all he asked. The same one you turned over to Spear Of The Great Waters (Pilate), the governor from the People of Iron (Romans), to be put on trial for his life. The same one you turned your back on, in front of Spear Of The Great Waters (Pilate), when he wanted to release him.

[14] "But you turned your back on the Holy and Upright One and then asked for a violent murderer to be set free. [15] In doing so you killed the Maker Of Life! But, the Giver Of Breath brought him back to life from the dead! This we have seen with our own eyes.

[16] "It is only because of Creator Sets Free (Jesus), and all that his name represents, that this man stands before you healed and strong now. You can see for yourselves what trusting in Creator Sets Free (Jesus) has done for him."

This Is What the Prophets Foretold

Stands On The Rock (Peter) continued to speak boldly.

[17] "Fellow Tribal Members," he said, "I understand that neither you nor your leaders knew what they were doing *when they had Creator Sets Free (Jesus) killed*. [18] But this is how the Great Spirit fulfilled all that the prophets foretold when they spoke of the suffering of the Chosen One.

[19] "You must think in a new way and return to the Great Spirit to walk this new path he has chosen for us all. Then you will be healed of your broken ways, [20] and Creator will shine his face on you and give you cool fresh water to drink from his river of life. He will then give to you the one he selected to be his Chosen One—Creator Sets Free (Jesus), [21] who has gone up into the world above to remain there until the time comes when Creator will restore all things.

"Creator spoke of these things long ago through his holy prophets. [22] Listen to the words of Drawn From The Water (Moses): 'The Great Spirit Chief will raise up a prophet from among the tribes, in the same manner he raised me up. You must listen to this prophet and do all he says, [23] for any among the tribes who fail to follow his ways will come to a bad end.'[l]

[24] "All the prophets—Creator Hears Him (Samuel) and all who spoke in the generations that followed—told about these very days we are living in. [25] Every Tribal Member is a descendant of those prophets and of the Peace Treaty Creator made with our ancestors. Did not the Great Spirit promise our ancestor Father Of Many Nations (Abraham) that through his descendants he would bless all the families who dwell on earth?

[26] "*That day has come!* The Great Spirit has raised up his servant, Creator Sets Free (Jesus), and sent him first to the tribes of Wrestles With Creator (Israel) to bless you and turn you back from your worthless evil ways."

---

l 3:23 Deuteronomy 18:15,18,19

Arrested and Imprisoned

4 While Stands On The Rock (Peter) and He Shows Goodwill (John) were speaking to the people, the head Lodge Soldier, along with the Upright Ones (Sadducees) and some holy men, came up to them. 2 They were offended because the message bearers were telling the people that the rising from the dead had begun with Creator Sets Free (Jesus). 3 They took hold of Stands On The Rock (Peter) and He Shows Goodwill (John) *to bring them to the council*, but because it was late in the day, they held them in prison until the next day. 4 But a large number of over five thousand men who heard Stands On The Rock (Peter) speak believed the message!

Facing the Grand Council

5 On the following day the headmen, elders and scroll keepers held a council in Village of Peace (Jerusalem). 6 Both Walks Humbly (Annas) the head high priest and Hollow In The Rock (Caiaphas) sat in the council along with He Shows Goodwill (John), Man Fighter (Alexander) and other members of the family of the chief holy man. 7 They brought Stands On The Rock (Peter) and He Shows Goodwill (John) to sit before them to give an answer to the council.

"Where did the power to heal this man come from? What is the name of the one you represent? Tell us!" they demanded.

8 The Holy Spirit rose up inside Stands On The Rock (Peter).

"Headmen and elders among the people," he said with boldness, 9 "if we are being questioned today before this council about the kindness we showed to a man who could not walk, by healing him, 10 then let all the tribes of Wrestles With Creator (Israel) know the truth. It is because of the name of Creator Sets Free (Jesus) the Chosen One, and all he represents, that this man stands before you healed and whole! Yes! The same Creator Sets Free (Jesus) from Seed Planter Village (Nazareth) whom you killed on the cross. The Maker Of Life has brought him back to life from the world of the dead. 11 He is 'the log you builders threw away, that has become the Chief Pole.'*m* 12 No one else can restore us. No other human being can represent the Great Spirit and carry in his name the kind of power required to rescue us and set us free."

The Council Decides

13 When the council saw the courage of Stands On The Rock (Peter) and He Shows Goodwill (John), they were amazed to find that they were common and unschooled men. And they took notice that they had walked the road with Creator Sets Free (Jesus). 14 But what could they say? The man who had been healed was standing right there with them! 15 They ordered them to wait outside of the council house while they decided what to do with them.

As the men were taken outside, the council lowered their voices and looked around at each other with troubled faces.

m 4:11 Psalm 118:22

[16] "What should we do with these men?" they asked. "Anyone living in Village of Peace (Jerusalem) can see that a powerful sign has been done by them. We cannot deny this. [17] But to keep this from spreading to more people, we must warn them to no longer represent Creator Sets Free (Jesus) or to speak to anyone in his name."

[18] The council agreed and summoned the message bearers to face their decision. They warned them, "You must never again say anything representing Creator Sets Free (Jesus) or instruct others in his teachings."

[19] Stands On The Rock (Peter) and He Shows Goodwill (John) disagreed with the council's decision.

"We will let you decide for yourselves whether or not we should follow the Great Spirit or weak human beings like yourselves," they said with boldness. [20] "But we cannot stop speaking about what we have seen with our own eyes and heard with our own ears!"

The council could not believe their ears! How could these backward people from Circle of Nations (Galilee) stand up to them!

[21] So the council warned and threatened them again, but released them and let them go on their way. The council dared not do anything to punish them, because the people were giving thanks to Creator for this powerful sign. [22] For the man who had been healed was over forty winters old.

The Message Bearers Return

[23] Stands On The Rock (Peter) and He Shows Goodwill (John) went back to their newly formed family and told them what had happened to them and what the council had decided. [24] When the family members heard this, they formed a circle around the message bearers, joined their hearts together, and sent their voices to the Great Spirit.

Prayer for Help

"O Great Father of the sky above and the earth below, of the great waters and all that is in them," they prayed, "hear our cry. [25] Long ago your Holy Spirit spoke these words through our ancestor Much Loved One (David), who served you:

" 'Why did the Nations, in their great anger, make empty threats? Why did the people waste their time forming useless plans? [26] The war chiefs of the land took their stand, and the war councils schemed together. But who were they planning to make war with? It was against the Great Spirit Chief and his Chosen One!'[n]

[27] *"This prophecy found its full meaning here in Village of Peace (Jerusalem). The truth of it is plain to see, for right here in the Village of Peace (Jerusalem) they gathered together and took their stand against your Holy Servant, Creator Sets Free (Jesus). Chief Looks Brave (Herod) and Spear Of The Great Waters (Pontius Pilate) together with*

---

n **4:26** Psalm 2:1-2

the People of Iron (Romans)⁰ and the tribes of Wrestles With Creator (Israel) 28 did what you, in your great wisdom, had decided long ago would be done.

29 "So we ask, O Great One, look down and see their threats against us. Help us to be brave and tell your story well 30 by performing many powerful signs as we represent your Holy Servant, Creator Sets Free (Jesus)."

31 When they finished praying, the place where they had gathered began to rumble and shake. The Holy Spirit filled them *with his power*, and with brave and strong hearts they began to tell Creator's Story!

They Share Their Possessions

32 With one heart and mind all who trusted in Creator Sets Free (Jesus) shared their possessions with each other. No one claimed their belongings to be only for themselves. 33 The message bearers, with great power, told about how Creator Sets Free (Jesus), their Wisdomkeeper, had defeated death and returned to life. Creator's great kindness was covering all of them *like a warm blanket,* 34 and no one among them was in need. Those who owned houses or land sold them and brought what they had gained 35 and gave it to the message bearers, who then made sure everyone had what they needed.

36 There was a man among them named He Gives More (Joseph), who was also given the name Son Of Comfort (Barnabas) by the message bearers. He was from the tribe of Holy Men (Levites), who was born in Island of Flowers (Cyprus). 37 He sold a piece of land that was his, and brought the money and gave it to the message bearers.

Lying to the Holy Spirit

5 1-2 There was a man named Gift Of Goodwill (Ananias) who, along with his wife Stone Of Beauty (Sapphira), sold some of their land. He, with his wife knowing about it, gave the money to the message bearers. *They let them think they had given all,* but they *secretly* held back some for themselves.

3 But Stands On The Rock (Peter) said to Gift Of Goodwill (Ananias), "Why did you let Accuser (Satan), that evil trickster snake, fill your heart to lie to the Holy Spirit? You have kept back some of the money from the sale of your land for yourself! 4 You did not have to sell your land, and even after selling it you still could do whatever you wanted. So why did you try to deceive us? You have lied not *only* to human beings but to the Great Spirit himself!"

5 When Gift Of Goodwill (Ananias) heard this, he fell to the ground and breathed out his last breath. Great fear and awe fell upon all who heard what had happened. 6 Some of the young men wrapped his body in a blanket, carried him out and buried him.

7 About three hours later the wife of Gift Of Goodwill (Ananias) came

---

o 4:27 Outside Nations

in, but she did not know what had happened.

⁸ Stands On The Rock (Peter) asked her, "Was this how much you sold the land for?"

"Yes," she said, "That is the right amount."

⁹ Stands On The Rock (Peter) then said to her, "How could both of you agree to put Creator's Spirit to the test? Look! The ones who buried your husband are coming to do the same for you."

¹⁰ Right then she fell down in front of him and breathed her last. The young men came in, and when they saw she had crossed over to death, they carried her away and buried her next to her husband. ¹¹ Once again great fear and awe took hold of all in the Sacred Family and also of all who heard what had happened.

Signs and Wonders Continue

¹² The message bearers were performing many powerful signs among the people. The people were all gathering together under the entryway *at the Sacred Lodge* named after the great chief Stands In Peace (Solomon). ¹³ The people respected them greatly, but many did not dare to join in with them. ¹⁴ Even so, the crowds grew and more and more people found faith in Creator and his Son.

¹⁵ The people carried the sick into the village pathways and laid them on their sleeping bundles and mats so that when Stands On The Rock (Peter) walked by, his shadow might fall on them. ¹⁶ The crowds came from the villages near Village of Peace (Jerusalem). They brought the sick and the ones tormented by evil spirits—and all of them were healed!

Opposition From the Spiritual Leaders

¹⁷ When the chief holy man and other spiritual leaders of the Upright Ones (Sadducees) heard what was happening, the fire of jealousy burned in their bellies; ¹⁸ so they took hold of the message bearers and put them in the local jail. ¹⁹ But a spirit-messenger from Creator came in the night and set them free.

²⁰ "Go and stand in the Sacred Lodge," the spirit-messenger instructed them, "and speak all the words of this new life to the people."

²¹ They did what they were told and went to the Sacred Lodge, and just as the sun was rising, they began to teach the people.

When the chief holy man arrived, along with the spiritual leaders, they called together the Grand Council—the elders of the tribes of Wrestles With Creator (Israel). They sent some Lodge Soldiers to the local jail to have the message bearers brought before the council. ²² When the Lodge Soldiers arrived at the jail, they could not find the prisoners, so they returned to report to the Grand Council.

²³ "When we arrived at the jail," they said to the council, "we found the jail doors locked and guarded. But when we opened the doors, there was no one to be found!"

24 The head Lodge Soldier and the head holy men could not believe their ears! While they were wondering about this, 25 a messenger came up to them.

"Look!" the messenger said, "the ones you put in jail are standing in the Sacred Lodge and teaching the people!"

26 The head Lodge Soldier, along with his soldiers, went to arrest the message bearers again, but not by force, for they were afraid the people might throw stones at them.

They Stand Before the Grand Council

27 So they took the message bearers to stand before the Grand Council to be questioned by the chief holy man.

28 "We clearly instructed you not to speak representing this man's name or his teaching. Now Village of Peace (Jerusalem) has been filled with your teaching. Do you mean to bring this man's blood upon our heads *by blaming us for his death*?"

Standing Strong

29 Stands On The Rock (Peter) and the other message bearers answered back, "We must obey the Great Spirit instead of *weak* human beings. 30 The Great Spirit of our ancestors has raised up Creator Sets Free (Jesus), the one you killed by hanging him on a tree. 31 Creator has honored him to the highest place, at his own right hand to be our Chief, the one who will set us free and give us a new way of thinking. This is how we, the people of the tribes

of Wrestles With Creator (Israel), will be set free from our bad hearts and broken ways. 32 We have seen these things with our own eyes! The Holy Spirit also agrees with these things, the one Creator will give to those who walk in his ways."

Wise Words from a Council Member

33 When the Grand Council heard this, the anger in them burned like a fire—they wanted to kill them. 34 But then, Creator Has Honored (Gamaliel) stood up to speak. He was a highly respected council member, a Separated One (Pharisee) and a teacher of Tribal Law. He instructed them to remove the message bearers outside for a while.

35 Then he said to the council, "You men of the tribes of Wrestles With Creator (Israel), think carefully about what you plan to do with these men. 36 Remember when Flows With Water (Theudas), made himself out to be a great one, with a following of four hundred men? He was killed and all his followers were scattered and came to nothing. 37 After him, Speaks Well Of (Judas) from Circle of Nations (Galilee) rose up during the days of the census. He also had many follow him, but he was also killed and his followers scattered.

38 "This is my counsel to you: Let these men go and trouble them no longer. If what they do is a weak human idea, then it will come to nothing. 39 But if Creator is with them, you will not be able to stand against them, and you may find yourselves fighting the Great Spirit!"

The Message Bearers
are Released

The Grand Council listened to his wisdom. [40] They brought the message bearers back in, beat them with a whip, and instructed them to speak no longer in the name of Creator Sets Free (Jesus) *or represent his teachings.*

[41] So the message bearers left the Grand Council. Their hearts were glad that they had been considered worthy to suffer dishonor for the reputation of Creator Sets Free (Jesus). [42] Day by day, in the Sacred Lodge and from house to house, they kept telling the Good Story about Creator Sets Free (Jesus) and showing the truth that he is the Chosen One.

The Sacred Family Grows

6 In those days, when the Sacred Family was growing in number, the Tribal Members who spoke the language of the Wisdom Seekers (Greeks) grumbled against the Tribal Members who spoke their own language. They complained *to the twelve* that their widows were being overlooked during the daily meals. [2] So the twelve message bearers invited everyone to a council meeting, and said:

"It is not a good thing for us to give so much of our time to seeing over these meals, for then we have little or no time to teach about Creator's message. [3] So choose seven men of good reputation, who are filled with Creator's Spirit and wisdom, who will serve in our place. [4] Then we can give ourselves to prayer and to the *teaching of Creator's* message."

[5] This seemed like a good thing to all the people, so they chose Many Feathers (Stephen), a man strong in his faith and full of the Holy Spirit. They also chose Friend Of Horses (Philip), Head Singer (Prochorus), Man Of Victory (Nicanor), Man of Honor (Timon), Stands Close By (Parmenas), and He Overcomes (Nicolas), an outsider from Stands Against (Antioch) who had been taken into the tribes of Wrestles With Creator (Israel). [6] They stood these men before the message bearers, who then placed their hands on them and sent their voices to the Great Spirit.

[7] Creator's message was told far and wide. In Village Of Peace (Jerusalem) the number of followers continued to grow, and many holy men believed and began to walk in this new way.

Many Feathers
Taken Captive

[8] Many Feathers (Stephen), who was filled with Creator's good medicine, was performing powerful signs among the people. [9] But some men, from what is called the gathering house of Men Set Free, opposed him. They were Tribal Members from Strong Wall (Cyrene), Village of Defense (Alexandria), Turns Over (Cilicia), and from the territory of Rising Sun (Asia). [10] Even though they stood against Many Feathers (Stephen) with strong words, they were not strong enough to defeat the wisdom given to him by the Spirit.

[11] So they talked some men into telling lies about him.

"We have heard him speak against Drawn From The Water (Moses) and against the Great Spirit!" they said to the people, elders and scroll keepers.

12 This turned them against Many Feathers (Stephen), so they took hold of him and brought him before the Grand Council. 13 Then they brought in the ones who were falsely accusing him to speak to the council.

"This man keeps speaking against the Sacred Lodge and against our Tribal Law," they said to the Grand Council. 14 "We heard him say that Creator Sets Free (Jesus) from Seed Planter Village (Nazareth) will bring an end to this holy place and change the tribal traditions given to us by Drawn From The Water (Moses)."

15 But all who were sitting in the Council were staring at the face of Many Feathers (Stephen) because his face looked like the face of a spirit-messenger.

Many Feathers Answers the Council

7 "Are these things spoken against you true?" the chief holy man asked him.

2 This was his answer: "Fellow Tribal Members, my brothers and fathers, hear what I have to say! The Great Mystery, the one who shines like the sun, appeared to our ancestor Father Of Many Nations (Abraham) while he was still living in Land Between Two Rivers (Mesopotamia), before he pitched his tipi at Dry Mountain (Haran).

3 "'Leave your people and the land of your ancestors,' Creator instructed him, 'and go to the land that I will show to you.'p

4 "So he went out from the people of the land of Field of Spirits (Chaldeans) and pitched his tipi at Dry Mountain (Haran) until his father crossed over to death. Creator then moved him to the land where you now live, 5 but he found no place to live there, not even a piece of ground to set his foot on. It was there that Creator promised him and his descendants a lasting home—even though he had no children.

6 "The Great Spirit told him that his descendants would be wanderers in a land of strangers, who will force them to work hard for them, and mistreat them for four hundred winters. 7 'But I will decide against this nation that forced them to be slaves,' Creator promised, 'and when they are set free, they will honor and serve me in this land.'q

8 "Creator gave to Father Of Many Nations (Abraham) the Peace Treaty that was sealed with the cutting of the flesh ceremony.r Then Father Of Many Nations (Abraham) became the father of He Made Us Laugh (Isaac) and eight days after he was born performed the cutting of the flesh ceremony on him. He Made Us Laugh (Isaac) became the father of Heel Grabber (Jacob), and he

---

p 7:3 Genesis 12:1   q 7:7 Genesis 15:13,14   r 7:8 Circumcision

became the father of the twelve ancestors of our nation.

9 "Our ancestors became jealous of He Gives More (Joseph) and sold him as a slave into Black Land (Egypt), but the Great Spirit stood with him and 10 set him free from all his troubles. Creator then honored him in the eyes of Great House (Pharaoh), the ruler of Black Land (Egypt), who made him a ruler over Black Land (Egypt) and his own family.

11 "A time of hunger came upon Black Land (Egypt) and Lowland (Canaan). It was a time of great suffering for our ancestors, for they could not find enough food. 12 When Heel Grabber (Jacob) heard that there was grain in Black Land (Egypt), he sent his sons—our ancestors—there to trade for some. 13 Then, when Heel Grabber (Jacob) sent them a second time, their brother, He Gives More (Joseph), *that they had sold as a slave*, made himself known to them. 14 Then He Gives More (Joseph) sent a message to his father Heel Grabber (Jacob) and welcomed him and all his family—seventy-five in all—to come to Black Land (Egypt) *under his protection.*

15 "So Heel Grabber (Jacob) pitched his tipi in Black Land (Egypt). It was there that he and our ancestors all crossed over to death. 16 Their bones were later moved to Burden Carrier (Shechem) and placed in a burial cave that Father Of Many Nations (Abraham) had traded for from the sons of Red Donkey (Hamor).

17 "*Many generations later,* when the time had come for the Great Spirit to keep his promise to Father Of Many Nations (Abraham), the number of our people in Black Land (Egypt) had grown from small clans to a great tribe. 18 But a new ruler arose in Black Land (Egypt) that did not know about He Gives More (Joseph). 19 This new ruler was the one who oppressed our people and forced them to leave their newborn children outside to die, *to make our numbers smaller.*

20 "It was during this time that Drawn From The Water (Moses) was born—a beautiful baby. Creator's eye was on this one! For three moons his family fed and cared for him. 21 When the time came that they had to leave him outside to die, the daughter of Great House (Pharaoh) rescued him and raised him as her own son. 22 So that is how Drawn From The Water (Moses) was taught all the wisdom of the people of Black Land (Egypt) and became powerful in his words and in all that he did.

23 "When he was a full grown man of forty winters, he decided to visit his tribal family—the descendants of Wrestles With Creator (Israel). 24 When he saw one of them being mistreated, he came to his defense and, on fire for justice, he struck down the man of Black Land (Egypt). 25 He thought his tribal family would understand that the Great Spirit had sent him to set them free—but they did not.

26 "The following day Drawn From the Water (Moses) saw two

Tribal Members fighting and tried to make peace between them.

"'Men!' he said to them. 'You are brothers. Why do you want to hurt each other?'

27 "But the one who had attacked his fellow Tribal Member pushed Drawn From The Water (Moses) away from him.

"'Who made you our ruler and judge?' the man said *in anger.* 28 'Do you want to kill me the way you killed that man of Black Land (Egypt) yesterday?'

29 "When he heard the man's words, Drawn From The Water (Moses) ran from there as fast as he could, and went to live as an outsider among the people in Land of Conflict (Midian). It was there that he had two sons.

30 "Forty winters later, in the desert wilderness near Mountain of Small Trees (Sinai), a spirit-messenger appeared to him in the flames of a burning thorn bush. 31 When Drawn From The Water (Moses) saw it, he wondered what it was. As he came close to see it better, he heard the voice of Creator.

32 "'I am the Great Spirit of your ancestors—of Father Of Many Nations (Abraham), and of He Made Us Laugh (Isaac), and of Heel Grabber (Jacob).'s

"Drawn From The Water (Moses) began to tremble *with fear* and he dared not to even look at the bush.

33 "'Take your moccasins off and let your feet touch the earth,'

Creator said to him, 'for the ground you are standing on is sacred.'"

With trembling hands Drawn From The Water (Moses) took off his moccasins. His knees grew weak as he stood before the fire of the Great Spirit and listened as Creator continued to speak.

34 "'With my own eyes I have seen the way my people have suffered in Black Land (Egypt). I have heard their deep sighs and groanings, and I have come down to set them free. Come now, it is time to go, for I am sending you back to Black Land (Egypt).'t

35 "So Creator sent back the same man who had been rejected by his own people when they said, 'Who made you our ruler and judge?' Through the spirit-messenger, who appeared to him in the burning thorn bush, the Great Spirit sent Drawn From The Water (Moses) to be both their ruler and the one who would pay the price to set them free. 36 With the powerful signs and omens he performed in Black Land (Egypt), at the Red Sea, and in the desert wilderness, he set them free and guided them through the desert wilderness for forty winters.

37 "Drawn From The Water (Moses) was the same one who said to the descendants of Wrestles With Creator (Israel), 'The Great Spirit will raise up a prophet like me from among your own people.' 38 When our ancestors were gathered together in the desert wilderness, Drawn From The Water (Moses) was there with them. On the Mountain

---

s 7:32 Exodus 3:6   t 7:34 Exodus 3:5,7,8,10

of Small Trees (Sinai) a spirit-messenger from Creator spoke to him. It was there that he and our ancestors were given the words of life which have been handed down to us.

39 "But our ancestors were not willing to follow his guidance. They turned away from him and turned their hearts back to the ways of Black Land (Egypt). 40 They said to Light Bearer (Aaron), *the brother of Drawn From The Water (Moses)*, 'We do not know what has become of Drawn From The Water (Moses), so carve for us an image of spirit-beings who can guide us.'

41 "So they formed an image shaped like a calf, offered ceremonial sacrifices to it, and celebrated what their own hands had formed. 42 But the Maker Of Life turned his face away from them, and then handed them over to serve the evil warrior-spirits who rule in the dark spirit-world above and around us. The book of the prophets speaks about this:

"'Was it to me that you offered ceremonial sacrifices for forty winters in the desert?' Creator asked the family-descendants of Wrestles With Creator (Israel). 'No! 43 Instead you carried an altar for Child-Burning Spirit (Moloch) and one for Wandering Star Spirit (Rephan). These were images you formed with your own hands that you chose to serve. So, because you have chosen this path, I will make you walk it to Village Of Confusion (Babylon).'*u*

44 "Our ancestors carried the Sacred Tent of Creator's Peace Treaty with them during their desert wanderings. The Great Spirit gave Drawn From The Water (Moses) a vision for this Sacred Tent and the full instructions on how to make it. 45 When the time came to enter the Land of Promise, our ancestors carried this Sacred Tent with them as He Sets Free (Joshua) led the way. The Great Spirit removed the Outside Nations from the land, and our ancestors took possession of it. The Sacred Tent remained there until the days of Much Loved One (David). 46 Creator's great kindness rested upon Much Loved One (David), so he asked if he could build a Lodge for the Great Spirit of Heel Grabber (Jacob). 47 But it was his son Stands In Peace (Solomon) who built a Lodge for him.

48 "But the One Above Us All does not live in Lodges built by human hands, for the prophet *Creator Will Help Us (Isaiah)* has said, 49 'The world above is my seat-of-honor and the earth below is a resting place for my feet. Could you build me a Lodge like this?' says the Great Spirit. 'One that I could rest in? 50 Have I not formed all of these things with my own hands?'"*v*

A great boldness rose up in Many Feathers (Stephen) as he made his stand before the Grand Council. A look of fire came from his eyes as he raised his voice and spoke from his heart.

51 "You are a bullheaded people! Your hearts of stone and deaf ears

---

u 7:43 Amos 5:25-27   v 7:50 Isaiah 66:49-50

have made you no different than the nations around you. Just like your ancestors, you continue to oppose the Holy Spirit. 52 Did not your ancestors hunt down, torture and kill the prophets who foretold the coming of the Upright One? You have now become his betrayers and murderers! 53 You!— the ones to whom our Tribal Law was given by spirit-messengers—a Law that you have not followed!"

The Grand Council Has Him Killed

54 When the council heard these words, they were filled with rage and ground their teeth in anger and frustration at him. 55 But then the Holy Spirit filled Many Feathers (Stephen) with a great vision. He looked up into the world above and saw a bright light shining from the Great Spirit, and standing next to him at his right hand was Creator Sets Free (Jesus)!

56 "Look!" he said, "I can see into the world above! The sky has opened and there at the right hand of the Great Spirit is the True Human Being!"

57 But they put their hands over their ears and screamed out loud as they all rushed together to take hold of him. 58 They dragged him outside of the village and began to throw stones at him to kill him. Those who spoke against him laid their outer garments at the feet of a young man whose name was Man Who Asks (Saul).

59 As they threw the stones at Many Feathers (Stephen), he was sending his voice to the Great Spirit.

"Creator Sets Free (Jesus) my Honored Chief," he called out to Creator. "Welcome my spirit *as I come to you!*"

60 He then fell to his knees and cried out with a loud voice, "Honored One, do not hold this wrong against them!"

Then, with a final breath, he fell to sleep and crossed over to death.

A Great Persecution Begins

8 Man Who Asks (Saul) stood in agreement with the death of Many Feathers (Stephen), and on that same day a great persecution of the Sacred Family in Village of Peace (Jerusalem) began. All except for the message bearers were scattered about in the territories of the Land of Promise (Judea) and High Mountain (Samaria). 2 With loud cries and many tears, some good-hearted men buried Many Feathers (Stephen). 3 But Man Who Asks (Saul) was bringing great harm to the Sacred Family. Going from house to house he dragged both men and women away to put them in prison.

Friend Of Horses Goes to High Place

4 Everywhere the ones who had been scattered went, they told others the story *about Creator Sets Free (Jesus)*. 5 Friend Of Horses (Philip) went to a village in High Place (Samaria) and began to tell them about the Chosen One. 6 When the people heard him and saw the powerful signs that he did, they all agreed to listen to what Friend

Of Horses (Philip) had to say. 7 The evil spirits shrieked out loud as he forced them out and many who could not walk or move about were healed. 8 This filled the hearts of the people of that village with great joy!

A Bad Medicine Man Believes

9 In that same village there was a man named One Who Hears (Simon), who had practiced bad medicine[w] and had made himself out to be someone great. 10 He had a reputation among the people, both small and great, that he was the power of the Great Spirit. 11 His reputation came from the bad medicine he amazed them with.

12 But when Friend Of Horses (Philip) told them about Creator's Good Road and the name and reputation of Creator Sets Free (Jesus) the Chosen One, both men and women put their trust in him and participated in the purification ceremony. 13 Even One Who Hears (Simon) believed and participated in the ceremony. After the ceremony he stayed close to Friend Of Horses (Philip), for he was amazed at the powerful signs and miracles he saw.

Some Message Bearers Come to Pray

14 The message bearers in Village of Peace (Jerusalem) heard that the people in High Place (Samaria) had welcomed Creator's message. So they sent Stands On The Rock (Peter) and He Shows Goodwill (John) to them. 15 The two went there and prayed for them to receive the Holy Spirit; 16 for they had only participated in the purification ceremony representing[x] the Honored One, Creator Sets Free (Jesus), and the Spirit had not yet come down upon them.

One Who Hears Learns a Lesson

17 When Stands On The Rock (Peter) and He Shows Goodwill (John) placed their hands on them *and prayed*, they received the Holy Spirit. 18 But One Who Hears (Simon), when he saw that the Holy Spirit came through the hands of the message bearers, offered them money to get this power.

19 "Give me also this power," he said to them, "so that anyone I place my hands on will receive the Holy Spirit."

20 "Both you and your money are on a path to a bad end," Stands On The Rock (Peter) warned him, "because you thought Creator's gift could be bought with money! 21 This message has found no home in you, for your heart is not straight before the Great Spirit. 22 Turn away from these evil thoughts and pray that, if possible, Creator will forgive you for this wrong way of thinking. 23 For I see that a bitter root has poisoned you and an evil power has captured your thinking."

24 "Pray to the Creator for me!" One Who Hears (Simon) said *with a trembling voice*, "so that nothing you have said will happen to me."

---

w 8:9 Lit., magic or sorcery   x 8:16 Lit., in the name of

25 So Stands On The Rock (Peter) and He Shows Goodwill (John) continued to speak Creator's words of truth and then returned to Village Of Peace (Jerusalem). On the way they told the Good Story about Creator Sets Free (Jesus) to many more people in the villages of High Place (Samaria).

A Spirit Messenger Speaks

26 A spirit-messenger from Creator came and spoke to Friend Of Horses (Philip).

"Rise up," the spirit-messenger told him, "and go south on the road that will take you from Village of Peace (Jerusalem) to Strong Place (Gaza)."

This road goes through the desert wilderness. 27-28 *So Friend Of Horses (Philip) followed the guidance of the spirit-messenger.* He got up and began to go toward the south.

Man from Eyes of Fire

While on the road, he came across a man from Eyes of Fire (Ethiopia). He had great authority because he was a trusted official[y] of the female chief of Eyes of Fire (Ethiopia) and managed all her wealth and possessions. This man had traveled to Village of Peace (Jerusalem) to participate in the Lodge ceremonies and was returning home.

As this man was traveling, he was sitting in a fancy horse-drawn covered wagon[z] and reading from the Sacred Teachings of the prophet Creator Will Help Us (Isaiah).

29 The Spirit *of Creator* said to Friend Of Horses (Philip), "Go and walk next to this covered wagon."

30 So Friend Of Horses (Philip) ran to where the man was and overheard him reading from the prophecies of Creator Will Help Us (Isaiah).

"Do you understand what you are reading?" Friend Of Horses (Philip) asked him.

31 "How can I," the man answered, "unless someone guides me?"

So he welcomed Friend Of Horses (Philip) to sit with him. 32 The man was reading these words from the Sacred Teachings:

"Like a sheep led to the slaughter or like a lamb being sheared, he was silent and did not open his mouth. 33 He was shamed and denied a fair trial. No one even imagined he had a future, for he was cut down in the prime of his life."[a]

34 "I ask you," the man said to Friend Of Horses (Philip), "is the prophet speaking about himself or someone else?"

35 Then Friend Of Horses (Philip) *took a deep breath,* opened his mouth and began from that prophecy[b] to tell him the Good Story about Creator Sets Free (Jesus). 36 As they traveled the road, they came to a watering hole.

---

y 8:27-28 These trusted officials, called eunuchs, were men who could not physically father children. They were often given positions of trust by ancient rulers.   z 8:27-28 Lit., chariot
a 8:33 Isaiah 53:7-8   b 8:35 Lit., Scripture

Purification Ceremony

"Look!" the man said, "There is much water here. Why should I not participate in the purification ceremony?"

[37] "If from your heart you truly believe," Friend Of Horses (Philip) answered, "you may."

"I believe that Creator Sets Free (Jesus) is the Son of the Great Spirit," the man replied.[c]

[38] He instructed them to stop the carriage and they both waded out into the water, and Friend Of Horses (Philip) performed the purification ceremony for him. [39] When they came up from the water, Creator's Spirit snatched Friend Of Horses (Philip) away from the man's sight; so he continued on his journey with a glad heart.

But what happened to Friend Of Horses (Philip)?

[40] He found himself in Strong Fort (Azotus), and as he walked throughout the territory, he told everyone the Good Story until he arrived at Chief Village (Caesarea).

A Rampage of Threats and Murder

9 Man Who Asks (Saul) was on a rampage, breathing threats and murder against the followers of the Honored One, Creator Sets Free (Jesus). He went to the Head High Priest [2] and asked for written documents to give to the tribal gathering houses in the village of Running Horse (Damascus). This would permit him to take any followers of the Way, men or women, bind them in chains and take them to Village of Peace (Jerusalem).

Voice From the World Above

[3] So on his way to Running Horse (Damascus), just as he came near the village, without warning a light from the world above shone down all around him. [4] He fell to the ground and then heard a voice speaking.

"Man Who Asks (Saul), Man Who Asks (Saul)," the voice called out his name twice, "Why are you pursuing and mistreating me?"

Man Who Asks (Saul) trembled with fear at the sound of the voice that was coming from the blinding light.

[5] "Honored One," he asked, "Who are you?"

"I am Creator Sets Free (Jesus)," the voice answered, "the one you are pursuing and mistreating. [6] Now stand to your feet and go into the village. There you will be told what you must do."

[7] The men who were traveling with him stood silent saying nothing, for they heard the voice but saw no one. [8] Man Who Asks (Saul) stood to his feet and opened his eyes, but he could not see. The ones who were with him took him by the hand and guided him into the village of Running Horse (Damascus). [9] He stayed there without

---

c 8:37 Most ancient manuscripts leave out verse 37.

eating or drinking, and after three days he still could not see.

Guidance From a Sacred Vision

[10] Now in that village there was a man named Gift Of Goodwill (Ananias), a follower of Creator Sets Free (Jesus). He was given a sacred vision from the Great Spirit.

"Gift Of Goodwill (Ananias)!" the voice called out to him in the vision.

"I am here, Honored One!" he answered back.

[11] "Get up and go to the house of Speaks Well Of (Judas), on the village pathway called Straight. There you must ask for a man from Tree Village (Tarsus) named Man Who Asks (Saul). He is praying right now. [12] In a vision he has seen a man with your name come to him and lay his hands on him so that he might see again."

[13] "Honored One," Gift Of Goodwill (Ananias) answered him back, "I have heard of this man and how much harm he has done to your holy people in Village of Peace (Jerusalem). [14] The head holy men have given him the authority to put in prison all who call upon your name."

[15] "Go to him," Creator Sets Free (Jesus) answered him, "for I have chosen this man to represent me to the Outside Nations, to their rulers and to the tribes of Wrestles With Creator (Israel). [16] I will show him how much he must suffer in order to represent who I am."[d]

Gift Of Goodwill Follows the Vision

[17] Gift Of Goodwill (Ananias) followed the guidance given to him in the vision and went to the house, and there he placed his hands on Man Who Asks (Saul).

"Man Who Asks (Saul), my brother," he said to him, "Creator Sets Free (Jesus), our Honored Chief, the one who appeared to you on the road you came here on, has sent me to you so you may see again and be filled with his Holy Spirit."

[18] Right then something like fish scales fell from his eyes and he could see again! Then he stood up and went to participate in the purification ceremony. [19] After that he ate some food and his strength returned. He stayed in the village of Running Horse (Damascus) for a few days with some followers of Creator Sets Free (Jesus).

He Begins to Tell the Story

[20] Right away he went to the local gathering houses and began to tell them that Creator Sets Free (Jesus) is the Son of the Great Spirit, [21] and all who heard him could not believe their ears!

"Is this not the man who in Village of Peace (Jerusalem) was making war against the ones who called upon this name?" they asked. "Did he not come here to take them bound to the head holy men?"

[22] But Man Who Asks (Saul) became more powerful in his speech, proving that Creator Sets

---

d 9:16 Lit., for the sake of my name

Free (Jesus) was the Chosen One, leaving the local Tribal Leaders confused and unable to argue against him.

The Plot to Kill
Man Who Asks

23 A few days later the Tribal Leaders formed a council to put him to death, 24 but he found out what they were planning. They kept watch day and night at the village gates so they could take and kill him. 25 But some of his followers snuck him out at night by lowering him down in a basket from an opening in the village walls.

26 He went to Village of Peace (Jerusalem) and tried to join together with the followers of Creator Sets Free (Jesus), but they were afraid and did not trust that he was a true follower. 27 But Son Of Comfort (Barnabas) came alongside of him and took him to the message bearers.

Man Who Asks (Saul) then told them the story of what happened on the road, how he had seen and heard the voice of the Honored One. He also told them that he had been representing Creator Sets Free (Jesus) and speaking out boldly to the Tribal Members in the village of Running Horse (Damascus).

Speaking Boldly

28 So Man Who Asks (Saul) stayed with them. He walked the roads all around Village of Peace (Jerusalem) representing Creator Sets Free (Jesus) by speaking out boldly about him.

29 He spoke to the Greek-speaking Tribal Leaders arguing with them, but it just made them look for a way to kill him. 30 When the members of the Sacred Family heard about this, they took him away to Chief Village (Caesarea) and from there sent him to Tree Village (Tarsus).

31 Finally, the Sacred Family in the territory of the Land of Promise (Judea), Circle of Nations (Galilee) and High Place (Samaria) were at peace and growing strong. As they walked in a sacred manner with great respect for Creator, the Holy Spirit comforted them and made their numbers grow.

A Powerful Healing

32 Stands On The Rock (Peter) was walking the road from place to place. On his journey he came upon Creator's holy ones who lived in the village of Almond Tree (Lydda). 33 There he found a man named Man Of Honor (Aeneas), who could not move his body and had been unable to leave his bed for eight winters.

34 "Man Of Honor (Aeneas)," Stands On The Rock (Peter) said to him, "Creator Sets Free (Jesus) the Chosen One heals you! Stand up and fold up your bed blankets."

The man stood right up, 35 and all who lived in Almond Tree (Lydda) and those who lived in Flatland (Sharon) saw him and turned their hearts to Creator's Honored One.

A Respected Woman Crosses Over

³⁶ Now in the nearby Village of Beauty (Joppa) there lived a follower of Creator Sets Free (Jesus) whose name was Deer Woman (Tabitha), which is translated into our tribal language as Deer Eyes (Dorcas). She was a doer of many good deeds and always gave to the ones who had little. ³⁷ During the time that Stands On The Rock (Peter) was in Almond Tree (Lydda), she became ill and crossed over to death; so they ceremonially washed her body and laid her in an upstairs room.

³⁸ Since Almond Tree (Lydda) is near to Village of Beauty (Joppa), the followers there sent two men to Stands On The Rock (Peter) begging him to come right away.

³⁹ Stands On The Rock (Peter) got right up and went with the men. When they arrived, they took him to where her body lay in the upstairs room. The widows came and stood next to him. The tears rolled down their faces as they showed him the *beautiful* garments Deer Eyes (Dorcas) had made when she was with them.

Power Over Death

⁴⁰ Stands On The Rock (Peter) sent them all outside. He then fell to his knees and sent his voice to the Great Spirit. After he prayed, he turned toward the dead body of the woman.

"Deer Woman (Tabitha)," he said to her, "get up!"

She opened her eyes, and when she saw Stands On The Rock (Peter),

she sat up. ⁴¹ He reached out his hand to her and helped her up. He then called all the holy ones and the widows and stood her before them—alive! ⁴² Word of this spread throughout all of Village of Beauty (Joppa) and many put their trust in the Honored One, *Creator Sets Free (Jesus).*

⁴³ Then Stands On The Rock (Peter) stayed a good number of days in Village of Beauty (Joppa) in the home of He Hears (Simon), a tanner of leather.

A Powerful Vision

10 Now there lived a man in Chief Village (Caesarea) whose name was Little Horn (Cornelius). He was a head soldier in the Young Bulls (Italian) band of the People Of Iron (Romans). ² He was a spiritual man who had deep respect for the Great Spirit. He, along with all his family, gave with a big heart to the poor and prayed to Creator at all times.

³ One day, in the middle of the afternoon, he had a sacred vision. He could clearly see a spirit-messenger from Creator coming toward him.

"Little Horn (Cornelius)!" the messenger said to him.

⁴ Little Horn (Cornelius) could only stare at the spirit-messenger and tremble with fear.

"What is it you want, Honored One?" he asked the messenger.

"Your prayers and gifts of kindness have been remembered; they have risen like sweet smelling smoke to the Great Spirit. ⁵Now you must send messengers to Village of Beauty (Joppa) to find One Who Hears (Simon), who is also named Stands On The Rock (Peter) and ask him to come to your home. ⁶He is lodging at a house near the great waters at the home of He Hears (Simon), the tanner."

⁷After the spirit-messenger who spoke to him had left, Little Horn (Cornelius) called two servants and a trusted soldier from the ones who were under his command. ⁸After he told them everything they needed to know, he sent them to Village of Beauty (Joppa).

Another Sacred Vision

⁹On the next day, as the messengers were traveling and coming close to the village, Stands On The Rock (Peter) climbed up onto the *flat* roof of the house to send his voice to Creator. It was about midday. ¹⁰He became hungry and wanted something to eat; but as they were cooking the food, he fell into a trance and had a sacred vision.

¹¹He saw an opening in the sky and something like a large soft blanket that was being lowered to the ground by its four corners. ¹²On the blanket were all kinds of four-legged animals, creeping things from the ground, and winged-ones who soar in the sky.

¹³"Stands On The Rock (Peter), rise up!" a voice said to him, "Kill—as an offering—and eat."ᵉ

This would have been a hard thing for Stands On The Rock (Peter) to hear, because their Tribal Law forbade them to ceremonially offer or eat any unclean animal, and many of these animals were unclean or impure.

¹⁴"I cannot, O Honored One!" he answered. "I have never eaten anything impure or unclean."

¹⁵Then the Voice spoke to him a second time, "What the Great Spirit has made clean, you must not consider impure."

¹⁶This was repeated three times, and then the blanket was taken right back up into the world above.

The Messengers From Little Horn Arrive

¹⁷Stands On The Rock (Peter) was troubled, trying to understand the meaning of the vision. At the same time the men who were sent by Little Horn (Cornelius) stood at the gate ¹⁸and called out to see if Stands On The Rock (Peter) was lodging there.

¹⁹While Stands On The Rock (Peter) was meditating on the vision, the *Holy* Spirit said to him, "Look, three men are searching for you. ²⁰Now rise up, go down into the house, and do not hesitate to go with these men, because I have sent for them."

²¹So Stands On The Rock (Peter) went down from the rooftop to where the men were, and said to them, "I am the one you are looking for. What is it you want from me?"

e 10:13 Romans 15:16

22 "Little Horn (Cornelius), who is a head soldier[f] of the People of Iron (Romans), sent us. He is a man in good standing who has deep respect for the Great Spirit and is well spoken of by all in your Tribal Nation. He was instructed by a sacred spirit-messenger to send messengers to you, to ask you to come to his house so he can hear your words."

He Goes With the Messengers

23 Stands On The Rock (Peter) then welcomed them into the house and gave them lodging for the night. The next day he and some of his spiritual brothers from Village of Beauty (Joppa) went with him.

24 On the following day they came to Chief Village (Caesarea). Little Horn (Cornelius), who was waiting for them to come, had gathered together many relatives and close friends.

In the House of Outsiders

25 As soon as Stands On The Rock (Peter) came into the house, Little Horn (Cornelius) dropped to his knees and began to pray to him.[g] 26 But Stands On The Rock (Peter) made him stand up on his feet.

"Stand up!" he said to him, "I am only a weak human being, just as you are."

27 Stands On The Rock (Peter) kept talking to him as they went inside the house. There he saw all the people who had gathered to hear him.

This was the first time Stands On The Rock (Peter) had ever been in the home of someone from another nation. These people were considered to be outsiders and unholy. This was new territory that he was walking into, so he took a deep breath and began to speak to them.

28 "As all of you must know," he said to them, "it is against our Law for a Tribal Member like myself to have anything to do with someone from an Outside nation. But Creator has helped me to see that I should not consider anyone to be impure or unclean. 29 So when I was asked to come here, I did not hesitate to come. So tell me, why have you sent for me?"

Little Horn Tells His Story

30 Little Horn (Cornelius) spoke up and said to him, "It has now been four days to this very hour. In the middle of the afternoon, while I was praying, I looked up and saw a man standing before me, and his garments were shining bright.

31 "'Little Horn (Cornelius),' he said to me, 'your prayer has been heard and your gifts to the poor have risen like sweet smelling smoke before the Great Spirit. He has remembered what you have done. 32 Send messengers to Village of Beauty (Joppa) to One Who Hears (Simon), who is also named Stands On The Rock (Peter) and ask him to come. He is lodging at the house of He Hears (Simon), a tanner of hides, who lives near the great waters.'

---

f 10:22 Lit., centurion   g 10:25 Lit., worship him

[33] "I sent for you right away, and I thank you for coming. So we have all gathered here, in the sight of the Great Spirit, to hear what Creator has instructed you to tell us."

Stands On The Rock Speaks to All

[34] Stands On The Rock (Peter) *took another deep breath,* opened his mouth and began to speak to all who had gathered: "I speak from my heart, I now see that Creator does not favor one human being over another. [35] He accepts people of all nations who have a deep respect for him and do what is right.

[36] "This is the message he has given to the tribes of Wrestles With Creator (Israel), a message of peace that comes through Creator Sets Free (Jesus) the Chosen One. He is the one who has been honored above all others!

[37] "You must have heard about it. It all began with the purification ceremony announced by He Shows Goodwill (John) in Circle of Nations (Galilee). From there his message has spread *like wildfire* throughout the Land of Promise (Judea).

[38] "It is the story of how the Great Spirit chose Creator Sets Free (Jesus) from Seed Planter Village (Nazareth), and how the power of Holy Spirit came to rest upon him. How he walked the land, with Creator at his side, doing good and healing all who were pushed down and crushed by the evil trickster.

[39] "We are his message bearers, telling the truth about all that he did in the territory of our Tribal Members and in Village of Peace (Jerusalem), where they had him killed by hanging him on a tree. [40] He is the one that Creator, on the third day, brought back to life from the world of the dead. He then appeared, [41] not to everyone, but to all those he chose ahead of time to be truth-tellers—to us, the ones who ate and drank with him after he returned to life from the dead.

[42] "He has instructed us to tell this story in a sacred manner, so that all people will know that Creator Sets Free (Jesus) has been chosen by the Great Spirit to decide the fate of the living and the dead. [43] All the *ancient* prophets have spoken of him, that all who put their trust in him, and all that he represents, will be released from their bad hearts and broken ways."

The Holy Spirit Comes Down

[44] While Stands On The Rock (Peter) was still speaking, the Holy Spirit came down upon all who were listening to his words. [45-46] They began to speak in *new* languages and give praise and honor to the Great Spirit. This amazed the Tribal Members[h] who came with Stands On The Rock (Peter), for they could hear *and see with their own eyes,* that even upon people from Outside Nations, the gift of the Holy Spirit had been poured out.

Then Stands On The Rock (Peter) said to all, [47] "Who can now refuse

---

h 10:45-46 Lit., the circumcised, a designation for a Tribal Member (Jew)

water for these people to participate in the purification ceremony? For they have received the Holy Spirit in the same manner that we did."

48 So he instructed them to participate in the purification ceremony in the name of the Chosen One Creator Sets Free (Jesus) *and all he represents, welcoming them into the Sacred Family.*

After that they asked Stands On The Rock (Peter) to remain with them for a number of days.

Stands On The Rock is Questioned

11 Back in the Land of Promise (Judea) the message bearers and other followers of Creator Sets Free (Jesus) heard that people from the Outside Nations had welcomed Creator's message. 2 So when Stands On The Rock (Peter) returned to Village of Peace (Jerusalem), the *strict* Tribal Members[i] there began to question him.

3 "How is it that you went into the house of outsiders[j] and ate with them?" they asked.

Stands On The Rock Retells His Story

4 So he told them, step by step, the journey he had been on.

5 "In the Village of Beauty (Joppa), where I was lodging, I was sending my voice to the Great Spirit. I went into a trance and was given a sacred vision. I saw something that looked like a large soft blanket coming down from the sky, being lowered by its four corners. As it came near to me, 6 I looked into it wondering what it was. I saw four-legged animals of the land, wild animals, snakes, creeping things, and winged-ones who soar in the sky.

7 "Then I heard a Voice say, 'Stands On The Rock (Peter), kill—as an offering—and eat.'

8 "'I cannot! O Honored One,' I answered, 'I have never eaten anything impure or unclean.'

9 "Then the Voice from the world above spoke to me a second time, 'If Creator has made it clean, then you must not consider it impure.'

10 "This happened three times. Then the blanket was taken back up into the world above. 11 Right then three men who had been sent to me from Chief Village (Caesarea) arrived at the house where we were lodging. 12 The Spirit told me to have no doubts about going with them. So I and six spiritual brothers went to the man's house and were welcomed inside.

13 "The man of the house told us how he had seen a spirit-messenger standing in his house. The messenger told him to send a message to Village of Beauty (Joppa) to One Who Hears (Simon), who is also named Stands On The Rock (Peter), 14 who will tell you and all your family and friends how to be set free and made whole.

15 "Just as I was beginning to speak to them, the Holy Spirit came down upon them in the

---

i 11:2 Lit., those of the circumcision   j 11:3 Lit., uncircumcised men

same manner he did for us at first. ¹⁶ Then I remembered what our Wisdomkeeper had said to us: 'He Shows Goodwill (John) performed the purification ceremony with water, but you will participate in the purification ceremony with the Holy Spirit.'

¹⁷ "If Creator gave them the same gift he gave to us when we put our trust in Creator Sets Free (Jesus), the Chosen One and our Honored Chief, who was I to stand in the way of the Great Spirit?"

¹⁸ When they heard these words, they sat there in silence with nothing to say. Then they gave honor to Creator.

"So then," they said *with wondering voices*, "the Great Spirit has also given the Outside Nations the way to return to the path of life."

Telling the Good Story

¹⁹ The ones who had been scattered because of the persecution that began when Many Feathers (Stephen) was killed had made their way as far as Land of Palm Trees (Phoenicia), Island of Flowers (Cyprus) and Stands Against (Antioch). They were telling the Good Story, but only to the Tribal Members, not to anyone from the Outside Nations.

²⁰ But there were others, men from Island of Flowers (Cyprus) and Strong Wall (Cyrene), who came to Stands Against (Antioch) and began to tell the Wisdom Seekers (Greeks) from Outside Nations about Creator Sets Free (Jesus), our Honored Chief. ²¹ The strong hand of the Great

Spirit was with them and a large number of them trusted in our Honored One.

²² Word of this came to the ears of the Sacred Family in Village of Peace (Jerusalem). ²³⁻²⁴ So they sent to them Son Of Comfort (Barnabas), a good-hearted man who was full of the Holy Spirit and faith. When he saw Creator's great kindness at work in them, it made his heart glad. He then spoke wise counsel to them, telling them to have brave hearts and to stand strong, looking to the Honored One.

There were so many new followers there that Son Of Comfort (Barnabas) knew he needed more help.

²⁵ So he went to Tree Village (Tarsus) to look for Man Who Asks (Saul). ²⁶ When he found him, he took him back to Stands Against (Antioch). For a whole year they gathered there, together with the Sacred Family. There they taught a large number of people. It was in the village of Stands Against (Antioch) that the followers of Creator Sets Free (Jesus) were first called Followers of the Chosen One.

²⁷ It was in those days that some prophets came down from Village of Peace (Jerusalem) to the village of Stands Against (Antioch). ²⁸ One of them, named Grasshopper (Agabus), foretold by the Spirit that soon there would be a shortage of food all over the territory of the People of Iron (Romans). This happened during the rule of Walks With A Limp (Claudius).

29 So the followers who lived in Stands Against (Antioch) decided to send help to the Sacred Family in the Land of Promise (Judea)—as much as they could spare. 30 Son Of Comfort (Barnabas) and Man Who Asks (Saul) hand-carried the gifts to the elders.

More Persecution

12 During those days, Looks Brave (Herod) k used his power as chief to bring harm to the Sacred Family. 2 He had He Takes Over (James) the brother of He Shows Goodwill (John) killed with the long knife. 3 When he found out that this pleased the *corrupt* Tribal Leaders, he decided to take Stands On The Rock (Peter) captive also—during the festival of Bread Without Yeast. 4 After capturing him, he put him in prison and assigned sixteen soldiers to guard him—four at a time. Looks Brave (Herod) planned to bring him before the people during the Passover festival.

Rescued by a Spirit-Messenger

5 But while Stands On The Rock (Peter) was in prison, the Sacred Family prayed for him with strong hearts as they sent their voices to the Great Spirit.

6 On the night before Looks Brave (Herod) was planning to bring him before the people, Stands On The Rock (Peter) was sound asleep between two soldiers who were guarding him. He was bound with two chains and more guards were guarding the prison gate.

7 Out of nowhere a spirit-messenger from Creator appeared and a light shone all around them. The spirit-messenger nudged Stands On The Rock (Peter) in his side to wake him up.

"Get up quickly!" the messenger instructed him, and right then the chains fell from his hands. 8 "Tighten your sash and put on your moccasins," he added. He did so and the messenger said, "Now put on your outer garment and follow me."

9 Stands On The Rock (Peter) went out with the spirit-messenger, but he thought he was having a vision and did not know it was really happening. 10 They had passed by the first guard, then the second, when they came to the iron gate that leads into the village. The gate opened by itself, they walked down a village path, and right then the messenger left him.

He rubbed his eyes and looked around and finally realized that he was not in a vision. This was really happening!

11 After his thoughts cleared up, he said to himself, "Now I know for sure that Creator has sent his spirit-messenger to rescue me from the hand of Looks Brave (Herod) and from all that the Tribal Members thought would happen to me."

---

k 12:1 This is the great grandson of Looks Brave (Herod) the Great who tried to kill Creator Sets Free (Jesus) when he was a baby.

At the House of Brooding Tears

¹²So Stands On The Rock (Peter) went to the home of Brooding Tears (Mary), the mother of He Shows Goodwill (John), who is also named War Club (Mark). Many of the Sacred Family had gathered there praying *for him.*

¹³He knocked at the gate outside the door, and a servant girl named Rose Bush (Rhoda) went to answer. ¹⁴When she recognized the voice of Stands On The Rock (Peter), she ran back inside without opening the gate and told everyone it was Stands On The Rock (Peter) who was at the gate.

¹⁵"You have lost your mind!" they said to her, but she assured them that it was he.

"It must be his spirit-messenger," they kept saying to each other.

¹⁶Meanwhile Stands On The Rock (Peter) was still knocking at the gate; and when they opened the door and saw him at the gate, they could not believe their eyes. ¹⁷Stands On The Rock (Peter) motioned to them with his hand to be silent; he then told them how Creator had rescued him from the prison.

"Tell He Takes Over (James) and the others what has happened," he said to them. He then he left to go to another place.

¹⁸The next morning the soldiers who were guarding Stands On The Rock (Peter) were in a big uproar, for he was gone! ¹⁹Looks Brave (Herod) came and searched for him also. When he could not find him, he questioned the guards and then ordered them to be put to death. He then traveled down from the Land of Promise (Judea) to Chief Village (Caesarea) and stayed there.

Eaten by Worms

²⁰Looks Brave (Herod) was angry with the people of Rock Land (Tyre) and Hunting Grounds (Sidon), so they sent some messengers to him to make peace, for their people depended on the food that came from the land Looks Brave (Herod) ruled over. The messengers won the favor of Budding Branch (Blastus), the most trusted servant of Looks Brave (Herod).

²¹After that Looks Brave (Herod) chose a day to make his decision about this matter. He put on his chiefly regalia and sat down on the Seat of Deciding to make a talk of many words.

²²The crowd began to shout, "This is not the voice of a man, but of a great spirit!"

²³Because Looks Brave (Herod) did not give the honor over to the Great Spirit, a spirit-messenger from Creator struck him down. He was then eaten by worms and crossed over to death.

²⁴Meanwhile, Creator's message continued to grow strong among the people and to spread far and wide. ²⁵*Their task was now complete, so* Son Of Comfort (Barnabas) and Man Who Asks (Saul) returned from Village of Peace (Jerusalem) to Stands Against (Antioch) taking with them He Shows Goodwill (John) who was also named War Club (Mark).

Prophets and Teachers

13 There were prophets and teachers among the Sacred Family that gathered in Stands Against (Antioch). There was Son Of Comfort (Barnabas), Creator Hears (Simeon) who was also called Black Man (Niger), also Bright Light (Lucius) from Strong Wall (Cyrene), Man Of Comfort (Manaen) who was taken into the family of Chief Looks Brave (Herod),[l] and Man Who Asks (Saul).

2 They were performing their ceremonies to Creator and going without food when the Holy Spirit spoke to them, "Set apart Son Of Comfort (Barnabas) and Man Who Asks (Saul), so they can do what I have chosen them to do."

New Message Bearers Sent Out

3 So after they continued to go without food and pray, they laid their hands on them and sent them on their way. 4 Then Son Of Comfort (Barnabas) and Man Who Asks (Saul) followed the guidance of the Holy Spirit and journeyed to Crashing Waves (Seleucia). From there they canoed to Island of Flowers (Cyprus).

5 When they came to Village of Salt (Salamis), they went to the local tribal gathering house. There, with the help of He Shows Goodwill (John), they began to share Creator's message with them.

Conflict With a False Prophet

6 They traveled the whole island as far as Foaming Water (Paphos). There they met a man named Son Of Creator Sets Free (Bar-Jesus), a Tribal Member and false prophet who practiced bad-medicine. 7 He was with the local official[m] of the People of Iron (Romans), whose name was Small One Who Serves (Sergius Paulus), a man of understanding, who had sent for Son Of Comfort (Barnabas) and Man Who Asks (Saul) to hear Creator's message from them.

8 But the bad medicine-man, who was also called Wise One (Elymas) in the local language, opposed them and tried to turn the official from believing their message. 9 Then Man Who Asks (Saul), with the power of the Holy Spirit, looked straight into his eyes.

10 "You son of the evil trickster!" he spoke sharply to Wise One (Elymas). "You who speak with a forked tongue! You are the enemy of all that is good and right. When will you ever stop making Creator's straight paths crooked? 11 Keep your eyes open *while you can*; for Creator's hand is against you, and for a while your eyes will not see, even the light of the sun."

As soon as Man Who Asks (Saul) finished speaking, a mist of darkness came upon him and he stumbled about looking for someone to take him by the hand. 12 When the official saw what happened *to the bad medicine-man*, he believed and was struck with wonder at the lesson Creator had given.

---

l 13:1 Lit., Herod the tetrarch, meaning ruler of one of four parts of a territory.   m 13:7 Proconsul

They Continue
Their Journey

[13] At Foaming Water (Paphos) Small Man (Paul)[n] and the ones who were with him set out in their canoes and journeyed to Earth Village (Perga) in the territory of Many Tribes (Pamphylia). From there He Shows Goodwill (John) left them and returned to Village of Peace (Jerusalem).

Small Man Tells
the Good Story

[14] But Small Man (Paul) and the others continued on and went to another village named Stands Against (Antioch) in the territory of Tree Sap (Pisidia). On the next Day of Resting they went into the local tribal gathering house and sat down. [15] After the people read out loud from the Law and the Prophets, the headmen of the gathering house sent a message to them.

"Fellow Tribal Members," the message said, "If there is anything you want to say to encourage the people, please speak up."

[16] So Small Man (Paul) stood up, motioned with his hands and said:

"Men from the tribes of Wrestles With Creator (Israel) and all who have deep respect for the Great Spirit, listen to me now! [17] The Great Spirit of our people chose to make our ancestors into a great nation when they were still *slaves* in Black Land (Egypt). He then lifted them up with his strong arm and led them out into the desert wilderness. [18] There he put up with their ways for forty winters. [19] He then defeated seven nations in the territory of Lowland (Canaan) and gave their land to the tribes of Wrestles With Creator (Israel) for the generations that would follow.[o] [20] All this took about four hundred and fifty winters in all.

"After that he gave them spiritual leaders[p] until the days of the prophet Creator Hears Him (Samuel). [21] When they asked for an earthly chief, Creator gave them Man Who Asks (Saul) the son of Sets His Trap (Kish) from the tribe of Son Of My Right Hand (Benjamin), who was their chief for forty winters.

[22] "After removing him as chief, Creator chose Much Loved One (David) to be the chief of our ancestors. This is what he said about him: 'I have found one who makes my heart glad, who will do all that I ask of him. He is Much Loved One (David) son of Original Man (Jesse).'

[23] "Creator has kept his promise to the tribes of Wrestles With Creator (Israel) and has raised up a descendant of Much Loved One (David) to be the one to set his people free *from their bad hearts and wrongdoings*. This descendant is Creator Sets Free (Jesus).

[24] "Before Creator Sets Free (Jesus) came to us, Creator first sent He Shows Goodwill (John), who announced a purification ceremony to return our tribes to the right way of thinking and walking. [25] When

---

n 13:13 This is where Man Who Asks (Saul) takes on the name Small Man (Paul). Paul is the Greek form of Saul.   o 13:19 Lit., as an inheritance   p 13:20 Lit., judges

the work of He Shows Goodwill (John) was coming to an end, he said many times, 'Do you think I am the Chosen One? I am not. I am not worthy to untie the moccasins of the one who is coming after I am done.'

26 "My fellow members of the Sacred Family, descendants of Father Of Many Nations (Abraham), and all who have deep respect for the Great Spirit, it is to *all of* us that this message has been given—to set us free and make us whole.

27-28 "It was the people who live in Village Of Peace (Jerusalem), and their leaders, who had him put to death because they did not recognize him. Even though they failed to understand the words of the prophets, which are read out loud on every Day of Resting, they fulfilled them when they had Spear Of The Great Waters (Pilate) put him to death—even though he had done nothing wrong.

29 "Then, when they did all that was foretold about him, they lowered him from the tree and laid him in a burial cave. 30 But the Great Spirit brought him back to life, 31 and for many days he was seen by the ones who had walked the road with him from Circle of Nations (Galilee) to Village of Peace (Jerusalem). They are now his truth-tellers to the tribes of Wrestles With Creator (Israel).

The Promise Has Come True

32 "Today, we are here to tell you this Good Story that completes the promise that was made to our ancestors: 33 The Giver Of Life has made his promise come true for us, their descendants, by raising up Creator Sets Free (Jesus), just as it says in the second Sacred Song (Psalm):

"'You are my Son. Today I have become your Father.'q

34 "To show that he would raise up Creator Sets Free (Jesus) from the dead, to never die again, here is what he said:

"'I will gift you with the sacred promises spoken to Much Loved One (David).'r

35 "And, here is another verse from the Book of Sacred Songs (Psalms):

"'You will not let the body of your Holy One return to the ground.'s

36 "It is clear that Much Loved One (David), after he served Creator's purpose for the people of his own day, crossed over into the death-sleep, was buried with his ancestors, and his body returned to the ground. 37 But the body of the one that Creator raised up did not return to the ground.

Final Words

38-39 "My fellow Tribal Members, know this: It is through Creator Sets Free (Jesus) that we are released from our bad hearts and broken ways. Whoever trusts in him is set free and put into good standing with Creator. This is something the Law given by Drawn From The Water (Moses) could never do.

40 "So then," *Small Man (Paul) said as he finished his talk,* "make sure that

---

q **13:33** Psalm 2:7   r **13:34** Isaiah 55:3   s **13:35** Psalm 16:10

another thing the prophets foretold does not happen to you: [41] 'Watch out, you who laugh and scorn! You will die in your amazement, for I am doing something you will not believe even when you are told that it has happened!'[t]"

The People Want to Hear More

[42] As they were leaving, the people begged them to stay and talk with them again on the next Day of Resting. [43] After the meeting at the gathering house ended, many of the Tribal Members and others who had been ceremonially taken into the tribe followed after Small Man (Paul) and Son Of Comfort (Barnabas), who urged them to keep walking in Creator's great kindness.

A Light to the Outside Nations

[44] Seven days later, on the following Day of Resting, almost the whole village gathered together to hear Creator's word. [45] But the local Tribal Members became jealous when they saw how large the crowd was. They spoke lies against Small Man (Paul) and argued against everything he said. But both Small Man (Paul) and Son of Comfort (Barnabas) stood up to them.

[46] "It was of great importance," they said with strong hearts, "that we would bring Creator's message to our Tribal Members first. But now that you have shown no respect for this message and decided that you are not worthy of the life of the world to come, we will turn to the people from other nations. [47] For this is what the Great Spirit instructed us to do when he said: 'I have chosen you to be a light to all nations, so that all who live upon the earth may know Creator's power to rescue and make them whole.'[u]"

[48] When the ones who were from other nations heard this, it made their hearts glad and they honored Creator's message; and they all—the ones who long ago had been chosen for the life of the world to come, that never fades—put their trust in the message.

[49] So Creator's message spread throughout the whole territory. [50] But the Tribal Members stirred up the spiritual leaders, both the women and men, against Small Man (Paul) and Son Of Comfort (Barnabas) and forced them out of that area. [51] So they shook the dust from their moccasins, as a sign against them, and went from there to Spirit Village (Iconium).

[52] The followers of Creator Sets Free (Jesus) were filled with joy and with the Holy Spirit.

Conflict in Spirit Village

14 The same thing happened at Spirit Village (Iconium). Small Man (Paul) and Son Of Comfort (Barnabas) went to the local tribal gathering house and spoke with such powerful words that many

---

t 13:41 Habakkuk 1:5   u 13:47 Isaiah 49:6

Tribal Members and Outsiders[v] put their trust in Creator Sets Free (Jesus).

2 But the Tribal Members who did not believe poisoned the minds of the people from Outside Nations and turned them against their new family members. 3 So the message bearers, Small Man (Paul) and Son Of Comfort (Barnabas), remained there a long time and spoke with boldness about the Honored One. Through their hands Creator did many wonderful and powerful signs, confirming the message of his great kindness.

4 But the people of Spirit Village (Iconium) were split apart; some stood with the Tribal Members and some with the message bearers. 5-6 But when the message bearers heard that some of the Tribal Members and Outsiders, along with their rulers, were planning to harm them and even stone them to death, they fled for safety. They went to the villages of She Wolf (Lycaonia), Set Free (Lystra), Skin Tanner (Derbe) and their surrounding territories 7 —telling the Good Story wherever they went.

A Powerful Healing

8 Now in the village of Set Free (Lystra) sat a man who was born with bad feet and unable to walk. 9 He sat listening as Small Man (Paul) was speaking. Small Man (Paul) looked closely at the man and saw that he had faith to be healed.

10 "Stand up on your feet!" he said with a loud voice.

The man jumped to his feet and began walking.

11 When the crowd of people saw what Small Man (Paul) had done, they all began to shout in their local language, "Powerful spirits[w] have come down to us in the form of human beings!"

12 Son Of Comfort (Barnabas) they called Skyfather (Zeus), and Small Man (Paul) they called High Messenger (Hermes) because he was the chief speaker. 13 The lodge of Skyfather (Zeus) was at the village gate, and the holy man of the lodge, along with the people, brought out cattle wearing ceremonial wreaths to make an offering to Small Man (Paul) and Son Of Comfort (Barnabas).

14 When the two message bearers heard what was happening, *in humble desperation* they tore their clothes and rushed out to the center of the crowd.

15 "Fellow human beings!" they shouted. "Why are you doing this? We are only weak two-leggeds like yourselves. We came to tell you the Good Story so you would turn away from these empty ways *and turn* to the Great Spirit, who is the maker of the sky, the earth, the great waters, and everything in them. 16 In past generations he permitted all nations to walk in their own ways, 17 yet in his goodness he gave each of us signs of his existence. He gave us rain from the sky above and seasons of harvest to feed us and make our hearts glad."

18 Even these words barely kept the people from sacrificing an

---

v **14:1** Greeks   w **14:11** Lit., gods

offering to them. [19] But then some Tribal Members from Stands Against (Antioch) and Spirit Village (Iconium) came and turned the people against Small Man (Paul). So they threw stones at him and dragged him outside the village, thinking he was dead. [20] But when some followers gathered around him, he got up and returned to the village. The next day he and Son Of Comfort (Barnabas) left to go to the village of Skin Tanner (Derbe).

They Finish Their Journey

[21] After telling the Good Story in that village and making many new followers, they made their way back through the village of Set Free (Lystra), then on to Spirit Village (Iconium), and then back to Stands Against (Antioch) *where they began their journeys.*

[22] *On the way* they strengthened the hearts of the *new* followers, telling them to stand tall as they walked this path of faith.

"Following Creator's Good Road to the end," they counseled them, "is a difficult path with many hardships."

[23] They chose elders to *watch over* every Sacred Family gathering. After praying and going without food, they dedicated them to the Honored One in whom they had put their trust.

[24] On their journey they walked *back* through the territory of Tree Sap (Pisidia) and Many Tribes (Pamphylia). [25] There in Earth Village (Perga) they told the Good Story[x] to the people before traveling on to the village of Grows More (Attalia).

[26] From there they traveled by canoe[y] to Stands Against (Antioch) where, by Creator's great kindness, they had been sent out on this journey that was now complete.

[27] After arriving, they gathered the Sacred Family together and told the story of all that Creator had done among them—how he had opened a pathway of faith for all Nations. [28] And they remained there with the Sacred Family for a long time.

The Council at Village of Peace

15 *While Small Man (Paul) and Son Of Comfort (Barnabas) were in Stands Against (Antioch),* some men came down from the Land of Promise (Judea) and began to teach the followers there.

They said, "Unless you have participated in the traditional cutting of the flesh ceremony,[z] given by Drawn From The Water (Moses), you cannot be set free and made whole."

[2] But Small Man (Paul) and Son Of Comfort (Barnabas) did not agree with them and had a strong argument with them. It was decided that Small Man (Paul) and Son Of Comfort (Barnabas), along with a few others, would go to the message bearers and elders at Village of Peace (Jerusalem) to settle this among them. [3] So having been sent on their way by the Sacred Family, they traveled through Land of Palm Trees (Phoenicia) and High Place (Samaria). As they traveled,

---

x 14:25 Lit., spoke the word   **y 14:26** Lit., sailed   **z 15:1** Lit., circumcision and also in verse 5

they told how the Outside Nations had come to faith. This made the hearts of all the followers glad.

⁴ When they came to Village of Peace (Jerusalem), the message bearers, elders, and the Sacred Family welcomed them. So they told them the stories of all that the Great Spirit had done through them. ⁵ But some of the Sacred Family members who belonged to the band of the Separated Ones (Pharisees) stood up among them *to make their voice heard.*

"The Outside Nations," said the Separated Ones (Pharisees), "must participate in the cutting of the flesh ceremony, and be required to follow our Tribal Law given by Drawn From The Water (Moses)."

⁶ The message bearers and elders sat in council together to discuss this matter. ⁷ After much talk and debate, Stands On The Rock (Peter) stood up among them.

"My fellow members of the Sacred Family," he said to all, "you know that a good while ago Creator chose me to be the one to help the Outside Nations come to faith by telling them the Good Story. ⁸ The Knower Of Hearts made this clear when he gave them the Holy Spirit in the same manner as he did for us. ⁹ The Great Spirit made no difference between us and them, purifying their hearts when they trusted in him. ¹⁰ So why put Creator to the test by putting a burden on their shoulders that neither our ancestors nor we have been able to carry?

¹¹ "So then," *Stands On The Rock (Peter) finished,* "we believe it is because of the great kindness of Creator Sets Free (Jesus), the Chosen One, that we will be set free and made whole. It is the same for us and them!"

¹² Silence fell upon all who had gathered there as they listened to Son Of Comfort (Barnabas) and Small Man (Paul) tell about the wondrous and powerful signs the Great Spirit had done through them when they were with the Outside Nations.

More Discussion

¹³ When they were finished speaking, He Takes Over (James) stood up and spoke to the gathering:

"My fellow Tribal Members, hear what I have to say. ¹⁴ One Who Hears (Simon) has spoken well to remind us of how the Great Spirit first showed *to us* his concern for the Outside Nations, by choosing from among them those who would represent him. ¹⁵ This agrees with the words of the prophets *from long ago.*

"It is written in the Sacred Teachings, ¹⁶ 'At that time I will return and repair the Sacred Tent of Much Loved One (David) that has fallen to the ground. I will raise it up from its tattered ruins and mend its tears, ¹⁷ so that the rest of mankind may search for the Great Spirit—all the Outside Nations who have *also* been chosen to represent me. This is what Creator is saying, ¹⁸ for he made these things known long ago.'ᵃ

---

a 15:18 Some ancient manuscripts read: For the Great Spirit knew long ago what he would do.

[19] "So, as I see it, we should not put stones in the path of the ones in these Outside Nations who are turning to the Great Spirit. [20] Here is the message we should send to them: that they should stay away from things offered to evil spirits,[b] from sexual impurity, from the meat of a strangled animal, and from *drinking* blood. [21] For from ancient times the ways of Drawn From The Water (Moses) have been taught in every village, and his words are read out loud in the tribal gathering houses on every Day of Resting."

The Council Decides

[22] Then the message bearers, the elders, and all of the Sacred Family agreed that it was a good thing to choose some men, along with Small Man (Paul) and Son Of Comfort (Barnabas), to take a message to Stands Against (Antioch). They chose Speaks Well Of (Judas) who is also called Son Of Resting (Barsabbas) and Woods Man (Silas), spiritual leaders among the Sacred Family.

The Council Writes a Message

[23] Here is the message they sent in a letter: "Greetings, from the message bearers and elders of the Sacred Family, to our brothers *and sisters* who are from the Outside Nations in the villages of Stands Against (Antioch), Bright Sun (Syria) and Turns Over (Cilicia).

[24] "We heard that some of our people came to you, even though we did not send them, and that they said things that troubled and confused you. [25] We all agreed it would be good to send some men to represent us—along with our much loved Son Of Comfort (Barnabas) and Small Man (Paul). [26] These are men who have risked their lives representing Creator Sets Free (Jesus), the Chosen One and our Honored Chief. [27] So we sent Speaks Well Of (Judas) and Woods Man (Silas) to tell you the same things we have written.

[28] "So then, it seemed good to the Holy Spirit and to us to place on you no burden other than these necessary things: [29] that you stay away from things offered to evil spirits, from *drinking* blood, from the meat of strangled animals, and from sexual impurity. If you stay away from these things you will be walking in a good way. Safe journeys to you."

The Message is Sent

[30] So they sent the messengers to Stands Against (Antioch). [31] When they gathered everyone together and read the message, their hearts were encouraged and made glad. [32] Speaks Well Of (Judas) and Woods Man (Silas), who were also prophets, lifted their spirits and made their hearts strong with many words.

The Messengers Return to Village of Peace

[33] After some time there, they sent the messengers back with a blessing of peace upon those who had sent

---

b 15:20 Lit., idols

them.^c ³⁵ But Small Man (Paul) and Son Of Comfort (Barnabas) remained in Stands Against (Antioch). There, along with many others, they taught the message of the Good Story about the Honored One.

Separate Ways

³⁶ After they had stayed there for a while, Small Man (Paul) said to Son Of Comfort (Barnabas), "Come with me and we will visit the Sacred Family in every village where we taught Creator's message—and see how well they are doing."

³⁷ Now Son Of Comfort (Barnabas) wanted He Shows Goodwill (John), who is also named War Club (Mark), to go with them. ³⁸ But Small Man (Paul) did not think it wise, for he had deserted them in the territory of Many Tribes (Pamphylia) and did not complete the work.

³⁹ Their argument became so strong that they split apart and went their separate ways. Son Of Comfort (Barnabas) took War Club (Mark) and set out in a canoe^d for Island of Flowers (Cyprus), ⁴⁰ but Small Man (Paul) chose Woods Man (Silas). So they were given Creator's blessing by the Sacred Family and set out ⁴¹ traveling through Bright Sun (Syria) and Turns Over (Cilicia). There they gave strength to the Sacred Family gatherings *in that territory.*

He Gives Honor
Joins the Journey

16 Small Man (Paul) also went to the village of Skin Tanner (Derbe) and then to Set Free (Lystra). In that village was a follower named He Gives Honor (Timothy). His mother was a Tribal Woman who trusted *in Creator Sets Free (Jesus),* and his father was from an Outside Nation.^e ² He Gives Honor (Timothy) was well spoken of by the Sacred Family at Set Free (Lystra) and Spirit Village (Iconium).

³ Small Man (Paul) wanted to take He Gives Honor (Timothy) with him, so he performed the cutting of the flesh ceremony for him,^f because of the Tribal People in the area who knew his father was from an Outside Nation.^g

⁴ As they journeyed through the villages, they instructed the Sacred Families to follow the decisions of the message bearers and elders who were in Village of Peace (Jerusalem). ⁵ So the Sacred Families were made strong in the faith, and their numbers grew larger each day.

Guidance From
the Holy Spirit

⁶ Small Man (Paul) and He Gives Honor (Timothy) continued their journey through the territory of Dry Wood (Phrygia) and Land of Strangers (Galatia), for the Holy Spirit had held them back from telling the Good Story^h in the territory of Rising Sun (Asia). ⁷ When they came to Land of Beech Trees (Mysia), they tried to go to Rushing Storm (Bithynia), but the Spirit of Creator Sets Free (Jesus) would not permit them. ⁸ So they went around

c 15:33 Other manuscripts add verse 34: But Woods Man (Silas) thought it good to remain.
d 15:39 Lit., sailed   e 16:1 Greek   f 16:3 Lit., circumcised him   g 16:3 Greek   h 16:6 Lit., speaking the word

Land of Beech Trees (Mysia) and traveled on to the village of Cut Through (Troas).

⁹ During the night Small Man (Paul) had a vision in which he saw a man from Land of Tall People (Macedonia) standing in front of him. The man was begging him and saying, "Come over to our land and help us!"

¹⁰ When the vision was done, right away we tried to go into the Land of Tall People (Macedonia), trusting that Creator had chosen us to tell the Good Story to them.

¹¹ So we set off in our canoe ⁱ straight from Cut Through (Troas) to Sign of Rags (Samothrace). The next day we came to New Village (Neapolis), ¹² and from there we went on to Horse Village (Philippi), the chief village of Land of Tall People (Macedonia) under the rule of the People of Iron (Romans). There we remained for a number of days.

Welcomed by a Woman of Faith

¹³ Then on the Day of Resting we went outside of the village gate to a nearby river to find a place to send our voices to the Great Spirit. We sat down on the riverbank and spoke to some women who had gathered there. ¹⁴ One of the women there, named Bitter Fruit (Lydia), was a trader in purple cloths and had great respect for Creator. As Small Man (Paul) spoke, she listened closely to the message, and Creator opened her heart. ¹⁵ She

and her family then participated in the purification ceremony.

"If you consider me to be one who trusts in our Honored Chief," she said to us firmly, "then you must come and stay at my house." And she would not take no for an answer.

They Force Out an Evil Spirit

¹⁶ As we were on our way to where we gathered for prayer, a slave-girl who had an evil snake spirit met us. ʲ She brought her owners much gain by fortune-telling.

¹⁷ She began to follow after Small Man (Paul) and shout out loud, "These men, who serve the Great Spirit who is above all, are showing us the way to be set free and made whole."

¹⁸ She did this for many days. *By so doing,* she greatly troubled Small Man (Paul), who finally turned and spoke to the *evil* spirit, "As one who represents Creator Sets Free (Jesus), the Chosen One, I tell you now to come out of this woman!"

¹⁹ Right away the spirit left her. When her owners saw that the hope of their gain was gone, they took hold of Small Man (Paul) and Woods Man (Silas) and dragged them to the village rulers at the trading post.

Arrested and Imprisoned

²⁰ They brought them before the village council and said, "These men are from the tribes of Wrestles

---

i 16:11 Lit., set sail   j 16:16 Lit., spirit of python

With Creator (Israel). They are bringing trouble to our village 21 by trying to force their tribal customs on us. Since we are of the People of Iron (Romans), we are not permitted to accept or follow these customs."

22 The people who had gathered there also began to speak against them, so the village council stripped their clothes off them and gave orders for them to be beaten with sticks. 23 When they finished beating them, they threw them into prison and told the headman of the prison to lock them up. 24 So he followed his instructions, put them deep into the prison and locked their feet in iron shackles.

An Earthquake Opens Prison Doors

25 In the middle of the night Small Man (Paul) and Woods Man (Silas) were sending up prayers and singing sacred songs to the Great Spirit. The other prisoners were listening, 26 when suddenly the earth began to shake violently, and the stones holding the prison up began to tremble. Right then the prison doors were opened and everyone's iron shackles fell off.

The Headman Becomes a Follower

27 When the headman of the prison woke up and saw all the prison doors standing open, he took his long knife and was going to kill himself, for he thought all the prisoners had escaped.

28 But Small Man (Paul) shouted out to him, "Do not harm yourself, we are all here!"

29 The headman of the prison asked for a torch, and trembling with fear he rushed inside and fell down before Small Man (Paul) and Woods Man (Silas).

30 He then took them outside and said, "What must I do to be set free and made whole?"

31 "Put your trust in Creator Sets Free (Jesus), our Honored Chief," they said to him. "He will make you whole and set you and all your family free *to follow him.*"

32 Then they told Creator's Good Story to him and all his family. 33 It was still late in the night, but the headman took Small Man (Paul) and Woods Man (Silas) and washed their wounds. Then right away the headman and his family all participated in the purification ceremony. 34 He then invited them into his home and fed them. His heart was glad because he and all his family had put their trust in the Great Spirit.

The Council Releases Them

35 In the morning the village council sent messengers, saying, "Release these men."

36 So the headman of the prison told Small Man (Paul), "The council has instructed me to release you, so you may go in peace."

37 But Small Man (Paul) said, "We are citizens of the People of Iron (Romans)! They have beaten us before the village without a trial and thrown us in prison, and now they would send us away in secret?

No! Let them come here and take us out themselves!"

38 The messengers went back and reported what they said to the village council. When they heard that they were citizens of the People of Iron (Romans), they were afraid. 39 So they came and apologized to them, released them and asked them to leave the village. 40 So after they left the prison, they went to the home of Bitter Fruit (Lydia). There they encouraged the Sacred Family, and *then left to continue their journey.*

The Message Brings Comfort and Conflict

17 After traveling through Circle Village (Amphipolis) and Village of Destroyer (Apollonia), they came to a Tribal Gathering House at the village of False Victory (Thessalonica). 2 As was his custom, Small Man (Paul) went to the gathering house on the next three Days of Resting. He tried to convince them from the Sacred Teachings, 3 explaining and proving to them that the Chosen One had to suffer and then rise again from the dead.

Then he said to them, "Creator Sets Free (Jesus), the one I have been telling you about, is the Chosen One!"

4 Some of them were won over and joined with Small Man (Paul) and Woods Man (Silas), including a large number from the Outside Nations[k] who had deep respect for

Creator and also many of the local headwomen.

5 But the Tribal Members became jealous. Banding together with some troublemakers from the trading post, they gathered a crowd and caused an uprising in the village. They broke into the house of a man named Healer (Jason), looking for Small Man (Paul) and Woods Man (Silas) so they could bring them before the people. 6 Not finding them there, they took hold of Healer (Jason) and some of the other Sacred Family members and dragged them before the village council.

"The ones who have turned the world upside down," they shouted, "have also come here! 7 And Healer (Jason) has welcomed them into his house. They are going against the laws of the Ruler of the People of Iron (Caesar), by saying there is another Ruler—Creator Sets Free (Jesus)."

8 This troubled the people and the village council, 9 so after taking payment as a promise from Healer (Jason) and the others *that there would be no more trouble,* they let them go.

Small Man is Sent Away

10 Right away, under the cover of night, members of the Sacred Family sent Small Man (Paul) and Woods Man (Silas) to Much Water (Berea). When they arrived, they went to the local Tribal Gathering House. 11 The Tribal Members there were more honorable than the ones in False Victory (Thessalonica), for they welcomed the message with

k 17:4 Greeks

glad hearts, and each day they searched the Sacred Teachings to see if their message agreed. [12] In this way many Tribal Members came to the faith, including honored women and men from the Outside Nations.[l]

[13] When the Tribal Members from False Victory (Thessalonica) found out that Small Man (Paul) was telling the Sacred Story in Much Water (Berea), they also came there to stir up the crowds and make trouble for them. [14] So right away the Sacred Family sent Small Man (Paul) away to the great sea, but Woods Man (Silas) and He Gives Honor (Timothy) remained behind.

[15] The ones who went with Small Man (Paul) took him to Wondering Place (Athens). Small Man (Paul) told them to send Woods Man (Silas) and He Gives Honor (Timothy) to him right away, and so they went back to Much Water (Berea).

Small Man at Wondering Place

[16] While Small Man (Paul) was waiting for them at Wondering Place (Athens), he saw that this large village was filled with images of powerful spirit beings. [17] So every day at the tribal gathering house he would argue with the Tribal Members, and at the trading posts he would talk with any spiritual people who happened to be there. [18] Some traditional wisdom seekers[m] also argued with him.

Others wondered, "What is this babbler saying?" While others said, "He seems to be talking about strange and powerful spirits."

Small Man Speaks at Mars Hill

They said this because he was telling them the Good Story about Creator Sets Free (Jesus) and his rising from the dead. [19] So they took him to the council at Mars Hill (Areopagus).

"Explain this new teaching to us," they asked him, [20] "for your message is strange to us, and we want to know its meaning."

[21] The people who lived in Wondering Place (Athens) would spend all their time telling or hearing about some new thing.

[22] So Small Man (Paul) stood up in the center of Mars Hill (Areopagus) and said, "People of Wondering Place (Athens), I can see that in all things you are a very spiritual people. [23] As I walked around, I saw some of your sacred objects. One altar had this message carved into it:

DEDICATED TO
AN UNKNOWN
POWERFUL SPIRIT

"So then, the one you sacredly honor without knowing is the one I will make known to you. [24] The Great Spirit is the one who created the universe and all things in it. Since he is the rightful ruler of the world above and the earth below, he does not live in lodges built by human hands. [25] Creator does not really need human beings to do

l 17:12 Greeks   m 17:18 Epicureans and Stoics

things for him, since he is the one who gives all people life and breath and everything we need.

26 "Beginning with the first human being, he made all tribes and nations. He wanted people to live all over the face of the earth. He decided ahead of time when and where each tribe would live. 27 He did this so that all people could look for him and find the trail that leads to him. Creator is not far away from any one of us. 28 It is through him that we live, walk, and have our being.

"As some of your song-makers have said, 'We are children of the Great Spirit.' 29 Since we are his children, we should not think that he is made of gold or silver or wood or stones. He is not like the carvings that people have thought up in their minds and made with their hands.

30 "In times past Creator overlooked this empty way of thinking. But now he wants all people everywhere to return to the right way of thinking, 31 because he has chosen a day when he will decide, for all people, who has done right and who has done wrong. He has chosen a man who will do this and has shown all people who he is by bringing him back to life again from the dead."

32 When they heard about the rising from the dead, some mocked him, but others said, "We will hear you again about this."

33 So Small Man (Paul) went on his way. 34 Some of the people believed and joined with him, including one of the council members of Mars Hill (Areopagus) named Shining Tree (Dionysius) and a woman named Good Wife (Damaris), along with a few others.

Small Man at Village of Pleasure

18 Small Man (Paul) left from Wondering Place (Athens) and went to Village of Pleasure (Corinth). 2 There he found a Tribal Member named Strong Eagle (Aquila) who lived in the territory of Black Waters (Pontus). He and his wife Lives Long (Priscilla) had recently moved from Land of Young Horses (Italy) because Walks With A Limp (Claudius), the Ruler of the People of Iron (Caesar), had ordered the removal of all Tribal Members from that territory.

3 Small Man (Paul) found out they were both tentmakers, as he was, so he lodged with them and joined them in their work. 4 Then on every Day of Resting he debated with his local Tribal Members and the Wisdom Seekers (Greeks), trying to convince them *about Creator Sets Free (Jesus)*.

5 After Woods Man (Silas) and He Gives Honor (Timothy) came from Land of Tall People (Macedonia), Small Man (Paul) became like a man on fire—trying to convince his Tribal Members that Creator Sets Free (Jesus) was the Chosen One. 6 But when they stood against him and spoke evil of him, he shook the dust from his clothes.

"You have decided your own fate!" he told them. "I have done all I can do. From now on I will go to the Outside Nations."

The Headman Believes

7 So he left them and went to the house of Stands Upright With Fire (Titius Justus), a man with deep respect for Creator and whose house was next door to the Tribal Gathering House. 8 A man named Curly Hair (Crispus), who was headman of the Gathering House, put his trust in our Honored Chief, and both he and his family participated in the purification ceremony. When others who lived in Village of Pleasure (Corinth) heard about this, they also believed and participated in the purification ceremony.

9 During the night Creator spoke to Small Man (Paul) in a sacred vision.

"Do not fear!" he said to him. "Keep speaking and do not be silent, 10 for I am standing with you. No one will harm you, for I have many people in this village."

11 So Small Man (Paul) stayed there for one year and six moons, teaching Creator's message to the people.

An Uprising Against Small Man

12 During the days when Rooster (Gallio) was the governor of Land of Sorrow (Achaia), the Tribal Members joined together in an attack on Small Man (Paul) and took him before the governor to accuse him of wrongdoing.

13 "This man is convincing people to serve the Great Spirit in ways that go against our Tribal Law," they accused.

14 But before Small Man (Paul) could open his mouth to defend himself, the governor spoke to the Tribal Members.

"If a wrong had been done or some kind of evil had been committed, then I would hear your accusations," he said to them, 15 "but if this is simply a question about words and names and how to interpret your own Laws, then you must decide for yourselves. I want nothing to do with deciding these things."

16 So he sent them away from his council house. 17 The Tribal Members then took Strong Protector (Sosthenes), the headman of the gathering house, and began to beat him right in front of the governor. But he turned his head the other way.

Small Man's Journey

18 After staying there for a number of days, Small Man (Paul) said farewell to the Sacred Family. Then he, along with Lives Long (Priscilla) and Strong Eagle (Aquila), set off in a canoe to Bright Sun (Syria). At Small Seed Village (Cenchreae) Small Man (Paul) ceremonially shaved his head because he had made a solemn promise.

19 From there they traveled to Village of Desired One (Ephesus). Small Man (Paul) left his traveling friends in the village, but he went to the local Tribal Gathering House to speak with the Tribal Members there. 20 They asked him to stay, but he turned them down and said his farewells.

²¹ "If Creator permits it," he told them, "I will return."

He then set out from the village by canoe. ²² He came to land at Chief Village (Caesarea), greeted the Sacred Family there, and then made his way to Stands Against (Antioch).

²³ He stayed there a number of days, then left and walked here and there, strengthening the hearts of the Sacred Family members throughout the territory of Land of Strangers (Galatia) and Dry Wood (Phrygia).

Back in the Village of Desired One

²⁴ There was a Tribal Member named He Tears Down (Apollos) from Village of Defense (Alexandria) who came to Village of Desired One (Ephesus). He was a powerful wisdom speaker who had a deep understanding of the Sacred Teachings. ²⁵ Even though he had only participated in the purification ceremony of He Shows Goodwill (John), he was well instructed in the Way of the Honored One, and a fire burned in his spirit as he spoke clearly about Creator Sets Free (Jesus).

²⁶ At the local Tribal Gathering House he began to speak openly; but when Lives Long (Priscilla) and Strong Eagle (Aquila) heard him speak, they took him aside and helped him see Creator's Way more clearly. ²⁷ Then, when he desired to go to Land of Sorrow (Achaia), the Sacred Family sent along a message to instruct the followers there to welcome him. When he arrived, he was a great help to the ones who had trusted in Creator's great kindness, ²⁸ for he spoke powerfully to his Tribal Members proving to them from the Sacred Teachings that Creator Sets Free (Jesus) was the Chosen One.

Village of Desired One

19 While He Tears Down (Apollos) was at Village of Pleasure (Corinth), Small Man (Paul) journeyed through the inland territories and arrived at Village of Desired One (Ephesus), where he found some followers.

² "When you put your trust in Creator Sets Free (Jesus)," Small Man (Paul) asked them, "did you receive the Holy Spirit?"

"What do you mean?" they replied. "We have not even heard about this 'Holy Spirit.'"

³ "What kind of purification ceremony did you participate in?" he asked.

"It was the purification ceremony performed by He Shows Goodwill (John)," they answered.

⁴ "He Shows Goodwill (John) performed a purification ceremony for the ones who returned to Creator's right ways of thinking and doing," Small Man (Paul) said to them. "In this way they would be ready to put their trust in Creator Sets Free (Jesus)—the one he was preparing the way for."

⁵ When they heard this, they participated in the purification ceremony represented by the name

of our Honored Chief—Creator Sets Free (Jesus). ⁶⁻⁷Small Man (Paul) then laid his hands on the men, about twelve in all, and they spoke in languages *they had not learned* and prophesied when the Holy Spirit came down upon them.

Small Man Tells the Good Story

⁸Then for three moons Small Man (Paul) went to their Tribal Gathering House and spoke out boldly to convince the people living there about Creator's Good Road. ⁹But some, who were stubborn, with hearts like stone, refused to believe, and spoke evil of the Way to all who gathered there.

So Small Man (Paul) left there. Taking with him the new followers, he went to the teaching-lodge of Harsh Ruler (Tyrannus) to teach there. ¹⁰He continued this for two winters, until all the Tribal Members and Wisdom Seekers (Greeks) who lived in the territory of Rising Sun (Asia) had heard the message about our Honored One.

Powerful Signs and Wonders

¹¹Through the hands of Small Man (Paul), Creator was doing some unusual powerful signs. ¹²Face cloths and sashes that had touched his body were taken to heal the sick and force out evil spirits.

¹³Then some Tribal Members who traveled about forcing out evil spirits tried to use the name of Creator Sets Free (Jesus) over those with evil spirits, saying, "I force you out by the sacred power of Creator Sets Free (Jesus), the one whom Small Man (Paul) proclaims."

¹⁴These men were the seven sons of Weak Hand (Sceva), a Tribal Member who was *representing himself as* a chief holy man.

¹⁵But the evil spirit spoke back to them, "I know of Creator Sets Free (Jesus) and I have heard of Small Man (Paul), but who are you?"

¹⁶Then the man with the evil spirit jumped on them and so overpowered them that they ran from the house naked, bruised and bleeding.

¹⁷Word spread to all the Tribal Members and the Wisdom Seekers (Greeks) who lived in Village of Desired One (Ephesus). Great awe and respect came upon all, and the name of Creator Sets Free (Jesus) was spoken of with honor.

¹⁸Many who had chosen to follow Creator Sets Free (Jesus) came forward and admitted to their evil practices. ¹⁹A number of them who had practiced bad medicine gathered their books and burned them in the sight of all. These books were found to be worth about fifty thousand silver coins.ⁿ ²⁰In this way Creator's message grew strong and spread like wildfire.

²¹After this, Small Man (Paul) decided in his spirit that he should travel through Land of Tall People (Macedonia) and Land of Sorrow (Achaia) and then on to Village of Peace (Jerusalem). "After that," he

---

n 19:19 Each coin was worth a day's wages.

said, "I must also go to Village Of Iron (Rome)" 22 So he sent his two helpers, He Gives Honor (Timothy) and Much Desired (Erastus), ahead of him to Land of Tall People (Macedonia), while he remained for a time in Rising Sun (Asia).

An Uprising in the Village

23 Now during that time there was a great uprising at Village of Desire (Ephesus) about the Way. 24 There was a man there named Corn Spirit (Demetrius), who worked with silver and made little silver lodges for the spirit-image named Fertility Woman (Artemis). His work helped support many of the artists who traded there. 25 He gathered them together, along with the others who also worked with silver.

"Fellow workers," he said to them, "you all know that this work we do provides for us. 26 You have all seen and heard what this Small Man (Paul) has done, not only in our village, but also in most of Rising Sun (Asia). He has convinced many people to turn away from our spirit-images, saying that spirit-images made by hands are not powerful spirits."

The crowd began to grumble and grow restless as he continued to speak.

27 "We are in danger that the work we do will be looked down on, and that the sacred lodge of the spirit-image of Fertility Woman, the one whom all in Rising Sun (Asia) and the world bows down to, will be seen as worthless, and her great beauty and power will fall to the ground."

28 When the crowd heard this, a great anger filled their hearts, and they shouted, "Great is Fertility Woman (Artemus) of Village of Desired One (Ephesus)!"

29 The whole village was thrown into confusion. With one purpose they ran into the teaching-lodge, dragging with them Glad Heart (Gaius) and Good Chief (Aristarchus) from Land of Tall People (Macedonia), who were traveling with Small Man (Paul).

30 Small Man (Paul) wanted to go into the crowd, but the other followers would not let him. 31 Also, some of the village leaders who were friendly towards him sent word for him not to come into the teaching-lodge.

32 The gathering became one of turmoil and confusion. Some were shouting one thing, some another. Most did not even know why they had gathered!

33 Some of the Tribal Members in the crowd pushed Man Fighter (Alexander) to the front, instructing him *what to say*. He motioned with his hand that he wanted to speak, 34 but when they saw that he was a man of the tribes of Wrestles With Creator (Israel), they cried out with one voice:

"Great is Fertility Woman (Artemis) of Village of Desired One (Ephesus)!!"

Over and over again, for about two hours, they kept shouting, 35 until the village scroll keeper finally quieted them down.

"People of Village of Desired One (Ephesus)," he said to all, "who among us does not know that the people of Village of Desired One (Ephesus) are the sacred lodge keepers of the great Fertility Woman (Artemis) and of her spirit-image that fell from the world above? 36 Since these things cannot be denied, you should lower your voices and do nothing without thinking clearly first.

37 "The men you have brought here are not lodge-thieves, neither do they speak against Fertility Woman (Artemis). 38 If Corn Spirit (Demetrius) and the other artists with him want to accuse anyone, let them bring these accusations to the village council or the local officials. 39 Anything else should also be brought to the village council meeting. 40 For we are in danger today of being charged with causing an uprising, with no good reason for it."

41 After saying this, he sent the crowd away.

Small Man Continues His Travels

20 After the uprising had calmed down, Small Man (Paul) gathered the local Sacred Family members together to strengthen their hearts and say his farewell to them. He then left for Land of Tall People (Macedonia).

2 As he traveled through that territory, with many words he lifted the hearts of the members of the Sacred Family who lived there.

He then came to Land of Wisdom Seekers (Greece) 3 and stayed there for three moons. Just as he was about to set out in his canoe to Bright Sun (Syria), the Tribal Members there hatched a plot against him, so he decided to return through Land of Tall People (Macedonia).

Small Man's Traveling Friends

4 Here are the names of the men who went with him: Defends His Father (Sopater) the son of Red Fire (Pyrrhus) from Much Water (Berea), Good Chief (Aristarchus) and Second Blessing (Secundus) from False Victory (Thessalonica), also Glad Heart (Gaius) from Skin Tanner (Derbe), He Gives Honor (Timothy), and He Is At Ease (Tychicus) and He Eats Well (Trophimus) from Rising Sun (Asia).

5 These men traveled ahead of us and were waiting for us at Cut Through (Troas). 6 They had to wait five days because we stayed for the Festival of Bread Without Yeast. Then we set out by canoe from Horse Village (Philippi) and joined with them at Cut Through (Troas) and stayed there for seven days.

Power Over Death

7 It was the first day of the week, when we gather to eat our sacred meal together. o Small Man (Paul) was doing the talking because he planned to leave the next day. He was long-winded and kept talking until the middle of the

o 20:7 Lit., break bread

night. 8 There were many torches burning in the upper room of the house where we had all gathered.

The number of people and the torches in this room, using up the air, may have made some people sleepy or lightheaded.

9 As Small Man (Paul) spoke on and on, a young man named Greatly Blessed (Eutychus), who was sitting on the window ledge, began to sink into a deep sleep. When the sleep overcame him, he fell from the third floor window and was found dead. 10 Small Man (Paul) went down, bent over the young man, and put his arms around him.

"Do not fear!" he said to all, "his life has returned to him."

11 So Small Man (Paul) went back to the upper room, ate the ceremonial meal with them and continued speaking until sunrise. He then went on his way, 12 and with glad hearts they took the young man home alive!

More Travels

13 We all climbed into our canoes and headed to Move Toward (Assos), where we would take Small Man (Paul) aboard, for he decided to travel there on land. 14 So he met us there and joined us as we went on to Bent Horn (Mitylene). 15 We set off from there, and on the following day we came to shore across from Snow Island (Chios). The next day we touched shore at Sand Cliff (Samos), and the day after that we came to White Sheep Wool (Miletus).

16 We did not stop at Village of Desired One (Ephesus), because Small Man (Paul) was in a hurry to get to Village of Peace (Jerusalem), if possible, for the Festival of Weeks,*p* and did not want to take the time to go to Rising Sun (Asia).

17 From White Sheep Wool (Miletus), Small Man (Paul) sent a messenger to Village of Desired One (Ephesus) to ask the elders of the Sacred Family to come to him. 18 When they came, this is what he said to them:

"You all know how I lived among you the whole time I was with you, from the first day that I set foot in the territory of Rising Sun (Asia). 19 I did all Creator asked of me with a humble heart, as I walked a trail of tears when the Tribal Members schemed against me. 20 You also know that I held back nothing that would help you, as I taught openly and from house to house. 21 I spoke truth in a sacred manner to both the Tribal Members and the Wisdom Seekers (Greeks), as I told them about turning their thoughts and hearts to the Great Spirit by trusting their lives to Creator Sets Free, our Honored Chief.

22 "And now, a captive of the Spirit, I am on my way to Village of Peace (Jerusalem). I do not know what will happen to me there. 23 I only know the Holy Spirit has made it clear to me that in every village I will be hunted down and taken captive. 24 But my life means nothing to me. I only want to finish walking the road the Maker of Life has set before me, telling the Good

Story of his great kindness as I follow Creator Sets Free (Jesus), my Honored Chief.

25 "I now know that none of you will see my face again. You are the ones I have taught clearly about the Good Road. 26 Hear me this day! I speak from my heart, I am no longer responsible for any of you, 27 for I held back nothing from you. All that Creator has made known to me, I have given to you.

28 "Stay alert and care for one another. The Holy Spirit has given you elders the task of watching over his people. Like shepherds that guard the sheep, you will watch over his Sacred Family, the ones he paid the highest price for— his own life-blood.

29 "I know that after I am gone savage wolves will sneak in who care nothing for the sheep. 30 Even some of your own elders will rise up and lead people down a false path, just to have their own followers. 31 So I tell you again—stay alert! Do not forget that night and day, for three winters, I kept giving you wise counsel and warning each of you with many tears.

32 "I now give you over to the Great Spirit's care and to the message of his great kindness—a message that will make you stand strong and give you his promised blessings, together with all the ones he has made holy.

33 "I never asked anyone for their silver, gold or fine clothes. 34 You all have seen that I worked hard with my own hands to provide for myself and for the ones who traveled with me. 35 In this way, I have walked a path for you to follow, working hard to give help to the weak. We must never forget the words of Creator Sets Free (Jesus), when he said, 'Giving to others is a greater blessing than receiving from others.'"

36 When Small Man (Paul) had finished speaking, he knelt down beside the elders of the Sacred Family and sent his voice to the Great Spirit. 37 With many tears they put their arms around his neck and kissed him. 38 Their greatest sorrow was from his words, "You will not see my face again."

Then they walked with him to our canoe *to see us on our way.*

Journey to Village of Peace

21 After we had torn ourselves away from them we set out in our canoe and followed the shortest distance to the island of High Point (Cos). On the next day we went to Rose Island (Rhodes), and then to Walked Over (Patara). 2 From there we found a large canoe that was headed for Land of Palm Trees (Phoenicia) and travelled with them. 3 We could see Island of Flowers (Cyprus) to our left as we traveled on toward Bright Sun (Syria) and then went to shore at Rock Land (Tyre) to unload trading goods from the canoe.

4 We looked for members of the Sacred Family *who lived there,* and, after finding them, we stayed with them for seven days. Guided by the Spirit, they kept telling Small

Man (Paul) not to go to Village of
Peace (Jerusalem). [5] At the end of our
time with them, as we were on our
way to leave, the men of the Sacred
Family, along with their wives and
children, followed us outside of
the village. We all knelt down at
the shoreline, sent our voice to the
Great Spirit, [6] and said our farewells.
We then climbed into the canoe as
they went back to their homes.

[7] From Rock Land (Tyre) we
continued on to Village of War
(Ptolemais). We were welcomed by
the Sacred Family and stayed the
rest of the day with them. [8] The
next day we left and went to
Chief Village (Caesarea) and lodged
there at the home of Friend Of
Horses (Philip), a teller of the Good
Story and one of the seven. [9] Now
Friend of Horses (Philip) had four
unmarried daughters who spoke
words from the Holy Spirit. [q]

*Friend of Horses (Philip) was
one of the seven who had been
chosen by the message bearers in
Village of Peace (Jerusalem) to be
in charge of serving the meals. He
also went about telling the Good
Story in High Place (Samaria).* [r]

[10] We stayed there a number of
days. During our stay a prophet
named Grasshopper (Agabus) came
to us from Land of Promise (Judea).
[11] He took the sash from Small Man's
(Paul's) waist and tied it around his
own feet and hands.

"This is what the Holy Spirit is
saying," he prophesied. "'The
Tribal Leaders in Village of Peace
(Jerusalem) will do the same to the

owner of this sash; they will tie him
up and turn him over to the People
of Iron (Romans)[s]'."

[12] When we, along with the Sacred
Family there, heard this, we all
urged Small Man (Paul) not to go to
Village of Peace (Jerusalem).

[13] "Why are you weeping and
breaking my heart?" he said to
them. "I am representing our
Honored Chief, Creator Sets Free
(Jesus). I am ready, not only to be
tied up, but even to die for him in
Village of Peace (Jerusalem)."

[14] Nothing we could say would
change his mind. "Let Creator's
will be done," we said, and then
remained silent.

Arrival at Village of Peace

[15] We then prepared to leave on
our journey to Village of Peace
(Jerusalem). [16] Some of the Sacred
Family members from Chief
Village (Caesarea) traveled with us,
along with a longtime follower
named He Will Remember (Mnason),
from Island of Flowers (Cyprus),
in whose house we would stay.
[17] When we arrived at Village of
Peace (Jerusalem), the Sacred Family
welcomed us with glad hearts.

Meeting With the Council

[18] The next day Small Man (Paul)
went with us to meet with He Takes
Over (James) and the elders who
were with him. [19] After giving them
a respectful greeting, he told them
about all the things Creator had done
as he had worked among the Outside

---

q 21:9 Lit., prophesied   r 21:9 See Acts Chapter 6 and 8.   s 21:11 Lit., Gentiles

Nations. ²⁰ When they heard this, they gave praise to the Great Spirit.

"Our brother," they said to him, "you can see how many thousands of our Tribal Members have become followers of Creator Sets Free (Jesus), and how our Tribal Law *given by Drawn From the Water (Moses)* burns like a fire in them!"

But then their manner changed and their voices lowered as they looked around and then back to Small Man (Paul).

²¹ "They have heard that you are teaching our Tribal Members who live among the Outside Nations to turn away from Drawn From the Water (Moses), that they should not perform the cutting of the flesh ceremony for their children or follow our tribal traditions. ²² What will happen when they find out you are here? What can be done?"

But it seemed that they already had made plans about what to do.

²³ "Listen, and do what we say," they said to him. "We have four men who have taken a solemn vow for dedication. ²⁴ Go and join with them in this vow and provide for the shaving of their heads. In this way you will show everyone that these rumors are false and that you still walk in our traditional Tribal Law.ᵗ"

This was the Law of Dedication (Nazarite). Those men and women who make this solemn vow to the Great Spirit must drink no wine, vinegar or strong drink and eat no grapes or the juice of grapes.

Among other things they also must not touch a dead person or cut their hair or beard during all the days of this vow. The vow must be kept for at least thirty days. After the days of the vow are complete, they must shave their heads in a holy ceremony at the Sacred Lodge in Village of Peace (Jerusalem).

He Takes Over (James) continued giving instructions to Small Man (Paul).

²⁵ "As for the ones from the Outside Nations who have trusted in Creator Sets Free (Jesus), we sent them a message with our decision: that they should stay away from things offered to evil spirits,ᵘ from *drinking* blood, from the meat of a strangled animal, and from sexual impurity."

²⁶ So the next day Small Man (Paul) went with the men to the Sacred Lodge. He purified himself with them and told them the number of days before the vow would be complete and the sacrifice that would be offered for them.

Small Man Taken Captive

²⁷ Seven days later, when the time was complete, *Small Man (Paul) returned to the Sacred Lodge.* There were some of his Tribal Members there from Rising Sun (Asia). When they saw him in the Sacred Lodge, they took hold of him and began to stir up the crowd against him.

²⁸ "Fellow Tribal Members!" they shouted out to the crowd. "Help us! This is the man who teaches

---

t 21:24 Numbers 6:1-21   u 21:25 Lit., idols

everywhere against our people, our Tribal Law, and this *Holy* Place! Even worse, he has brought Wisdom Seekers (Greeks) into the Lodge and has defiled this Holy Place."

²⁹ They said this because they had seen He Eats Well (Trophimus) from Village of Desired One (Ephesus) with Small Man (Paul) in Village of Peace (Jerusalem), and thought he had brought him into the Sacred Lodge.

³⁰ The village was in an uproar! A group of people came together, took hold of Small Man (Paul), dragged him outside of the Lodge, closed the gates behind him—and tried to kill him.

³¹ A messenger went from them and told the local head soldier of the People of Iron (Romans) that there was an uprising in the Village of Peace (Jerusalem). ³² At once he took some soldiers and their officers with him and ran to where they were attacking Small Man (Paul). When they saw the head soldier and his men, they stopped beating Small Man (Paul).

³³ The head soldier arrested him and had him bound with two chains of iron. He then asked the crowd who this man was and what he had done. ³⁴ Some in the crowd shouted one thing and some another. Since the head soldier could not figure out what happened, he decided to take Small Man (Paul) back to the headquarters. ³⁵ The crowd became so violent that Small Man (Paul) had to be carried up the stairs.

³⁶ "Take him away!" they shouted over and over again as they pressed close following behind the soldiers.

³⁷ Just before they got to the soldiers headquarters, Small Man (Paul) turned to the head soldier and spoke in the soldier's language.

"Is it permitted for me to speak to you?" he asked.

³⁸ "You speak the language of the Wisdom Seekers (Greeks)," he replied. "Then you are not the man from Black Land (Egypt) who some time ago caused an uprising and took four thousand assassins out into the desert wilderness."

³⁹ "I am a Tribal Man of the tribes of Wrestles With Creator (Israel)," Small Man (Paul) answered, "from Tree Village (Tarsus) in the territory of Turns Over (Cilicia), a citizen of a well known village."

He now had the full attention of the head soldier, so he made a request.

"I beg you," he said to the head soldier, "let me speak to my people!"

⁴⁰ The head soldier gave him permission, so Small Man (Paul) stood on the steps overlooking the crowd and motioned his hand to the people. A great hush settled over them, so Small Man (Paul), speaking in the language of his own people, *took a deep breath and with respect* began to speak to them.

Small Man Speaks to the Crowd

22 "My fellow Tribal Members, my fathers," he said, "hear me now as I explain myself to you."

² When the people heard him speak in their native language, they quieted down even more.

3 "I am a fellow Tribal Man, born in Tree Village (Tarsus) in the territory of Turns Over (Cilicia), but I was raised in Village of Peace (Jerusalem) and was taught at the feet of Creator Has Honored (Gamaliel). I learned to closely follow all of our traditional Tribal Laws, and a fire for the Great Spirit burned in my belly, just as it does in yours today.

4 "I hunted down and even killed the followers of this Way. I put both men and women in iron chains and took them to prison. 5 Our chief holy man and the whole council of elders are witnesses to the truth of what I say. For I asked for and received written authority to give to the local Tribal Council in Running Horse (Damascus), with instructions to capture any followers of the Way and take them to Village of Peace (Jerusalem) to be punished.

6 "It was midday on the journey to Running Horse (Damascus). As I came near the village, suddenly a bright light from the world above shined down all around me. 7 I fell to the ground and heard a voice speaking to me *and twice calling out my name.*

"'Man Who Asks (Saul), Man Who Asks (Saul),' the voice said, 'why are you pursuing and mistreating me?'

8 "Honored One," I asked, "Who are you?"

"'I am Creator Sets Free (Jesus) from Seed Planter Village (Nazareth),' the voice answered, 'the one you are pursuing and mistreating.'

9 "The men who were traveling with me saw the light, but did not hear the voice of the one speaking to me.

10 "Honored One," I asked, "what is it you want me to do?"

"'Stand to your feet and go into the village,' he said to me, 'and there you will be told all that I want you to do.'

11 "Since I was still unable to see because of the bright light, the men with me led me by the hand to Running Horse (Damascus).

Small Man and Gift Of Goodwill

12 "A man named Gift Of Goodwill (Ananias), who had deep respect for our Tribal Law and had a good reputation among our Tribal Members who lived there, 13 came and stood beside me.

"'Man Who Asks (Saul), my brother,' he said to me, 'look up and see again!'

"I looked up and right then sight returned to my eyes!

14 "Then he said to me, 'The Great Spirit of our ancestors has chosen you to know his will, to see the Upright One and hear his voice, spoken from his own mouth. 15 You will tell all people the truth of what you have seen and heard. 16 What are you waiting for? Rise up and participate in the purification ceremony, washing you clean from your broken ways, as you call out to him, trusting in all that his name represents.'

17 "*Sometime later,* after I had returned to Village of Peace (Jerusalem), I was in the Sacred Lodge sending my voice to the Great Spirit.

I fell into a sacred vision [18] and saw Creator Sets Free (Jesus).

"'You must hurry and leave Village Of Peace (Jerusalem) right away,' he said to me, 'for they will not believe what you tell them about me.'

[19] "'Honored One,' I said to him, 'they know that I used to go from one Gathering House to another, capturing and whipping the ones who trusted in you. [20] When the blood of Many Feathers (Stephen) your truth-teller was being shed, they saw that I was standing in agreement and guarding their garments while they killed him.'

[21] "'Go!' he said to me, 'I am sending you far away to other nations.'"

The Crowd Turns Against Him

[22] The Tribal Members listened to him, up until this last word.

"Away with this one!" they shouted, "He has no right to even live on this earth!"

[23] The crowd was wailing out loud! They tore off their outer garments and threw dust into the air. [24] The head soldier ordered his men to take Small Man (Paul) back to their headquarters with instructions to beat him with whips until he told them the reason the crowd was so angry with him.

[25] But as they stretched him out and prepared to whip him, Small Man (Paul) turned to the head soldier standing there.

"Does your law permit you to whip a citizen of the People of Iron (Romans)," he asked, "without a fair trial?"

[26] Hearing this, the head soldier reported to his head officer.

"What are you doing?" he asked, "This man is a citizen of the People of Iron (Romans)."

[27] The head officer went to Small Man (Paul).

"Tell me," he asked, "Are you a citizen of the People of Iron (Romans)?"

"Yes, I am," Small Man (Paul) replied.

[28] "I paid a high price to become a citizen," the officer said to him.

"But I was born a citizen of the People of Iron (Romans)," Small Man (Paul) replied.

[29] Right away the soldiers who were about to question him backed away. Fear came upon the head officer as he realized that he had bound a citizen of the People of Iron (Romans) in chains.

Before the Grand Council

[30] But the head officer wanted to know what Small Man (Paul) was being accused of by the Tribal Members, so, before releasing him, he instructed the Head Priests and the Grand Council to meet. He then brought in Small Man (Paul) and stood him before them.

He Speaks to the Grand Council

23 Small Man (Paul) looked deeply into the eyes of the members of the Grand Council.

"My fellow Tribal Members," he said to the Council, "All my life I have walked in a good way, with a pure heart before the Great Spirit."

2 *Hearing this,* Gift Of Goodwill (Ananias) the chief holy man ordered the ones standing near Small Man (Paul) to strike his mouth.

3 "Creator will strike you, you false-faced pretender!" Small Man (Paul) said back to him. "Do you sit there using our own Tribal Law to decide my fate, and then break the same Law by ordering me struck?"

4 The ones standing near him said, "How dare you speak in a disrespectful manner to Creator's chief holy man?"

5 "Fellow Tribal Members," he replied, "I did not recognize that he was the chief holy man, for it is written in the Sacred Teachings, 'You must not speak against a leader of your people.'ᵛ"

6 Small Man (Paul), knowing that both the Upright Ones (Sadducees) and the Separated Ones (Pharisees) sat on the Grand Council, said to them, "My fellow Tribal Members, I am a Separated One (Pharisee). It is because of my hope that the dead will rise to life again that I am on trial here today."

The Council is Divided

7 When he said this, an argument broke out between the Separated Ones (Pharisees) and the Upright Ones (Sadducees). This created a division in the Council, 8 for the Upright Ones (Sadducees) say the dead will not rise and that there are no spirits or spirit-messengers, but the Separated Ones (Pharisees) believe in them all.

9 The arguments grew louder and louder. Then some scroll keepers who were among the Separated Ones (Pharisees) stood up and voiced their argument forcefully.

"We find no reason to condemn this man," they cried out. "It could be that a spirit or spirit-messenger has spoken to him!"

10 The division broke out into violence. The head officer, afraid that Small Man (Paul) would be torn apart by them, ordered his soldiers to take him by force and bring him back to their headquarters.

11 That night Creator Sets Free (Jesus) came and stood near him *in a sacred vision.*

"Be strong of heart," he said to him, "for in the same manner you have represented me in Village of Peace (Jerusalem), you must also represent me in Village of Iron (Rome)."

The Plot to Kill Small Man

12 Early the next day, some of the Tribal Members schemed together against Small Man (Paul). They bound themselves in a solemn promise that they would not eat or drink until they had killed him. 13 There were more than forty men who bound themselves to each other in this twisted plan. 14 They went to the Head Priests and elders and said:

"We have bound ourselves with a solemn promise to neither eat nor

---

v 23:5 Exodus 22:28

drink until we have killed Small Man (Paul). ¹⁵ So we want you and the council to ask the head officer to bring him to you. Tell him that you plan to ask Small Man (Paul) some more questions. We will then be ready to ambush him on the way and kill him."

Warning From a Nephew

¹⁶ But when Small Man's (Paul's) nephew heard about the ambush, he snuck into the place where Small Man (Paul) was being held and warned him.

¹⁷ Small Man (Paul) then called out to one of the head soldiers, "This young man has something important to report, so take him to your head officer."

¹⁸ Hearing this, the head soldier took him to the head officer.

"The prisoner Small Man (Paul) asked me to bring this young man to you. He has something important to tell you."

¹⁹ So the head officer took the young man aside, and asked, "What is it you want to report to me?"

²⁰ "Some Tribal Members from the council have agreed to ask you to bring Small Man (Paul) as if they want to question him some more," he told the head officer. ²¹ "But do not let them fool you, for there are more than forty men waiting to ambush him on the way. They have bound themselves by a solemn promise to neither eat nor drink until they have killed him. They are ready now and waiting for you to agree to bring him."

²² The head officer told the young man to say nothing, sent him away, ²³ and then called two head soldiers to himself.

Small Man Sent to the Governor

"I want you to be ready by the third hour of the night," he instructed them. "Gather seventy horsemen and two hundred spearmen and take them as far as Chief Village (Caesarea)."

²⁴ He also provided a horse and horsemen for Small Man (Paul), to bring him safely to Lucky Man (Felix), the governor for the People of Iron (Romans).

²⁵ He then he wrote a letter to *send with them* to give to the governor:

²⁶ "Greetings from Limping Man Who Sets Free (Claudius Lysias) to the most noble Lucky Man (Felix), governor representing the People of Iron (Romans).

²⁷ "This man, *who has been brought before you,* was taken captive by the Tribal People, who were about to kill him. But when I learned that he was *also* a citizen of the People of Iron (Romans), I had my soldiers rescue him. ²⁸ To find out what he was accused of, I took him before their Grand Council. ²⁹ I learned that he was being accused of matters relating to their own tribal laws, but nothing deserving death or imprisonment. ³⁰ When I was told of a plot against this man, I had him sent to you at once, and told his accusers to bring their accusations to you."

³¹ So the soldiers, following their instructions, took Small Man (Paul)

by night to First Ancestor Village (Antipatris). 32 On the next day the soldiers let the horsemen take him further, while they returned to headquarters. 33 When the horsemen came to Chief Village (Caesarea), they gave the letter to the governor and turned Small Man (Paul) over to him. 34 After reading the letter, the governor asked which territory he was from. Learning that Small Man (Paul) was from Turns Over (Cilicia), he agreed to hear his case.

35 "I will make my decision," he said to Small Man (Paul), "after your accusers arrive."

He then ordered that Small Man (Paul) should be kept under guard in their headquarters, *which used to be* the lodge of Looks Brave (Herod), *the bad hearted chief of the tribes of Wrestles With Creator (Israel).*

Small Man Accused

24 Five days later Gift Of Goodwill (Ananias) the chief holy man, along with some of the elders and a legal expert named Third (Tertullus), came before Lucky Man (Felix), and with many words they brought to him their accusations against Small Man (Paul). 2 When they brought Small Man (Paul) before them, the legal expert began to accuse him.

"O Most Honored Lucky Man (Felix)," he began his speech, "our hearts are glad that under your guidance we have had many winters of peace. Because of your wisdom, many good changes have come to the people, 3 changes that we fully welcome with glad and open hearts. 4 So we beg you, in your kindness, to hear our short complaint.

5 "We have found this man to be a troublemaker who, all over the world, stirs up our Tribal People in a bad way. He is a headman of the wayward band called Seed Planters (Nazarenes). 6 When he tried to defile our Sacred Lodge, we arrested him *w*and would have judged him by our own Tribal Law. 7 But the head officer Limping Man Who Sets Free (Claudius Lysias) came and forcefully took him out of our hands. He then ordered his accusers to come to you. 8 When you question him for yourself, you will learn from him that we speak the truth."

9 The Tribal Members who were there also joined in the accusations, saying it was all true.

10 The governor then motioned for Small Man (Paul) to speak.

"I know that for many winters you have been a judge over this nation," Small Man (Paul) said. "My heart is glad that I can clear the air regarding these things. 11 As you will find out from others, it has not been more than twelve days since I went to Village Of Peace (Jerusalem) to offer my prayers and participate in traditional ceremonies at the Sacred Lodge.

---

w 24:6 The remainder of verse 6 and verse 7 following, are not included in many ancient manuscripts.

¹² "No one there found me making trouble or stirring up a crowd—not at the Sacred Lodge, the Gathering House, or in the village. ¹³ No one here can prove the accusations they now bring against me.

¹⁴ "But I speak from my heart, I am only guilty of following the Way, which they say is false. But this is the Way I follow the Great Spirit of my ancestors. This Way is in agreement with the Law of my people and what has been foretold by our prophets. ¹⁵ This gives me the same hope in Creator that my accusers have— that all who have died, both those who do good and those who do bad, will rise to life again. ¹⁶ Knowing this, my aim is to walk with a clear heart toward the Great Spirit and my fellow human beings.

¹⁷ "After being away for a number of winters, I returned to Village Of Peace (Jerusalem). I brought gifts for the poor of my nation, as well as ceremonial offerings. ¹⁸ When they found me, I was in the Sacred Lodge participating in a ceremony—with no crowd or disturbance. ¹⁹ There were some Tribal Members from Rising Sun (Asia) who were there at that time. If they have any accusation against me, they are the ones who should make it.

²⁰ "Let these men who are here tell you what I did wrong when I stood before the council. ²¹ The only thing they can say against me is what I said to them: 'I am on trial today because I believe in the rising of the dead!'"

²² But Lucky Man (Felix), who knew more about the Way, delayed his decision.

"I will make my decision," he said, "when Limping Man Who Sets Free (Claudius Lysias) arrives."

²³ He then ordered the head soldier to keep Small Man (Paul) under guard, but to give him some freedom and permit his friends to care for his needs.

²⁴ A number of days later Lucky Man (Felix) returned with Tender Woman (Drusilla) his wife, who was a member of the tribes of Wrestles With Creator (Israel). He had Small Man (Paul) brought to him, and he *and his wife* listened to him tell about his trust in Creator Sets Free (Jesus), the Chosen One. ²⁵ They talked back and forth about Creator's right ways, about self-control and about the judgment that was to come. But Lucky Man (Felix) became afraid.

"Leave me for now," he said. "I will send for you when I have more time to talk."

²⁶ He was hoping that Small Man (Paul) would offer him a bribe, so from time to time he would send for him and talk with him; *but Small Man (Paul) remained under guard.* ²⁷ Two winters later Lucky Man (Felix) was replaced as governor by Pig Festival (Porcius Festus). Then to gain favor with the Tribal Members, he left Small Man (Paul) in prison.

Small Man Put on Trial

25 Three days after Festival (Festus) arrived, he went from Chief Village (Caesarea) to Village of Peace (Jerusalem). ² So the head holy men and other Tribal Leaders *wasted no time* and brought to him their accusations against

Small Man (Paul). They begged him, ³ as a favor to their nation, to have Small Man (Paul) returned to Village of Peace (Jerusalem); for they were hatching a plot to have him killed along the way.

⁴ "Small Man (Paul) is being guarded in Chief Village (Cesarea)," Festival (Festus) said to them, "and I am returning there soon. ⁵ Have your Tribal Leaders travel with me. If this man has done wrong, I will hear your accusations against him there."

⁶ So after eight or ten more days he left for Chief Village (Cesarea). The next day he sat down in his council chair, where he would decide this case, and ordered Small Man (Paul) to be brought before him. ⁷ As soon as he arrived, the Tribal Members who had come from Village of Peace (Jerusalem) circled around him and began to make accusations against him that they could not prove.

⁸ Small Man (Paul) stood up and said, "I have not spoken against our Tribal Law, our Sacred Lodge, or against the Ruler of the People of Iron (Caesar)."

⁹ But then Festival (Festus), wishing to gain the favor of the Tribal Leaders, responded to Small Man (Paul) and asked, "Do you wish to stand trial before me in Village of Peace (Jerusalem)?"

Small Man (Paul) could see right through him.

¹⁰ "I am making my stand here, before you, at the council chair of the People of Iron (Romans). This is where the decision about me should be made. By now, it should be clear to you that I have done nothing wrong against my own people."

Small Man (Paul) paused to draw strength from deep within. He made up his mind to do what was right and follow the path Creator had set before him.

¹¹ "If I have done anything to deserve death," he continued, "I will not try to escape. But if their accusations are false, you have no power to turn me over to them. I appeal to the Ruler of the People of Iron (Caesar)."

¹² Festival (Festus), after speaking to his council, said to him, "You have made your appeal to the Ruler of the People of Iron (Caesar), and to him you will now go."

Small Man and Chief Wildhorse

Chief Wildhorse (Agrippa) was a Tribal Member who ruled over some of the territory near Circle of Nations (Galilee) under the power of the People of Iron (Romans). He was the son of Looks Brave (Herod) also named Wildhorse (Agrippa) and the great grandson of Looks Brave (Herod) called The Great.

¹³ A number of days later Chief Wildhorse (Agrippa), along with his sister Bringer Of Victory (Bernice), came to pay their respects to *the new governor* Festival (Festus). ¹⁴ Since they were lodging with him for a number of days, he explained to the chief about the accusations

made against Small Man (Paul) by the Tribal Leaders.

"There is a man here who was left by Lucky Man (Felix) as a prisoner. [15] When I went to Village of Peace (Jerusalem), the head holy men and the Tribal Elders told me about him. They wanted me to find him guilty. [16] I informed them that the laws of the People of Iron (Romans) would not permit me to hand over anyone until they could stand face to face with their accusers and make a defense for themselves.

[17] "So when they came here I wasted no time, and on the next day I sat as head of the council and sent for him to stand trial. [18] I expected to hear from his accusers about some great evil, [19] but instead their accusations were about their own spiritual ways and about a man named Creator Sets Free (Jesus), who was dead but who Small Man (Paul) said was alive.

[20] "Since I knew nothing about these things, I asked if he wished to go to Village of Peace (Jerusalem) and face his accusers there. [21] But he appealed his case to the Ruler of the People of Iron (Caesar) and to be kept under guard until I could send him to our Ruler for his decision."

[22] Wildhorse (Agrippa) then said to Festival (Festus), "I would also like to hear from this man for myself."

"You will hear him tomorrow," Festival (Festus) replied.

Small Man Before Chief Wildhorse

[23] The next day Wildhorse (Agrippa) and Bringer Of Victory (Bernice), making a big show of it, came into the council room along with the head officers and leaders of the village. Festival (Festus) gave the order, and Small Man (Paul) was brought in.

[24] "Chief Wildhorse (Agrippa) and all who are here," the governor said, "standing before you is the man whom the whole Tribal Nation has asked me to condemn to death; [25] but I have not found him guilty of anything deserving death. And since he has appealed to the Ruler of the People of Iron (Caesar), I will send him to Village of Iron (Rome).

[26] "But, since I am not sure what message to send to my Ruler about him, I have decided to bring him to you all, and above all to you, Chief Wildhorse (Agrippa), so you can give me counsel in this matter. [27] For it seems unwise to me to send a prisoner there without a clear report of the accusations made against him."

Small Man Tells His Story

26 Then Wildhorse (Agrippa) said to Small Man (Paul), "You are permitted to speak and tell your side of this story."

So Small Man (Paul) stretched out his hand and began to tell his side of the story:

[2] "Chief Wildhorse (Agrippa), since my accusers are all Tribal Members, *like yourself,* it seems good to me that I can defend myself before you today, [3] mainly because you know so well how we disagree about many of our Tribal traditions. So I

humbly ask that you to listen to me with patience.

4 "All our Tribal People know the manner I have walked, even from the days of my youth, when I lived among our people in Village of Peace (Jerusalem). 5 They have known from the first, if they will admit to it, that I walked in the way of a Separated One (Pharisee)—the most demanding of all our spiritual paths.

6 "The reason I stand here on trial before you today is my hope in the promise made by the Great Spirit to our ancestors— 7 a promise our twelve tribes solemnly strive for as they serve him night and day with prayers and ceremonies. It is for this hope, O honored chief, that I stand here accused by our Tribal Leaders! 8 Why would any of our people find it impossible to believe that the Great Spirit raises the dead?

9 "At first, I myself was convinced that I should do as much harm as I could to destroy the reputation of Creator Sets Free (Jesus) of Seed Planter Village (Nazareth). 10 This is what I did in Village of Peace (Jerusalem): I obtained permission from the Head Priests to capture and put many of Creator's holy ones into prison. Not only that, but I voted against them when they were being killed. 11 In all our gathering houses I violently punished them, trying to force them to speak against Creator Sets Free (Jesus). Like a threatening storm I took out my anger on them, even pursuing them to faraway places."

Small Man Tells His Sacred Vision

12 "On one of these journeys I was on my way to Running Horse (Damascus) with the full approval and authority of the head holy men. 13 Then at midday, O honored chief, I saw a light from the world above shining down on me and my fellow travelers. 14 We all had fallen to the ground when I heard a voice speaking to me in our Tribal language.

"'Man Who Asks (Saul), Man Who Asks (Saul),' the voice called my name twice, and asked, 'why are you pursuing and mistreating me? It is a hard and painful thing to fight against me, like a horse pushing back against the spurs.'

15 "'Honored One,' I said back to the voice, 'who are you?'

"'I am Creator Sets Free (Jesus),' the voice answered, 'the one you are pursuing and mistreating. 16 Now rise up! Stand to your feet! I have chosen you to be my servant—a witness—that will tell others what you have seen with your own eyes and what I will reveal to you.

17 "'I will rescue you from your own people and from the Outside Nations—the ones to whom I am sending you— 18 to open their eyes so they may turn from the path of darkness to walk the road of life, and turn away from the power of the Accuser (Satan) to the power of the Great Spirit, and so that they may be released and set free from their bad hearts and wrongdoings. In this way they will find their

place among all who are made holy by trusting in me.'

Small Man Finishes His Story

¹⁹ "So then, Chief Wildhorse (Agrippa), I was true to this sacred vision. ²⁰ I told everyone—first to those in Running Horse (Damascus), then to the people in Village of Peace (Jerusalem) and to all in the territory of the Land of Promise (Judea), and also to the Outside Nations—that they should change their thinking, return to Creator's ways, and walk in a manner worthy of this change of heart.

²¹ "This was the reason that these Tribal Members took hold of me at the Sacred Lodge and tried to kill me. ²² Up to this day, with the help of the Great Spirit, I have told the truth to both small and great. I have said only what was foretold by the ancient prophets and by Drawn From The Water (Moses): ²³ that the Chosen One must suffer, and then, being the first to rise from the dead, he would be the light-bearer— shining both on our people and on the Outside Nations."

²⁴ Right then, as Small Man (Paul) was still speaking, Festival (Festus) interrupted.

"Small Man (Paul)," he shouted, "You are sick in the head! Your much learning is twisting your mind!"

²⁵ "O most noble Festival (Festus)," Small Man (Paul) replied, "what I am saying is clear and understandable. ²⁶ Chief Wildhorse (Agrippa) understands these things, so I am speaking boldly to him and holding nothing back. I am convinced that he is aware of all that I speak of, for none of these things happened in a cave."

Small Man (Paul) then turned and faced Chief Wildhorse (Agrippa).

²⁷ "Chief Wildhorse (Agrippa)," he boldly asked, "do you believe in what the prophets have spoken? I know that you do!"

²⁸ "Do you think I could in such a short time be talked into becoming a Follower of the Chosen One?" he replied.

²⁹ "I pray to the Great Spirit that, whether in a short time or long, all who hear me today would become as I am—except for these chains."

³⁰ *After hearing these words* Chief Wildhorse (Agrippa) stood to his feet. The governor and Bringer Of Victory (Bernice) and all the others stood up with him.

³¹ They left the room, and after talking together they said, "This man has done nothing that deserves prison or death."

³² Then Chief Wildhorse (Agrippa) said to the governor, "This man could have been set free if he had not appealed to the Ruler of the People of Iron (Caesar)."

Voyage of Trouble

27 They decided to send Small Man (Paul) by a great canoe to Land of Young Horses (Italy).

Village of Iron (Rome), the headquarters of the Ruler of the People of Iron (Caesar), was in the territory of Land of Young Horses (Italy).

So Small Man (Paul), along with some other prisoners, was turned over to a head soldier of the Royal Guard, named Soft Haired Man (Julius). ² At Harbor of Death (Adramyttium) we climbed aboard a canoe which was going our way, making stops at harbors along the shoreline of Rising Sun (Asia). So we launched out into the great waters. A man named Good Chief (Aristarchus) from False Victory (Thessalonica), in the territory of the Land of Tall People (Macedonia), also journeyed with us.

³ On the following day we came ashore at Hunting Grounds (Sidon). There Soft Haired Man (Julius) was kind to Small Man (Paul) and permitted him to go to his friends so they could care for him.

⁴ From there we launched out again into the great waters, but remained close to the shoreline of the Island of Flowers (Cyprus), for the winds were strong against us. ⁵ From there we crossed the open waters near Turns Over (Cilicia) and Many Tribes (Pamphylia), and then came to land at Weeping Waters (Myra) in the territory of Land of Wolves (Lycia).

⁶ At Weeping Waters (Myra) the head soldier found a great wooden sea canoe on its way from Man Fighter (Alexandria) to Land of Young Horses (Italy) that would give us passage, so we climbed aboard. ⁷ For a number of days we paddled along slowly until with difficulty we came near Old Village (Cnidus). The wind was against us and began to force us off course, so we remained close to the shoreline of Beast Island (Crete) near Village of Garments (Salmone). ⁸ From there we struggled along the shoreline until we came to a place called Good Harbor, near Shaggy Village (Lasea).

⁹ The journey was no longer safe. Too much time had passed, for the tribal Festival of Release from Wrongdoingsˣ had already passed. So Small Man (Paul) gave them this advice:

¹⁰ "Fellow travelers," he said to them, "I can see that this journey ahead of us will end in injury and loss, not only of the canoe and its goods, but also of our lives."

¹¹ But the head soldier was more convinced by the headman of the canoe than by the words of Small Man (Paul). ¹² And because the harbor was not a good place to stay the winter, a greater number of people decided it was best to launch out into the great waters and try to reach Palm Tree (Phoenix). This was a harbor on the shore of Beast Island (Crete), facing both to the southwest and to the northwest.

¹³ But then, when a gentle south wind began to blow, they thought they could reach their journey's end. So they prepared their canoe and launched out into the great waters again. They stayed close to the shoreline of Beast Island (Crete) for safety, ¹⁴ but it was not long before a violent wind roared down from the island—a wind they call "The Northeaster."

---

x 27:9 Day of Atonement, a festival of the tribes of Wrestles With Creator (Israel)

15 The canoe was caught in the wind, and when we could make no headway against it, we gave up trying and let it force us along. 16 Then, when we came under some cliffs, we were finally able to get the canoe under control. 17 We roped the life-raft we were towing behind us to the side of the canoe, and then tied the ropes around the canoe to hold it together. Then, fearing we would be caught in the shallow sandbars,y we lowered our anchor rock and let the canoe be dragged along by the fierce winds.

18 But the next day, after being pounded by the storm, they began to throw the goods overboard. 19 Then, on the third day, with their bare hands they threw the benches and whatever else they could findz into the water. 20 For many days the storm continued to rage, the sun did not shine, nor could the stars be seen at night. All hope of being rescued was gone.

Visited by a Spirit-Messenger

21 After they had gone for many days without food, Small Man (Paul) stood up among them.

"Fellow travelers," he said to them, "if you would have listened to me and not set out from Beast Island (Crete), you would not have suffered this injury and loss. 22 But I say to you now, do not lose your courage. For even though our canoe will be lost, not one of us will lose our lives. 23 Last night a spirit-messenger from the Great Spirit, the one I belong to and serve, stood by my side.

24 " 'Do not fear,' he said to me, 'for you must stand before the Ruler of the People of Iron (Caesar). So look and see! The Giver of Life has gifted you with the lives of all who journey with you!' "

The men just stared at Small Man (Paul) with wondering eyes and said nothing. So he once again spoke courage into their hearts.

25 "Be strong of heart," Small Man (Paul) said to them, "for I have faith that the Great Spirit will do everything he told me. 26 But we will have to find an island to land on."

They Come Near Land

27 It had now been fourteen nights that we had been driven about by the wind and waves of the Sea With No Wood (Adriatic Sea). In the middle of the night, the men who guided the canoe could feel that we were near land. 28 They began to test the depth of the water; it was as deep as a tall tree.a Then a short distance later they tested it again and found that it was not as deep.b

29 Since they knew the shoreline was rocky, they were afraid we might run into a large rock under the water, so they dropped four anchor rocks from the back of the canoe and prayed for the sun to rise.

Some of the Men Try to Escape

30 But then, some of the men, trying to escape, untied the life-

---

y 27:17 Lit., Syrtis, meaning shoal, shallow sandbars or reefs   z 27:19 Lit., equipment, tackle, gear
a 27:28 About 120 ft   b 27:28 About 90 ft

raft and lowered it into the water, pretending they were putting out more anchor rocks.

Small Man (Paul) saw what they were doing and went to the head soldier.

31 "If these men leave the canoe," he said to him and the other soldiers, "You will not be saved *and all will be lost.*"

32 So the soldiers cut the leather straps from the life-raft and let it drift away.

He Encourages the Men

33 Just before the sun began to rise, Small Man (Paul) urged everyone to eat something.

"For fourteen days now you have been constantly worrying and have not eaten any food," he said to them. 34 "Please eat something now. You will need it to survive. *Do not fear! No one will die or be harmed;* not even one hair from your heads will be lost."

35 After he said this, he took a loaf of bread, and giving thanks to the Great Spirit in front of them all, he broke it and began to eat. 36 This gave the men courage, so they also began to eat.

37 All in all there were two hundred and seventy-six persons in this great wooden canoe. 38 When they finished eating, they tossed the rest of the grain over the side to lighten the canoe.

Sunrise and a Rough Landing

39 When daylight came, they did not recognize the shoreline, but they could see a bay with a beach. They decided to try to run the canoe up into the sandy beach, if possible. 40 So they cut the ropes to the anchor rocks and left them in the water. At the same time they untied the ropes holding the rudders in place. Then they set the men to the paddles, and they paddled with all their might[c] heading toward the beach.

41 But on the way the canoe struck a sandbar and stayed there, stuck in the sand, and the front of the canoe began to break from the force of the waves. 42 The soldiers made a plan to kill the prisoners so none could escape by swimming away. 43 But the head soldier, wanting to spare the life of Small Man (Paul), stopped them. He ordered the ones who could swim to jump overboard and swim to land. 44 The rest he sent floating on wooden poles and pieces of the canoe. In this way all who were aboard made it safely to the land.

A Warm Welcome

28 After everyone was safe on the shore, we found out that this land was called Island of Honey (Malta). 2 The indigenous people there showed great kindness to us. It was raining and cold, so they built us a warm fire and welcomed us all.

Snake Bite

3 Small Man (Paul) gathered a bundle of sticks and threw them on the fire, but the heat forced out

---

c 27:40 Lit., They put up the sails into the wind.

a poisonous snake that bit into his hand and would not let go.

4 When the local natives saw the snake hanging from his hand, they said, "This man must be a murderer. Even though he escaped from the great waters, the spirit who rights wrongs will not let him live."

5 Then Small Man (Paul) shook the snake from his hand into the fire, and nothing bad happened to him. 6 The local people were sure that he would swell up or fall down dead. They waited a long time, but when they saw that nothing bad had come to him, they changed their minds and said he must be a powerful spirit.

Small Man Heals the Sick

7 There was a piece of land belonging to From The People (Publius), the chief of the island. He welcomed us into his home for three days and took care of all our needs. 8 At that time the father of From The People (Publius) was sick in bed with a high fever and a bloody stool. Small Man (Paul) went to see him and, after praying, laid his hands on the man and healed him.

9 After that, the rest of the island natives who were sick came to Small Man (Paul), and they were also healed. 10 The people honored us with many gifts, and when we were leaving, they loaded our canoe with all that we needed.

Arrival at Village of Iron

11 Three months later we again launched out into the great waters in another very large wooden canoe.

This canoe was made by the people from Man Fighter (Alexandria). The front of the canoe was carved into the images of two powerful look-alike spirits—Bright Light (Castor) and Much Sweet (Pollux).

12 We came to land at Smelly Swamp (Syracuse) and lodged there for three days. 13 From there we launched out and came to Royal Place (Rhegium). The next day, with the help of a south wind, we arrived at Deep Water Hole (Puteoli). 14 It was there that we found some Sacred Family members, who welcomed us to stay with them for seven days.

After that we left again toward Village of Iron (Rome). 15 The Sacred Family members who lived there, when they heard we were coming, came to greet us from as far away as the Great Trading Post (Forum of Appius) and the Three Lodging Houses along the Great Trail (Appian Way). When Small Man (Paul) saw them, he gave thanks to the Great Spirit and his heart was strengthened. 16 Then, upon our arrival to Village of Iron (Rome), Small Man (Paul) was permitted to live by himself with a soldier to guard him.

He Meets the Local Council

17 Three days later Small Man (Paul) asked to meet with the local Tribal Leaders. When they had gathered together, he told them the story of what had happened to him.

He stood there in chains under the guard of a soldier of the People of Iron (Romans). Yet he spoke with dignity as he faced the leaders of his own people.

"Fellow Tribal Members," he said to them, "I have done nothing against our people or the traditions of our ancestors, but even so I was arrested in Village of Peace (Jerusalem) and handed over to the People of Iron (Romans). ¹⁸They questioned me and were about to release me, since I had done nothing deserving death. ¹⁹But when our Tribal Leaders refused to agree, I had no choice but to appeal to the Ruler of the People of Iron (Caesar)—not that I have any accusation to bring against my own people.

²⁰ "It is for this very reason that I have asked to see and speak with you, for I wear these chains because I have the same hope held by all the tribes of Wrestles With Creator (Israel)."

Small Man (Paul) then stopped speaking, looked calmly into their faces, and waited for them to reply.

²¹ "No one from the Land of Promise (Judea) has come with a bad report, nor have we have received any written message about you from them. ²²But we want to hear how you see this new way*ᵈ* that some are following, for we know that people everywhere speak against this way."

Sent to the Outside Nations

²³They made plans to meet again with Small Man (Paul) on another day. When that day came, they arrived in large numbers at the place where he was lodging. From sunrise to sunset, using the Law of Drawn From The Water (Moses) and the teachings of the Prophets, he spoke many words to clearly show them the truth about Creator's Good Road and about Creator Sets Free (Jesus).

²⁴Some were convinced by his words, but others refused to believe. ²⁵So they disagreed with each other and began to leave after Small Man (Paul) said these last words to them:

"The Holy Spirit was right when he spoke these words through the prophet Creator Will Help Us (Isaiah):

²⁶ "Go and tell this people, 'You will hear but not understand, you will see but not know what you are seeing, ²⁷because the heart of this people has become like stone. Their ears have grown dull and they have closed their eyes. If only they would open their ears and eyes, then their heart would understand, and they would return to me and be healed.*ᵉ*'"

Final Words

A look of sorrow came over the face of Small Man (Paul) as he watched his own people turn and walk away.

²⁸ "So let it be known to you," he said to them, "that this message about the Great Spirit's plan to rescue and make whole has been sent to the Outside Nations—and they will listen!"

---

d 28:22 Lit., sect, a group with differing and questionable beliefs   e 28:27 Isaiah 6:9-10

²⁹ Hearing this, the Tribal Members argued fiercely with one another as they walked away.*

³⁰ Small Man (Paul) continued to live in his own rented house and welcomed all who came to him.

³¹ With great boldness he spoke openly about Creator's Good Road and kept teaching others about our Honored Chief—Creator Sets Free (Jesus), the Chosen One.

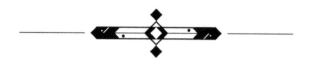

---

f **28:29** Some ancient manuscripts do not include verse 29.

FIRST NATIONS VERSION

In the last days...

"The Great Spirit will be the one to stand between many nations to show them the pathway of peace. His guidance will teach them how to make their weapons of war into tools to work the ground and grow good medicine. Their spears will be made into planting sticks and their tomahawks will be used to trim the vines. Nations will no longer lift up the arrow and the bow to fight against other nations. They will never again learn the ways of war, but will walk together on a path of peace."

From the Great Spirit
To the tribes of Wrestles With Creator

Isaiah Two Four

Small Man

To Village of Desired One

Ephesians

FIRST NATIONS VERSION

FIRST NATIONS VERSION

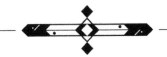

Small Man
To Village of Desired One
(Ephesians)

Greetings

1 From Small Man (Paul), chosen by the Great Spirit to be a message bearer for Creator Sets Free (Jesus).

To the Great Spirit's holy people who live in Village of Desired One (Ephesus)—the ones who walk the good path following the Chosen One:

² Great kindness and peace to you from the Father above and from our Honored Chief Creator Sets Free (Jesus), who is the Chosen One.

Chosen for Great Kindness

³ All blessings belong to the Great Spirit, who is the Father of Creator Sets Free (Jesus). From the spirit world above he has gifted us with all spiritual blessings found in the Chosen One.

⁴ In the same way, before he made all things and because of his great love, the Maker Of Life chose to make us pure and holy in his eyes. ⁵ He also decided ahead of time, through Creator Sets Free (Jesus), to take us into his family, fulfilling his purpose and making his heart glad. ⁶ This great kindness he has shown us brings honor to him and gives us a highly honored place, together with his much loved Son.

⁷⁻⁸ By paying the highest price— offering his own life-blood—the Chosen One released us from a great captivity caused by our bad hearts and broken ways. He poured out all of this overflowing kindness on us, showing how wise and understanding he is.

Hidden Wisdom Made Clear

⁹ It makes Creator's heart glad to show us the hidden wisdom of his plan *for all of creation*, now made clear through the Chosen One. ¹⁰ This is how Creator brings all things to completion. He makes all things in the world above and on the earth below come together and find their full meaning and original purpose in the Chosen One.

¹¹⁻¹² The Chosen One has shared with us all that he has been given.

This was Creator's plan that he decided long ago to accomplish—a wise and powerful vision he saw within himself. Creator is working out all the details, fitting everything into his purpose, so that we, *who are from the tribes of Wrestles With Creator (Israel),* who have first put our hope in the Chosen One, will bring praise and honor to him.

[13] And now, not only we, but all other Nations who have heard the truth of this message, can participate in his plan. This is the Good Story that sets all people free.

When we trusted in the Chosen One, he marked us as his own by giving us his promised Holy Spirit. [14] He did this to make sure that we, the people he paid a great price for, will receive all that he has planned for us. This brings great praise and honor to him.

Sending Up Prayers

[15] Ever since I heard of the trust you have in Creator Sets Free (Jesus) and your deep love for all of his holy people, [16] I have never stopped giving thanks for you, remembering you when I send my voice to the Great Spirit.

[17] I pray that the Father of honor and beauty, who is the Great Spirit of our Honored Chief Creator Sets Free (Jesus), will gift you with a spirit of wisdom to know him deeply and understand his mysterious ways.

[18] I am asking him to shine his light into your hearts so you can clearly see the hope he has chosen us for and the beautiful treasure he has in us—his holy people.

[19] I pray he will show how much greater his power is for all who put their trust in him. [20] This is the same power he used when he brought the Chosen One back to life from the dead and gave him the place of honor at his right hand— [21] a high spiritual place greater than all rulers, authorities, and powers; a place higher and stronger than all names that can be named, not only in this world but also in the one that is coming.

[22] This is how he brought all things, seen and unseen, under his loving power and made him the Elder[a] of his Sacred Family. [23] This Sacred Family is his body *on earth* made whole by the one who gives everything and everyone their full meaning and purpose.

A Dark Path

2 We all once walked a dark and crooked path that led us to death. [2] Our broken ways caused us to miss the mark and wander from the good path, following the worthless ways of this world.

We all once walked this dark path of the evil one who rules the spiritual atmosphere of this world, that evil spirit who is at work in disobedient human beings. [3] This is how all of us once lived when we followed our uncontrolled emotions fed by bodily desires and dark thoughts. These broken ways became our natural condition, and,

---

a 1:22 Lit., Head

like the rest of mankind, we were children deserving *Creator's* anger.

From Death to Life

[4] But the Great Spirit, who is kind and forgiving, because of his deep love, [5] raised us up from *spiritual* death. Even though we were walking on the road of death, he made us alive again with the Chosen One. This is what it means to be rescued by the gift of his great kindness.

[6] He lifted us up with him to the highest place in the world above and put us on a seat of honor alongside the Chosen One. [7] He did this to show us the overflowing greatness of his kindness and mercy, not only in this world but also in the one that is coming—all because of what the Chosen One has done.

A Great Gift

[8] It is by trusting in his great kindness that we have been made whole[b]—not because of any good thing we have done, but only by accepting a gift that we could never earn. [9] In this way, no one can brag or boast about themselves, but only humbly give thanks. [10] We are like clay in his hands, molded from the Chosen One, made to be like him, and walking the ancient pathways he originally created us for.

Outsiders and Insiders

[11] You Nations must not forget that before you knew the Chosen One you were not natural born[c] members of the tribes of Wrestles With Creator (Israel). You were called "the outsiders"[d] by the ones who call themselves "the insiders."[e] But remember, the sign that marks them as "insiders" is cut into their flesh with human hands.

[12] You Nations did not share in the promises or the Peace Treaty that the Great Spirit made with those tribes. You were out from under their special care and protection—unaware of and apart from the Chosen One. You shared no common hope and were outside of the help Creator gave to them in this world.

He is our Great Peace

[13] But no more! Even though you Nations were far away, you have now been made close by the life-blood offered by Creator Sets Free (Jesus), the Chosen One. [14] He is our great peace, who has brought the people of all Nations together with the tribes of Wrestles With Creator (Israel), making them into one new people by removing the barrier that separated us.

[15] In his own human body he removed the hostility between us when he did away with the rules and requirements of our Tribal Law that separated us. This is the way he recreates people—making one new humanity out of the two. This brings us all together in the path of peace.

---

b 2:8 The Greek word here means to rescue, deliver, set free, or make whole. c 2:11 Lit., Gentiles in the flesh. d 2:11 The Uncircumcision e 2:11 The Circumcision

A Clear Path

16 Even though we behaved like enemies, we are now friends with the Great Spirit and with one another. When Creator Sets Free (Jesus) died on the cross, those things that made us enemies died with him. We are now joined together as one people in one body. 17 He brought this Good Story of peace and harmony to people who were far away from him and to people who were close to him. 18 Because of him we both have a clear path, through one Spirit, to the Father from above.

A New Sacred Lodge

19 Now we are all his holy people and members of one new nation. No one is on the outside of this great family that our Father is creating. We are all related to one another and initiated into Creator's Lodge that is built together with wooden poles— 20 the message bearers and prophets of old. Creator Sets Free (Jesus) is the main pole binding us together, 21 like branches being weaved into his Sacred Lodge. 22 Joined together in this way, we all become a dwelling place for his Spirit.

A Great Mystery Revealed

3 Because I, Small Man (Paul), follow the Chosen One and represent you Nations in this way, I have been arrested and put in chains. 2 I am sure you have heard how the Great Spirit chose me, because of his great kindness, to be a wisdomkeeper to all Nations. 3 Creator chose me, by a sacred vision, to make known this hidden wisdom that I have already spoken about.

4 When you hear this message, you will understand how I see the mystery of the Chosen One. 5 This mystery was not known to our ancestors in the same way his Spirit has now told it to his holy message bearers and prophets.

6 This mystery is that the people of all Nations have equal share in the inheritance of the tribes of Wrestles With Creator (Israel). They have full membership in the same body and are included in the promise made by the Chosen One as told in the Good Story.

Chosen to Tell the Good Story

7 The gift of Creator's great kindness came to me in a powerful way, and created in me a desire to serve this Good Story. 8 Even though I am small and weak among his holy people, he still chose me to tell all Nations about the mysterious treasures he has hidden in the Chosen One, 9 and about the unfolding of this ancient plan—a great mystery that was hidden away for many ages in Creator's heart. 10 So that now, through his Sacred Family, his great wisdom, which is like a rainbow with many colors, will be made known to the powers and rulers in the *unseen* world above.

11 This Good Story gives full meaning to the ancient purpose he planned before he created all things. This purpose has now been

made clear though the Chosen One, Creator Sets Free (Jesus). [12] Our trust in him opens the way and gives us strong hearts to move close to the Great Spirit. [13] So do not become weak of heart when you hear about how much I am suffering for you, which is proof of your great worth.

A Humble Prayer

[14] This is the reason I bow down on my knees and humble myself before the Father above, [15] from whom all families, clans and tribes, in this world and in the world above, are named.

[16] This is my prayer for you: that from the great treasures of his beauty, Creator will gift you with the Spirit's mighty power and strengthen you in your inner being. [17] In this way the Chosen One will make his home in your heart.

I pray that as you trust in him, your roots will go deep into the soil of his great love, [18] and that from these roots you will draw the strength and courage needed to walk this sacred path together with all his holy people. This path of love is higher than the stars, deeper than the great waters, wider than the sky. Yes, this love comes from and reaches to all the directions.

I pray that you would feel how deep the Chosen One's great love is— [19] a love that goes beyond our small and weak ways of thinking. This love fills us with the Great Spirit—the one who fills all things. [20] I am praying to the Maker of Life who, by his great power working in us, can do far more than what we ask for, more than our small minds can imagine.

[21] May his Sacred Family and the Chosen One bring honor to him across all generations, to the time beyond the end of all days. May it be so!

A Humble Path

4 Because I walk the road with our Honored Chief, I have been made a prisoner. I now call on you to join me in representing him in a good way as you follow the path he has chosen for you. [2] Walk with a humble and gentle spirit, patiently showing love and respect to each other. [3] Let his Spirit weave you together in peace as you dance in step with one another in the great circle of life.

[4] *In this circle* we are joined together in one body, by one Spirit, chosen to follow one purpose. [5] There is only one Honored Chief, one common faith, and one purification ceremony. [6] There is one Great Spirit and Father of us all, who is above all, and who works in and through all.

The Headdress of the Chosen One

[7] His great kindness has gifted each of us from the headdress[f] of the Chosen One. [8] That is why it is said, "When he was lifted up on high, he captured many warriors, took their spoils of war and gave them back to the people."[g]

---

f 4:7 The headdress was worn among many tribes to represent victory in battle and good deeds accomplished. Here it is used as a metaphor of the Chosen One's victory.   g 4:8 Psalm 68:18

[9] What does "he was lifted up" mean? It could only mean that he had to first come down, into the lowest parts of the earth, [10] so he could be lifted up, to the highest place, and be the one who would restore all things.

Walking the Good Road in Harmony

[11] He gifted us with message bearers, prophets, tellers of the Good Story, and wisdomkeepers,[h] who watch over us like a shepherd watches over his sheep. [12] These gifts were given to prepare Creator's holy people for the work of helping others and to make the body of the Chosen One strong [13] until we all follow the Good Road[i] in harmony with each other because we know and understand who Creator's Son is.

We will then be like the Chosen One—mature human beings, living and walking in his ways, and fully reflecting who he is. [14] No longer will we be like children who are tossed about by the waves and follow every voice they hear in the wind. We will no longer listen to the human tricksters with their forked tongues.

[15] Instead, as true human beings, we will walk out this truth on the path of love. When we become fully grown, we will be like the Chosen One, joined together with him in the same way a body is connected to its head. [16] Every joint in this body is needed to hold it together and help it grow. When all the parts work together the way they should, then the body grows strong in the love of the Great Spirit.

Representing our Honored Chief

[17] I say this to you as one who represents our Honored Chief. You must no longer walk the dark path of the Nations *who have chosen their own ways.* [18] Their minds have no good thoughts, because the darkness has taken away their ability to see and think clearly. Their hearts have become as hard as stone and can no longer beat with the life that comes from the Great Spirit. [19] This takes them down the path of greed and selfish pleasure, leading to an impure life. [20] This is not the path you learned from the Chosen One, [21] for the true path to walk is only found in Creator Sets Free (Jesus).

[22] Take off that worn out and stained outfit of your past life with its selfish desires and worthless ways of thinking. It no longer represents who you are. [23] You are now true human beings, with a new way of seeing and thinking. [24] Put on the regalia of your new life; for you have been made new, created again to look like the one who made you, standing in a good way, and walking a true and sacred path.

Living in Harmony

[25] We are all members of one body—*one tribe,* so we must speak truth and be honest with each other, leaving the path of falsehood far behind.

---

h 4:11 Teachers   i 4:13 The faith

26 There are times when anger is the right thing, but do not let your anger turn into rage, for it will burn like a wildfire. Work things out before the sun sets that day— 27 or the evil one may use it to burn up all the good things in your life.*j*

There is no room for thieves on this sacred path. 28 The ones among you who have stolen and taken what is not yours must learn to do good, working hard with their hands. In this way they will not only have enough for themselves, but also something to help others.

Do Not Grieve the Holy Spirit

29 Keep a close watch over the words you speak, for our mouths can be full of worthless and empty talk that will bring death to others. Let your words be full of wisdom and goodwill that will give strength and bring healing to the ones who hear you. 30 In this way the Creator's Holy Spirit will not be grieved—for it is he who marks you as his own and keeps you safe for the day when all things will be complete.*k*

31 Let Creator pull the bitter roots from your heart, for they feed the rage and anger that takes you down a path of fighting, hurting and speaking evil of your fellow human beings. 32 Instead, show goodwill and kindness to others, by releasing them from the things they have done wrong; for this is what the Great Spirit, through the Chosen One, has done for you.

Walking His Road

5 We must follow in the steps of the Great Spirit, for we are his much loved children. 2 Walk the road of love, following the path of the Chosen One, who loved us and offered up his life to the Great Spirit like the smoke of burning sage.

3 Sexual relations are sacred. They must be kept pure, and free from uncontrolled desire. As his holy people, we must follow Creator's purpose and plan for human beings who represent him. 4 Sexual relations should be spoken of with respect, no foolish talk or dirty jokes; instead give thanks *for this sacred gift of creating new life.*

5 Listen closely, no one who walks an impure path of uncontrolled desires participates in the Good Road of the Chosen One and the Great Spirit. The ones who walk in this way follow lying spirits that take them down a dark path, far from the sacred ways of the Great Spirit. 6 Do not listen to their empty words and forked tongues, for the Great Spirit's anger will be shown to the ones who follow these ways. 7 Do not walk with them on a path that leads to a bad end.

Darkness and Light

8 As weak human beings, you were once empty and full of darkness, but now that Creator's Spirit lives in you, you are beings full of light. 9 Walk in the light, and all things good and right and true will shine out from you. 10 This will prove you

---

j 4:27 Psalm 4:4   k 4:30 The day of redemption or restoration

are his children—the ones who seek for ways to make his heart glad.

[11] Turn away from the path of darkness with its worthless ways, instead let your light shine into the darkness to show the way out. [12] The shameful things done under the blanket of night should not even be spoken of, [13] for the light shines into the darkness and takes the mask off its empty ways. It is like the sunrise that pushes back the night and brings the light of a new day. [14] This is why it is said, "Wake up, O sleeper, come back from the dead, and the Chosen One will shine on you!"

The Way of Wisdom

[15] Walk with your eyes wide open, and make wise use of your time, [16] for the evil days we live in are full of worthless and troubled ways. [17] Keep foolishness far from you, *and welcome the ways of wisdom,* for then you will clearly see the path Creator has chosen for you.

[18] It is not wise to become a drunk, for it will lead you to a life of emptiness and sorrow. Instead, drink deeply of Creator's Spirit, *and he will lead you into a life of beauty and harmony.*

[19] *At your gatherings,* tell the ancient stories and sing the traditional songs. Sing spiritual songs from your heart *as you dance before the Great Spirit,* [20] giving thanks to our Father the Creator, as you represent our Honored Chief, Creator Sets Free (Jesus)— the Chosen One.

Wisdom for Husbands and Wives

[21] If you have respect for the Chosen One, then have respect for each other. [22] Wives, honor your husbands in the same way you honor the Great Spirit. [23] Just as the Chosen One guides and protects his Sacred Family as his own body when they put their trust in him, [24] so a wife should, in the same way, follow the loving guidance of her husband in all these things.

[25] Husbands, love your wives just as the Chosen One loved and gave his life for his Sacred Family. [26] He did this to give them a place of honor and dignity above all others—washing all with the purifying water of the word he speaks over them. [27] He will clothe his Sacred Family with the regalia of beauty and harmony with no wrinkles or stains, *like a bride dressed for her wedding day.* [28] This is the manner in which husbands should love their wives, as their own bodies; for the one who loves his wife, loves himself. [29-30] For no one hates his own body, but instead takes good care of it, just as the Chosen One does for his Sacred Family. For we are members of his body, of his flesh, and of his bones.

[31] "For this purpose a man must leave his father and mother, so he can join with his wife, and the two will become one body."[l] [32] This is a great mystery, but I am telling you that it is about the Chosen One and his Sacred Family. [33] So each man should love his wife as himself,

l 5:31 Genesis 2:24

treat her as he wants her to treat him, and each wife is to give respect to her husband.

Further Instructions on Respect

6 Children, it is the right thing to follow the guidance of your parents, for this is what Creator wants. [2] "Honor your father and mother"—for this is the first instruction in our Tribal Law that carries a promise with it— [3] "that it will go well with you, and you will live long on the land."[m]

[4] Fathers, if you push your children too hard, it will only make them angry. Instead, help them to grow strong in the ways of the Great Spirit.

[5] Slaves, do everything your earthly masters tell you to do; show great respect to them in the same way you serve the Chosen One. Do this from a strong and pure heart, [6] not just to look good to your earthly master, [7] but as if you were serving our Honored Chief, [8] knowing that Creator will see and honor all who serve others, no matter if they are slaves or free.

[9] Masters, do not use threats, but treat your slaves with the same respect you would give to the Great Spirit; for he is your master from the world above as well as theirs, and he will not favor one over another.

Preparing for Spiritual Warfare

[10] Last of all, *I must remind you that we are all fighting in a spiritual* battle. *We are weak human beings, so* let your strength come from our Great Warrior Chief. [11] The only way to stand strong against the war plans of the evil trickster[n] is to put on Creator's war garments. [12] *But remember,* we are not fighting against human beings. Our battle is against the evil rulers, the dark powers, and the spiritual forces of the unseen world above and around us.

[13] Once you are fully dressed for this war, you will be able to stand your ground in this day of the enemy's evil rule. You are now ready to make your stand— so stand strong. [14] Wrap the sash of truth around your waist, cover your heart with the breastplate of making wrongs right again, [15] and put on your feet the moccasins of Creator's peace *treaty,* so you will always be ready to tell the Good Story *as you walk the road of life.* [16] Then you must raise high the shield of trusting in Creator; this will put out the flaming arrows of the evil one. *Don't forget to* [17] put on the headdress of Creator's power to rescue and set free, and use the long knife of the Spirit—which is the word of Creator *coming from your mouth.*

[18] All of this is done by prayer, sending your voice to the Great Spirit, asking him for all that is needed. As you pray with the help of the Spirit, stay alert and keep all of Creator's holy people in your thoughts—praying for their needs. [19] Also ask Creator to give

---

m 6:3 Deuteronomy 5:16   n 6:11 The devil

me the right words to speak and the courage to make known the mystery of Creator's Good Story. ²⁰ This is the reason I now represent the Great Spirit as a captive in chains. So pray that I will speak with boldness and not hold back.

Final Words

²¹⁻²² So you will know how I am doing, I am sending He Is At Ease (Tychicus), a much loved spiritual brother and one who serves others as a gift from Creator. He will let you know how we are doing so your hearts can be lifted up and strengthened.

²³ Peace be to all the spiritual family members, along with love and trust from the Great Spirit, who is our Father, and from our Wisdomkeeper, Creator Sets Free (Jesus), the Chosen One.

²⁴ May Creator's great kindness rest on all who love the Chosen One, with a love that will never grow old or fade away.

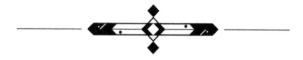

FIRST NATIONS VERSION

History, Context and Key Terms

To help the reader with the historical and cultural context, we are including some background information here. While this is not comprehensive, it should provide guidance to help set the story in its proper context. The Bible is a book the writing of which spans several millennia, and by the time of Creator Sets Free (Jesus) many thousands of years of history had already passed.

Also, there are many important key terms in Bible translation. The translators have worked with both Biblical and cultural consultants to determine the most appropriate ways to translate these key terms for general relevance to our First Nations people. Below are just a few of many important key terms with some explanation of why these terms were chosen.

Glossary of Key Terms

Creator Sets Free (Jesus)

The name Jesus was a common name in first century Palestine. The name Jesus finds its roots in the Hebrew language. His name in Hebrew is Yeshua, (pronounced yeh-shoo-wah). The name comes from two words. The first is Yah, the shortened form of Yahweh, the Hebrew name for the Great Spirit. The second comes from a word that means to rescue, deliver, save or simply 'set free'—Yah Sets Free. From the Hebrew to the Greek of the New Testament, Yeshua became Iesous (pronounced yeh-soos). From the Greek to the English, Iesous became Jesus.

The tribes of Wrestles With Creator (Israel) in Biblical times gave names that had meaning. For example Abraham means Father Of Many Nations. This is similar to the traditions of our First Nations people, so we decided to follow this practice in the First Nations Version. We have chosen to call Jesus by the translated meaning of his name, which is Creator Sets Free. This is a rendering of his name in English, as it would have been heard and understood in the language of his own people. We have also done this with all other names found in the New Testament.

Chosen One (Christ)

The Great Spirit spoke to the tribes of Wrestles With Creator (Israel) through many prophets. These prophets spoke of a coming deliverer called the Messiah, which means the Anointed One. From the Greek language of the New Testament, Messiah is translated in English as Christ, which means the same thing. This Messiah, or Christ, was to be the Great Spirit's Chosen One to set his people free. In this retelling of this Good Story, we use the term 'Chosen One' in place of 'Christ' since few English-speaking people understand the meaning of the word Christ. Scripture uses the term Chosen One to refer to Creator Sets Free (Jesus) in many English translations. See Luke 9:35.

True Human Being (Son of Man)

Creator Sets Free (Jesus) most often referred to himself as the Son of Man, which we translate as True Human Being. This title is full of meaning from the Old Testament Scriptures. In the book of Ezekiel it is used over 90 times, and simply means a human being. There, it is not meant to be a title of prestige, but of humility. In using this title, Creator Sets Free (Jesus) is presenting himself as a common human being—as one of us.

In the book of Daniel the title Son of Man takes on an expanded meaning. Daniel sees a vision of one like a son of man coming before the Ancient of Days on the clouds of heaven. This Son of Man is given authority, glory and sovereign power from the Great Spirit. His rule is over all peoples and languages and his chiefly rule will never come to an end. Even though he is a human being, he will be worshiped. See Daniel 7:13-14.

So, Creator Sets Free (Jesus) as the Son of Man shows us that the Good Road or Kingdom of God is a kingdom of humility, love and service to others. He is a common man and at the same time the almighty Creator who alone is worthy of worship. As Son of God he is divine; as Son of Man he is a true human being.

We have the used the title True Human Being for Son of Man. For he is one of us; he is what a human being should truly be like. As we walk the road with him, we are on the path to becoming true human beings.

Apostle (Message Bearer)

The Greek word translated as 'apostle' literally means 'sent one.' It is used of the carrier of an official message, similar to the idea of an ambassador. These 'sent ones' not only carried a message but also carried with it the authority of the person or nation sending them. In this translation we have translated 'apostle' as 'message bearer.'

Bad Hearts and Broken Ways (Sin)

For many of our First Nations people the English word 'sin' evokes the memories of boarding school where 'sin' was often the length of our hair, or speaking in our native language, or anything related to our cultures. The Biblical concept of sin is expressed in the Greek word 'hamartia' which means to miss the mark, or fail to do what is right. In other words, not living in the ways Creator made us to live. This is best expressed in Romans 3:23: "For all have sinned and fall short of Creator's glory." All human beings are broken and fail to live in Creator's ways. Some try but fail, some do not even try, and others give themselves over to evil ways. We have translated 'sin' as either 'bad hearts,' 'wrongdoings' or 'broken ways,' depending on which best fits the context.

Day of Resting (Sabbath)

The instructions from the Law given by Drawn From The Water (Moses) included a day of resting called the Sabbath, which means rest. This was to honor the Great Spirit who created all things in six days and then rested on the seventh. From sunset Friday until sunset Saturday no work was to be done. Also, how far a person could walk was limited by this law. The proper interpretation and practice of this Day of Resting became one of the main points of controversy between the spiritual leaders and Creator Sets Free (Jesus).

Good Road (Kingdom of God)

Today, many First Nations tribes speak of the 'good way' or 'red road' as a way to understand a way of life that seeks to live in harmony with the Great Spirit's plan for all of creation. To live in harmony with fellow human beings and all of creation could be called 'walking the good road.'

With the advice of some of our Native America friends and the insights from the prominent American Indian theologian, George E. Tinker,[a] we have chosen to translate the 'Kingdom of God' as the 'Good Road.' Creator Sets Free (Jesus) came to call us to walk in a new way, a way of beauty and harmony, that reflects the government of God/Heaven. To walk the road with Creator Sets Free (Jesus) is to be on this path.

Gathering Houses (Synagogues)

In the time of the Gospel story, the Tribal People usually had a village meeting place called the synagogue, which simply means gathering place. The synagogue was used primarily for religious purposes, such as the study of the Scriptures and prayer, but also for local village council meetings. We have chosen to call the 'synagogues' simply 'gathering houses.'

Holy Men (Priests)

According the Law of Drawn From The Water (Moses) only men were permitted to be priests. By this same Law priests could only be chosen from one tribe—He Brings Together (Levi). We have translated 'priest' in the following ways: for the 'high priest' we chose 'chief holy man,' for the 'chief priests' we chose 'head priests,' and for 'priest' we chose 'holy man.'

Outcasts (Sinners)

The Separated Ones (Pharisees) identified certain people as 'sinners.' This word carries a more disturbing meaning than just someone who sins. These 'sinners' were the 'outcasts' of their society and designated as such by an oppressive interpretation of Tribal Law. These outcasts were not permitted to enter the gathering houses and were despised by the Separated Ones (Pharisees). Outcasts included tribal tax collectors, prostitutes, people who ate and drank too much, those with diseases that made them ceremonially unclean, and all Gentiles (non-Tribal Members).

Outside Nations (Gentiles)

The members of the tribes of Wrestles With Creator (Israel) called all people from other nations 'Gentiles.' In this translation for the word 'Gentiles' we have used 'Nations,' 'other nations,' 'Outside Nations,' 'Outsider,' and occasionally 'People of Iron' when referring to the Romans, who were also Gentiles.

Purification Ceremony (Baptism)

In the time of Creator Sets Free (Jesus), baptism in water was a cultural and spiritual practice among the people. Baptism was a sacred ceremony among the tribes of Wrestles With Creator (Israel) symbolizing purification or cleansing. It also was used as an initiation rite into the spiritual and social community. To be baptized in the name of someone was to accept their teachings and become identified with them. Baptism was most often practiced by immersing a person in flowing water, which is why rivers were often used. In this translation we have chosen to call 'baptism' the 'purification ceremony.'

Spiritual Leaders

In the time of Creator Sets Free (Jesus) the tribes of Wrestles With Creator (Israel) were divided into many different religious groups with differing beliefs. The members of these religious groups had set themselves up as the spiritual leaders of tribes of Wrestles With Creator (Israel).

Separated Ones (Pharisees) are mentioned most often. The title 'Pharisees' means 'separated ones'. The Pharisees were the most vocal and influential of the spiritual leaders and held a very strict and oppressive interpretation of Tribal Law. As their name indicates, they separated themselves from those they deemed to be sinners and pressured others to do the same. We have translated 'Pharisees' as 'Separated Ones'.

Upright Ones (Sadducees), which means 'righteous or upright ones', were often rich and held positions of power within their religious and political establishments. They differ from the Separated Ones (Pharisees) in several ways. Most significantly they did not believe in spirits or in a resurrection from the dead. We have translated the 'Sadducees' as 'Upright Ones.'

Scroll Keepers (scribes and lawyers) are mentioned quite often in the Gospels, and both titles describe the same group. The scribes were the keepers of the Sacred Scrolls, the Scriptures. Since they knew how to write, they became scroll copiers, making copies of the Scriptures. Since they spent so much time reading and writing the Scriptures, they became experts in the interpretation of the Tribal Law. We have translated 'scribes' as 'scroll keepers'.

Friends of Herod (Herodians) are believed to be a small group that supported the family dynasty and political interests of Chief Looks Brave (Herod). The Herodians were tribal members. We have paraphrased the 'Herodians' as 'Friends of Looks Brave'.

Men On Fire (Zealots) are indirectly referred to in the Gospels. Zealot means one who is on fire or full of zeal. In practice, however, the Zealots were insurrectionists using violent terrorist methods. Many of the Zealots were openly rebellious against Rome and wanted to lead a violent uprising against the Romans. Son Of His Father (Barabbas) was most likely a Zealot, and one of the followers of Creator Sets Free (Jesus) appears to have been a former Zealot (Simon the Zealot). Some historians speculate that Speaks Well Of (Judas), the betrayer, may have also been a Zealot. We have not offered a translation other than for Simon the Zealot, referring to him as One Who Listens (Simon), the Man On Fire (Zealot).

Sacred or Ceremonial Lodge (Temple)

Under Chief Much Loved One (King David), Creator instructed the nation to build a Sacred Lodge in Village of Peace (Jerusalem). This would be a permanent structure to replace the tent, also called the tabernacle, that was used when the tribes were wandering in the wilderness. Creator did not allow Much Loved One (David) to build this Sacred Lodge because he was a man of violence and warfare.

The first Sacred Lodge was built by Stands In Peace (Solomon), the son of Much Loved One (David), and later destroyed by the people of Village of Confusion (Babylon). When they returned from their exile, a second Lodge was built, but it was smaller and much less impressive. Leading up to the time of Creator Sets Free (Jesus), Chief Looks Brave (Herod the Great) had used his fantastic wealth to further rebuild the Lodge and try to restore much of its ancient glory. This Lodge contained four courtyards—the Court of the holy men, the Court of the tribes of Wrestles With Creator (Israel), the Court of the Women, and the Court of the Outside Nations (Gentiles). In this version we have translated 'Temple' as 'Lodge' or 'Sacred Lodge' or 'Ceremonial Lodge.'

The Holy Place was another inner chamber within the Sacred Lodge, connected to the Most Holy Place and separated by a very thick curtain. The Holy Place was entered often by priests who performed daily ceremonies and offered morning and evening prayers.

The Most Holy Place, also called the Holy of Holies, was the innermost chamber of the Lodge, a small room separated from the Holy Place by a very thick curtain. It contained sacred objects from their tribal history. No one was allowed to see behind this curtain except the chief holy man—and then only once a year, when he entered for a special ceremony. Most scholars agree that it was this curtain that was torn in two, from top to bottom, when Creator Sets Free (Jesus) gave up his spirit.

Sacred Family (Church)

Most English translations translate the Greek word 'ekklesia' as 'church.' This word literally means 'called out ones' and was used for community gatherings, whether religious, social or governmental. We have chosen 'Sacred Family' for this translation, highlighting the relational aspect of this sacred gathering of the followers of Creator Sets Free (Jesus). This meaning is reflected in several Scriptures where the 'ekklesia' is called a 'household,' Greek 'oikos' meaning a family member or one living in the same house. 1 Timothy 3:15, Ephesians 2:19, and 1 Peter 4:17 are examples of this. We have also used 'Sacred Family' or 'Sacred Family members' in many places where 'brothers' is used. This was a familial term referring to both men and women as believers in Creator Sets Free (Jesus), making them members of the 'ekklesia' or 'Sacred Family.'

Spiritual Warfare

In Ephesians Chapter 6 there is a section on the 'war garments' of Creator, also called the 'armor of God.' It is important to understand that this warfare is not a physical battle or a contest of brute power between the Great Spirit and Accuser (Satan), even though it affects things in this natural world. Rather, it is a war of ideas (2 Cor 10:3-6). The powerful weapon Creator gives us is his Word of Truth that reveals the truth about the Great Spirit and his love for all of mankind.

Tribal Tax Collectors (Tax Collectors)

Tax collectors were often Tribal Members who contracted with the People of Iron (Romans) for the procurement of taxes. They could force the people, under the threat of violence, to pay them. To make a living, they had to collect more than what was due. And they often became extremely rich off the suffering of the people and were hated by everyone. We have chosen to call them 'tribal tax collectors.'

Tribal Members (Jews)

The people of the tribes of Wrestles With Creator (Israel) were also called 'Jews' in the Bible. The name 'Jew' comes from the time when tribes of Wrestles With Creator (Israel) were divided into two nations. The Northern nation was called 'Israel' and consisted of ten tribes. The Southern nation was called Judah and consisted of two tribes. The name 'Jew' is simply a reference to 'Judah' and became a way of referring to all the tribes. We have simply used 'Tribal Members' and 'Tribal People,' or, when the context seemed appropriate, 'spiritual leaders' or 'tribal leaders,' to translate 'Jews.'

Valley of Smoldering Fire (Gehenna)

Gehenna is a Greek word that refers to the Valley of Hinnom also known as Valley of the Son of Hinnom. In the history of the tribes of Wrestles With Creator (Israel), some from the tribes sacrificed their children to an evil spirit named Powerful Ruler (Molech). They would burn them in an oven of fire and then throw their burnt bodies into the Valley of Hinnom or Place of Burning (Topheth). The name 'Gehenna' became a metaphor for fiery judgment and destruction (Jeremiah 7:31-32).

Wisdomkeeper (Rabbi)

In the time of Creator Sets Free (Jesus) there were spiritual leaders who traveled about gaining followers. These leaders were often called rabbis, meaning teacher. They functioned as a sage or wisdom keeper as they taught their interpretation of the written and oral torah (Jewish laws). Creator Sets Free (Jesus) was called 'rabbi' in the Gospels. It is a title of respect and honor, and rabbis were held in high esteem even though they held no official status. In our translation we have used 'wisdomkeeper' for 'rabbi.' When appropriate we also used this title for 'lord' when people addressed Creator Sets Free (Jesus) in this honorable way.

From Vision to Print

We hope you have enjoyed reading this edition of the First Nations Version New Testament. Our hope is to finish the entire New Testament by the end of 2018. This project is the beginning of the fulfillment of a dream that began on the Hopi Indian Reservation in Northern Arizona over ten years ago.

A good way to stay informed on our progress is to join our Facebook page:

www.facebook.com/FirstNationsVersion

You can also visit the following websites to read more about our vision and how you can support us:

www.firstnationsversion.com

www.onebook.ca/projects/fnv

This book will be available for purchase in the US on Amazon.com and in Canada on Amazon.ca.

We also hope to have a free smartphone app that will include Luke, Acts and Ephesians in the near future.